D0554434

DEC   2001

DEMCO

ESTES PARK
PUBLIC LIBRARY

Muscular Christianity

Muscular Christianity

MANHOOD AND SPORTS
IN PROTESTANT AMERICA,
1880–1920

Clifford Putney

HARVARD UNIVERSITY PRESS
Cambridge, Massachusetts, and London, England   2001

Copyright © 2001 by the President and Fellows of Harvard College
All rights reserved
Printed in the United States of America

Library of Congress Cataloging-in-Publication Data

Putney, Clifford, 1963–
  Muscular Christianity : manhood and sports in Protestant America, 1880–1920 /
Clifford Putney.
     p.   cm.
  Includes bibliographical references and index.
  ISBN 0-674-00634-8 (alk. paper)
     1. Protestant churches—United States—History.   2. Masculinity—Religious
  aspects—Christianity—History.   3. Sports—Religious aspects—Christianity—History.
  4. Masculinity—United States—History.   5. Sports—United States—History.
  6. United States—Church history.   7. United States—Social life and
  customs—1865–1918.   I. Title.

BR517 .P88 2001
280′.4′097309034—dc21   2001024680

To my parents,
Richard Spencer Putney
and
Audrey Wallace Putney

Contents

Illustrations

Acknowledgments

I am deeply grateful for the support that enabled me to write this book. Much of this support came from Brandeis University, which awarded me a Crown Fellowship and a dissertation writing grant. These allowed me to complete "Muscular Christianity," my Ph.D. dissertation in American history. The dissertation was carefully read by my excellent advisors, Morton Keller of Brandeis, Richard Fox of Boston University, and James Kloppenberg of Brandeis (now of Harvard). Their knowledgeable suggestions were very helpful to me.

Also helpful were a number of resourceful librarians and archivists, including Andrea Hinding and David Carmichael of the Kautz Family YMCA Archives, Douglas Brown of Groton School, Diana Yount of Andover Newton Theological School, and Laura Whitney, Gloria Korsman, and Clifford Wunderlich of Harvard Divinity School. These and other expert bibliophiles helped me to gain access to materials on muscular Christianity at institutions such as the Kautz Family YMCA Archives in Minneapolis, the Chicago Research Library, the Harvard College Library, the Schlesinger Library at Radcliffe, the Springfield College Library (which has an excellent collection of early physical education periodicals), and the member libraries of the Boston Theological Institute (a consortium that includes Andover Newton and Harvard Divinity School).

I am indebted to the above-mentioned institutions, and also to the editors of *Anglican and Episcopal History (AEH)*. A portion of Chapter 3 originally appeared as "Men and Religion" in *AEH* 63:4 (December 1994), 451–467; thanks to the editors for permission to use that article here.

Thanks also to the friends, colleagues, and family members whose emotional support and encouragement enabled me to finish my dissertation and later this book. I am especially grateful to my parents, who provided me with writing space during the summers; my housemate, Susan Jones, who put up with my kvetching; and Professor Mark Carnes of Barnard College, who read and reread my text. His comments and the advice I received from excellent editors such as Donna Bouvier at Harvard University Press helped me to convert my dissertation into a book that will, I hope, raise people's interest in the subject of muscular Christianity.

Introduction

Among all the marvelous advances of Christianity either
within this organization [the YMCA] or without it, in this
land and century or any other lands and ages, the future
historian of the church of Christ will place this movement of
carrying the gospel to the body as one of the most epoch
making.

—G. STANLEY HALL (1902)

Between 1880 and 1920, American Protestants in many denominations witnessed the flourishing in their pulpits and seminaries of a
strain of religiosity known, both admiringly and pejoratively, as
"muscular Christianity." Converts to this creed included Josiah
Strong, a Social Gospel minister who thought bodily strength a pre-
requisite for doing good; G. Stanley Hall, a pioneer psychologist who
wished to reinvigorate "old-stock" Americans; and President Theodore Roosevelt, an advocate of strenuous religion for "the Strenuous
Life." These and other stalwart supporters of Christian manliness
hoped to energize the churches and to counteract the supposedly enervating effects of urban living. To realize their aims, they promulgated
competitive sports, physical education, and other staples of modern-
day life.

Muscular Christians were active not only in America but also in
England, where the term "muscular Christianity" arose in the 1850s
to describe the novels of Thomas Hughes and Charles Kingsley. Both
of these men believed that the Anglican Church of their day was becoming overly tolerant of physical weakness and effeminacy. To reverse this perceived trend, Hughes and Kingsley worked to infuse Anglicanism with enough health and manliness to make it a suitable
agent for British imperialism. Their ideas were also exported to America, where they were received with enthusiasm by Unitarian minister
Thomas Wentworth Higginson. In a seminal 1858 *Atlantic Monthly*

article entitled "Saints, and Their Bodies," Higginson praised Hughes and Kingsley for being supportive of health and manliness. He also wished that health and manliness were more evident in America's Protestant churches, which he viewed as unhealthy and unmanly.[1]

Higginson's view was not without some basis in fact. American Protestant churches in the colonial and antebellum periods may indeed have fostered ill health, since they tended to view artificial exercise as an immoral waste of time. In addition, since the late seventeenth century Protestant churches in America have had more female than male adherents.[2] This gender imbalance troubled antebellum Southern male evangelicals, whose churches were frequently viewed as unmanly.[3] It also troubled Northern male evangelical sponsors of the so-called "Businessmen's Awakening," a revival that flourished in several cities from 1857 to 1858.[4] Designed to bring men into church, the Businessmen's Awakening in some ways resembled the first American Young Men's Christian Associations, which were formed in the 1850s partly in order to fill the churches with young men.

The Businessmen's Awakening and the YMCAs were connected not only by their focus on men but also by their association with evangelist Dwight L. Moody, who as a young entrepreneur in Chicago participated in both the Businessmen's Awakening and the Chicago YMCA. Later in life, Moody became a full-time evangelist, traveling around the country and preaching (as one historian contends) primarily to men.[5] Moody also held a series of conferences for religious workers in the vicinity of Northfield, Massachusetts. These conferences, the first of which was held in 1885, helped to advance muscular Christianity in America by bringing together Christian athletes such as football hero Amos Alonzo Stagg, who, like Moody, believed that religion and sports were compatible.[6]

The fact that Moody promoted religion and sport at his Northfield conferences has led two historians to call him "the champion of an indigenous American brand of muscular Christianity."[7] If muscular Christianity is defined as a Christian commitment to health and manliness, there is no doubt that Moody was intimately affiliated with muscular Christian institutions such as the YMCA and the Northfield conferences. But whether Moody himself was a muscular Christian is a debatable question. Unlike some of the religious workers whom he hosted at Northfield, Moody was fond of sentimental Victorian hymns that emphasized motherhood and the nurturing side of

Christ.[8] He also had enough room in his ministry for women, many of whom flocked to the Moody Bible Institute in Chicago and Moody's school for girls in Northfield, Massachusetts.[9]

Moody's tolerance for women in religion differentiated him from strident muscular Christians such as G. Stanley Hall, who talked loudly around 1900 about the existence of a "woman peril" in the churches. Believers in this peril were concerned not only about the disproportionate number of women in church but also about the "feminizing" influence that churchwomen supposedly had on various aspects of Victorian religion, including denominational hymn books, which muscular Christians found overly sentimental; popular images of Jesus, which they viewed as overly feminine; and the ministry, which they believed was full of effeminate men. The muscular Christians' aversion to sentimentality, refinement, and other stereotypically feminine traits was not shared by everyone. But their contention that stereotypically feminine traits characterized much of Victorian religion is hard to refute.

The prevalence of stereotypically feminine traits within American Protestant churches during the Victorian period has been well documented by Ann Douglas, who views the ecclesiastical enshrinement of feminine tastes as a reflection of women's power within the churches.[10] This power will be discussed in Chapters 1 and 3, in which I contend that muscular Christianity was in part a male reaction against women's religious leadership. The strength of that leadership undoubtedly irritated a number of men, and it probably helped to retard the spread of muscular Christianity, which did not really take off in America until the closing decades of the nineteenth century. Before that time, according to Benjamin Rader, talk of "Christian manliness" came mainly from "old-stock" eastern patricians such as Thomas Wentworth Higginson. But in the closing decades of the nineteenth century, "the popularity of Christian manliness began to extend beyond the eastern elite to middle-status Protestants, even to those of an evangelical temperament."[11]

The spread of muscular Christianity in the closing decades of the nineteenth century resulted from numerous factors, including athletic developments, such as a decline in the evangelical Christian antipathy toward sports, the adoption by most YMCAs of athletic programs, and the invention by YMCA men of "character-building" sports such as basketball and volleyball. Also helping to advance muscular Christianity in the late nineteenth century was an imperialistic urge to extend American Christianity overseas in a forceful way. This could hardly be done by "womanly" missionaries, argued muscular Christians, who called upon "manly men" to spread the Gospel not only in "heathen" lands but also in American churches, especially those that were supposedly suffering from an excess of Victorian sentimentality.

The muscular Christian call for manly men was a loud one. But the call for manly men in the Progressive Era did not emanate only from muscular Christians; it also emanated from secular figures in politics, academia, and the press, many of whom joined muscular Christians in bemoaning what Ann Douglas calls "the feminization of American culture": the nineteenth-century relegation to women of such cultural responsibilities as the teaching of children, the instillment of religion and the determination of artistic merit.[12]

One sign of men's dissatisfaction with feminized culture was the enormous popularity in nineteenth-century America of fraternal lodges such as the Masons, the Odd Fellows, and the Red Men. These purveyors of good fellowship did not hold with the Victorian cult of domesticity and its contention that true happiness was to be found only in the company of one's wife and children. Instead, they served, in the opinion of Mark Carnes, as refuges from the home, providing an environment wherein "unsung" male virtues were praised and respected.[13]

Lodge members may have viewed Victorian domesticity as a threat. But a more material threat to manly men was the late-nineteenth-century emergence in America of large corporations, with their plethora of midlevel management positions. These sedentary office jobs did not provide the same opportunity for exercise as farm or factory work. Nor did the resultant weakening of men's musculature escape the notice of contemporary writers, many of whom began to bemoan "the decline of the race" and the softness inherent in "overcivilization."

Alarmed by the prospect of "overcivilized" middle- and upper-class managerial types being toppled by lower-class workers and muscular immigrants, many Progressive Era reformers hurried to endorse artificial exercise, outdoor camping, and other methods of strengthening America's elite. They also inveighed against city living, woman teachers, and other things that were supposedly sapping the vitality of American males, particularly males of "Anglo-Saxon" lineage. If Anglo-Saxon men wanted to retain their dominant position in American society, preached various reformers, then they would have to follow the example set by Theodore Roosevelt, who transformed himself via boxing and barbells from a sickly house-bound teenager into the rough-riding, safari-going, big-stick-wielding Bull Moose of legend.

Roosevelt's transformation and his efforts to make American culture more vigorous and manly have recently begun to interest historians such as Gail Bederman, Mark Carnes, Clyde Griffen, Kevin White, Michael Kimmel, and E. Anthony Rotundo. These pioneers in the emergent field of "men's history" agree that in the late nineteenth and early twentieth centuries middle-class American Protestant white men were beset by a number of challenges, including such perceived threats to their status as non-Protestant immigration, the women's rights movement, and the ability of big business to wipe out the "little guy." As a result of these challenges, there arose what some are calling a "masculinity crisis" in the Progressive Era, a period when various male intellectuals, uncertain about their place in society, struggled to come up with a new model for manhood. The old model prescribed by the Victorians had stressed stoicism, gentility, and self-denial. But these traits in the opinion of many Progressives did not really enable native-born, middle-class white men to maintain their authority in an era when immigrant politicians, articulate suffragists, and powerful monopolists were on the ascendant.

Convinced that the archetypal buttoned-down Victorian gentleman was ill-equipped to handle the challenges posed by modernity, many Progressives proposed a new model for manhood, one that stressed action rather than reflection and aggression rather than gentility. To describe their new ideal man, his supporters even adopted a new word, the adjective "masculine," which as Gail Bederman points out did not come into general usage until the 1890s.[14] Before that decade, admirable men were often described as "manly." But since the word "manly" sometimes meant "civilized" in the Victorian period, it lost some of its cachet in the Progressive Era, when "overcivilization" was attacked by men such as G. Stanley Hall, who believed in the primacy of "primitive" instincts and emotions. Hall and other proponents of what E. Anthony Rotundo calls "passionate manhood" never abandoned the term "manly."[15] But they did supplement it with the word "masculine," which in their minds connoted the sort of raw male power needed to combat disruptive changes in society.

To ensure that this power did not vanish from the "Anglo-Saxon race," many old-stock Progressives sought to instill manliness in their sons. Their task was abetted by nature-oriented institutions such as the newly formed Boy Scouts, which took "sissified" boys from the suburbs and sent them on rigorous trips into the forest. These forest outings were designed to endow white boys with "brute strength" and basic survival skills. But their encouragement of primitiveness within white boys raised a difficult question: If primitiveness was a valuable quality in white boys, then why was it often used as a term to denigrate nonwhite cultures?

This question placed many white Progressives in a quandary. On the one hand they wanted to encourage primitiveness in their sons. On the other hand they wanted to deplore primitiveness in other cultures. But their dilemma, while puzzling, was not insoluble. For as Gail Bederman points out, the developmental theories put forward by Progressive Era educators such as G. Stanley Hall explained that primitiveness was not a permanent condition—at least not for whites. Nonwhites in Hall's opinion might languish forever in a state of permanent primitiveness. But primitiveness for white boys was supposedly just a phase through which they had to pass. If white boys gained the requisite amount of strength and hardihood in their primitive phase, Hall averred, then they could go on to master the intricacies of civilization without fear of nervous collapse.[16]

Hall's developmental theory was exceedingly popular at the beginning of the twentieth century, largely because it enabled Progressives to combine primitivism with a sense of cultural superiority. But it was not only Hall's developmental theory that enabled Progressives to combine conflicting attitudes toward civilization; it was also muscular Christianity. Like Hall's theory, muscular Christianity laid stress on the importance of having a muscular, "preindustrial" body. This body, however, was not simply meant to do preindustrial chores such as hunting and farming; it had a higher purpose. Instead of just being a tool for labor, the body was viewed by muscular Christians as a tool for good, an agent to be used on behalf of social progress and world uplift.

The muscular Christian notion of using primitive bodies to advance civilized ideals enjoyed widespread popularity during the Progressive Era. But the centrality of muscular Christianity in Progressive Era thought has been largely overlooked by historians. Men's historians in particular have said relatively little about muscular Christian participation in the early-twentieth-century campaign to "defeminize" American culture.[17] Their inattention to muscular Christianity (which Rotundo has called "the peak of absurdity") may reflect the fact that nineteenth-century American Protestant churches have seldom been seen as bastions of aggressive masculinity.[18] Instead of being portrayed as pro-masculine, the churches have generally been portrayed as pro-feminine by historians such as James Turner, who contends that many nineteenth-century intellectuals simply abandoned Protestantism after concluding that it had become too "unmanly."[19]

While historians such as Turner are right to call the Protestant churches purveyors of domesticity, molders of idealized femininity, and the like, they are wrong to imply that the churches were devoid of manly men. They forget that not everyone connected with mainline Protestantism supported Victorian sentimentality, as evidenced by the abundance of Progressive Era ministers and laymen who advocated replacing "feminized" Christianity with a more masculine faith. These opponents of feminized religion were not only active in well-known organizations such as the Boy Scouts and the YMCA; they were also instrumental in forming "surprisingly underexploited" bodies such as the Protestant church brotherhoods, the Student Volunteer Movement, the Knights of King Arthur, and the Men and Religion Forward movement, all of which worked hard to make Christianity a religion to which "he-men" and boys might proudly belong.[20] Although a few books have been written about these lesser-known groups, most have been uncritical treatments, concerned more with their subject institutions than with muscular Christianity as a whole.

In an attempt to focus attention on muscular Christianity as a whole, this book provides an overview of the muscular Christian movement in America at its historical peak, roughly from 1880 to 1920. After 1920, pacifism, cynicism, church decline, and the devaluation of male friendships combined to undercut muscular Christianity—at least within the mainline Protestant churches. But in the forty years before 1920, an extraordinary amount of talk within Protestant churches focused on the need to rescue American manhood from sloth and effeminacy.

Muscular Christian talk of rescuing American manhood will undoubtedly prompt some to ask how inclusive the term "American manhood" really was. This is a good question, the answer to which is somewhat ambiguous. The evidence presented in this book suggests that when white muscular Christians spoke of "American manhood," they generally had in mind some sort of Anglo-Saxon ideal. But not all muscular Christians were white, as Nina Mjagkij points out in her work on black YMCA leaders. These individuals (who remained segregated from the main body of the "Y" until 1946) not only aimed to achieve "true manhood"; they also "advocated exercise as a means to prevent the decline of the physical male prowess of the members of their own race."[21]

Middle-class black muscular Christians may have been as concerned as their white counterparts about the enervating effects of sedentary living. But Nina Mjagkij points out that while white muscular Christians viewed physical weakness as a threat to their continued enjoyment of power, black muscular Christians viewed it as an impediment to their achievement of civil rights. As a result, writes Mjagkij, black muscular Christians intent on achieving social justice often sounded less reactionary than white muscular Christians, whose fear of cultural obsolescence sometimes led them to lash out at immigrants and people of color.[22]

Black muscular Christianity's divergence from white muscular Christianity was not only qualitative; it was also quantitative, since Progressive Era black Protestant churches were decidedly less inclined than Progressive Era white Protestant churches to worry about the dangers of effeminacy in religion. That at any rate is the contention of church historian Evelyn Brooks Higginbotham, who argues that while white churchmen debated with white churchwomen about whether Christ was more masculine than feminine, black churchmen and -women set the issue of Christ's masculinity aside in order to concentrate exclusively on achieving "racial self-determination."[23] Higginbotham's case for the harmoniousness of gender relations in Progressive Era black churches is perhaps a bit overstated, but her assertion that the masculinist rhetoric of muscular Christianity flourished more in white churches than in black ones does square with the evidence I have found. That evidence points to the fact that muscular Christianity in the Progressive Era was primarily a white Christian phenomenon, though it undoubtedly influenced non-Christian groups such as the YMCA-inspired Young Men's Hebrew Association, which practiced what novelist Max Nordau called "Muskeljudentum," or Muscular Jewry.[24]

If American muscular Christianity was primarily a white Christian phenomenon, then some people will wonder whether the U.S. Catholic Church embraced muscular Christianity. The answer, according to Father Patrick Kelly, is that the Church did embrace muscular Christianity, but not until the latter part of the twentieth century, when it finally saw the religious value of sports. In the three centuries that preceded the twentieth century, writes Kelly, the Catholic Church "lost the ability to see God" in sports. As a result, it was "cut off from the development of modern sport."[25]

Kelly's contention that sports and Catholicism did not really mix until the twentieth century is challenged by Christa Klein, who writes that sports were adopted in the latter half of the nineteenth century by at least two Catholic boys' schools, St. John's College (Fordham) and St. Francis Xavier. These schools, according to Klein, were led by Jesuits who noted the rise of muscular Christianity in the Protestant educational establishment. In response, the Jesuits at Fordham and Xavier developed a doctrine in the 1890s that Klein calls "Muscular Catholicism." Like Protestant muscular Christianity, Muscular Catholicism stressed the importance of being a healthy athlete. But Muscular Catholicism in Klein's view was not nearly as male-centric as Protestant muscular Christianity, which according to Klein "polarized masculine and feminine roles to an extent completely unknown in Catholic hagiography."[26]

Klein's definition of Protestant muscular Christianity as an entirely male-centric phenomenon is refuted to some degree by Chapter 6 of this book, which argues that some aspects of Protestant muscular Christianity appealed to women in the Girl Scouts, the Camp Fire Girls, and the Young Women's Christian Association. As for her assertion that Muscular Catholicism celebrated both "masculine and feminine character traits," it will not be challenged here, since this book focuses largely, though not exclusively, on the spread of muscular Christianity among middle- to upper-class white Protestants.[27]

Of the white Protestants who initially embraced muscular Christianity in the United States, most came from the North, particularly the urban Northeast, and most belonged to what E. Digby Baltzell called "the Protestant establishment": a collection of such disproportionally influential mainline churches as the Congregationalists, Disciples, Episcopalians, American Baptists, Northern Presbyterians, and Northern Methodists.[28] Other, more theologically conservative churches were not implacably hostile to muscular Christianity (which eventually caught on in fundamentalist circles and lasted there far longer than in the mainline churches), but it was clearly white, liberal churchmen who espoused the movement first.[29]

Today liberal churchmen tend to avoid muscular Christian rhetoric, and they emphasize instead the importance of gender neutral terminology in their sermons and hymns. Muscular Christianity appears to have disappeared, too, from the Young Men's Christian Association, whose clientele now consists not only of young Protestant men but also of women, the elderly, Catholics, and non-Christians.[30] As for other muscular Christian organizations such as the Brotherhood of St. Andrew and the Knights of King Arthur, they are all but extinct. But their demise does not mean that muscular Christianity has ceased to exist. Members of the Men and Religion Forward movement may no longer be around to preach the virtues of muscular Christianity, but their faith in the power of manly athletes to overcome society's ills lives on, as evidenced by the emergence of such neo–muscular Christian groups as the Promise Keepers and the Fellowship of Christian Athletes.[31]

CHAPTER ONE

The Birth of a Movement

> We don't want to see the virtuous young man always have
> shoulders that slope like those of a champagne bottle, while
> the young man who is not virtuous is allowed to monopolize
> the burly strength which must be possessed by every great and
> masterful nation.
>
> —THEODORE ROOSEVELT (1897)

Muscular Christianity can be defined simply as a Christian commitment to health and manliness. Its origins can be traced to the New Testament, which sanctions manly exertion (Mark 11:15) and physical health (1 Cor. 6:19–20). But while muscular Christianity has always been an element in Christianity, it has not always been a major element. The early Church sometimes praised health and manliness, but it was much more concerned with achieving salvation, and it preached that men could achieve salvation without being healthy and husky. This doctrine seemingly squared with the Gospels, and it reigned supreme within the Church for centuries. It did inspire criticism, however, and that criticism was especially fierce in the nineteenth and early twentieth centuries, when droves of Protestant ministers in England and America concluded that men were not truly Christians unless they were healthy and "manly" (a term used to connote strength, endurance, and other stereotypically male attributes).

Charles Kingsley and Thomas Hughes

The phrase "muscular Christianity" probably first appeared in an 1857 English review of Charles Kingsley's novel *Two Years Ago* (1857).[1] One year later, the same phrase was used to describe *Tom Brown's School Days*, an 1856 novel about life at Rugby by Kingsley's friend, fellow Englishman Thomas Hughes.[2] Soon the press in

general was calling both writers muscular Christians and also apply-
ing that label to the genre they inspired: adventure novels replete with
high principles and manly Christian heroes.[3]

Hughes and Kingsley had much in common. Both men espoused
Christian Socialism and disliked evangelical Methodism (which
Kingsley termed "Manichaean" or otherworldly).[4] Both also deplored
the effect of industrialism on English society and wondered if traditional morality were sufficient to cope with it. But Hughes and Kingsley were not without difference. For one thing, Kingsley wrote more
prolifically than Hughes, and he was a clergyman whereas Hughes
was not. Kingsley also deserves more credit than Hughes for equip-
ping English muscular Christianity with a cohesive and conscious philosophy, consisting equally of athleticism, patriotism, and religion.

When addressing the last of these subjects, Kingsley underscored
his opposition to two important developments facing the Anglican
Church, of which he was a member: the Catholic-leaning Oxford
Movement on the right and dissenting evangelicalism on the left (the
latter represented in fiction by George Eliot's praying miser, Silas
Marner). Kingsley, who identified with the "Broad Church" wing of
the Anglican Church, viewed both the High Church and the dissenting parties as too exclusive.[5] He furthermore accused them of idolatry,
with the Anglo-Catholics placing Mary before Christ and the evangelicals (in Hughes's words) "putting the Book in the place of Him of
whom it testifies."[6]

On a less theological note, Kingsley employed the Christian Socialist teachings of his mentor, F. D. Maurice, to censure Anglican extrem-
ists right and left for fleeing "from the world instead of trying to mend
it." Given that life was a battle, he reasoned, then should not Christians be at its center? Should not they value the qualities of "man-
fulness" and "usefulness" above those of contemplativeness and introspection?[7] The answer was yes, Kingsley wrote, though he was
not content to let matters rest there. For while he considered
"Manichaeism" a sin of omission, he also thought it a positive harm.
In particular, he blamed the celibacy and asceticism of some Anglo-
Catholic clerics for undercutting family values and for producing a
dangerous "fastidious, maundering, die-away effeminacy," the ideal
not of God, but of "affected, artificial, sly, shifty" rogues.[8]

Kingsley disliked asceticism as much for its physical enervation as
for its distractions from civic duty. In his mind, people's bodies existed
not to be abused or ignored, but rather to be consecrated in God's ser-

vice. Hence the need to support those activities (such as athletics) likely to enhance the body's serviceability. This argument may have failed to sway either Tractarians or Evangelicals (the latter of whom harbored toward athletics, in George Eliot's words, "a certain suspicion as of plague infection,")[9] but Kingsley cleaved to it steadily, crediting his own participation in the time-honored sports of "snipe shooting, and rowing, and jack-fishing" with giving him the "strength and hardihood" necessary to do God's work.[10]

For those still unconvinced, Kingsley pointed to athleticism's social benefits. Chief among these was its ability to ameliorate English class differences. Ill feelings could be overcome through camaraderie on the playing field, wrote George Trevelyan (a latter-day Kingslean); and undoubtedly had "the French noblesse . . . been capable of playing cricket with their peasants, their chateaux would never have been burnt."[11]

By benefiting Britannia internally, athletics stood to benefit her externally as well. For if the country were ever to fulfill its imperial ambitions, its authorities could not "allow English people to grow up puny, stunted, and diseased."[12] Nor could they condone the enfeeblement of those prospective colonial administrators—the middle and upper-middle classes—who in Kingsley's mind were "lacking in that experience of pain and endurance necessary to bring out the masculine qualities."[13]

This preoccupation with empire-building constitutes the third element in Kingsley's ethos after pro-athletics and anti-Manichaeism. It also helps to distinguish somewhat his version of muscular Christianity from that of latter-day Americans. For while the latter envisioned divine health becoming available to all nations, Kingsley spoke primarily to the English, telling them they were a chosen people "in covenant with God."[14]

To illustrate this chosenness, Kingsley compared England's present-day rule in the world with that of earlier (in Kingsley's mind prototypically English) groups such as the Israelites, the Goths, and the Saxons. Small as these groups were, Kingsley maintained that they nonetheless possessed those essential qualities of manliness, clean-living, and worshipfulness before God that in the end enabled them to triumph over (or in the case of the Saxons at least discomfit) their larger but less manly opponents, the Philistines, the Romans, and the Normans.

In Kingsley's teleological worldview, the victories of the Goths et alia merely presaged that great and final victory promised England, then the leading player in God's unfolding historical drama. But England's achieving its imperial destiny still depended on three things: its remembering the lessons of the past, its resisting being drawn into such cul-de-sacs as Manichaeism, and its cleaving to a Christianity compatible not so much with peace as with war, which Kingsley celebrated in "Brave Words to Brave Soldiers," a tract circulated among English fighters in the Crimean War.

Kingsley's view of Christianity, athletics, and patriotism found expression in his many novels: historical novels like the 1855 *Westward Ho!* (about the discovery of the New World) and novels with contemporary settings like the 1851 *Yeast* (about the revivifying effects of sport). These novels, whether historical or contemporary, contained barely veiled social commentary. They were "novels with a purpose," as the Victorians called such literature, and they generally pitted aesthetic villains against athletic heroes, or "brain-hewer(s)" as were called the protagonists in Kingsley's 1866 Saxon epic, *Hereward the Wake*.[15]

Of all his characters, Kingsley was especially fond of "manly models" for the English clergy: rugged, amiable fellows like the "sporting parson" Panurgus O'Blareaway in *Yeast*,[16] or actual warriors like ship's chaplain Jack Brimblecombe in *Westward Ho!* Kingsley even managed in his 1853 novel *Hypatia* to make a fifth-century Alexandrian bishop, Synesius, appear the very image of a fox-hunting country parson.

Unfortunately for Kingsley, his portrayal of monasticism in *Hypatia* was so unflattering that John Henry (later Cardinal) Newman, England's most famous convert to Roman Catholicism, felt compelled to respond. To repudiate *Hypatia*'s inaccuracies, Newman gave, in his 1856 novel *Callista*, an alternative account of early Christianity. For Newman, early Christianity's greatest heroes were not manly men, but martyred women. These women achieved salvation not by conquering but by transcending the world; and Newman believed that anyone who thought otherwise ought honestly to embrace Islam (a faith that squared with Kingsley's celebration of worldly power).[17]

On the heels of Newman's publication of *Callista* came the famous and prolonged Newman-Kingsley debate, which pitted Newman's vision of the world as a place fraught with snares and pitfalls against Kingsley's vision of it as a great character-builder. The debate became quite rancorous in 1864, when Kingsley, who hated "popery," accused Newman publicly of deviousness and of espousing an unmanly faith.[18] In response to this "gratuitous slander," Newman wrote *Apologia Pro Vita Sua* in 1864.[19] A magisterial defense of Catholicism, the book won the Newman-Kingsley debate for Newman, at least insofar as most intellectuals were concerned. Looking back years later, an anthologist of Kingsley refused even to speak of "his miserable dual with Cardinal Newman, wherein he was so shamefully worsted."[20]

The general view of Kingsley's being bested by Newman was not shared by Kingsley's ally Thomas Hughes, who in some ways went further and did more in support of Kingsley's ideals than did Kingsley himself.[21] Both men had been called "muscular Christians," but Kingsley never fully embraced the term, viewing it merely as "a clever expression, spoken in jest."[22] Hughes, however, viewed "muscular Christians" as people who used their bodies for "the advancement of all righteous causes."[23] He also celebrated muscular Christianity (in spirit if not in name) in *Tom Brown's School Days,* a book whose phenomenal popularity made Hughes an even better known spokesman for Christian manliness than Kingsley.[24]

Tom Brown's School Days was not Hughes's only work, but it was arguably his greatest, far surpassing in sales such later offerings as *Tom Brown at Oxford* and *The Manliness of Christ* (wherein Hughes claimed that if Christianity could not be made more manly, it "will go to the wall").[25] Among the book's staunchest advocates were Victorian educators, who liked its propagation of the muscular Christian values of fellowship, honor, and service—a socializing code "designed," as one historian writes, "to teach England and English boys that one can be the best looking, best-playing, and most popular, and still be humble."[26]

Schoolboys probably read *Tom Brown's School Days* less for its "sporting values" than for its tales of sport. Nonetheless they undoubtedly appreciated the book's addressing them and their concerns directly, and not (as was the case with so much of Victorian children's literature) from some lofty, morally superior vantage point. Possibly, too, boys did not mind overmuch the book's lack of saintly female exemplars (another literary convention), who disappear after an opening scene in which Tom's harassment of the servants and obvious "inaptitude for female guidance" lead to his being sent off to the all-male Rugby School.[27]

Awaiting Tom at Rugby is what might well be called a muscular Christian hierarchy of goodness. On the bottom rung of this moral ladder stands the bully Flashman, who can boast of strength but not of the goodness necessary to use that strength appropriately. Next comes Tom's pious but ineffectual friend, Arthur. And then comes Tom himself, whose combination of strength and piety mark him as an embryonic Christian gentleman.

Above Tom on the moral ladder at Rugby are only God and God's representative, the school's headmaster, whom Tom calls "the Doctor." This character was based on a real person, Thomas Arnold, who had been Hughes's headmaster at Rugby in the 1830s. Thanks to his influence on Hughes (who credited Arnold with instilling in him "a strong religious faith and loyalty to Christ")[28] and thanks also to his greatly expanding the English public school system, the real Dr. Arnold occupies an important place in the annals of muscular Christianity—although his was a Christianity more austere, less hearty, and less inextricably linked with sports than his protégé's.[29]

Like Charles Kingsley (another admirer of the Doctor), Arnold deplored the effects of nonconformity and Tractarianism on English society. And he shared with the generation prior to Kingsley's a horror of revolution (especially the French) and of the excesses of democracy and individualism. Whenever the quest for equal rights conflicted with social harmony, wrote Arnold, the former must be forfeited; for "equality is the dream of a madman, or the passion of a fiend."[30]

Arnold supported the English union of church and state (believing it to invest morality with power), and he preached incessantly the virtues of duty: duty to one's school, to one's king, and to God. Moreover, he sought to implement his vision of the ideal society at Rugby, where he was headmaster from 1828 to 1841. It was a daunting task Arnold set himself: nothing less than imposing order and morality upon the otherwise disordered and amoral life of boys.

Ultimately, the means Arnold hit upon for turning out Christian gentlemen was organized sports, whose rules, chains of command, and strenuosity made them ideal teachers of duty and hard work. Sports were also viewed by Arnold as a means of channeling and dispersing those boyish energies (particularly sexual energies) which, if left unchecked, might result either in masturbation ("the deadly habit") or in other illicit behavior.[31]

To many of the students who participated in Rugby's pioneering use of sports, and who heard Arnold preach in chapel, the Doctor seemed almost godlike—a concrete manifestation of virtue and authority. Others, particularly later in the century, remembered the Doctor (or at least the Doctor as cultural icon) much less fondly. Representative of the first view was Thomas Hughes, who in *Tom Brown's School Days* described Arnold as "a man whom we felt to be, with all his heart and soul and strength, striving against whatever was mean and unmanly and unrighteous in our little world." Representative of the later, less flattering view was Bertrand Russell, who thought that Arnold "sacrificed intellect to virtue" as an educational goal.[32]

The late Victorian devaluation of Arnold's pedagogical reputation corresponded with a devaluation of English muscular Christianity as a whole. One reason for this was that by century's end many of those tasks for which muscular Christians had girded their loins (empire-building, the reformation of public schools, and so on) were no longer challenges but comfortably established facts. At the same time, while men like Russell no longer recalled the chaos and grinding pedantry characteristic of the pre-Arnoldian style of education depicted by Henry Fielding in *Tom Jones,* they certainly knew firsthand the abuses of muscular Christian pedagogy, with its anti-intellectualism, insistence on conformity, and equation of might with right.

Those hostile to muscular Christianity included Victorian writers such as Gerard Manley Hopkins and post-Victorian writers such as E. M. Forster (Forster's criticism of the doctrine being that it produced men with "well-developed bodies . . . and undeveloped hearts"). Another opponent of muscular Christianity was Evelyn Waugh's older brother, Alec, who was expelled from Sherborne for homosexuality, and who later in a novel condemned English schoolmen for causing boys to worship manliness "at the shrine of the god of Athleticism" while continuing to label as unwholesome the logical outgrowth of such worship.[33]

Admittedly there were some serious literary inheritors to the mantle of Hughes and Kingsley. One was Edward George Bulwer-Lytton (inventor of the immortal line "It was a dark and stormy night") whose 1873 novel *Kenelm Chillingly* features an aristocratic protagonist who, unaided and alone, ventures forth into the world intent on physically rectifying evil. A second claimant to the muscular Christian style was G. A. Lawrence, author of such vigorous adventures as *Guy Livingstone* (1857) and *Sword and Gown* (1859). Finally deserving of mention is, of course, Rudyard Kipling, who thought it "the white man's burden" to advance Christianity and civilization.

But while all these authors employed Kingslean themes of manliness and derring-do, they failed wholly to do justice to Kingsley's vision of *principled* strength. Bulwer-Lytton's Kenelm Chillingly, for example, is no Kingslean hero, acting out of public spirit and with an eye toward bettering his fellow man; rather he appears moody, and with the typical aristocrat's unconcern for outward justification. G. A. Lawrence's novels likewise lack Kinglsey's idealism, and seem to include Christianity more as an afterthought than as a foundation stone.[34] As for Kipling, his outlook seems more fatalistic than Christian. Nor is his famous admission "You're a better man than I am, Gunga Din" much in the muscular Christian vein, implying as it does that while the English have might, the natives (at least occasionally) are right.

All things considered, English muscular Christianity fared better in institutions than in literature. It was especially useful in the public schools, where unruly boys were disciplined through athletics, and through athletic metaphors were taught the essential manliness—and therefore palatability—of Christ.[35] Missionary organizations also saw the value of athletics, not only in reaching boys, but also in evangelizing foreigners. That at least was the belief of the famous "Cambridge Seven," a group of Christian athletes who left England in 1885 for China's Inland Mission. Led by internationally renowned cricketer C. T. Studd (whose father, in an interesting instance of transatlantic cross-pollination, had been converted by American evangelist Dwight L. Moody), the Cambridge Seven stressed their athletic prowess and their ability to unlock the hearts and minds of China's "heathen" masses.[36]

While the Cambridge Seven were entertaining the Chinese, muscular Christianity was influencing such paradenominational organizations as George Williams's Young Men's Christian Association (founded 1844), William Alexander's Boys' Brigade (founded 1883), and Lord Baden-Powell's Boy Scouts (founded 1907). For the Boy Scouts (at least in England) muscular Christianity appeared only in its most rarified form—Baden-Powell's ambition being less to bring boys to Christ than to promote in them a general wholesomeness and reverence for king and country. With the Boys' Brigade, however, Christianity and church worship were essential, the club's object being to advance through military drill "all that tends toward a true Christian manliness."[37] As for the YMCA, at first its purpose was simply the evangelization of young men in the cities through traditional means: tent meetings, street-corner preaching, and pamphleteering.

But once the New York City "Y" pioneered the use of gymnasia as a means of Christian outreach in 1869, English YMCAs generally followed suit.

In the end, however, institutions proved scarcely better than authors at preserving Kingsley's delicate balance between athleticism, patriotism, and Christianity. For just as chapel bromides about God and country too easily shaded off into "a litany of Nationalism," school sports began to be played as much for themselves as for their allegedly Christian benefits.[38] By 1888, one English author was complaining that whereas the early Victorians had not appreciated sports enough, "the pendulum of popular taste has perhaps swung a little too far in the opposite direction, and the athlete is made almost a demigod."[39]

In response to the problem of immoral athleticism, Thomas Hughes called in 1880 for "a revival of the muscular Christianity of twenty-five years ago";[40] but unfortunately for him, that revival never happened—at least not in England. America proved a different story; for as one historian of English muscular Christianity notes: "it has been in America that muscular Christianity and its institutionalized cult of youth . . . found the widest acceptance."[41]

America's Response to Kingsley and Hughes

Educated, mid-nineteenth-century Americans were exposed to English muscular Christianity almost from its inception, a fact not surprising given their tendency toward Anglophilia and access to muscular Christian novels.[42] On the heels of this initial exposure came Thomas Hughes's tour of America in the early 1870s, during which time he addressed Harvard College on "Muscular Christianity and Its Proper Limits."[43] Afterward, Hughes helped to found the colony of Rugby, Tennessee, which from 1880 to 1887 served to teach muscular Christianity to the sons of English immigrants.[44]

When Hughes died in 1896, fashionable New York City preacher David J. Burrell devoted an entire sermon to "Tom Brown at Rugby." Seven years later, Unitarian minister Jenkin L. Jones commemorated Hughes's coining of the term "the manliness of Christ." Believing "the phrase [to suggest] a too long neglected element in piety," Jones agreed with Hughes that "Jesus warrants no sensuous rhapsodies about what is called downy couches, spread by angel hands, but rather a spirited muscular piety, a splendid kind of stand-on-your-feet trust."[45]

Such glowing ownership of muscular Christianity was commonplace during the era of Theodore Roosevelt, who viewed *Tom Brown's School Days* as one of the two books that every boy should read.[46] But when the Hughes book first reached America in the late 1850s, many Americans were unused to the book's central premise: the idea that sports built Christian character. That idea was completely foreign to the inheritors of the Calvinist tradition in America, wrote Unitarian minister Edward Everett Hale in 1857. "To play at cricket was a sin, in the eyes of the fathers," he recalled, "as much as to dance or to play on an ungodly instrument."[47] As a result of such attitudes, Washington Gladden grew up in the 1840s thinking "that if I became a Christian it would be wrong for me to play ball."[48]

The puritanical view of sport as a sinful diversion "lingers to this day," wrote Hale. It prevented Americans from taking time off from work for recreation; and this overemphasis on work helped to explain why so many Americans were "haggard" and "overwrought." Antebellum America's "fascination with work" also produced what Hale called an "absolute indifference . . . to matters of physical health," which he felt was largely responsible for the rarity in America of healthy pastimes such as cricket and rowing.[49] Such "muscle-building sports" were commonplace in Britain, noted the *New York Herald* in 1859, and their comparative absence in America was a matter for grave concern, considering that it "undoubtedly tended to reduce our young men to effeminacy."[50]

The absence of sports in antebellum America troubled not only the *New York Herald* but also the Reverend Horace Bushnell, a liberal Congregationalist who was one of the earliest critics of the puritanical strain in American culture. In his highly influential *Christian Nurture*, Bushnell condemned Calvinists for their undue emphasis on work and repentance. He said nothing in the original 1847 edition of *Christian Nurture* about using play to avoid overwork, but he brought up the subject of play in his 1861 revision, declaring that "religion is to be the friend of play" even on the Sabbath.[51]

Bushnell was joined in his celebration of play by Ralph Waldo Emerson, who was among the first to fault Americans for their lack of physical exercise. Writing to a friend in 1843, the Sage of Concord observed that Americans seemed to lack the healthfulness that characterized the "robust" Englishman.[52] Four years later, Emerson actually visited England, and this visit reinforced his impression that America possessed more invalids than England. The visit also inspired Emerson in 1857 to publish *English Traits,* a book in which he portrayed the typical Englishman as a "wealthy, juicy, broadchested creature," destined ultimately to manage affairs all over the globe.[53]

English Traits was not wholly effusive about the English, for while Emerson admired their physiques, he heavily criticized their religion. Anglicanism, to the Transcendentalist Emerson, smacked too much of complacency and hoary ritual. And though the Anglican clergy were laudable for their manliness ("when out of their gowns," Emerson noted, they "would turn their backs on no man") they were nonetheless guilty of overstressing the importance of conformity and of telling their parishioners "By taste are ye saved."[54]

More appreciative than Emerson of the connection between Anglicanism and health was Thomas Wentworth Higginson, a Unitarian minister whom one historian has called America's premier "muscular Christian."[55] In an 1858 *Atlantic Monthly* article entitled "Saints, and Their Bodies," Higginson praised Kingsley's "Broad Church" movement, with its emphasis on "breadth of shoulders, as well as of doctrines." Also singled out for praise was *Tom Brown's School Days,* whose "charm," Higginson thought, "lies simply in the healthy boy's-life, which it exhibits, and in the recognition of physical culture, which is so novel to Americans."[56]

Having complimented the English for their adoption of sports, Higginson went on to criticize Americans for their "deficiency of physical health." As evidence of this deficiency, he pointed not only to the valetudinarianism of America's women and professional men, but also to the fact that "one seldom notices a ruddy face in the schoolroom, without tracing it back to Transatlantic origin." The absence of healthy people in America was in large part the fault of the Protestant churches, wrote Higginson, particularly those churches that taught "that physical vigor and sanctity were incompatible." In preaching such nonsense, Higginson concluded, the churches were separating themselves "from the strong life of the age." They were filling the ministry with men who lacked "a vigorous, manly life," and they were encouraging parents to "say of their pallid, puny, sedentary, lifeless, joyless little offspring, 'He is born for a minister,' while the ruddy, the brave, and the strong are as promptly assigned to a secular career!"[57]

By calling for more health and manliness in the churches, and by praising the works of Hughes and Kingsley, Higginson helped to inaugurate the muscular Christianity movement in America. Joining Higginson were other liberal Protestant clergymen such as the Reverend Henry Ward Beecher, who was among the first to advocate building gymnasiums within YMCAs.[58] Using religious property for recreational purposes must have seemed outlandish to old-style Calvinists, but physical fitness advocate Moses Coit Tyler promoted the idea in his 1869 book *The Brawnville Papers.* "Every village that has two churches now should just put both congregations together, to worship in one building and to practice gymnastics in the other," wrote Tyler. The change would produce healthier Christians, and then "there would be more godliness in this land, and more manliness, too; the fashionable theology would be shamed out of its disgraceful Paganisms; and the diseased rubbish which was shot upon Christianity by forlorn old monks who had the stomach ache would be carted off by the scavenger."[59]

The Tyler plan for making gyms out of churches was undoubtedly too extreme for Hughes and Kingsley. But their ideas about Christian manliness clearly appealed to Tyler, who spent time as an itinerant gymnast in England before becoming America's first professor of U.S. history.[60] Whether or not Tyler picked up muscular Christianity in England, he was at least familiar with the term. For him "muscular Christianity" meant "Christianity applied to the treatment and use of our bodies," but for the *North Carolina Presbyterian* "muscular Christianity" held a slightly different meaning. "We like this phrase, though it is 'new coined,'" noted the journal in 1867, "because it expresses the idea of that robustness and vigor which ought to characterize those who are strong in the Lord and the power of His might. It is suggestive of force and that high-strung, nervous energy which by constant exercise has developed its possessor into the stature of a perfect man in Christ Jesus."[61]

While the Presbyterian journal's view of muscular Christianity as a character builder differed from Tyler's view of it as a body builder, both the journal and Tyler clearly held muscular Christianity in high esteem. They shared that view with the *New York Times,* which in response to the construction in 1869 of the first YMCA gymnasium in New York City wrote that the move represented a necessary "concession to the muscular Christianity of the time."[62] By using the term in a positive way, journals such as the *Times* and the *North Carolina Pres-*

byterian demonstrated that the ideas of Hughes and Kingsley had taken root in America by the late 1860s. But not everyone greeted this development with joy. One of the many detractors of muscular Christianity was a writer for the *Sunday Times* of Boston, who made fun of Dwight L. Moody in 1877 by calling him a "muscular Christian," a term for which *The Friend,* a Hawaiian missionary journal, also had little appetite.[63] "We all understand the kind of thing which is meant by people who talk of Muscular Christianity," observed *The Friend,* which went on to criticize muscular Christianity's supporters for thinking that "the grandeur of the character is increased by the combination of thorough blackguardism with high physical qualifications."[64]

Opposition to muscular Christianity was particularly virulent within American academia, wrote one Amherst College professor. Eventually that opposition was replaced by an appreciation for the sanctity of health, he continued, but there was a time in the mid-nineteenth century when "Muscular Christianity was not in favor with the elect."[65] That disfavor on the part of the establishment toward muscular Christianity was evident when Charles Kingsley died in 1875. In response to Kingsley's death, the *Illustrated Christian Weekly* in New York observed rather caustically that the man had been more of a novelist than a theologian. The paper also stated that Kingsley's view of the Christian as "a man who fears God and can walk a thousand miles in a thousand days" was "certainly very defective."[66]

The fact that there was resistance to muscular Christianity in America is undeniable. That resistance, which was particularly strong before 1880, stemmed from a number of factors, one of them being the Civil War. At first glance, the war appears to have strengthened muscular Christianity by giving rise to such militant Christian songs as "The Battle Hymn of the Republic." But the war actually undermined muscular Christianity in America by certifying the manliness of innumerable men. Those men demonstrated their manhood on the battlefield; and having done so, they had scant need to demonstrate it again on the playing field. Their heroism was confirmed, and they could afford to scoff at muscular Christian remedies for unmanliness.[67]

Also retarding the spread of muscular Christianity in America was the country's economy. Unlike the English economy, which by the time of Hughes and Kingsley had become heavily industrialized, the

ESTES PARK
PUBLIC LIBRARY

American economy remained primarily agricultural until well after the Civil War. This meant that most Americans in the mid-nineteenth century were used to farming and engaging in hard physical labor. They may have worried about overusing their muscles, but concern for underuse was uncommon. When it surfaced in antebellum America, it came mainly from unusually privileged people such as Thomas Wentworth Higginson in the industrialized Northeast.

Higginson's fear of American decrepitude led him to eulogize exercise. But his efforts to promote exercise as an alternative to decrepitude stirred up opposition from within those evangelical Protestant churches that Charles Kingsley had described as "Manichaean," or body-denying. Those churches, which held sway in America to a far greater degree than in England, did not object to physical exertion when it was linked to production. But exercising one's muscles for no particular end except health struck many Protestants in the mid-nineteenth century as an immoral waste of time. As a result, exercise enthusiasts such as the Reverend Edward Everett Hale found it socially impossible to engage in the sports they loved. They could exercise their muscles while gardening, wrote Hale; for that was an acceptable use of time. "But if I spend a tenth part of the same time in playing ball, or in skating, or in rowing," he added, "my reputation as a man of industry, or even of sense, under our artificial canons, would be gone."[68]

Making it socially difficult to engage in sports was but one way whereby evangelical Protestant churches slowed down the growth of muscular Christianity in America. Another impediment was their love of feminine iconography. This love had grown over the course of the early nineteenth century, and by midcentury the churches, particularly those in the Northeast, were channeling much of their energy into praising such stereotypically "female" traits as nurturance, refinement, and sensitivity. In praising such traits, they naturally clashed with the muscular Christians, who tended to glorify such stereotypically "male" traits as strength, courage, and endurance.

The celebration of manly virtues never disappeared from Victorian churches in America, but those churches tended to champion femininity. Why they did so is a question perhaps best answered by Ann Douglas, who argues in her well-known "feminization" thesis that as career-minded antebellum men increasingly chose business over leadership in the churches, church leadership fell into the hands of less "manly" men (mainly ministers) and women. These two groups then established a symbiotic relationship. While women supported ministers following the disestablishment of churches in the early national period, ministers praised women for their womanly qualities. Ministers also created sermons that likened women to angels, depictions of Christ that emphasized his "feminine" character, and arguments that supported women's spiritual leadership within the home. As a result, writes Douglas, women were culturally if not politically empowered, and nineteenth-century American culture as a whole was substantially "feminized."[69]

Testimony corroborating Douglas's "feminization" thesis comes from Barbara Welter, who argues that nineteenth-century American Protestant churches were "more domesticated, more emotional, more soft and accommodating—in a word, more 'feminine' than their Puritan forebears."[70] As a result, observed English traveler Frances Trollope, America was unique, for there was surely no other country in the world "where religion had so strong a hold upon the women or a slighter hold upon the men."[71]

Faced with such an inhospitable climate, early muscular Christians might have foreseen that their success in America depended on certain conditions. First, fears of American "degeneracy" had to spread well beyond liberal Protestant ministers in New England such as Thomas Wentworth Higginson. Second, evangelical Protestants had to accept the virtues of leading a "strenuous life" replete with exercise. Third (and perhaps most important) there had to arise great dissatisfaction with the "feminization" of American Protestantism. As long as the majority joined Harriet Beecher Stowe in praising religion most for its being "comfortable," "poetical," "pretty," "sweet," and "dear," muscular Christianity stood little chance.[72] And as long as Protestant theology dwelt primarily on transcendence, and its art primarily on death, hostility would persist toward Charles Kingsley's "manly" notion of staring life square in the face.[73]

Overcivilization

Fortunately for muscular Christian expansionists, the triumphant reign of the ladies' journals, lyceum lecturers, and similar purveyors of Protestant refinement did not long remain unquestioned. Following the Civil War, and especially after 1880, Anglo male critics began wondering openly whether America might be paying too high a price for concerted highmindedness and for its attendant constraints in behavior. In particular, they charged the custodians of sentimental Protestant culture (the Alcotts, Beechers, Childs, Sigourneys, et alia) with having left the realities of earthly living—with having become, in a word, "overcivilized."

Witnesses to the baleful effects of overcivilization on America's upper classes included historian Henry C. Merwin and (more importantly) rebel patrician Theodore Roosevelt—safari hunter, future president, and author of *The Strenuous Life* (1901). According to these men, overcivilization meant excessive, body-denying intellectualism, the fruit of which was emasculation—physical and cultural. Merwin admitted to having little respect for the so-called "respectable" American, whom he termed "a creature who is what we call oversophisticated and effete—a being in whom the springs of action are, in a greater or less degree, paralyzed or perverted by the undue prominence of the intellect." Roosevelt heartily concurred with these sentiments, observing that there was a "general tendency among people of culture and education . . . to neglect and even look down on the rougher and manlier virtues, so that an advanced state of intellectual development is too often associated with a certain effeminacy of character."[74]

Roosevelt's critique of Gilded Age culture was harsh, but an even harsher critique came from Basil Ransom, a character in Henry James's novel *The Bostonians* (1886). Referring to the urban Victorian environment into which he had moved, the Southern-born Ransom confesses to feeling that "the whole generation is womanized; the masculine tone is passing out of the world; it's a feminine, a nervous, hysterical, chattering, canting age, an age of hollow phrases and fake delicacy and exaggerated solicitudes and coddled sensibilities, which, if we don't look out, will usher in a reign of mediocrity, of the feeblest and flattest and the most pretentious that has ever been."[75] This "chattering, canting age" described by Ransom drew blame not only for causing effeminacy in men but also for fostering "neurasthenia," or nerve sickness. Following its conception as a term in 1880 by neurologist George Beard, neurasthenia quickly became the diagnosis of choice for sufferers of hysteria, depression, and anxiety. And although these conditions were nothing new, their omnipresence in postbellum America seemed truly remarkable.[76]

"On every street, at every corner we meet the neurasthenics," declared the *North American Review* in 1908.[77] These, together with the people who analyzed them, included "the majority of well-known cultural producers of the time"—novelists such as Wharton, Howells, and Dreiser; artists such as Sargent, Eakins, and Remington; philosophers such as Royce, Santayana, and James; reformers such as Addams, Riis, and Muir; and cultural icons such as Mother Jones and Helen Keller.[78] Even Theodore Roosevelt, big game hunter that he eventually became, started out life as a neurasthenic child, a "tall, thin lad with bright eyes and legs like pipestems."[79]

Symptoms commonly associated with neurasthenia included headaches, backaches, worry, hypochondria, melancholia, digestive irregularities, nervous exhaustion, and "irritable weakness."[80] But of all their ailments, neurasthenics generally viewed paralysis of the will as the most debilitating. Such paralysis ("immobilizing, self-punishing repression," as T. J. Jackson Lears describes it)[81] might, if left unchecked, curtail the sufferer's productivity; or it might, providing the sufferer were wealthy enough, lead to one of those aimless European sojourns best represented in autobiography by Henry Adams, and in fiction by the character Peter Alden in George Santayana's *The Last Puritan*.

Often nervous paralytics sought the advice of a doctor, only to be told that they needed "complete rest"—a solution that seems in retrospect the worst possible. Had the deeply depressed Jane Addams taken this "respectable" course, implies a biographer, and not found fulfillment in settlement work, it is doubtful whether she could long have endured.[82] Nor would readers of Charlotte Perkins Gilman's *The Yellow Wall Paper* be subjected to such a horrific ending had the story's heroine, a neurasthenic woman following a "rest cure," been allowed to leave her room.[83]

Few psychologists today, of course, if faced with nineteenth-century neurasthenia, would recommend rest cures. Instead, they would likely follow Freud in attributing the disease not so much to overwork as to culturally thwarted sexual impulses. But though this may often have been true (the case of Alice James springs to mind), T. J. Jackson Lears cautions against viewing neurasthenia as simply the product of sexual repression. As much as anything, he writes, neurasthenia reflected people's aversion to and unfulfillment with the "evasive banality" of late-nineteenth-century American culture: that combination of material complacence, exaggerated refinement, and spiritual hypocrisy over which Basil Ransom so despaired.[84]

In a recent addendum to Lears's "evasive banality" thesis, Tom Lutz writes that besides revealing the emptiness of people's lives, neurasthenia served as "a marker of status and social acceptability." For one thing, doctors believed that the disease afflicted only the most highly developed races, and among these, only the most religiously "advanced" (proof of the latter being that "no Catholic country is very nervous"). For another thing, neurasthenia pervaded America's governing elite, and though most (including Theodore Roosevelt) thought this reason to lament, some (the more romantically inclined) could not help cherishing the imagined scenario wherein civilization's few pale guardians bravely contemplated "la deluge."[85]

Still, whatever the *spiritual* explanations for neurasthenia and the overcivilization scare—whether they were symptoms of overrefinement, reactions to cultural "weightlessness," or perverse forms of self-congratulation—their groundedness in late-nineteenth-century *material* conditions cannot be forgotten. As Richard Hofstadter pointed out long ago in his celebrated "status anxiety" argument, changes within the socioeconomic makeup of late-nineteenth-century America alone could have sufficed to produce nervousness among the nation's traditional middle and upper classes over the perceived imperilment of their hitherto dominant cultural rule.[86]

Foremost among the external developments considered a threat by America's "oldline" cultural arbiters (and by that Hofstadter meant not only small-town Protestant professionals but also old-moneyed urban elites) was the expansion of the cities. Estimates are that cities increased 50 percent in size during the 1880s, a rate six times faster than that of the 1870s;[87] and for those accustomed, as were many Protestants, to equating city living with all manner of vice, such growth seemed immoral. Indeed, Fred Smith of the Men and Religion Forward movement considered conditions in America's cities "shocking" enough to require the president to "call for a period of national prayer and repentance."[88]

Adding to worries about "city rot" was evidence of rural decline. For countless decades, the countryside had been counted on to offset urban wickedness, but Progressive Era reformers expressed concern that the countryside was not what it had once been. "As everyone knows," explained Myron Scudder of the Men and Religion Forward movement, "our country districts have long been suffering depletion. Even now," he observed, "multitudes of the better classes are busy exchanging their country homes for homes in the city," depriving their offspring of the chance to develop the superior "farm bred mind" needed to oversee America's cities, businesses, universities, and churches.[89]

While Scudder worried about rural depopulation, other defenders of Protestant hegemony felt threatened by an influx of immigrants. Largely non-"Western" and non-Protestant in character (especially after 1880) this influx was often taken by Anglos as a sign of their cultural displacement. At the very least, warned Cornell professor Edward Hitchcock, Jr., Americans weakened by "neurasthenia" were vulnerable to race "mingling" and to the loss of their distinctive Anglo-Saxon heritage.[90]

More sanguine about WASP tenacity was Congregationalist minister Frank Crane. But even he acknowledged that overcoming the immigrant's fondness for "the saloon, gambling devices, desecration of the Sabbath, profanity, vice and crime" would be difficult, especially given his "ominous" alienation from "the agencies of purity and sobriety, morality and love of justice."[91]

If the immigrant, the city, and rural depopulation constituted the first three horsemen of the nativist apocalypse, many considered the "modern woman" to be the fourth. Inevitably, critics differed as to who this creature was, but in general they saw her presaging "the invasion of man's domain by women."[92] As one journalist put it, "Woman has made her way to the smoking room and has mounted the bicycle. She began to adopt masculine attire, and nothing but her own taste stopped her."[93]

Whether America was actually beset by cigar-smoking, pants-wearing women is, of course, open to debate. But it is true that the number of women white-collar workers trebled between 1900 and 1920[94] and that many, including psychologist G. Stanley Hall, educator Lilburn Merrill, and Episcopal bishop Henry C. Potter of New York, found this development objectionable on medical, educative, and moral grounds.

Hall maintained throughout his work that it was the chief function of womanhood to bear and raise children; hence his characterization of the carefree "Gibson girl" as a "medical monstrosity." Merrill underscored more the supreme unattractiveness of the archetypal "woman lecturer," whose "cheeks were furrowed by a soul out of sorts because of the mistake that had been made in creating her a woman."[95]

As for Potter, he counted "the modern young girl . . . among the other freaks and eccentricities of our modern social order." She had left her home, he wrote, finding it "dull and irksome," and from there had fallen prey to "every silly ambition and every grotesque imagination that could find a lodgment in any weak and undisciplined mind." In short, "she has gone to hell!"[96]

As intemperate as Anglo-Protestant commentators could sometimes be about outsiders, and about the encroachments of urban vice, evidence suggests they were no less concerned over internal threats. After all, furor over change seldom erupts from those wholly confident of their capacity for resistance; and in truth many Protestants felt they lacked that capacity. The pervasiveness of neurasthenia helped convince them of their weakened condition, as did a number of other, more tangible factors, all supposedly implicated in the Anglo race's growing physical, cultural, and moral enfeeblement.

Cities came in for a good share of the blame, this time not as breeders of crime but as sappers of white-collar vitality. "A hundred years ago," observed a writer for *Harper's* in 1889,

> there was more done to make our men and women hale and vigorous than there is to-day. Over eighty per cent of all our men then were farming, hunting, or fishing, rising early, out all day in the pure, bracing air, giving many muscles very active work, eating wholesome food, retiring early, and so laying in a good stock of vitality and health. But now hardly forty per cent are farmers, and nearly all the rest are at callings—mercantile, mechanical, or professional—which do almost nothing to make one sturdy and enduring.[97]

Joining in the antiurban refrain were psychologists William James and G. Stanley Hall. James for his part confessed to feeling his flesh "creep" at the thought that one day technological advances would make physical exertion unnecessary. Physical vigor "will always be needed," he avowed, "to furnish the background of sanity, serenity, and cheerfulness to life." Hall concurred; only he wondered whether city life allowed for physical recreation, and whether the public understood its necessity. "The trouble is," wrote Hall, "that too few realize what physical vigor is in man or woman, and how dangerously near weakness often is to wickedness."[98]

The physical enervation of its young—particularly its male young—proved especially compelling to America's Protestant establishment, who occasionally entertained fears of well-bred but overeducated weaklings succumbing before muscular immigrant hordes. Oliver Wendell Holmes, for example, decried the existence in cities of "such a set of black-coated, stiff-jointed, soft-muscled, paste-complexioned youth as . . . never before sprung from loins of Anglo-Saxon lineage." J. F. A. Adams believed that public schools would have to initiate physical training if Anglo-Saxons were to "save our race from physical degeneracy." And Luther Gulick of the YMCA estimated that "exclusive intellectual education at the expense of the rest of the man soon works a ruin that we are all of us only too familiar with; results in this direction frequently come about in one generation of this one-sided development, but more usually in two or three. Thus we account for the poor children that so frequently come from good stock."[99]

Some degeneracy theorists did not think the problem one of reduced health in boys through academic one-sidedness; rather, they stressed corruption of boys' character by women teachers (who by 1920 made up 80 percent of the precollege teaching force).[100] Between 1908 and 1915, articles on education with the "woman peril" as their theme appeared in the *Atlantic Monthly, World's Work,* and the *American Physical Education Review,* the first lamenting "the feminizing influence of woman teachers on manners and morals and general attitude toward life";[101] the second blaming female teachers for incidents of "rowdyism";[102] and the third regretting the presence of "old maids" on college faculties.[103] By far the most eloquent case, however, against women teachers surfaced in a 1914 *Educational Review* article. Here the author argued, "To put a boy . . . under woman tutelage at his most impressionable, character-forming age is to render violence to nature and a gross wrong and inequity to the boy; it is to do violence to that most precious possession, his masculine nature—in a large sense, his soul."[104]

Turn-of-the-century feminine influence in areas other than education likewise drew hostile scrutiny. In publishing, for example, Silas Weir Mitchell joked that "the monthly [magazines] are getting so lady-like that naturally they will soon menstruate." Kentucky author James Lane Allen felt similarly about novelists. For too long, he wrote, writers had labored under "the Feminine" as opposed to "the Masculine Principle," producing "a literature of the overcivilized, the hyper-fastidious . . . the fragile, the trivial, the rarified, [and] the bloodless."[105]

Theodore Roosevelt thought abandonment of the "Masculine Principle" particularly crippling when it came to politics. As he remembered it, reform efforts in the Gilded Age went nowhere because the reformers themselves were "gentlemen who were very nice, very refined, who shook their heads over political corruption and discussed it in drawing rooms and parlors, but who were wholly unable to grapple with real men in real life."[106]

All in all, critics charged, if gender rules could not be straightened out, and if substitutes (moral and physical) could not be found for life on the farm, chaos loomed. Some spoke of imminent "race suicide" caused by the cessation of marriage between people of the "right sort." Others, including naval expert and Christian apologist Alfred Thayer Mahan, noted America's resemblance to ancient Rome—or at least Rome after it had, in Mahan's words, abandoned its "strong masculine impulse" and "degenerated into that worship of comfort, wealth, and general softness, which is the ideal of the peace prophets of to-day."[107]

Among those most eager to rectify overcivilization were progressive-minded Protestant clergy, who wondered to what extent their churches were involved in the devitalization (or "feminization") of American culture, and whether it was possible for them to atone. One minister so concerned was the Reverend Charles Macfarland, secretary of the Federal Council of Churches, who observed that "much of our ministry is dying, or is dead, of culture." It was like "a great dynamo," he added, "without any connection to the felts and wheels."[108]

Macfarland accused educated Protestants of abandoning their historic leadership role, and of showing indifference to socioeconomic concerns. People in cities were electing their own men and not "men of culture," he wrote, in large part because "men of culture . . . have not been sufficiently in touch, in sympathy, with the feelings, the wants, the needs, the hearts, the minds of those whose destinies have been placed in their hands."[109]

Richard S. Storrs of Union College likewise observed church influence on the wane, although he attributed it less to congregational indifference than to clerical unmanliness. "More frequently . . . than anything else," he wrote, unmanliness "deprives the cultivated preacher of religion of any such commanding power as belonged to the men, less largely instructed, but more stalwart in spirit, who made pulpits famous half a century ago."[110]

Compounding the social shortcomings of the Church was what historian Paul Carter calls "the spiritual crisis of the Gilded Age," which included doubts about the continued relevance of Christianity itself.[111] These doubts persisted despite newer, more humanistic conceptions of God, and despite Herculean attempts to reconcile theology with modern scientific principles such as Darwinism.[112] Indeed, efforts to modernize the Gospel may actually have aggravated what T. J. Jackson Lears calls (after Nietzsche) the "weightlessness" of late-nineteenth-century culture, a culture whose "spiritual blandness" and "moral impotence" furthered people's longing "for intense experience to give some definition, some distinct outline and substance to their vaporous lives."[113]

The Strenuous Life

Late-nineteenth-century fears concerning Anglo-Protestant obsolescence, the disenchantment with Victorian culture, and a reaction against urban "corruption" paved the way for what one minister termed that "recent rational revival of righteousness," the Progressive Movement.[114] Viewed by the journals *Outlook, Current Literature,* and *Nineteenth Century* as "a great moral upheaval," Progressivism consisted of a number of reformist drives, not the least of which was "The Cult of the Strenuous Life."[115]

Eager to redeem the nation from "slackness," devotees of the Strenuous Life emphasized duty, bodily vigor, action over reflection, experience over "book learning," and pragmatic idealism over romantic sentimentality. They also endowed their program with a highly "masculine" vocabulary, eschewing such hitherto popular "feminine" terms as "heartfelt," "soulful," and the like. At the height of their fame, proponents of the Strenuous Life influenced many areas of American culture, including politics, recreation, literature, science, education, and religion.

No one better championed the Strenuous Life than the term's originator, Theodore Roosevelt. An asthmatic, spectacled child descended from a patrician New York family, the future president initially seemed to confirm every dire prediction concerning WASP malaise. But a searing adolescent experience during which he was beaten up by two boys who called him a "highbrow" persuaded him to remake himself. As a result, he took up gymnastics and shooting, was taught boxing by an ex-prizefighter, and later purchased a large ranch in the Dakotas, where, in the words of the Reverend Christian Reisner, "he studied in God's out-of-doors amidst primitive conditions and 'nature-cured' men."[116]

Upon returning to civilization (according to Reisner, like Moses from Mt. Sinai) Roosevelt flouted genteel convention and immersed himself in the corrupt world of New York State politics.[117] He chose politics as his particular field of "strenuous endeavor" (he thought everyone should have one) because of its challenge, and because he saw politics as a manly proving ground whereupon those who were decent and law-abiding "should not let those who stand for evil have all the virile qualities."[118]

Roosevelt wished to set an example for other "sons of the rich" (lately grown "soft," noted Reisner, "and given to slothful ease"); and in this he achieved success. One newspaper in particular noted that after Roosevelt upbraided the New York City Club for naïveté in politics, members there "took the tops of their canes out of their mouths, tapped the floor with the other end and threw away their lighted cigarettes" (cigarette smoking then being considered an effeminate habit).[119]

New York City's Irish political bosses proved harder to impress. Many thought Roosevelt a "sissy," since he continued to exhibit, despite his inward transformation, all the outward markings of a confirmed "dude": a Harvard education, eyeglasses worn at the end of a black silk cord, impeccable clothes, grammatical English, and "a comically high-pitched voice."[120] But when those same bosses, angered by Roosevelt's reforms, hired a thug named Stubby Lewis to rough him up, "the trained boxer gave 'Stubby' the beating of his life."[121]

Roosevelt's beating of Stubby Lewis captured the imagination of those fearful of immigrant takeover and tired of genteel restraint. Subsequent exploits, such as the storming of San Juan Hill, amply confirmed the soon-to-be-president's place as an apostle of WASP rejuvenation. Roosevelt himself took this role seriously, preaching variously the virtues of athleticism, the outdoors as a remedy for urban life, improved character as an impediment to vice, and the necessity of opposing "race suicide."[122]

Topping Roosevelt's list of social restoratives, however, was the Spanish-American War, which he saw as a chance to assert America's eminence in world councils while cleansing the Western Hemisphere of a used-up power.[123] Roosevelt also viewed U.S. victory in the conflict as evidence (in Senator Albert Beveridge's words) of God's having "marked the American people as His chosen nation to finally lead in the redemption of the world."[124]

But for Roosevelt the most exalted justification for war was neither geopolitical nor missionary. Instead, it involved war's ennobling effects on the human frame—its imposition of discipline and its forging of courage and mettle. This was especially crucial for an America that to the Rough Rider's mind showed signs of "losing the fighting edge," lapsing into "mere animal sloth and ease," and succumbing to a "gradual failure of vitality."[125]

Overestimating Roosevelt's appeal—warlike and otherwise—to Protestant America would be hard to do. To many he seemed the standard-bearer of Progressivism and something of a savior besides.[126] Such was Roosevelt in the eyes of his followers that in 1912 they adopted "Onward Christian Soldiers" as a song for the Bull Moose campaign.[127] And when Roosevelt died in 1919, the Boy Scouts of America spoke of him in terms befitting a messiah. "He was frail," the BSA recalled; "he made himself a tower of strength. He was timid; he made himself a lion of courage. He was a dreamer; he became one of the great doers of all time." Furthermore, "he broke a nation's slumber with his cry, and it rose up. He touched the eyes of blind men with a flame and gave them vision. Souls became swords through him, swords became servants of God."[128]

Among Theodore Roosevelt's greatest legacies were substantially improved national park and forest systems—beneficiaries of the president's belief in the revivifying effects of outdoor life. Roosevelt was not alone in this belief; for as cities grew and the frontier shrank, people evinced increasing respect toward nature, which *Outlook* magazine described in 1903 as "the middle ground between God and man" and "the playground of the soul."[129]

Nature worship helped to popularize nature writers such as Daniel Beard and new leisure-time magazines such as *Forest and Stream* (1873), *Outing* (1885), *Field and Stream* (1897), and *Outdoor Life* (1897). Nature worship also influenced to some degree men's fashions, which tended to emulate the athletic, outdoor lifestyle.[130] But nowhere was nature worship more seminal than in organized camping, which emerged for boys in the 1880s and for girls some thirty years later. Churches, interestingly enough, helped inaugurate the movement, it being their contention that city boys needed fresh air in order to avoid "moral deterioration."[131]

The first church camp (founded in 1880 and only the second boys' summer camp in America) was located on Gardner's Island, Rhode Island. Its founder, the Reverend George W. Hinckley, a self-described "apostle of fresh air," later justified camping on the grounds that "The race was dying; dying of its own stupidity; dying from in-doorness." In 1882, a second church camp appeared: Camp Harvard in Rindge, New Hampshire. Three years later, the YMCA opened its first camp, Camp Bald Head, in Orange Lake, New York. But "it was not until 1890," observed camp historian Henry Gibson, "that the organized camp idea caught the imagination of leaders of boy life."[132] After that, "camps for boys [sprang up] like mushrooms."[133]

At the same time camps took city children to the countryside, the Playground Association of America aimed at bringing the countryside to city children. Founded in 1906 by Henry S. Curtis and Luther Gulick, with Gulick as president, Theodore Roosevelt as honorary president, and Jacob Riis as honorary vice-president, the PAA solidified the growing "Play Movement," whose concerns, as Curtis explained them, were urbanization, overwork, neurasthenia, "racial decay," the tendency in cities toward criminality, and (last but not least) the intellectual bankruptcy of ascetic Christianity.[134]

Additional, no less compelling, reasons for forming playgrounds in cities were advanced by Association presidents Luther Gulick and Joseph Lee. Lee thought playgrounds an "antidote to civilization," which he described as tragic, disease-ridden, and ultimately unfulfilling. Open air, danger, ruggedness, and participation in team sports were prerequisites for full humanity in boys, he wrote, and their absence had transformed America into an unidealistic, listless "race of money makers" and mere sports spectators.[135]

Somewhat less apocalyptically, Gulick stressed the effectiveness of playgrounds at drawing young people from dance halls and movie palaces, and at teaching them "the happy and wholesome use of leisure time." Yet he, too, thought recreation vital to national well-being since, if history was right, "those nations which devoted their leisure to re-creating health and building up beautiful bodies have tended to survive, while those which turned, in the marginal hours, to dissipation have written for us the history of national downfall."[136]

Playground enthusiasts were not the only ones enamored of roughness and "reality," and hostile toward modernism, with its gray bureaucratic structures; artists of the Roosevelt era were, too. For craftsmen (particularly those of the Arts and Crafts movement) the challenge was to create by hand, incorporating nature whenever possible (see, for example, the wood furniture in Old Faithful Lodge). For architects, whether Gothic Revivalists or Prairie Schoolers, the issue was authenticity: planning buildings reminiscent of a distinct time or place.

In literature, the perfumed decadence of Oscar Wilde was in disrepute, as was the comparatively tough "domestic realism" of Henry James and William Dean Howells (whose grandniece actually wrote him in 1906 complaining about the lack of virility in his novels).[137] What seemed to please critics more than the domestic realists were "manly" novelists such as Jack London, Stephen Crane, Theodore Dreiser, Frank Norris, and (on a lesser plane) Zane Grey, all of whom were exponents of action, honesty, and adventure. Older adventure writers such as Sir Walter Scott and Rudyard Kipling also received tribute, one reviewer complimenting the latter on his style and on his imperviousness to feminine influence.[138]

Scientists as well as humanists were converts to the Strenuous Life, and if the latter upheld movement goals in writing, the former verified them in the lab. One "scientist" concerned with invigorating America was G. Stanley Hall, who authored numerous works on how to make "men more manly and women more womanly."[139] Another expert opposed to physical desuetude and gender deviation was Dr. Eugene Talbot, whose archetypal "degenerates" included unmarried women, cigarette smokers, and boys who played with dolls.[140]

More supportive of strenuosity overall, however, within science—particularly social science—was the movement away from theories of purely natural selection. By 1908, as one authority put it, "a voluminous literature . . . has quite completely relegated heredity influence into an oblivion of insignificance," thus establishing "the all-importance of environment in the making of character."[141]

By admitting the efficacy of human engineering (that is, "character building"), science lent validity to Progressive attempts at race revitalization, city reclamation, and the recasting of immigrants in the "American" mold. It also participated directly in these attempts, primarily through the newly established field of eugenics, which one practitioner described in 1910 as "rational scientific human breeding for the welfare of the race" and a cure for "the unnatural conditions with which modern civilization has surrounded us."[142]

G. Stanley Hall defined eugenics more simply as the "art of breeding as applied to man." But he also thought it revolutionary insofar as it combined scientific methods with moral intent, thus helping to bridge the nineteenth-century gap between science and religion.[143] Emboldened by Hall's idea that breeding was a moral topic, eugenicists and eugenically minded groups such as the American Purity League and the American Society of Sanitary and Moral Prophylaxis (both representative of the social hygiene movement) spoke with comparative candor about such hitherto off-color subjects as pregnancy, venereal disease, and "the Social Peril" (i.e., prostitution).[144]

Another subject deemed "moral" by eugenicists was physical training, called by one authority the nation's most "wholesome racial habit."[145] Indeed, so important was this considered for the nation's well-being that many demanded it be made mandatory in the public schools, something that first occurred statewide in Ohio (1892), then in Illinois (1895) and North Dakota (1899).[146] Colleges also began making physical training mandatory in the 1890s, although Harvard refused to do so until after World War I, its rationale being that "in an institution where attendance at chapel and lectures is optional, it has not seemed advisable to require attendance at physical exercises."[147]

Few schools did more on behalf of youthful bodies than those in Philadelphia, where physical training was considered a subset of moral education. Charles K. Taylor, who directed the city's Department of Moral Education, thought it "ten times more important for children to know that destruction came upon Rome because the people became physically weak and morally corrupt than it is to study the names of the successive Caesars." He also considered it his duty to succeed where the churches "had utterly failed": namely by connecting "in a practical way the physical and mental life with the moral."[148]

One of Taylor's notable "experiment[s] in character building" involved making boys wear buttons that designated them the possessors of either first-class, second-class, or third-class physiques. Any boy wanting to join extracurricular activities had to wear a button, Taylor explained, and naturally the dishonor attached to being anything less than first-class would induce him to become stronger.[149]

Taylor and educators like him believed that the importance of physical education demanded a shift in educational priorities. Their contention was that there existed too much mind-body dualism within the academy and that this had to be overcome if students were ever to achieve what the Reverend Elwood Worcester called "the fundamental dogma of modern psychology": "the unity of mind and body."[150]

Yale mathematics professor Eugene L. Richards went further, arguing that the end product of education should not be knowledge, but rather "power, vigor." After all, he reasoned, history proved that "all those races which declined, went down before races of stronger physical power. The corruption of the body by sloth and effeminate luxury was followed by a mental decline, just as softness and weakness of mind . . . have always gone hand in hand with enervated, enfeebled bodies."[151]

The heightened importance of brawn over brains led a Harvard Phi Beta Kappa speaker to observe in 1894 that the ideal college man was not, as in days gone by, an introspective, religious type with a "towering forehead, from which the hair was carefully brushed backwards and upwards to give the full effect to his remarkable phrenological development." Instead, collegiate heroes of the Nineties were apt to be men of "mass" and "power"—stars of the gridiron or captains of crew.[152]

Not everyone approved this change in college models from serious scholar to vigorous "all-around man." But Charles W. Eliot, the president of Harvard from 1869 to 1909, applauded it. A former athlete himself, Eliot held "bodily wholesomeness and vitality" to be the "one indispensable foundation for the satisfactions of life" (including "domestic joy," "professional success," and an "honorable career"). Moreover, he strongly disagreed with "all attempts"—not excluding religious ones—"to draw a line between bodily satisfactions on the one hand and mental or spiritual satisfaction on the other."[153]

Thirteen years into his presidency, Eliot reported to the Harvard trustees that, as a result of athletic and curricular reforms, "the ideal student has been transformed from a stooping, weak, and sickly youth into one well-formed, robust, and healthy." In 1905 he reiterated that "nowadays a scholar is not a recluse, or a weakling incapable of strenuous pursuits." Instead he was the owner of "a tough and alert body" who "masters some books . . . and then pushes beyond," heading toward the goal of progressive reform.[154]

Muscular Christianity and the Social Gospel

As the call of the Strenuous Life reverberated in the secular society, many urged the Protestant churches to get in sync with the times. Instead of clinging to the sentimentalized Christianity of the past, editorialized *Century Magazine* in 1896, the churches ought to embrace a "vigorous, robust, muscular Christianity . . . devoid of all the et cetera of creed," a Christianity "which shows the character and manliness of Christ."[155] Such a Christianity could be found, many thought, in the Social Gospel movement, which swept through mainline Protestant churches in the late nineteenth and early twentieth centuries.

Proponents of the Social Gospel were particularly plentiful at Oberlin College in Ohio. A "cradle for the fledgling physical education profession and the muscular Christian movement," Oberlin reflected the religious sensibilities of its president, Henry Churchill King, who criticized Protestant churches for belonging "to an amiable rather than a strenuous age." What was needed was a "new Puritanism," argued King—something to sweep away the religious "sentimentality" of a "vacillating, flabby, self-indulgent generation."[156] This new religion would have to be socially relevant, added the dean of Oberlin Theological Seminary, who explained, "There is a kind of civilized savageness in the terribly earnest mood of our age which will kill or abandon any institution that cannot prove its right to continued existence"—Protestant churches included.[157]

The need to be socially relevant lent force to the Social Gospellers, who addressed not only iniquitous labor conditions in industrial America but also Victorian cultural anxieties, including fears about physical weakness and weightlessness. Other turn-of-the-century religious figures, such as High Church Episcopalians, joined proponents of the Social Gospel movement in addressing Victorian cultural concerns, but whereas the High Churchmen dealt with urban problems by becoming medievalists and antimodernists, the Social Gospellers proposed to deal with urban problems directly. They also differed from their popular contemporaries the Christian Scientists, whose modern-day gnosticism (a rejection of physical problems) struck Henry C. King as escapist. "Christian brethren, this is life," he cried— "temptation, trial, struggle, conflict, possible victory—the strenuous life. You cannot cowardly give it up."[158]

In response to the call for strenuous service, the Social Gospellers helped to set up charitable agencies such as soup kitchens and homeless shelters. Their efforts on behalf of the urban poor earned them the respect of later secular historians, who tend to praise them for reversing the churches' old attitude toward social problems, which one authority says was marked prior to 1880 by "a spirit of good-natured apathy."[159] But the Social Gospellers were not just social problem solvers; they were also moralists. Many of their leaders, such as Congregationalist ministers Josiah Strong, Lyman Abbott, and Washington Gladden, grew up with small-town values and believed that those values ought to be replicated in America's cities.

Guided by their dream of evangelizing the cities, the Social Gospellers expressed an interest in reaching out to Catholic urban immigrants and teaching them such classic small-town Protestant virtues as temperance and delayed gratification. They also warned against inactivity on the part of urban churches. Such inactivity would spell disaster, wrote Josiah Strong. For there were "increasing indications that if the churches do not soon organize for the prosecution of social reform they will lose their opportunity for leadership and with it their great opportunity to regain their lost hold on the masses."[160]

To connect their religion with the masses, Social Gospellers wanted to make it more appealing. This desire led them to downplay the remote image of God the Father while concentrating "almost exclusively" on the more immediate figure of Jesus, whom they liked to portray as a rough-handed carpenter and social activist.[161] Social Gospellers also sought to popularize their religion by downplaying credal niceties and denominational exclusivity, encumbrances that Charles Kingsley had condemned fifty years earlier on behalf of the Broad Church movement.

Kingsley no doubt would have approved of the Social Gospellers. He certainly would have shared their fears about a gender imbalance within mainline American Protestantism. That imbalance had become truly remarkable by 1899, when women reportedly comprised three-quarters of the church's membership and nine-tenths of its attendance.[162] With so many more women than men in church, it was clear to many in the Social Gospel movement that the church was purveying an unmanly religion. "There is not enough of effort, of struggle in the typical church life of to-day to win young men to the church," explained Josiah Strong; for a "flowery bed of ease does not appeal to a fellow who has any manhood in him."[163]

Strong shared his view of the church as "effeminate" with a number of Social Gospel ministers. One was Carl Case, a Baptist, who wrote in 1906 that there existed "a feminine note in religion as in education, depriving it of its virility, prone to substitute a sentimental idea

of what ought to be for a candid recognition of what is . . . with an in-
ordinate desire to call everything by a fictitious name, dreaming that
life is beauty, not knowing that life is war."[164]

The issue of unmanliness in religion was not peripheral to the Social Gospel; it was central. That was why Social Gospel leaders devoted whole books to the subject, books such as Washington Gladden's *Straight Shots at Young Men* (1900), Josiah Strong's *The Times
and Young Men* (1901), and Harry E. Fosdick's *The Manhood of the
Master* (1913). Unifying these works was the argument that an unmanly church was incapable of enacting serious social reform. The
church that was "so emasculated that the devil turns away from it
with a smile" could accomplish nothing, explained one Presbyterian
minister. But a church with "virility" would ultimately be able to
"mold public opinion into hostility to political treachery and municipal rottenness."[165]

Having determined that the church was beset by a manhood problem, Social Gospellers came up with a solution: bring more men into
church. Every church needed to fill its pews with more "red-blooded
men," declared one Oberlin Theological Seminary official.[166] But how
best to do this was a question that puzzled the Social Gospellers.
Some, such as Walter Rauschenbusch, sought to bring men to church
by making Jesus look more manly. "There was nothing mushy, nothing sweetly effeminate about Jesus," asserted Rauschenbusch. For Jesus was a "man's man" who "turned again and again on the snarling
pack of his pious enemies and made them slink away." The essential
manliness of Jesus was unquestionable, agreed Josiah Strong. But the
issue for him was not whether Jesus was manly enough for men;
rather it was whether men were manly enough for Jesus. "The practical question for you," he told a young man, "is whether you are *man*
enough to become a genuine Christian—man enough to give up the
meanness of selfishness for the general good."[167]

Strong allowed that for young men truly to be attracted to the
church, changes aside from the elimination of Victorian hyper-
femininity would have to be made. The most important of these
changes was having the churches come to grips with physical reality.
If religion in the eighteenth century was not spiritual enough, Strong
argued, religion in the nineteenth century was not physical enough.
And this was unfortunate because a religion "which ignores the physical life becomes more or less mystical and effeminate, loses its virility,
and has little influence over men or affairs."[168]

Coming to grips with the physical life not only meant fixing up urban slums, wrote Strong; it also meant fixing up one's body. There needed to be "much greater respect for the human body," he reasoned, since "there can be little usefulness, little intelligence, little moral character, little happiness without the right sort of a body." For this reason, Strong disliked seeing unfit bodies all around him. There was something wrong "with the general physique of the race," he concluded, and he was not alone among Social Gospellers in thinking that the church was somehow at fault. For too long, argued the Reverend James Vance, Christians had been ignoring the Biblical "religion of the body," leaving the "impression . . . that Christianity strikes at physical development, or is, at best, indifferent to physical health and beauty."[169]

If the church wanted to uphold physical health, thought the Social Gospellers, then it had to accept sports and bodily exercise. This acceptance could simply take the form of ministerial support for sports, as it did when Washington Gladden urged "the young man who sits at the desk or leans over the counter all day" to take up either gymnastics or the bicycle. But some within the Social Gospel movement believed that modern conditions made it necessary for the church to take a more direct role in physical education. "Industry today is modifying human biology," causing "the enervation of physical and moral powers," observed George Fisher of the YMCA's Physical Education Department. Hence the need for churches and "Christian employers" alike to embark on a "new physiological evangelism," one whose outcome would be the reduction of working hours, an increase in exercise, and the improvement of personal hygiene.[170]

By forging an alliance between religion and the Progressives' cult of the Strenuous Life, the Social Gospellers thought they were doing good. However, their alliance had unintended consequences. Instead of strengthening religion, contends T. J. Jackson Lears, the Social Gospellers actually weakened it by eroding the boundaries between sacred and secular and by equating health and manliness with divinity. Such accomplishments, in Lears's opinion, helped foster a twentieth-century "therapeutic ethos": a belief in individual well-being for its own sake, and not as a means toward helping others.[171]

Considerable truth appends to Lears's criticisms of the Social Gospel at its most muscularly Christian. Nevertheless, it must be allowed that most Social Gospellers themselves generally eschewed the therapeutic ethos, preferring instead to associate good health with the fulfillment of some higher purpose. As Robert Handy notes, "The social gospel emphasized the motif of service to humanity," and for this reason its justifications for "right body keeping" tended to be along the lines of making oneself more serviceable.[172]

For his part, Henry C. King listed as the main reason for keeping in "superb health" the obligation of the Christian to "make his body the best instrument that he can make it for the spirit, the very best medium for the spirit to work through." Harvard chaplain Francis Peabody put it even more simply, calling "the healthy body . . . an agent of the Christian soul." But perhaps Josiah Strong came closest to epitomizing muscular Christianity when he wrote, "If the true Christian aim is service, not ecstasy, then that is the most Christian treatment of the body which fits it for the most perfect, the most abounding, the longest-continued service in upbuilding the kingdom of God."[173]

Ministers such as Strong belonged to a powerful movement in nineteenth-century Protestantism, a movement whose watchwords were health and manliness. This movement surfaced first in England, where it was fueled by the moralistic adventure tales of Thomas Hughes and Charles Kingsley, both of whom opposed asceticism and "effeminacy" within the Anglican Church. To make Anglicanism a religion suitable for the conquering British people, Hughes and Kingsley sought to equip it with rugged and manly qualities. They also exported their campaign for more health and manliness in the Church to antebellum America, where factors such as "feminized" Protestantism and Protestant opposition to sports prevented the ideas of Hughes and Kingsley from immediately taking hold. Postbellum changes in American society, however, placed health and manliness uppermost in the minds of many male Protestants, who viewed factors such as urbanization, Catholic immigration, and "neurasthenic decay" as threats not only to their health and manhood but also to their privileged social standing. To maintain that social standing, WASP leaders such as Theodore Roosevelt urged "old stock" Americans to revitalize themselves by embracing athleticism and aggressive male behavior as part of the Strenuous Life. WASP leaders also called on their churches to abandon the supposedly enervating tenets of "feminized" Protestantism and to replace those tenets with the Social Gospel, whose proponents echoed Hughes and Kingsley in calling for what can best be termed "muscular Christianity," a strenuous religion for the Strenuous Life.

CHAPTER TWO

God in the Gym

> Any religious experience that is connected with a weak or diseased body is to be regarded with suspicion. There can be no health, no thought, no moral feeling, no sound judgment, no vigorous action, except in connection with a sound body.
>
> —THE REVEREND DR. THEODORE MUNGER (1897)

Muscular Christians are undoubtedly best known for their celebration of bodies. Whether it was Thomas Hughes and his formation of Christian manhood on the playing fields of Rugby, G. Stanley Hall and his reconfiguration of Christianity along eugenic lines, or Josiah Strong and his defense of a physical basis wherefrom to do good, the centrality of the body within muscular Christian theology cannot be overlooked. Nor were bodily concerns peculiar to muscular Christians. Many nineteenth-century reformers, first in England, then in America, expressed faith in the power of strenuous activity to overcome the perceived moral defects of urbanization, cultural pluralism, and white-collar work. Many also hoped that through physical experience, and through the celebration of bodies, they might gain release from various body-denying and evangelically inspired social constraints.

An Upsurge in Athletics

Given the agitation for physical expression that characterized the late nineteenth century, it is not surprising that several historians of sport view the postbellum years as a golden age for athletic competition. Roberta Park notes the "remarkable interest" Americans paid to sport in the four decades prior to the foundation of the Playground Association of America in 1906. Robert Barney declares early experiments in sport by New England private academies to have been "but a pale prelude to what would follow in America's post–Civil War era." And Elmer Johnson says of the 1880s that "almost every sport, program feature, training institution, and operational principle of any consequence or enduring value had its origin in this period."[1]

Many of nineteenth-century America's sporting innovations were developed at elite colleges such as Yale, which formed the first college team (a rowing club) in 1843. Soon Harvard, Brown, Dartmouth, Trinity, and the University of Pennsylvania had rowing clubs; and in 1852 the first intercollegiate competition was held: a regatta between Harvard and Yale on Lake Winnipesaukee, New Hampshire. Other collegiate firsts included Amherst's building of a gymnasium in 1860 (an event precipitated by the deaths of two college seniors—allegedly from overstudy),[2] the spread of baseball in the 1860s, and the development of football and track in the 1870s. Basketball, tennis, and hockey arose in the 1890s, completing what John Higham calls the transformation of America's colleges into "theaters of organized physical combat."[3]

Another phenomenon contributing to what Higham terms the "dynamism" of the late nineteenth century was professional sport.[4] Long held to be, in the Brooklyn YMCA's words, "under questionable control, or in partnership with evil appliances," professional sport gained newfound respectability in the 1890s, if never quite winning the wholehearted "approval of Christian public sentiment."[5] Foremost in public esteem was baseball, whose first professional team was the Cincinnati Red Stockings (formed 1869) and whose first World Series was played in 1903. Professional football's popularity in no way approached that of baseball, or even cycling; yet by 1900 it was a solid presence in the Midwest, following a "primitive" 1890s beginning in western Pennsylvania. Even boxing, hitherto banned in most American cities, made steps in 1892 toward acceptance and legality through the adoption of Queensberry rules, which stipulated the wearing of gloves.[6]

Concurrent with the rise of sports was the rise of sports heroes: professional heroes like John L. Sullivan, college heroes like Princeton's Robert "Pop" Gailey ("a big-bodied, lion-hearted centre-rush on the '96 team [and] a man through and through"),[7] and fictional heroes like Frank Merriwell, who counted among his admirers Jack Dempsey, Woodrow Wilson, Babe Ruth, Al Smith, and Wendell Willkie.[8] Coaches, too, came in for their share of the glory, with journalist Richard Harding Davis calling football coach Walter Camp the most important man at Yale after the president (whose name Davis could not recall).[9]

In part people's admiration for athletes stemmed from the 1890s maturation of the newspaper sports page, which endowed athletes with widespread name recognition. In part it stemmed from fervor related to the Spanish-American War and the conviction of more than one journalist that it was athletics upon which victory depended, or more precisely an athletically proficient soldiery.[10] Still, sports worship was at base the product of people's preoccupation with physical fitness and virility. As Daniel Rodgers notes in his study of the ebbing Puritan work ethic, late-nineteenth-century readers appeared less appreciative than their forebears of stories featuring gritty entrepreneurs—men who retired from life and the world in order to build a better mousetrap. Instead, they wanted characters who lived, who were active and adventurous—characters like Frank Merriwell, Owen Johnson's *Stover at Yale,* and later the Hardy Boys.[11]

Sporting figures like these helped alleviate urban-related fears of unreality and encroaching softness. They demanded approbation, explained poet John P. Bocock, by virtue of their "brawn and sinew." "And they are but shining examples" he pursued

> Of the lads we all love and admire,
> Ready with muscles of iron
>   For the scrimmage of blood and fire;
> Ready to tackle the foeman
>   Alike upon land and on sea,
> Columbia, these are thy jewels,
> Thy heroes of battles to be![12]

Battling heroes, muscular combatants—these were athletic metaphors applicable only to men. Women were thought too delicate for professional sports, and women amateurs remained overshadowed by their male counterparts—that is, until the appearance of Olympic skating champion Sonja Henie in the late 1920s and 1930s. This is not to imply that women were unaffected by the rise in sport; quite the contrary. Most of the Seven Sister colleges developed physical education programs a scant decade or so after the Ivy League. Smith College, under the will of its benefactor Sophia Smith, was instructed to provide courses on "Gymnastics and Physical Culture" as well as on

"Evidences of Christianity." By 1877 the college could report that it had "regular exercises in lighter gymnastics and in the open air, under the direction of a competent lady teacher."[13]

Often the justifications for women's athletics were the same as those for men's: the need to overcome physically deleterious Victorian social constraints and the fear of "race suicide." Arguing the first point was Amherst professor John Tyler, who called "unhealthy habits of posture" in girls "a disgrace to our civilization" and who insisted on every girl's "right to a pleasing voice and a graceful carriage." Supportive of the second, more eugenic view was G. Stanley Hall, who thought judicious physical training essential if women were ever adequately to fulfill their "supreme function" of motherhood. In the end, reasoned fitness advocate Helen McKinstry, was not the importance of female athletics self-evident? For what man contemplating marriage would choose a "delicate, anaemic, hothouse plant type of girl" over a "strong, full-blooded, physically courageous woman, a companion for her husband on the golf links and a playmate with her children?"[14]

If McKinstry thought athletics essential for women, she nonetheless recommended against their engaging in competitive sports. Other experts writing in the 1906 issue of *American Physical Education Review* agreed: competitive sports were damaging to femininity and a threat to women's reproductive capabilities. "Strenuous training" and "general competition," Luther Gulick explained, while "a measure of manhood" for men, were for women "injurious to both body and mind." He added that "pleasure and recreation," kept within the school, should be the chief end of women's athletics. Frances Kellor, General Director of New York City's Inter-Municipal Research Committee, concurred, arguing that "aesthetics" and "joy" ought always to characterize the female athlete more than "the grim determination to win at any cost."[15]

Most outspoken on the subject was Harvard physical education maven Dudley Allen Sargent, who feared the female competitor's "tendency to become masculine in form and character" and who foresaw the day when "effeminate man will succumb to virile woman." To "postpone that time," he urged that woman's role in the "rougher sports" be confined to that of uplifter and that her knowledge of such sports be sufficient only to enable her "to be the sympathetic admirer of men and boys in their efforts to be strong, vigorous, and heroic."[16]

McKinstry, Gulick, and Sargent concluded that in lieu of competitive contact sports like football, baseball, boxing, or hockey, women ought to pursue more holistic, life-enhancing activities. For McKinstry this meant primarily swimming, tennis, skating, and "cross country tramping"—plus golf, archery, and horseback riding for those who could afford it. For Gulick it sufficed that "a city girl . . . be provided with outdoor exercise, with plays and games" (assuming these did not lead to "serious, public competition"). Finally, Sargent thought it most important that the sport in question produce "good carriage, perfect poise, self-command and exquisite grace and refinement."[17]

Recreational sports along the lines of those envisioned by McKinstry and company were, in short, deemed suitable for women, and indeed for men also—especially those kept from collegiate and professional sports by their health, age, or station. Much of America heeded the experts' advice, adding to what one journalist called "the widespread and steadily growing interest in amateur sports."[18]

Among the most popular amateur sports were lawn games like croquet, tennis (first played in America on Staten Island in 1874), and golf (imported from Scotland in 1888 by the St. Andrews Golf Club of Yonkers, New York). No sport, however, eclipsed cycling, a craze for which swept America following improvements made to the bicycle in the late 1870s. To advocates of female fitness, the bicycle was "doing more to improve the physical condition of the American woman, and therefore of the American people, than any other agency yet devised."[19] To simple pleasurers, it resembled a "modern Pegasus," a "favorite mount" upon which "you sweep through the air in freedom, speed, and joyous song, a rival to the bird."[20]

Such encomiums as these, however, left Gilded Age social critic Thorstein Veblen unimpressed. The "addiction to athletic sports" was not exceptional, he wrote; rather it was simply one piece of evidence among many that some vast economic sea change had occurred in America[21]—something scholars now describe as the shift from a paradigm of scarcity to a paradigm of abundance (that is, from an economy seeking avoidance of pain to one desirous of achieving pleasure).

The foremost beneficiary of this change, Veblen concluded, was the moneyed or "leisure class," industrialism's uppermost caste, a group whose function was the "conspicuous consumption" of material goods. Sports like yachting or polo abetted this function: they were flamboyant and they absorbed a great number of resources. The popularity of sports also caused Veblen to predict that one day capitalism might revert back to feudalism, since in his view there existed many parallels between the knight with his sword and the industrialist with his tennis racket. Both threw big parties and lived in baronial splendor. Both aspired to athletic prowess. And both engaged in these activities for the same reason: the intimidation of a potentially rebellious underclass.[22]

Veblen's relation of sport to social dominance, eye-opening for its time, is still intriguing today. Nonetheless, his theory in other respects is flawed. As one critic pointed out in the 1890s, sports were important not only to the rich, but also to the urban working and middle-classes. "Workers in stores and offices . . . typewriters, elevator boys, barbers, physicians, lawyers, and clergymen" were all playing vigorously, he wrote, and the fact that they were doing so "to an extent which is new to this generation" could not be "accounted for by any theories of a more numerous leisurely class."[23]

Nor were people's motives for exercising entirely social or economic. Instead some were therapeutic; others were spiritual. One clergyman writing anonymously to *The Wheelman* in 1882 even confessed that sports (in his case cycling) had saved his sanity, since just when it looked as though he had nothing left to look forward to but "monotony" and ill health, "[along] came my bicycle, and, as if by magic, away went the spirits that had tormented me so long, and as their cloven feet and writhing tails disappeared in the dark past I was met by the laughing, beautiful faces of the spirits of health and cheerfulness."[24]

Religion and Sport

At first glance it would seem that America's Protestant churches were ill positioned to participate in the burgeoning sports movement. After all, neither the Calvinist nor the evangelical theologies upon which most denominations were founded had ever trumpeted the glories of the flesh, let alone those of recreational sports. Instead, charged the Reverend A. Holmes in 1909, they fostered a "deadly enmity" between "the soul and the body"[25]—a judgment that many sports historians have since tended to endorse.[26]

Christianity's traditional mistrust of purely physical enjoyments, and perforce of physical recreation, dates back to its inception. Even before the Christian emperor Theodosius banned the Roman games in 394 A.D., St. Paul expressed his belief that "bodily exercise profiteth little" in comparison with godliness (1 Tim. 4:8). According to Paul (whom muscular Christian exegetes tried to portray as opposed to the body's mortification, not its exercise)[27] the Second Coming was imminent; therefore corporeal improvements were irrelevant.

The Parousia's postponement failed to sway the Church greatly with regard to the body. Indeed the Church Fathers' discovery of Plato early in the Middle Ages actually intensified their aversion to carnal amusements. Plato (whom one sports historian calls a "symbol of the betrayal of the body in Western Culture")[28] believed this world to be but an imperfect copy of the next. Accordingly, the medieval Church, which incorporated Platonism into its colleges and universities, supported a curriculum wherein physical education mattered little and academic reflection much. Not content with this, the Church also "persistently suppressed many sports and games."[29]

Catholic teaching regarding sports and the body reigned supreme until the Protestant Reformation, when two new approaches were proposed—the first almost approving of human physicality, the second condemning it. Representative of the more tolerant side of Protestantism was Martin Luther, who thought bodily functions a part of God's plan and who supported bodily exercise for reasons of public health and national defense.[30] Supportive of the more severe view was John Calvin, who even more passionately than the Catholics felt the flesh to be vile, but who unlike them proffered no remedy (given that no amount of fasting could forestall one's predestination toward heaven or hell).

Calvin's followers in the New World cleaved to his attitudes regarding sport and the body. In places such as New England, where Calvinists predominated in the colonial period, sports were restricted and clothing was regulated. In places such as colonial Virginia where Calvinists were less influential, dances and public gaming occurred to a degree unknown up North.[31] But this does not mean that sports were condoned by Virginia's established Anglican Church, which supported a law passed by the Virginia Assembly in 1619 that outlawed gaming at dice or cards and bound over "any person found idle . . . to compulsory work."[32]

When both Calvinism and church-state establishments declined in the aftermath of the Revolutionary War, the axes upon which Protestants based their aversion to the body shifted significantly. For clergy in the Congregational and Episcopal (formerly Anglican) Churches, where disestablishment meant less political power, powerlessness began to look more like a virtue; hence many of the things that powerlessness connoted (ethereality, ill-health, and the like) began to appear more virtuous.[33] Consequently, the healthy body, once thought to be the source of unwarranted pride, now indicated one's estrangement from the sublime.

Powerlessness appealed somewhat less forcefully to ascendant denominations such as the Methodists, who gravitated after the passage of the old order to Christian perfectionism, an idea that Calvinist pastors had striven to condemn. What perfectionism meant in relation to the body was clear. Whereas Calvinists viewed themselves as physically incapable of achieving their own salvation, antebellum Methodists believed in using their bodies for the betterment of themselves and the world. Antebellum Methodists remained highly doubtful, however, about using their bodies for sport, a fact that explains why in 1790 they "wisely banished every species of play" from Cokesbury College in Abingdon, Maryland.[34]

The Methodists were not the only ones to look down on sports in the antebellum period; so did more urbane Protestants, such as the Reverend Theodore Cuyler. The minister of New York's fashionable Market Street Dutch Reformed Church, Cuyler seemingly objected to sports not because they were sinful but because they were indecorous. Reading was "the first and purest of our recreations," he wrote in 1858. It was certainly preferable to a strenuous activity "that stimulates this nervous system of mine, until I become a walking maniac," for this sort of activity was "dangerous and in the last damnable."[35]

Though sophisticated ministers such as Cuyler undoubtedly differed in many respects from Methodist circuit-riders, both city ministers and rural evangelists had several reasons in common for distrusting play and recreation. According to historian Richard Swanson, these reasons were, first, the belief that recreation detracted from spiritual devotions; second, the belief that recreation was a waste of time; third, the belief that recreation had unsavory connections with taverns and gambling; and fourth, the belief that recreation would prove too addictive, given humanity's sinful nature.[36]

These beliefs were shared by most Protestant denominations in the antebellum period, but not apparently by the Church of Jesus Christ of Latter-day Saints—the Mormons. In keeping with one critic's characterization of them as the most success-oriented faith in America, the Mormons never had much difficulty equating health with godliness.[37] Nor were they against equating godliness with virility, since an early custom of the church was to examine for fullness the privy parts of prospective leaders.[38] The Mormon Church was the first to support Boy Scout troops, the first to erect a recreation hall wherein athletic competitions were held,[39] and the first to show, in the words of one admirer, "permanent recognition . . . of the bodily welfare of its adolescents."[40] Why exactly they pioneered these forms of organized uplift is difficult to explain. Possibly it devolved somehow from their belief in familial, as opposed to individual, salvation: the notion that more important even than inner goodness was outward conformity to the laws of God and society.

More representative than the Mormons of the Protestant view toward sport were the Disciples of Christ—a powerful group akin theologically and socially to the Methodists. Four men helped found the Disciples: Thomas Campbell (1763–1854), Alexander Campbell (1786–1866), Barton Stone (1772–1844), and Walter Scott (1786–1861). Of these four, only Alexander Campbell had much use for sport; the others thought it frivolous—if not downright ungodly. Stone urged the avoidance of "such groveling pleasures," while Thomas Campbell held sport to be in competition with Bible-reading and prayer. Stone also thought the body prey to "all the evils of mortality," while Thomas Campbell called it "degraded" and "a vile abode."[41]

Admittedly, Stone wanted ministers—and ministers' bodies—to be better looked after by their parishioners. He reasoned (in an interesting contrast to latter-day complaints about ministerial softness) that hard labor detracted from ministerial dignity and reduced the time available for study and reflection. "Our ministrations," he concluded, "would be more blessed to the people if we were enabled to live without such care and labor on our farms."[42]

Stone shared this negative attitude toward bodily exercise with many mainline clergy. It was a feeling that was deeply ingrained and in some cases slow to change, considering that many Southern Methodists maintained a hostile attitude toward sports such as football until the twentieth century.[43] Nevertheless, the decades following the

1870s witnessed a growing clerical acceptance of sport—first in the cities, then in the countryside. Foremost among the reasons for this change in attitude was the fate of unfit clergy, who appeared to be dying everywhere of "nervous diseases."[44] City preachers divorced from work on the farm were especially prone to neglecting their bodies, alleged one YMCA man, as evidenced by the fact that "the average middle-aged saint of the present day is not healthy looking, nor has he as well a shaped body as his framework would allow. He is in this condition through neglect of exercise, improper eating, etc. The saints must have stronger and more enduring bodies than they have to bear the burdens and heat of the day that soul-winning and earning their daily bread and butter cast upon their shoulders."[45]

The unhealthiness of urban clergy was clearly a matter for concern. But there were other factors conducive to a clerical acceptance of exercise, including the perception (warranted or not) that there existed too many Christians of the "weak, womanish, watery-eyed type" and not enough of the "rugged, rough and ready type."[46] The "physical weariness" resultant from city living also demanded clerical attention, wrote Henry C. King, since tired parishioners did not have "anything left of time and strength for church worship."[47] As for the medical benefits of exercise, clergymen who subscribed to any of the new mass-circulation magazines could not help being exposed to articles (such as a series started by *Harper's* in 1897) wherein scientists refuted old myths about the body and stressed the need for more holistic health care.[48]

Developments such as these led clergy to address human physicality and to approve what was in T. J. Jackson Lears's words a "fundamental reorientation" in Progressive Era American attitudes toward the human body.[49] The clergy not only acquiesced in this reorientation; they also actively promoted it, largely through the importation and spread of German biblical criticism.

Known as the "new theology," German criticism placed unparalleled stress on the humanity of Jesus, and on his plans for effecting salvation in this world. Consequently, noted the *Outlook* in 1914, "the emphasis of Christian endeavor to-day is on present rather than future redemption, and its approach to the spirit is more and more through the body." Thanks to the new theology, "the conceptions of the body as the enemy to the soul . . . are disappearing like the morning mist."[50]

Much of the success of the new theology rested, as William Hutchison points out, on the clergy's need to be "modern"—to keep abreast of the times.[51] Similarly, it was the wish to be modern that furthered clerical acceptance of sports and games. Many considered church participation in the sports revolution to be an institutional imperative. As *Current Opinion* remarked in 1914, "if the church wishes to hold its young people . . . it cannot ignore the recreation of its young people."[52] Or, as Herbert Gates explained more thoroughly in the introduction to his 1917 book *Recreation and the Church,* "People will play, thank God! We may play with them if we will, and thereby help them to realize the best that this instinct has to offer; or we may hold aloof, adopt an attitude of narrow, indiscriminate condemnation or at best of cold indifference, and allow the boys and girls to play on without us and without our sympathetic guidance."[53]

Gates's plea for "sympathetic guidance" echoed an argument fairly common in the early 1900s. That argument was the need for professionals (including ministers) to oversee sport in order to vouchsafe its high moral tone. A game such as football was capable of "developing the gentleman of ethical character and conduct," allowed Charles F. Thwing, president of Western Reserve University, but only so long as it embodied "elementary conditions of the ethical process." Once it betrayed this ideal (and there were many who agreed with Charles Eliot Norton that college athletics were "little short of a national disgrace"), reform—and reformers—seemed necessary.[54]

Additional arguments in support of an increased ministerial presence in athletics came in protest to the unchristian nature of the Physical Culture movement, which by the early 1900s was billing itself as the only true friend to the body. Not only had Physical Culture's founder, Bernarr Macfadden, called bodybuilding a "new religion" superior to the old; in addition he had condemned traditional Christianity for being overly "prudish" and repressive.[55] In response to this, and in reaction to Macfadden's sex manuals—which for the period were very explicit—some ministers felt compelled for the first time to preach on matters involving "personal purity" (about which more will be said in Chapter 4).

Others ventured that beyond quoting scripture at the muscleman, Christians ought to resemble him physically. This at least was the personal philosophy of "Pitching Parson" Allen Stockdale, who advised clergy to "lose the sickly white color of the speculative realm of study, and take on the more attractive brown of the actual life of men." Remember, he cautioned, "men are liable to lose respect for your traditional position when they lose respect for your muscles."[56]

Not everyone was as keen as Stockdale to enhance ministerial biceps. Nevertheless, many conceded the importance of health and the need for combining health with Christianity. Evidence of this came in various forms, including prep school addresses, college sermons, and YMCA periodicals—works whose authors might well be called "body as temple" theologians (1 Cor. 6:19–20). Unlike antebellum evangelicals, "body as temple" men generally avoided vilifying the body; instead, they praised it as a vehicle for good. They also, when preaching, played on certain themes: the compatibility of health and scripture, the need to glorify one's body, and the tendencies of health toward goodness and weakness toward evil.

The first of the "body as temple" men's themes—making health scriptural—largely involved the redepiction of biblical characters. These it seemed could no longer be thought of as antisocial aesthetes; rather, they had to have been strong, muscular fellows, proficient in sports and games. "Those whom God chose as leaders were men of strong physique," observed *Outlook* in 1914. "Moses was a strong man, else the march over the desert would have exhausted him, the anxiety of the exodus would have crushed him."[57] And just as Moses, so also Jesus (who "radiated good health"),[58] John ("a strong, eager, enthusiastic young man"),[59] Paul ("one of the great sport lovers of his day"),[60] and Samson (whose "mighty strength and . . . healthy and resolute and infectious good humor" were offset only by a lack of "personal purity").[61] Even the theologically conservative *Methodist Review* joined the chorus, permitting publication in 1885 of an article asserting that Christ's good health was "an essential factor in the scheme of salvation."[62]

The second tenet of "body as temple" theology, glorifying the body, refuted the idea of the body's being "sinful and weak," and instead insisted on its being "good and strong."[63] "Body as temple" theologians similarly claimed that religion was no foe of the body; rather, it was a friend. "What religion desires is not a truncated piece of man," explained Harvard chaplain Francis Peabody, "but a whole man, healthy, happy, natural, and free."[64] Or as the Right Reverend Charles H. Brent (Episcopal bishop to the Philippines) put it in his book *The Splendor of the Human Body*, bodies were manifestations of the soul, and their upkeep was a Christian duty. Christ occupied a body similar to ours, reasoned Brent; therefore "to dishonor our body is to dishonor His—to *crucify Him afresh and to put Him to an open shame.*"[65]

Because "body as temple" theologians considered upkeep of the body a virtue and its neglect a sin, many came perilously close to calling musclemen saints and the sick sinners. Exacerbating this tendency was the Social Gospel idea of salvation in this world, which seemed to require more doers than thinkers. Both assumptions—that strength reflected virtue and that the weak were somehow "slacking off"—surfaced repeatedly in "body as temple" publications, including an 1898 survey of twenty-three YMCA secretaries on "Why a Christian Man Should Take Regular Physical Exercise," which elicited such responses as "A strong mind in a strong body makes a better Christian" and "[Eating right bespeaks] Christlike spirit."[66] Conversely, wrote Elon College president W. A. Harper in 1915, "A man with a weak body in these stirring times, need not expect to attain any other than a mediocre position of usefulness, no matter how brilliant his mind or devout his purpose."[67]

At their most extreme, "body as temple" men completely dropped the traditional Christian emphasis on confessing weakness in oneself and forgiving it in others. "The holy man must be a whole man," insisted Professor John Tyler of Amherst, because it was (in the words of G. Stanley Hall) "the supreme destiny of man" to keep himself "always at the very tip-top of condition." The meek, who Jesus said shall inherit the earth, seemed not to count. The Reverend Dr. Frank Crane actually dismissed them as "mollycoddles," asserting that "the road to hell is crowded with the slouching, shuffling, blear-eyed, trembling morons."[68]

Church-Sport Associations

Religious leaders who supported a rapprochement between religion and sport insisted that it produce more than "body as temple" theology. They also wanted churches to take "moral leadership of athletics in America."[69] Arguments like that of YMCA physical education secretary George Fisher, who urged "the church [to] enlarge its scope of activities [and to] include activities hitherto not included as definitely religious,"[70] abounded circa 1900, and not without result. Certainly many clergymen now considered sports appropriate "adjuncts to social uplift"—occasionally to the point of thinking athletic prowess a better qualification for ministry than a seminary degree. Churches (at least liberal ones) also ceased calling sports "evil and licentious" and instead started using them "to the glory of Christ"[71]—largely through forging alliances with athletic leagues and playground associations, running their own sports programs, and remodeling their buildings to include basketball courts and other sports facilities.

One way by which ministers encouraged sports entailed not frowning when they were played on Sunday (a practice formerly taboo). In 1905 Episcopal bishop Henry C. Potter firmly declared Sunday play to be "a question for the individual"—even though twenty-seven years earlier he had expressed outrage at the predilection of immigrants for Sabbath-day sports and at their demand "that we shall waive the customs and repeal the laws that hallow our Lord's day."[72] Another minister claimed in a June 1900 *Outlook* article entitled "The Moral Side of Golf" that people had a right to play on Sunday. "The old prejudice against pleasure as being intrinsically evil has broken down nearly everywhere," he wrote. "The Puritan Sabbath has been definitely renounced."[73]

The possibility that recreation might one day crowd out religious worship altogether struck most liberal clergy as too far-fetched. Besides, religion and recreation were not opposites; they were twins. "Religion is recreational," insisted the Reverend Silas Persons; "preaching the Gospel, the glad tidings from God, and hearing it preached, is itself a recreation." And just as religion was recreational, it also supposedly conveyed the same therapeutic benefits as other forms of recreation—up to and not excluding vigorous muscle tone. Thus could Admiral Alfred T. Mahan characterize prayer as "inherently a force; demanding energy for its development and manifesting energy in its operation." And thus could the Reverend Dr. James Vance portray the Gospel as something that "makes the blood pulsate . . . sets the heart a-throbbing . . . [and] sweeps the nerves with celestial aspirations."[74]

Often ministers equating athletic with spiritual exultation knew whereof they spoke. In fact, clergy numbered among the first professionals to try amateur sports and to pronounce them "truly progressive."[75] That this move came not without controversy is attested to by a series of articles in the first (1882) issue of the pioneering sports journal *The Wheelman*. These articles—all written by clergymen and all on the subject of "Clergymen and the Bicycle"—uniformly congratulated ministers for their courage in cycling, while chastising backward congregants for thinking such doings "unseemly." In one article, the Reverend John L. Scudder, pastor of the Jersey City Tabernacle (Congregational), one of the first churches to offer athletics as part of its "bold ecclesiastical leap into the arena of sin,"[76] expressed his "firm belief . . . that if bicycles were more generally used by American preachers, there would be fewer hollow chests, round shoulders, sensitive stomachs, and torpid livers."[77] In another article, the Reverend S. L. Gracey observed that now that "the riding whip of the pioneer Bishop of America, Rev. Francis Asbury, lies in honored estate," bicycles had replaced circuit-riding as the means whereby clergymen got their exercise.[78]

Rivaling in novelty the preacher as athlete was that other postbellum phenomenon: the athlete as preacher. Of the latter, William ("Billy") Sunday no doubt ranks first. Born in 1862 to an Iowa bricklayer, the evangelist-to-be overcame a difficult childhood to play center field for the Chicago White Stockings (1883–1888). While still a ballplayer he came under the influence of street preachers and converted to Christianity—whereupon the Chicago YMCA asked him to be one of its emissaries to boys and men. After his baseball career ended in 1891, Sunday went to work full-time for the "Y"; later he set out on his own, touring small towns and cities across the Midwest. From there his rise to fame was meteoric: he made converts by the tens of thousands, enjoyed the patronage of J. D. Rockefeller, and had dinner with Presidents Roosevelt and Wilson.[79]

As a preacher, Sunday was very physical, doffing his coat, breaking furniture, and employing sports metaphors whenever possible. A few found such antics distasteful, not the least of whom was historian Richard Hofstadter, who blamed Sunday for ending the New England tradition of preacher-as-scholar. But others welcomed Sunday's claim that one could be both a Christian and a "real man." Among the latter was the ordination board of the Chicago Presbytery, who ordained Sunday in 1903 despite his lack of an education and despite his inability to answer many of their questions. In defense of their action, they explained that whereas they, for all their learning, could boast of few converts, Sunday, with his athletic build, could boast of thousands—thereby laying as great a claim to the title of "reverend" as anybody.

For his part, Sunday disdained even answering his critics. "What do I care," he once said, "if some puff-eyed little dibbly-dibbly preacher goes tibbly-tibblying around because I use plain Anglo-Saxon words? I want people to know what I mean and that's why I try to get down to where they live."[80]

Not all muscular Christians liked Sunday as much as the Chicago Presbytery. Some thought him not manly but coarse, while others considered him a blot on the ministry. A preacher-athlete far more appealing to these groups was the legendary "Grand Old Man" of football, Amos Alonzo Stagg. Born the same year as Sunday and also a Presbyterian, Stagg attended Yale, which he pitched to five baseball championships. Upon graduation in 1888, he declined several offers from major-league teams and instead entered Yale Divinity School. There he converted: from baseball to football (becoming good enough at the latter sport to be named to the first All-American team in 1889).[81]

Originally, Stagg hoped to become a minister. But after overhearing Student Volunteer Movement leader John R. Mott criticize his homiletic abilities, he decided perhaps his path as a Christian lay more in coaching than preaching.[82] Consequently, he followed the advice of Luther Gulick and transferred from Yale to the YMCA's physical training school in Springfield, Massachusetts. From Springfield he left in 1892 to become the first director of physical culture and athletics (and incidentally the first tenured athletic director of any kind) at the new University of Chicago, where he coached football for the next forty-one years. Stagg's contributions to football while at Chicago included the huddle, numbered uniforms, and a lighted playing field. He was also partially responsible (through such early-twentieth-century inventions as the "T" formation and the forward pass) for making football less injurious, thereby dissuading Theodore Roosevelt from banning the game.[83]

Throughout his remarkably long college football coaching career (1892–1960) Stagg, who lived to be 103, upheld Christian values in sport. He exhorted his players to "live clean" and forbade their indulgence in drinking, smoking, and profanity. He also opposed the emergence of professional football, which he thought turned colleges into "nurser[ies] for professional gladiators." The point of college athletics, Stagg thought, was man-making, and to this end he formed the first athletic-letter club in 1904. Named the Order of the C, this club required its members first to be gentlemen and sportsmen, second to be amateurs in spirit and act, and third to give their universities two years of community service.[84]

Christian athletes such as Stagg and Sunday served their cause in ways other than preaching and coaching. In fact, simply by being athletes and at the same time Christians they provided ministers with multiple homilies. Presbyterian missionary Robert Speer advocated using Christian athletes as models for young men in matters related to sex. He considered the life of golfer William Holabird ("a splendid athlete, with a life without spot or stain") particularly exemplary.[85] An equally fine specimen of Christian manhood was Harvard athlete Marshall P. Newell ('95), "who however the game might be going, played fair while he played strong."[86]

Newell and Holabird were individuals, but occasionally Christian athletes came in teams. This was true of the "Stubby Christians" football team Stagg coached for Springfield.[87] It was also true of the Princeton football team of 1893, which beat Yale 6–0 in an extraordinary Thanksgiving Day game. Afterward, noted a reporter, "One of the Princeton coaches came into the [locker] room . . . and holding up his arm for silence said, 'Boys, I want you to sing the doxology.' And standing as they were, naked and covered with mud and blood and perspiration, the eleven men who had won the championship sang the doxology from the beginning to the end as solemnly and as seriously, and, I am sure, as sincerely, as they ever did in their lives."[88]

Celebrating Christian athletes was but one way churches had of acknowledging the need for exercise in modern life. Another lay in allying with and molding athletic organizations. YMCA secretary George Fisher, writing in 1915, thought church-sport associations conceivably "the most potent factor for shaping athletics in North America."[89] The Reverend Charles Gillkey, writing in *Playground,* agreed, stressing that "religion and recreation belong together." The "alliance" between churches and recreational agencies made sense, he added, considering that both groups espoused "sunniness," "spontaneity," "playfulness," and "the creative impulse."[90]

Foremost among the recreational groups backed by the churches was Luther Gulick's Playground and Recreation Association (PRA). Committed to school recess and other innovative ideas, the PRA contributed enormously to the spread of public playgrounds, which one supporter called "the most religious institution[s] we have."[91] A second organization connected to the church was the American Association for the Advancement of Physical Education (created 1885), several of whose founders were clergymen. Third was the Sunday School Athletic Association (inspired in 1909 by the YMCA; later absorbed by the Federal Council of Churches), whose membership in 1915 included over one hundred urban churches.[92]

Protestant church participation in athletics could be direct as well as indirect, extending to the running of vacation Bible schools, athletic fields, community houses, and similar places. Josiah Strong, writing in 1900, thought it "remarkable" how churches were building "facilities for physical culture and recreation—a gymnasium, baths, very likely a swimming pool, and perhaps a bowling alley, which not long since would have been deemed sacrilegious."[93]

Sometimes church-owned facilities ranked among the finest recreational outlets in town. This was the case in St. Louis, which by 1923 had eleven churches with organized sports, nine with gymnasiums, eight with playgrounds, seven with play organizations for children, two with "recreation farms," and one with a summer camp. Even in the largest cities, where recreational opportunities were greater, church facilities stood out. In New York, for example, the Madison Avenue Presbyterian Church maintained two summer camps and boasted a parish house five stories high, replete with "full [athletic] equipment" for both sexes, two paid directors, and dozens of volunteer assistants.[94]

The uses to which religious organizations put their athletic facilities and summer camps varied. In 1897, the Southern Baptist Theological Seminary dedicated its new gym to the production of "broad-shouldered" ministers.[95] Twenty years later, the First Baptist Church of Pittsburgh, Pennsylvania, hired a professional gymnast for its gym and a superintendent and physician for its summer camp, to which it took "campers in squads from forty to sixty in uniform age and sex."[96]

Not surprisingly, the most elaborate recreation programs belonged to such churches as Trinity Episcopal in New York City, which had both a concern for green space and the financial wherewithal to operate several chapel churchyards as playgrounds.[97] But the church and recreation movement was neither entirely urban, nor was it entirely white. St. John's Church of Springfield, Massachusetts, was black-run, and it maintained a fifty-four-acre summer recreation farm, two athletic clubs, and a recreation program employing Springfield College men as directors.[98] "Wide-awake" country churches were similarly engaged, noted one playground expert, in "promoting wholesome recreation for the young."[99]

In a 1917 survey, several ministers conceded that the establishment of their church recreation programs was motivated by a combination of altruism and pragmatism. The Reverend Charles W. Shinn, educational director at the Ashland Avenue Baptist Church of Toledo, Ohio, claimed that athletics meant both "honesty in children" and "many additions to the church." The Reverend William R. Taylor, pastor of Rochester's Brick Presbyterian Church, agreed that recreational activities were capable of producing "healthier, stronger, lither, more efficient, purer bodies" while at the same time "increas[ing] interest in, and devotion to, the church and Sunday school." As for the effect of church athletics upon the community, the Reverend Albert W. Palmer of Plymouth Congregational Church in Oakland, California, boasted that "we have kept saloons out of our part of the city . . . [by] providing something better"—something that had placed "a remarkably high percentage of young people, especially young men, in our C. E. societies and church services."[100]

The fact that church recreational directors were highly idealistic is obvious. But in his study of the Pittsburgh Playground Association (an organization heavily funded by local churches), historian Francis Couvares contends that what really motivated recreation reformers was social control: the desire to enstamp Anglo-Protestant values on immigrant children by monitoring their play.[101] It is a valid point, since much pro-recreation rhetoric did indeed concentrate on "saving" urban waifs from allegedly bad influences (defined by one PRA leader as "sexual immorality and the white-slave traffic").[102] On the other hand, at least one minister highly influential in the recreation movement thought play more important to the churched than to the unchurched. "Our recreational work has not lured the irreligious into our church," he admitted. "We did not expect that it would. 'In vain is the net spread in the sight of any bird.'"[103]

Most likely, churches kept gyms for a variety of reasons: to "save" citified children, to raise church membership, and to ensure healthfulness. But behind all these reasons was the liberal religious notion that salvation lay as much through the body as through the soul. Without this notion, swimming pools would hardly have become "Christian" attractions. Nor would swing sets have appeared an effective means of molding character.

Crowning proof of this—that liberal churches were willing to view certain sports as inherently religious, and not simply as evangelical tools—came in the mid-1920s, with the proposed building of a "sports bay" (alcove) in New York City's Episcopal Cathedral of St. John the Divine. As originally conceived, the sports bay was to have had a stained glass window depicting twenty-six modern sports. In the wake of people's objections to the secularity of its boxing, wrestling, and horse-racing scenes, however, the design was changed to include such biblical events as Jacob wrestling the angel, David conquering Goliath, and St. Paul's injunction to run a good race.

Bishop William Manning (the "Cathedral Builder") defended the sports bay from its few critics on the grounds that sports were neither irreligious nor unaesthetic. Sports, he asserted, "have just as important place in our lives as our prayers. It is my opinion that the beautiful game of polo, in its place, is as pleasing to God as a beautiful service in a beautiful cathedral."[104]

The YMCA

Of all the organizations working to bring religion and sport closer together, none was more influential than the Young Men's Christian Association. Founded in 1844 by a London dry goods clerk named George Williams, the YMCA grew over the course of the century from a small collection of young evangelical Englishmen into an immensely powerful and wealthy international organization, credited by Union Seminary president Charles C. Hall with having reached "the highest level of efficiency attained by the moral and spiritual forces of our time."[105] The fascinating story of this transformation (documented best by C. Howard Hopkins in his monumental *History of the YMCA in North America*) can only be touched on briefly here, with special emphasis on the association's foray into physical training and the ways it reconciled this effort with Christian evangelism.

The first YMCA in the United States was the Boston Association, formed in 1851 through the efforts of Captain Thomas Sullivan, the Reverend Lyman Beecher, and others—mainly Baptists, Methodists, Episcopalians, and Congregationalists. Captain Sullivan wanted the Boston Association to resemble the English YMCAs he had read about: places equipped with comfortable furniture, a library, and a reading room where lectures and Bible classes might be held. To this end, he and his friends secured rooms on the corner of Washington and Summer Streets, and prevailed on the sentimental novelist Lydia Sigourney to write the dedication hymn.[106] Their aim, like that of many philanthropic ventures of the time, was domestic and rescue oriented. Specifically, it entailed providing a "home away from home" for Protestant young men newly arrived in the city, thereby ensuring that they did not suffer for want of Christian surroundings.

Soon after the creation of the Boston Association, other YMCAs sprang up in America's major cities. By 1853 there were twenty, by 1856 fifty-six, and by 1860 two hundred five. The first full-time employee, or "secretary," of the "Y" was John Wanamaker (later founder of America's first department store), who served the Philadelphia Association from 1857 to 1861. The first North American convention took place in 1854, when delegates from places as geographically diverse as Toronto and San Francisco met in Buffalo, New York, to form a central committee.

The Central Committee (later headquartered in New York and renamed the International Committee) undertook supervision of the YMCA's various home and foreign work departments and special associations. These groups by 1905 numbered twenty-two. They included such departments as that for Education and for Religious and Missionary Development and such associations as the Student Association and the Railroad Men's Association. There was also a special Colored Men's Association, whose existence reflected the racist belief of many whites within the YMCA that blacks ought not to be integrated into the main body of the "Y." Some individual Northern associations disagreed with racial segregation and began to integrate their facilities early in the twentieth century. But segregation persisted in some Southern associations until well after 1946, the year desegregation was made a national YMCA goal.[107]

Whether black or white, most YMCA members in the nineteenth and early twentieth centuries were young men under forty. Their numbers were significant: in 1912 roughly 1 out of every 181 Americans was either an active or an associate YMCA member. Active membership was defined by the Portland convention of 1869 to include only those who belonged to evangelical Protestant churches and who could subscribe to the foundational "Paris Basis" of 1855 (which stated in part that "The Young Men's Christian Associations seek to unite those young men who, regarding Jesus Christ as their God and Savior . . . desire to be His disciples in their doctrine and in their life").[108] Associate membership theoretically extended to all young men of good character, though those who took advantage of it were more often native than foreign born, and more often white-collar than blue-collar workers.[109]

Despite its evangelical church basis, the YMCA was for its time decidedly ecumenical, allowing Victorian sentimentality and missionary fervor to undercut the importance of strict religious credalism. Some conservative pastors viewed this ecumenicalism as a threat, and the "Y" as a rival organization, bound to head men off from church membership. To allay such fears, "Y" secretaries spoke throughout the nineteenth century of their being allies to the churches, capable of reaching men beyond the churches' orbit. They also maintained until 1925 that it was the YMCA's principal aim to direct men "into active membership in the church of their choice."[110]

Conservative pastors were right, however, to wonder about the YMCA's undiluted commitment to religious conversion. Long before 1925, the "Y" was showing as much concern for society as for souls, and its focus had expanded to include what *Harper's* described as "men begrimed with oil and smoke . . . [a] large and growing class of workers."[111] Springfield College president Laurence L. Doggett called this shift in emphasis, which he saw as taking place during the years 1870–1878, "the period of the adap[ta]tion of the work of the Association to the needs of young men." It was followed, he said, by a "period of expansion" (1878 onward) during which time wealthy businessmen, enamored of the YMCA's new plan to Christianize the laboring man, contributed millions of dollars toward programs and personnel, toward buildings (725 in the United States by 1912), and toward the establishment of three training schools: two in Springfield, Massachusetts (made into Springfield College); and one, George Williams, in Chicago.[112]

Characteristic of the YMCA during its period of expansion was a commitment to the ideals of the Strenuous Life: physical hardness, vigorous action, and the rejection of various genteel constraints. One expression of this commitment was the Association's popularization in the 1880s of outdoor camping. Another was its creation in 1883 of a White Cross Army, the first American organization that openly taught about sex.[113] The White Cross Army and outdoor camping helped the YMCA in its battle against male softness. But even more helpful in this battle were YMCA physical work and YMCA work with boys under sixteen. The former led to the creation of the Physical Work Department in 1887 and the latter (which individual associations began in the 1870s) led to the creation of the Boys' Work Department in 1900.

Boys' work for the "Y" meant moving away from its old "custodial" rule (keeping young men from sin) and the adoption of a more "progressive" goal—character building. Character building, as the name implies, required not the preservation of morals already taught, but rather the strengthening of boys so as to ward off degeneracy. Character builders thought it essential that the boy ("Y" men always spoke of the "boy," an embryonic man; never of the more androgynous "child") have his masculinity cultivated at the outset; otherwise he might never develop into a leader capable of asserting "American" values.[114]

An important facet of character building was physical exercise: strengthening the organism to enhance its capacity for doing good. And there existed no greater places for physical exercise in the Progressive Era than YMCA gymnasia (to which in 1900 nearly one-third of all "Y" members—or 80,373 men—belonged). The first "Y" gyms were impromptu affairs, sometimes located in church basements. But in 1869 three well-equipped gyms opened up in Washington, New York, and San Francisco. Ten years later, the Chicago Association converted one of its prayer meeting rooms into a gym, complete with vaulting bar, a set of parallel bars, a rowing machine, and other sports paraphernalia. By 1880 fifty-one associations maintained gyms and by 1900 four hundred fifty-five did so. Those that did not, noted Association secretary Sherwood Eddy, gradually "disappeared."[115]

At first YMCAs viewed their gymnasia as a means to save souls, not to build character. They thought them a likely snare for those young men for whom YMCA teas, tracts, and Bible readings held no allure. Even so, objections that athletics were unchristian dissuaded some YMCAs from ever trying them. The European associations, for example, often rejected physical work, one London secretary warning in the 1860s that "a Christian young man had better not compete in a swimming match, or indeed a match of any kind."[116] All in all, commented a 1914 history of YMCA physical education, "the work was misunderstood and at best was considered more largely as an asset for securing members and as a means of counteracting evil resorts rather than as a worthy factor in itself in the development of Christian manhood."[117]

Early YMCAs may not have stressed the religious nature of athletics, but they did view them as fulfilling an unmet need. The fact was, explained George Fisher, that the city man, the "de-natured man . . . must be made to feel intensely!"[118] Athletic facilities offered the best hope for this; but as these were, prior to the Association's colonization of them, "in the almost undisputed control of conscienceless men," they were avoided.[119] Then came the YMCA's building of swimming pools (the first, in 1885, appearing in Brooklyn), its gymnasia, and its sponsorship of rowing, hiking, and bike and baseball clubs. With these developments, it became increasingly respectable for Protestant men to repair their tired bodies.

Only two things remained to make pious Christians leery of entering YMCA gymnasia: an imperfect integration of athletics into YMCA programming and an atheistic physical directorship. Many early YMCA physical directors were ex-circus men, broken-down pugilists, and the like. Often they were openly scornful of both the YMCA's religious aims and its members' demand for light gymnastics as opposed to heavy lifting and circus stunts. Association secretaries responded by bemoaning the lack of Christian men available for directing sports and by praising effusively any whom they found. But the gap between those who prized the Association for its athletics and those who prized it for its mission defied easy reconciliation. As one "Y" leader observed in 1898:

> There is a natural antagonism between these two types of men which often amounts to contempt on the part of the stronger one. The breach daily widens—the nice, pious men rise to power in the reading-room, library, and reception room, the strong, hearty fellows in the gymnasium. Two factions exist—the one emphasizes too much the spirit, the other the body. One talks about the "physical department being unmanageable and a disgrace to the Association," the other about "the spider-legged, namby-pamby hypocrites in management who want them to play girls' games."[120]

Fortunately for the YMCA, there emerged in the latter half of the nineteenth century three individuals dedicated to narrowing the gap between athletics and Christianity. The first of these was Robert J. McBurney (1837–1898), who in 1862 assumed the secretaryship of the struggling New York YMCA, molding it within the decade into America's most influential "Y." McBurney never married; he devoted his whole life to the betterment of young men. He lived in the "Tower Room" of the Twenty-Third Street YMCA, which he helped build, and which he equipped with one of the Association's earliest, most munificent gyms. His greatest accomplishment, however, was the "Four-Fold Plan," the first clear rationale for combining athletics with evangelism. Proposed around 1869, it advocated ministry to all four aspects of a young man's life: bodily, social, spiritual, and intellectual.[121]

The next YMCA figure significantly to advance Christian athletics was Robert J. Roberts (1849–1920). A short, extremely muscular man able to lift a 120-pound dumbbell over his head with either hand, Roberts was a devout Baptist who in 1876 left his career as a mechanic and woodturner to work as a gymnastic superintendent for the Boston Association. There he coined the term "body building" and won plaudits as the Association's "first Christian physical director."[122] He also labored to switch the Boston organization's emphasis from heavy exercise to light gymnastics, concentrating on reducing office worker midriffs. Roberts's recreational philosophy, developed after a bad fall and calculated to attract the amateur gymnast, was that athletics should above all be "short, safe, easy, pleasing, and beneficial."[123]

In 1887 Roberts joined the physical education staff at what soon became Springfield College. His only other colleague on the faculty was Luther H. Gulick (1865–1918)—the greatest of YMCA philosophers. Gulick respected Roberts up to a point, but generally found him too slow and mechanical. He also expressed doubts about McBurney's Four-Fold Plan, which he thought overly compartmentalized. "There have been some very bad results already," he wrote late in the nineteenth century, "that we can trace to the four-fold conception of our work"—namely failure to invest "Y" athletics with moral purpose. Remember, he stressed, the gymnasium was neither "a trap to catch young men" nor something that existed "only for the bodies of its members." Instead, it belonged to the YMCA "as a fundamental and intrinsic part in the salvation of man."[124]

Gulick's importance to the "Y" warrants a review of his background. Born in Hawaii to a well-known family of Congregational missionaries, he grew up primarily in Japan, but at age fifteen left for Oberlin's preparatory school. There he suffered so greatly from headaches that he was eventually forced to drop out. This experience, coupled with a revelation about the interconnectedness of health and morals, decided him upon a career in physical education.[125] Consequently, he entered the Sargent School of Physical Training in Cambridge, Massachusetts, and after that received an M.D. from New York University Medical College.

Gulick's first two jobs, both starting in 1887, were with the YMCA—as director of physical training at Springfield College and as secretary for the International Committee's newly formed Physical Department. In both positions, he gained a reputation for humor and nonconformity, subjecting himself to various physical experiments and eschewing coat and tie for gray flannel shirts.[126] He also advocated unceasingly the cause of physical education, editing within the space of twenty years four movement journals (including the august *American Physical Education Review*) and writing five books, one of which he dedicated to Theodore Roosevelt.[127]

Many of Gulick's writings, like those of his friend, G. Stanley Hall, exuded faith in recreation, particularly as a curative for urban woes. But Gulick worried lest people's conventionalities preclude them from "recreating" even when they wanted to. "My own father," he recalled, "played but little as a boy. During later life he tried to play, but it was work. It was pathetic to see him try to play lawn tennis. It was easier and more agreeable for him to study Sanscrit than to bat a ball over a net."[128]

Hoping to convince Christians like his father of the moral value of play, Gulick originated the phrase "body, mind, spirit" (after Dt. 6:5) to describe the importance of symmetry to character. He also suggested an inverted red triangle to represent the "body, mind, spirit" idea and pushed for the YMCA to adopt it as its symbol. Many who thought Gulick an impractical visionary and the red triangle too reminiscent of a graven image resisted, and the motion went down to defeat in the North American conventions of 1889 and 1891. But Gulick persevered, starting a magazine called *The Triangle* and passing out buttons, and by the end of 1891 the red triangle was informally adopted as the YMCA's official seal.[129]

Gulick's subsequent contributions to Association athletics included basketball and volleyball (née mintonette), both of which premiered at Springfield. Basketball, developed in 1891 by the Reverend James Naismith at Gulick's behest, originally served as an indoor substitute for football. Volleyball, whose exhibition game Gulick scheduled in 1896, substituted in turn for basketball, which some businessmen found hard to play.

Both basketball and volleyball quickly spread throughout the Association and were carried overseas by YMCA missionaries. One reason for this was their compatibility with the Association's new athletic ideals: teamwork, ease of access, and applicability to all ages. Gulick also averred that whereas the old Robertsonian dumbbell drills were solitary and antisocial, sports like basketball and volleyball promoted sociability and "all-around development" (qualities, interestingly enough, that corporations were just beginning to prize in their professional/managerial employees).[130]

Because not everyone appreciated the idealism underlying basketball and volleyball, the YMCA moved in 1895 to reorganize and strengthen its Athletic League. "The Athletic League," explained Gulick, its first secretary, "is based on the idea that the influence of athletics upon character must be on the side of honesty and Christian courtesy."[131] To this end, the League promoted healthy amateurism and resisted the professionalization of sports (concern over which caused the Association in 1911 to sever its ties with the Amateur Athletic Union, which had proposed fielding professional teams). The League also circulated a "Clean Sports Roll" (written by Gulick), the particulars of which one "Y" man summed up in two words: "consecrated backbone."[132]

One by-product of Gulick's campaign to Christianize the gym was a closer relationship between the Association's Physical and Religious Departments. Bible Study secretary Fred Goodman, writing in 1915 on Bible study in the gym, acknowledged this, and concluded that "the risen Jesus is a member of every gymnasium class, of every athletic team in which there are Christians, whether we are conscious of it or not."[133] Physical directors for their part generally liked being thought essential "worker[s] in the Kingdom of God."[134] At least they appeared less averse to allowing Bible study in their gyms, and more willing to view physical training as somehow religious.[135]

Gulick himself did not remain long enough within the "Y" to witness the full blending of Christianity with athletics. In 1903 he left Springfield, and for the next three years he served as director of physical training in the public schools of New York City. Later in life he helped found several health and physical education societies, the American Folk Dance Society, and three organizations covered elsewhere in this volume: the Playground Association, the Boy Scouts, and the Camp Fire Girls (to whom he was known as Timanous, or "guiding spirit").[136] But it was in connection with the YMCA that Gulick most directly advanced the cause of muscular Christianity. Before Gulick, the "Y" had kept gymnastics subordinate to evangelism. After him, it held physical fitness, no less than religious conviction, responsible for leading men to Glory.

Thanks largely to pioneers such as Luther Gulick, the postbellum years were important ones for sport in America, years that witnessed the growth of college sports, the spread of amateur athletics, and a host of recreational firsts. Such "diversions" initially aroused considerable opposition from Protestant divines, but over time the mainline churches came to see sport as beneficial. This conversion was greatly abetted by pious athletic organizations such as the YMCA, which strove to regulate sports and Christianize athletic facilities. As a result of its efforts, the YMCA attracted numerous Christians to its gymnasia. It also urged those Christians to look upon the YMCA red triangle and sing "Body, mind, and spirit freed; No more bruised and blighted; Build the new humanity; Holy, strong united!"[137]

Freeing the body from the prejudices of the past was a significant accomplishment for the YMCA, which had worked since the late 1860s to break down the barriers between religion and sport. But the YMCA was not content simply to inject athleticism into Christianity. It also wanted to bring Christianity closer to men. Some men of dubious virility seemed content with the churches' "feminized" view of Jesus, observed the YMCA in the late nineteenth century. But "real men" appeared ready in the eyes of the Association for a genuinely "virile" religion—like the one described in the next chapter.

CHAPTER THREE

Men and Religion

Shout aloud the stirring summons
O'er the land from sea to sea,
Men are wanted, men of courage,
For the man of Galilee.
Men are wanted, men of purpose,
Men of high or low degree,
Each to be a fellow worker
With the man of Galilee.

—FROM *MANLY SONGS FOR CHRISTIAN MEN* (1910)

On October 12, 1908, President Theodore Roosevelt wrote to Student Volunteer Movement leader John R. Mott expressing approval of that group's efforts to recruit "more men of ability to lead the aggressive forces of Christianity." Strong, well-rounded Christians immune to both "hysteria" and "sentimentality" were definitely needed, the President said, to cope with America's industrial problems, with recent overseas acquisitions, and with the "unhealthy drift" toward the city.[1] But where were such heroic men to be found? Not in the seminaries, charged educators; these were full of pallid, overly cerebral types. Not in the pews, complained ministers; these were empty of men. Outside the YMCA, in fact, Christian manhood appeared threatened, weakened by decay from within and by encroaching feminization from without.

The Woman Peril in Religion

Recent histories of the Social Gospel by Janet Fishburn and Susan Curtis emphasize the importance within that movement of issues pertaining to manhood. Both authors recount how prominent Social Gospellers expressed dissatisfaction with the "feminized culture" of their day; how they felt themselves to be less than their fathers, who had fought in the Civil War; and how (in compensation) they conceived the Social Gospel, with its worldwide reformatory aims, to be, in the words of Methodist leader Fayette L. Thompson, "a vaster program than our fathers ever dreamed." Fishburn believes that the Social Gospel offered men the chance to "do good" and not be thought emasculate. "In a culture where the power of a good woman might serve the nation through her influence in the domestic sphere," she writes, "the 'strenuous life' of the good man might serve the nation through his influence in the public sphere."[2]

Undoubtedly Social Gospel proponents conceived theirs to be a manly enterprise (as explained in Chapter 1). But it was not only theologically liberal reformers who proposed making religion more manly; it was also conservative religious spokesmen such as the Reverend Jasper Massee, who in *Men and the Kingdom* (1912) decried women's omnipresence in religion—particularly the predominance of "immature and untrained women [Sunday school] teachers." "Religion is a man's job," he concluded, and it was high time for men to take leadership both of their churches and of their families' worship hours.[3]

Massee's concern over men's abandonment of their religious duties was not without some basis in fact. Membership statistics compiled in 1910 by the YMCA revealed that American churches were two-thirds female. Participation figures were even more lopsided.[4] A prominent Congregationalist writing in 1890 observed regretfully that despite examples of active and powerful laymen, "the mainstay of the modern church is its consecrated women."[5] Two decades later, Fayette L. Thompson confirmed that whereas "the masculine was once dominant in the church . . . that it is less so now is a matter of general knowledge."[6]

Men still filled most pulpits, of course. But women, eager for influence denied them in business and politics, predominated in day-to-day committee work, in visitations, and in the Sunday school movement.[7] Ann Douglas argues that women largely dictated the form of nineteenth-century Protestantism, softening harsh Calvinistic theologies and producing services reminiscent "of a sort of weekly Mother's Day."[8] As a result, wrote one observer, the churches were becoming so feminized that soon "there will not be men enough in heaven to sing bass, when 'the Song of Moses and the Lamb' is rendered by the redeemed before the Great White Throne."[9]

Men who remained in the church often risked being thought effeminate. And though this was not such a bad thing prior to the Civil War (when ministers frequently won praise for their sensitivity, refinement, and other "feminine" characteristics),[10] sensitive men in the Progressive Era were much less appreciated. One opponent of sentimental Christianity noted that there was an "imprudent classification which every healthy minister resents—'men, women, and clergymen.'"[11] A second lamented that "too often sissy fellows have paraded themselves as representatives of Christianity's crowning work and characterization, while the men of full-blood and ambition have quietly dropped out from such company."[12]

Observers considered the disappearance of masculinity from religion unfortunate for a number of reasons. One critic reflected that since divinity had both male and female sides, overlooking the male side "greatly enfeebled" the church.[13] Another maintained that women, for all their angelic qualities, were not thinkers; hence the church's crying need for male "brains."[14] The church could not do without "the beauty of its womanly virtues," conceded Fred Smith, an organizer of the Men and Religion Forward movement. "But Christianity is also essentially masculine, militant, warlike," he added, "and if these elements are not made manifest, men and boys will not be found in increasing numbers as participants in the life of the church."[15]

The most exhaustive critique of excess femininity in the churches was undoubtedly Carl Case's *The Masculine in Religion* (1906). Case, a Baptist minister with a Ph.D. from the University of Chicago, maintained that in overcoming "the narrow and constraining masculine elements" of the past (for example, Calvinism) Protestant churches had become overly "passive," overly concerned with "appearances"—in a word, overly "feminine." He also took issue with the idea that whereas religion was "natural" for women, it was "unnatural" for men.[16]

The businessman's absence from church resulted not from irreligion, Case wrote; rather it showed his dislike for cant and his reluctance to waste time. "Men do not find enough to do in the church of that which requires skill and courage," he explained. "There is too great a contrast between the strenuous business life to which they are accustomed and the lifeless committee work upon petty things to which they are invited."[17]

Case felt that as things stood, the social needs and spiritual aspirations of men were much better served by the lodge than by the church. Churches forced men to listen to ministers whom they might not respect; lodges offered men the chance to talk freely, and on timely subjects. Churches assigned men committee work that "belittles their manhood"; lodges undertook "weighty" charity work and assigned men to "important" positions. Church religion was too otherworldly and feminized; lodge religion was "practical" and fit "the legitimate demands of a man's religious nature." But "if the lodge satisfies men," Case concluded hopefully, "the church can do it. It can be a home of enjoyment, a means of fellowship and sociability, a place of activity, discussion, and responsibility, a satisfaction to the religious nature, far better than the lodge."[18]

More recent comparisons between church and lodge have been drawn by historians Mary Ann Clawson and Mark Carnes. Clawson sees lodge ritual (the secret handshakes, blood oaths, and so on) providing something liberal Protestantism lacked: celebration of the male virtues and affirmation of men's spirituality.[19] Carnes also notes the presence within Victorian lodges of "manly" ritualism. Lodges, he says, treated men as morally autonomous beings. Churches in contrast preached that men were inherently sinful, wholly in need of feminine aid for redemption.[20]

Whatever the truth of these observations, churches evidently saw themselves competing with lodges for men's allegiance and respect. They also understood church worship to be one of numerous activities available to men on any given Sunday, and that to remain viable church worship would have to be made more compelling.[21] From these realizations, Progressive Era ministers fashioned a call to worship whose chief aim was to attract men. It appealed to men in four ways: through their sense of discipline, through their sense of the practical, through their youthful passions, and through their desire for the heroic.

The church's appeal to discipline evolved from the idea that society during the Gilded Age had grown too "soft" and that as a result men were shirking their religious responsibilities. Back when ministers preached hellfire, noted *Scribner's* in 1899, men were "austere and narrow, but so virile, so indomitable and forceful, that their impress is even yet stamped deep upon our national character."[22] The laxity of modern men, by contrast, seemed to demand a religious "intcrpretation of manhood mainly resting upon discipline, as *contrasted with all softness and easy self-indulgence.*"²³

Disciplining religion meant making it more "practical," better able to fulfill people's immediate expectations. "This is a practical age," explained a Methodist pastor in 1911, "and needs wholesome truth set before it in vigorous and practical forms."²⁴ Unless churches lived down their reputation for "other-worldliness," commented another cleric, and leveled with "the matter-of-fact men of the counting-room, the shop, and the factory," they were lost; for men "want a religion which has some relation to things seen and temporal."²⁵

Proponents of "practical Christianity" conceived making the church more businesslike to be a challenge worthy of men—especially young and ambitious ones. Young men should draw inspiration from Christ's efforts to reform the church of His day, argued psychologist G. Stanley Hall, speaking before the International Committee of the YMCA in 1905. They must not be set back by "the timid apprehensions of graybeards," but must instead "defy" and "refute" them, ridding the church of everything "stagnant" and "sterile." Young men ought also to "stand erect on [their] own feet," Hall continued, and "free [themselves] from the conservatism of men of the past." Above all, they should know that their efforts were approved of by Jesus, who "comes to young men as to no others," and for whom "women, childhood, and old age are by nature a little less near."²⁶

While Hall asked young men to empathize with Christ, others asked them to be heroic on behalf of religion. Present-day churches made religion "too easy and too cheap," thought one YMCA speaker. But "promise young men battles instead of feasts, swords instead of prizes, campaigns instead of comforts, and the heroic which lies deep in every man will leap in response."²⁷ Those left cold by this challenge were redundant, added a spokesman for the Brotherhood of St. Andrew; for "the church and the world to-day are calling, not for puny, weak-backed, dyspeptic, priggish apologies for men, but for strong, masculine, muscular fellows, who can hold their own with any man."²⁸

One man who seemed to embody all the tenets of manly religion was Theodore Roosevelt. The President, wrote a biographer, early on eschewed mere show in religion, cleaving instead to the venerable if déclassé Dutch Reformed Church of his family, and attending that church (rather than the Episcopal cathedral) when in Washington.²⁹

He also taught Sunday school while a student at Harvard, at which time "piety and activity in the church were only expected of the effeminate or those anticipating an early death." Later in life, Roosevelt largely avoided religious disputation, though he frequently urged men to attend church services, took steps to see that soldiers did so during the Spanish-American War, supported American missionaries overseas, and publicly praised the work of the YMCA.[30]

Theologically, Roosevelt stood squarely behind the Social Gospel. "His is a militant faith," noted Jacob Riis, "bound on the mission of helping the world ahead." "Ascetic" Christianity by contrast repelled the President for being generally unhealthy, productive of low birth rates, and a threat to civilization.[31] "If we read the Bible aright," Roosevelt confided to his friend Riis, "we read a book which teaches us to go forth and do the work of the Lord in the world as we find it . . . That kind of work," he went on, "can be done only by the man who is neither a weakling nor a coward; by the man who in the fullest sense of the word is a true Christian, like Greatheart, Bunyan's hero."[32]

After Roosevelt's death in 1919, two prominent Methodist pastors elegized his masculine piety. The first, Christian Reisner, ventured that "religion was as natural to Mr. Roosevelt as breathing"—as natural as the President's "sturdy health."[33] The second, Ferdinand Iglehart, congratulated the President for having discovered religion despite his wealthy, urban background. "In entering life," Iglehart averred, Roosevelt "came to two roads, a broad one leading to destruction and a narrow one leading to heaven. He deliberately took God as his guide and Christ as his example, and at the age of sixteen entered the Army of the King and battled for the cause of righteousness till the day of his death."[34]

Captains of Christ

Powerful laymen such as Theodore Roosevelt advanced muscular Christianity by example. But most knew that reforming the church to make it more vigorous and manly depended at least in part on the efforts of clergy. Ministers might never match YMCA secretaries for versatility, conceded John D. Rockefeller, Jr.; they might never be able to wrestle, play billiards, and teach church history with "equal facility." Nevertheless, "the more of virility and of rugged manhood there is in the pulpit, the more will the vigorous men of the city be influenced by its message."[35]

Unhappily for exponents of a virile ministry, people's reigning image of the clergyman was of someone sensitive and refined, someone more comfortable at women's teas than at men's sporting competitions. It was an image at least somewhat accurate, notes Ann Douglas; for liberal ministers often were "mamma's boys" whose health was fragile and whose friendships were with women.[36] But while such "delicate" types might appeal to women, argued Oberlin president Henry C. King, men found them "especially repulsive." Men preferred ministers "of blood earnest spirit," he averred. Or, as the Reverend Dr. James Vance wrote in reference to the sentimental clergyman, "Where in all the sweep of freaks and failures, of mawkish sentiments and senseless blathery, can there be found an object to excite deeper disgust than one of these thin, vapid, affected, driveling little doodles dressed up in men's clothes, but without a thimbleful of brains in his pate or an ounce of manhood in his anatomy? He is worse than weak—he is a weaklet."[37]

Critics did concede that there were multiple reasons preventing "strong men" from entering the ministry. The Reverend Jenkin Lloyd Jones believed one of these reasons was the rise of alternative venues in which to do good: the public schools, settlement houses, and other social service agencies.[38] Others pointed to the declining status of the ministry vis-à-vis the secular professions. Between the years 1870 and 1906, they noted, the number of divinity students increased only 137 percent, whereas medical students rose by 302 percent, law students by 848 percent, and business students by a percentage greater than medicine and law combined.[39] Ministerial salaries also decreased relative to competing professions. As one Congregational minister wrote in 1909, "The clergyman's salary is provided from the savings of others who serve in the productive professions. The stipend is not usually large; it is somewhat uncertain. Altogether, these facts are apt to chill young men as they look forward to this service."[40]

The possibility of intellectual stultification seemed to some an even greater reason for avoiding ministry than low salaries. Jenkin Lloyd Jones confessed he understood the "high-minded" young man's repugnance for ministry, since various church "medieval[isms]" undoubtedly "menace[d]" that young man's "intellectual liberty."[41] An early-twentieth-century sociological study confirmed that placating hoary-minded parishioners and other "monotonous harrassments of the ministry" were "detrimental to intellectual growth."[42] "Picture the weak church in its darkest colors," wrote Dean Edward Bosworth of Oberlin Theological School: its chance for expansion small, its building "weather-worn," and its membership unwilling "to allow their minister small liberty to proclaim ideas . . . in the vernacular of modern thought." Ministry at such a church was not a career, he warned; it was a "hole." "And a man does not want to get into a hole. He wants to get into a field."[43]

A final roadblock to ministry was the profession's reputation for "womanliness." Such a stigma was particularly dissuasive for the "strong man," explained Dean Bosworth; for "he is a manly man, not a ladies' man or desirous to be ornamental at a pink tea."[44] Associating ministers exclusively with women was indeed irksome, agreed an eminent Congregationalist; nonetheless too often it was true. After all, the minister "has sometimes spent the forenoons with his books, and his afternoons with the women and children of the parish in his pastoral work, with no adequate provision for personal contacts with the men of his community."[45]

People's equation of ministry with self-sacrifice and their perception of ministers as womanly raise the question: why not women ministers? Women were active in the church, founding missionary boards and conducting charity work. Moreover, according to nineteenth-century stereotypes, they were naturally more religious than men—more giving of themselves, saintlier, and more "sympathetic."[46] This being the case, it made sense for women to preach, in order that their purifying influence might be extended.

In fact, women did achieve ordination in several denominations prior to the twentieth century. The first to do so was Antoinette Brown Blackwell, who in 1853 accepted a call to the Congregational church in South Butler, New York. Sects with collective ministries (Shakers and Quakers) gave women temporal authority even earlier. At the beginning of the twentieth century around 108 women were enrolled in Protestant seminaries (187 by 1904); and twenty years later the Congregationalists counted 100 women ministers, the Universalists 88, and the Unitarians 42.[47]

The first churches to ordain women tended to have three things in common: difficulty attracting male ministers, weak ties to centralized authority, and congregational polity (that is, lay government). This helps explain why the bulk of women ministers occupied rural Congregational, Universalist, and Unitarian pulpits (though even here, notes historian Cynthia Grant Tucker, concern over manliness in the

Progressive Era led to the purging of women ministers). Denominations whose polity was presbyterial or episcopal (that is, denominations with powerful hierarchies) mostly opposed women's ordination. The Methodist Episcopal Church (Northern) abolished the unofficial licensing of women to preach in 1880 and postponed ordaining women until 1956. Northern Presbyterians delayed women's ordination until 1955, Southern Presbyterians until 1964. Episcopalian women won ordination as deaconesses in 1964, but it was not until 1976 that they received full ordination as priests.[48]

Objections to women's preaching varied from age to age, but during the Progressive Era those objections were expressed by both liberals and conservatives. Conservatives not surprisingly based their case largely on scripture. Thus the Presbyterian minister Samuel Niccolls argued that while women "helpers" abounded in the Bible, they were subordinate to men, and admirable chiefly for their humility.[49] Liberals generally interpreted scripture more freely; and some, such as Jenkin Lloyd Jones, even thought that women's ordination was a good idea. Others, however, believed world uplift to be a "man's job," one requiring strength and fortitude. As John R. Mott put it, "The work of the ministry is so comprehensive that it requires strong men to carry it on."[50]

Mott and others argued that ministry ought not to be disassociated from manhood, but rather used as proof of it. They pointed to Christian leaders of the past—"men whose blood coursed strong and hot through their veins, fine specimens of muscular, soldiery Christianity"—as evidence that ministry "engender[ed] manliness."[51] One Chicago Presbyterian testified that by entering the ministry he had "vacated none of my masculine inheritances nor sidestepped any of the bequests that fall to red-blooded manhood." Instead, never had he felt himself "so overwhelmingly challenged to the full limit and variety of my distinctly masculine qualities as I do at this hour by the vast and baffling obligations of religion."[52]

Emphasizing the manliness of ministry struck reformers as a good idea, and one likely to attract young men. Hence when John R. Mott commissioned nine divines to write pamphlets urging young men to enter the ministry, everyone laid stress on contemporary problems and the manliness required for overcoming them. One writer depicted ministers as "brave, contemporary servants of the supreme interest of society," battling "degeneracy" and at the same time "send[ing] forth [their] appeal for reinforcements."[53] Another demanded men "strong" and "high-hearted" enough to withstand Christ's exacting specifications. "Who can face and conquer the monster evils of current life?" he asked. "Who can take this vast, complex modern age and unify its qualities, not destroy them but fulfill them in Christ?"[54]

An additional series of articles supportive of manlier ministries appeared in the first three volumes of *The American Journal of Religious Psychology* (1906–08). Written by David Spence Hill, a student of G. Stanley Hall at Clark University, they recommended seminary reform as the first step toward healthier churches. Hill thought seminaries "institution[s] out of harmony with the times," and he urged them to upgrade their curricula. In particular, he proposed cutting back on ancient languages, introducing modern subjects such as biology, and consolidating seminaries in the interest of scientific efficiency. He also wanted more "all-round men" on seminary faculties and fewer "book-worms, freaks, and geniuses."[55]

Two of Hill's proposed reforms aimed directly at producing manlier, more socially aware seminarians. The first recommended time off for "a year or two of actual participation with world-toilers." The second called on seminaries to eliminate most financial aid (productive of a "spineless dependence"). Forcing seminarians out of their cloisters and into "grimy contact" with the outside world would make them more "practical," Hill argued. Moreover, it promised to dissuade from ministry most "ritualists," "parasites," and "weaklings," leaving behind only those hearty souls "appreciat[ive] of the present and full of cheerful expectation for the future of the race."[56]

That new standards for ministry were forming seems apparent, and in fact questionnaires collected by Hill and Carl Case reveal this to have been the case. The responses to Case's questionnaire—delivered over the course of three pastorates to a wide spectrum of people— showed that men in particular wanted "shorter," "pithier" sermons and a more "masculine church service" ("a church service where strong, manly sermons are preached and songs sung which are full of vigor and vim").[57] Hill's questionnaire—sent in 1905 to several hundred diverse individuals—garnered 145 replies: 92 from females, 52 from males, and most from people under thirty years of age. Of the respondents, 130 detailed for Hill their conception of the "ideal minister," 80 saying he should be "benevolent" and 52 stressing instead his "manliness" and "strength." As for the ideal minister's physical appearance, Hill's respondents generally agreed that "he must be tall, stately, six feet, strong to look at, well proportioned, etc." His having "an imposing physique," in short, was important—"almost unanimously" so for younger respondents.[58]

Whether this penchant for muscular ministry was at all related to the successful dissemination of the YMCA's Christian ideal is difficult to say. Still, at least one "Y" man held the Association's crusade for health to be partially responsible for people's growing dissatisfaction with ministers whose bodies were "glaring[ly] defect[ive]." "Don't misunderstand me," he hastened to add, "I do not mean that it is requisite for a minister to have a handsome face, for that is something that he cannot entirely control; but I do say that a finely proportioned body, well developed chest, broad shoulders, and standing square on the feet, gives any man a decided advantage in any calling in life and especially in the ministry."[59]

That modern-day ministers ought to be veritable founts of strength and heartiness was certainly true, agreed Presbyterian layman William Scott. But it was not enough for ministers to secure their own manliness, he continued; they also had to found men's groups for the benefit of male parishioners. For without such groups, churches risked losing men to the saloon or the lodge, thereby proving that "no church to-day is fully alive to its mission that has not in connection with it some kind of men's organization, call it Club, League, Brotherhood, or what you will."[60]

Protestant Brotherhoods

The Brotherhood movement (a campaign to establish men's groups and Bible studies) flourished within Protestant churches from the early 1880s until World War I.[61] Its chief instigators were men such as Edwin J. Gardiner, who worried about the churches' losing their hold on young men. "There are . . . quite a number of men" in the church, Gardiner wrote in 1887, but "where are the young men?" Most likely they were reading "light novel[s]," he surmised, or sporting with their "materialistic" friends. Nor could he much blame them. After all, the young single man often received scant welcome in church. Ushers generally seated him in a back pew, people looked askance at his clothes, and sodalities planned not for his needs, but for the needs of women and families.[62]

Gardiner believed such inattention detracted from the "spiritual culture" of young men, and he warned that as things stood, America's future fathers would most likely be atheists. The way to reverse this situation, he believed, was through the efforts of church brotherhoods. A proper church brotherhood, he wrote, would greet young men with open arms; it would minister to their needs and acquaint them with a Christianity far less "passive" than any they had hitherto known. Proper brotherhoods moreover would be conducted by as well as for young men. Their leaders would be plain-spoken and energetic, able instinctively to apprehend the young man's "infirmities."[63]

Inspired by these and similar arguments, men's groups began to form throughout mainstream Protestantism. Local examples included the First Baptist Church Young Men's Social Union (Lansing, Michigan), the First Baptist Church Young Men's Club (St. Paul, Minnesota), the Ashland Avenue Baptist Church Young Men's Fraternity (Toledo, Ohio), the Memorial Baptist Church Young Men's Christian League (Los Angeles, California), the First Congregational Church Men's Club (Jersey City, New Jersey), the Central Congregational Church Men's Guild (Brooklyn, New York), the Broadway Tabernacle Church Men's League (New York City), the Markham Memorial Presbyterian Church Men's Club (St. Louis, Missouri), the Methodist Episcopal Church Young Men's Christian Brotherhood (Belvidere, Illinois), and the St. Matthew's Lutheran Church Young Men's Club (Philadelphia, Pennsylvania).[64]

Groups with a broader geographic base included the Sunday Evening Club (dedicated to improving turnout at Sunday services—and to the care of men's hats and coats in the vestry), the Young Men's Christian Union in Boston (Unitarianism's answer to the YMCA), the Pleasant Sunday Afternoon Club (another alternative to the YMCA, originating in England), the Young Men's Presbyterian Union of Chicago (an amalgamation of thirty-two young men's Bible classes) and the Baraca (Hebrew for "blessed") movement (which also encompassed a number of young men's Bible classes).[65]

The first church men's club to achieve national prominence was the Brotherhood of St. Andrew (Episcopalian). Named after the disciple who brought Simon to Christ, the organization was the brainchild of James L. Houghteling, who founded the order in 1883. A Yale graduate and son of a wealthy lumber merchant, Houghteling taught a

Bible class for young men at St. James Church in Chicago. It was there, he later recalled, that the Brotherhood of St. Andrew was born, largely in response to the arrival at St. James of a "strange" and "ancient drunkard" who claimed that he had once belonged to a (most likely British) young men's order called the Society of Andrew and Philip—Philip being the disciple who brought Nathaniel to Christ.[66] Inspired by the derelict's tale, Houghteling convinced his Bible class to rename itself the Brotherhood of St. Andrew and to take a greater interest in the poor and the homeless. He also asked his class to evangelize more young men and to reorganize along military lines. As a result, young men who arrived at St. James were greeted by a leader of the Brotherhood and directed to one of two aisles where the organization held pews. Each aisle had a "lieutenant," who in turn had under him several "privates," one or more to a pew. In addition, there was a "quartermaster," who kept Brotherhood pews supplied with hymnbooks and invitation cards.[67]

Inductees into the Brotherhood of St. Andrew pledged two things: to pray daily "for the spread of Christ's Kingdom among young men," and to bring at least one male friend per week to church or Bible study. New members received a cardboard folder containing the two rules, a certificate of membership, a summary of the objects of the order, recommendations, and brief prayers. Among these last was the Brotherhood's signature prayer, "a collect for Saint Andrew's Day," which read:

> Almighty and eternal Father, without whom nothing is strong, nothing is holy, we beseech Thee to inspire and sustain the prayers and efforts of the members of our Brotherhood and to hallow their lives; and grant that young men everywhere be brought into the Kingdom of Thy Son, and may be led from strength to strength until they attain unto the fulness of eternal life, through the same, Thy Son, Jesus Christ our Lord, Amen.[68]

Expansion of the Brotherhood was swift. By 1885 churches throughout Chicago boasted chapters, and in 1886 a national convention was held and a constitution drawn up. That same year saw foundation of the Brotherhood's journal, *St. Andrew's Cross* (circulation 7,000 in 1891). This organ published pieces advocating "service" and the establishment of strong bodies for such service.[69] It also worked to unify the organization's membership, which by 1903 had reached 9,000 (excluding boy members and members overseas).

The success of the Brotherhood of St. Andrew inspired several imitators. The largest of these was the Brotherhood of Andrew and Philip (founded 1888; membership in 1903: 25,000). This organization differed from the Brotherhood of St. Andrew in that it was interdenominational, with twenty-three member denominations. Otherwise it was nearly identical to the Brotherhood of St. Andrew (including copying the earlier organization's rules for prayer and service). Local branches of the Brotherhood of Andrew and Philip called themselves "manly" ministries "of young men for young men," and to an extent this was true.[70] But their founder and president, the Reverend Rufus W. Miller, wanted ultimately to "bring the young men of the congregation under the guidance and instruction of their natural leaders, the pastor and church officers."[71]

Many denominations with links to the Brotherhood of Andrew and Philip also had their own men's groups. Two of the more significant were the Presbyterian Brotherhood and the Brotherhood of St. Paul (Methodist). The Methodist brotherhood (founded 1896; membership in 1903: 25,000) continued in the tradition of its predecessors, the Brotherhood of Andrew and Philip and the Brotherhood of St. Andrew. Like the latter group, the Brotherhood of St. Paul had an active junior organization and employed military titles (Christ was the "great commander," pastors his "ranking officers"). Like the Brotherhood of Andrew and Philip, the Brotherhood of St. Paul evinced some ambiguity of purpose, promising at once to empower young men and to cement them firmly within the church. What distinguished the Brotherhood of St. Paul from other Protestant brotherhoods was its resemblance to the Masons, the Odd Fellows, and other secular fraternities. This resemblance primarily manifested itself in elaborate initiation ceremonies, in the establishment of mutual aid funds, and in the conferring of orders: the Order of Jerusalem for new members, the Order of Damascus for full members, and the Order of Rome (a strange title for Methodists) for members of two years' good standing.[72]

Presbyterians began serious discussion of men's brotherhoods in 1895. PCUSA (Presbyterian Church in the USA) General Assembly minutes that year noted that while churches had "sufficient organization of women and children and youth, the call is to be made for the organization of men." Thereafter PCUSA churches worked hard to found men's societies and Bible classes, and by 1906 there existed 500 of these organizations nationwide. That same year, these groups combined to form the Presbyterian Brotherhood (known from 1908–1911 as the Presbyterian Men's Movement). This organization convened several mass meetings of Presbyterian laymen, the most significant of which was the Men's Jubilee Congress (held May 23–27, 1903, in Pittsburgh, Pennsylvania). It also published its own journal, the *Men's Record,* an important chronicler of Presbyterian missions.[73]

In some instances, Christian brotherhoods operated outside the church. A good example of this was the Gideons, famous today for their hotel Bibles. Organized in 1899 at Janesville, Wisconsin, the Gideons (membership in 1903: 3,000) were commercial travelers who yearned for Christian community and "the elevation of manhood." In the absence of churches to which they could regularly go, these men formed state "camps" and held "camp-fires" as opposed to Sunday services. Their avowed aim was to evangelize other salesmen with whom they came into contact, and in this they were often successful. To quote Frank Cressey, author of *The Church and Young Men* (1903): "The rise and growth of the Gideons among a class of men commonly supposed to be largely outside of Christian influence, is a striking answer to those who affirm that Christianity is declining and that the church is losing power over the hearts of men."[74]

The Gideons were Protestant, as was most of the Brotherhood movement. Catholics, noted Cressey, appeared relatively uninterested in helping young men specifically, and in the matter of men's evangelism they were "doing . . . far less than their Protestant neighbors." One priest (and college president) whom Cressey interviewed even doubted whether the church ought to do anything new with regard to young men. "With us the great agencies for the spiritual betterment of young men are those established by God Himself," he explained, "namely, the holy sacraments."[75]

Many additional reasons existed for Catholic reticence in men's evangelism. Two of the most important were working conditions for Catholic males and the authority (or lack of authority) of women in the Catholic Church. With regard to the former, the tendency in fin de siècle America for Catholics to have physically demanding blue-collar jobs generally forestalled worries over physical degeneracy, and hence deflated appeals (such as those made in *St. Andrew's Cross* and other Protestant journals with white-collar readerships) for muscular Christianity and enhanced Christian manliness. As for the specter of women taking over the church, this also seemed less of a problem for Catholics than Protestants. After all, notes historian Peter McDonough, Catholic orders such as the Jesuits were bastions of male religiosity, eschewing the influence of both women and sentimentality; and if they talked little about "feminization," perhaps that was because they had never experienced it.[76]

The Catholics' complacent attitude toward Christian manliness put them at odds with the Brotherhood mainstream. But though their relation to the movement was marginal, it was by no means nonexistent, as evidenced by the emergence in the 1880s of several Catholic fraternities. These organizations (most patterned after already-existing Protestant ones) included the Knights of Columbus (a Catholic alternative to such secret societies as the Masons), the Catholic Order of Foresters (another Masonic alternative), the Knights of Father Matthew (a men's temperance society), and the Catholic Total Abstinence Union of America (which despite its name was a rather convivial group, with buildings containing gymnasiums, reading rooms, and billiard halls). There was also a Catholic equivalent to the YMCA called the Young Men's Institute, whose membership in 1903 numbered around 12,000.[77]

What chiefly distinguished Catholic groups from the Protestant brotherhoods was their subjection to clerical oversight and to the pope, who forbade Catholics membership in religious societies over which he had no control. But this subjection often was stronger in appearance than reality, and Catholic fraternities—compared with other nineteenth-century Catholic organizations—enjoyed enormous liberties. Indeed in some ways they presaged what historian Will Herberg called the "Protestantization" of American Catholicism: the investiture of authority in laymen and the valuing of religion for its sociability.[78]

The spread of Catholic church brotherhoods was greeted with enthusiasm by one Jesuit, who praised the brotherhoods for reinfusing religion with "recreational value" hitherto lost to Anglo-Saxonism due to Cromwell's tragic destruction of the monasteries—medieval prototypes of the modern-day community center.[79] Protestant brotherhoods also won encomiums, especially during their heyday, which peaked with the Men and Religion Forward movement of 1911–1912 (an event covered in Chapter 5). After this, notes a Presbyterian historian, enthusiasm for the Protestant men's movement gradually died down.[80]

Whatever their fate or purpose, brotherhoods left indelible marks on politics and society. "War *la outrance*" had been waged against the devil," affirmed brotherhood spokesman Frederick Leete; and there had been "magnificent and costly victories . . . over the powers which enthrall men and keep them from serving Christ." Among such victories, wrote Leete, were the Missoula, Montana, brotherhoods' Sunday closure of the saloons; the success of a Congregational brotherhood in reforming Minnesota's penal laws; and, most important, the "Better Brattleboro Campaign," a Vermont consortium of church brotherhoods "standing together on behalf of goodness."[81]

But for the brotherhoods, probably no work ranked higher than winning young men for Christ. It was inspiring, observed the St. James's chapter (Chicago) of the Brotherhood of St. Andrew, that due to aggressive recruitment, "Our seats are full, and any Sunday morning may be seen forty to fifty men sitting together in a solid phalanx, four or five to a pew, worshipping God and singing His praise, shoulder to shoulder."[82]

This eagerness for conversions (discussed more fully in Chapter 5) relates to a final, if somewhat peripheral, outgrowth of church brotherhoods: their creation of a market for books on "personal" (that is, men's) evangelism. The Progressive Era saw a spate of such works, among the most notable being Samuel M. Sayford's *Personal Work* (1899), J. H. Jowett's *Passion for Souls* (1900), H. Clay Trumbull's *Individual Work for Individuals* (1901), H. Wellington Wood's *Winning Men One by One* (1908), and Howard Begbie's *Souls in Action* (1911). Though these books have been largely forgotten, one brotherhood authority thought that their authors were every bit as important as Josiah Strong, Walter Rauschenbusch, and other proponents of the Social Gospel.[83]

Manly Christianity

Protestant brotherhoods did not restrict themselves to personal evangelism or to the cleanup of society. They also wanted to reform those churches that, to quote the October 1896 cover of *Men* (a YMCA journal), had become places Christ "would have hated"—places where "Jesus' cross has been taken out of his hands and smothered in flowers."[84] Such "elegant" churches ("repulsive" for their "exclusiveness") demanded change, opined President Henry King of Oberlin College, "at any cost to ritualism or ceremony." They especially needed to become more socially active in order to acquit Christ's commands and to effect his overall plans for humanity.[85]

Pleas such as these for churches to adopt the Social Gospel did not go unheeded. "Time was," acknowledged the Right Reverend Frank Wilson, an Episcopal Church historian, "when the Church was afflicted with a debilitating inertia and rested in her work almost to the point of laziness." Yet "today," he continued (writing in 1916), "new and energetic motives prompt her to increasingly vigorous activities." Midweek services, religious clubs, reform societies, and "organizations for clean amusement" were aborning with "a rushing, roaring energy" that was truly "astonishing"—so astonishing that Wilson urged caution lest churches by their clamor "drown out the voice of God which should guide the course of their efforts."[86]

Especially reflective of the new religious militancy was the Salvation Army, which began as a mission to East London's destitute. Originally called the Christian Mission, the Army took on its present name in 1878 when its leader, Wesleyan evangelist William Booth, was inspired to conduct Christian work on a military basis. The following year a British expatriate family (the Shirleys) instituted the first Salvation Army in America: the Salvation Factory of Philadelphia, Pennsylvania.[87]

The success of this venture encouraged Booth in 1880 to dispatch to America an official envoy composed of a uniformed male commissioner and seven "hallelujah lassies." Though they were mistaken by reporters for a traveling concert troupe when they disembarked at New York, the group quickly proved their evangelical intent, and by the end of the year had helped establish eight Salvation Army "corps" (six of them in Philadelphia). Ten years later, there were 410 corps in 35 states, and the Salvation Army was well on its way to becoming an American fixture.[88]

The mission of the Salvation Army was to the poorest of the poor, particularly alcoholics; and in its mission the Army found military nomenclature very useful. Terms such as "knee drill" for prayer, "prisoner" for convert, and so on not only attracted attention, explained Army historian Edward McKinley; they also convinced people that they were participating in a dynamic, victorious campaign. Other morale boosters included the Army's blue, red, and yellow flag (emblematic of its motto, "Blood and fire"), its trademark brass bands (first adopted in 1878), and its uniforms: black straw bonnets with red and blue bows for women and regulation military caps for men (these last ordered in 1891 to replace the rather eclectic mix of pith helmets, cowboy hats, toppers, and firemen's helmets formerly used by Army men as headgear).[89]

One area in which the Salvation Army did not shine was theology. The fact that its prospective converts were largely illiterate and its personnel themselves often uneducated had much to do with this; but an equally important reason for the Army's lack of theological lustre was its placement of action over theory. As an article in the first (1881) issue of the American Army's newspaper, *The War Cry*, put it, there had been "ten thousand times too much" Christian theorizing already. The time had come to "force war," and that meant transferring the Gospel from the churches to the slums and dispensing with "nonessentials" such as communion (a real pitfall for recovering alcoholics). War for the Salvation Army also meant feeding, clothing, and sheltering the poor by establishing farm colonies, orphanages, day nurseries, homes for prostitutes, and Christmas dinner and toy drives.[90]

Such commitment to Social Gospel reform impressed contemporaries and endeared the Salvation Army to the Protestant men's movement (whose attitude toward the Social Gospel was generally sympathetic). At the same time the Army, for all its works and militancy, cannot be considered part of the men's movement, first because its mission was not specifically directed to men, and second because its ranks were heavily female. Class and theological differences also separated the fundamentalistic Salvationists from the Congregationalists, Episcopalians, and other mainstream Protestants who made up the men's movement; and though men in these denominations admired the Army for its social achievements (Frank Cressey calling the Army's accomplishments "far in advance" of the established churches'),[91] they still thought it rather old-fashioned, chiefly because it continued to insist that salvation be imposed suddenly from without.

An external imposition of grace appealed very little to men's groups such as the YMCA, which sought salvation through a progressive buildup of character.[92] The YMCA also doubted whether bands and uniforms were the best way of attracting people to religion. If the churches truly wanted to bring in the masses, reasoned YMCA leaders, then they had to promote their most salable commodity, Jesus. His irresistible life story was being made clearer every day by advances in biblical archaeology and hermeneutics, wrote the Reverend Charles Jefferson, who concluded in 1908 that "we understand Jesus of Nazareth better than has any other generation of men that has ever lived."[93]

Accentuating the character of Christ made enormous sense to Progressive Era Protestant reformers, writes historian Robert Handy. These reformers may secretly have viewed Protestantism as a declining force, he argues, but they retained their faith in Christ as someone all could follow.[94] For this reason, Christ more than anyone else seemed fitted to lead both in religion and in the campaign for political uplift. After all, reasoned Harvard chaplain Francis Peabody, however disrespectful "social agitators" might be toward the church and its causes, Christ yet "commands their loyalty," for in him they saw realized "the ideal of manhood."[95]

Of course, if Christ were ever fully to lead, prevailing misconceptions of him had first to be exploded. Chief among these (at least for Social Gospellers) was the notion that he was somehow "effeminate and weak."[96] "Jesus was not a weakling," asserted G. Stanley Hall; his apprenticeship in carpentry alone must necessarily have caused "maximal muscle development."[97] Jesus "by the best standards of manhood" was manly, too, argued Carl Case, so manly in fact that he ought to be called "the supremely manly man."[98]

Another misconception reformers wished to dispel involved Christ's age: specifically images of him as either a helpless infant or a venerable sage. The Jesus whom we admire was not a baby, averred *St. Andrew's Cross;* nor was he a graybeard. Instead, he was a young man ("the greatest of all young men") who "finished His ministry on earth ere the dullness of age had diminished His vision or crippled His vigor."[99]

So "fresh" and "vital" indeed was Christ, wrote Scots theologian John Kelman in *Association Men,* that it made one wonder: had he perhaps discovered the "secret of perpetual youth"? In truth he had not; rather he *was* youth, youth incarnate, whose force had transformed "a *blasé* and outworn civilization" (Rome) and "sent it forth into the future with *the spirit of a boy.*" And "just as Christ made the aging Roman Empire young again," Kelman concluded, speaking now of foreign missions, "so we have seen a change come upon ancient lands in our own time. They were growing decrepit in their extreme old age, and now they are turning young, manifesting the new spirit of enterprise, the new powers of adaptation, imagination, and ingenuity, that are characteristic of youth, and setting forth on great national careers, not like decaying empires, but like little children. Jesus Christ, in those instances, shows himself *the author of a race that never grows old*—that is his secret."[100]

Not all reformers joined Kelman in pursuing biblical revisionism to the point of confusing Jesus Christ with Peter Pan. But their thoroughness in exploring hitherto unknown aspects of Christ's personality was impressive. Author-ministers Walter Rauschenbusch and Charles Jefferson in particular believed Jesus to have been the most "well-rounded" man ever, possessing qualities the modern-day businessman would do well to emulate.[101]

Personalizing Christ was essential, agreed Harvard chaplain Francis Peabody—particularly with regard to men. Men wanted a Christ whom they could respect, he argued, one who was "no gentle visionary," but rather "a Person whose dominating trait is force." Obviously this manly Christ had shown "consideration for women," especially his mother; "but for softness and sentimentality, such as characterizes the feminine man, there was no room in his rugged, nomadic, homeless life."[102]

Having ascertained Christ's robust manliness, Peabody went on to criticize artists for portraying the Saviour as a "pallid sufferer, stricken by the sins of the world."[103] Others agreed with Peabody, joining him in his criticism of religious art. One Congregationalist wondered openly whether the "long hair" and "woman's skirts" given to Jesus in stained glass windows could "produce in the minds of young men and boys the impression of a vigorous, heroic type of manliness which Jesus did really exhibit."[104] Another Congregationalist quizzed his readers on the degree to which they had been misled by Christian artists. "Has [Jesus] impressed you as subdued and meek, calm and effeminate?" he asked. "Have you seen him always as many a painter has painted him, pale and ghastly, sickly, emaciated? When you think of him do you think of some one thin and gaunt, weak and pallid? Not so did he seem to the people of his day."[105]

A particularly virulent critic of Christian art was Clark University president G. Stanley Hall, who in the two decades prior to World War I collected some eighty images of Jesus, which he showed to hundreds of students and acquaintances. Responses were generally unfavorable. From the men came comments like "looks sick, unwashed, sissy, ugly, feeble, posing, needs a square meal and exercise," and so on. Among the women (or at least among those whom Hall characterized as "honest"), reactions were equally adverse. Clearly, Hall concluded, artists had failed in "their duty": they had not commended Christ to the masses and had not made him conform to people's "ideal of what the manly man should be."[106]

Such calls for manlier renditions of Christ provoked several responses. Among the more significant was an art exhibition featuring ten portraits of Jesus, most of them manly. Funded by Cleveland businessmen and composed entirely of American artwork, the exhibit toured the country in 1906. One critic who saw it in New York praised especially a painting by Joseph Lauber, which showed "a virile and impassioned Christ, standing on a hill-top illumined by the rays of the sinking sun."[107]

A second medium for the manly Christ was the stained glass window. Images of Christ looking strong and purposive were common in Progressive Era church windows, as were saints garbed as knights and carrying swords. Such images, described by T. J. Jackson Lears as "an exhilarating fusion of martial virtue and religious faith," underscored the importance of Christian manliness, and in Lears's view also provided "a sharp counterpoint to the sordid commercial ethic of the gilded age."[108]

Equally indicative of Lears's revitalizing ethic were buildings in which the stained glass was housed: gothic churches of the high Victorian style. This style, popular in America from around 1870, differed from the "rarified" gothic of the early 1800s, writes architectural historian C. M. Smart, in that it was more "masculine," eschewing "the dainty and delicate in preference for the bold and impressive."[109] Its foremost American practitioners were architects Henry Richardson and Leopold Eidlitz, the designers respectively of Trinity Church in Boston (1872) and Christ Episcopal Cathedral in St. Louis (considered by Charles Kingsley to be America's most "churchly church").[110]

Even more important to reformers than icons or architecture was hymnody, the third major church art form. The chief objection to much of hymnody—particularly the gospel songs of Fanny Crosby—was its "nauseating sentimentalism" together with its otherworldliness.[111] "Many of the hymns that are flooding our market to-day are putrefaction," averred an irate music critic in 1910. "Imagine," she added, pointing to a modern songbook, "children of tender years singing such a wail as this":

> I should like to die, said Willie,
>   if my papa could die too,
> But he says he isn't ready
>   cause he has so much to do.
> And my little sister, Nellie,
>   says that I must surely die,
> And that she and mamma—then she stopped,
>   because it made me cry.
> There will be none but the holy—
>   I shall know no more of sin,
> There I'll see mamma and Nellie,
>   for I know he'll let them in;
> But I'll have to tell the angel
>   when I meet him at the door,
> That he must excuse my papa,
>   cause he couldn't leave the store.[112]

Overindulgence in such hymns was akin to drunkenness, thought hymnodist Charles Richards. Nonetheless, "Sunday schools and churches often sing such things till their spiritual vision is perverted, their spiritual strength emasculated, and their taste depraved."[113] Apparently male taste differs from that of "our sisters and daughters," observed the Reverend A. A. Pfanstiehl in 1898. For whereas women liked such "purposeless" and "sentimental" songs as "Gently Gliding Down the Stream of Time," men understood them to be "unmanly" and indicative of nothing quite so much as a "flabby soul."[114]

Instead of sentimental hymns with their emphasis on motherhood and death, would not it be better, reformers asked, to sing of brotherhood and of repairing this world? Indeed it would, answered the Reverend Frederick Gates in 1907. After all, he reasoned, "when youth and activity are the notes struck by our preachers today how discordant for them to bid their congregations sing 'My days are gliding swiftly by.'"[115]

Clearly people wanted hymns free of "exaggerated . . . feeling," noted Charles Richards in 1915, and thanks to changes in the hymnals they were getting them. In fact, churches increasingly were avoiding "a too frequent use of plaintive and melancholy songs, which imply that the harps are still to be hung upon the willows in a strange land." Instead, "They are singing songs of courage, of cheer, and of triumphant faith. They are not singing as much about heaven as they used to. They are singing more about the Kingdom here below which is to transform the earth into a heaven when the victories of Christ are complete. They are not singing songs of vague and dreamy sentimentality as of old. They are singing songs of character, of service, of brotherhood, of Christian patriotism, of aggressive missionary spirit, of the practical Christian life."[116]

A good example of this musical transition from sentimentality to aggressiveness was the YMCA hymnal. First issued in 1867, it originally contained such sentimental favorites as "Sweet Hour of Prayer" and "He Leadeth Me! O Blessed Thought." A committee formed in 1902 to revise the hymnal replaced these tunes with Social Gospel songs especially adapted for male voices. Its "attempt," it explained, was "to collect the best of those hymns . . . in which the emphasis is put upon the heroic, active masculine qualities rather than upon the passive virtues and states of mind and feeling."[117]

Another repository for manly hymns was the popular 1910 songbook *Manly Songs for Christian Men*. Especially "adapted to the needs of male singers," it featured such hearty songs of Christian progress as "Men Are Wanted":

> The days are evil and forces mighty
> Against the Christ now stand array'd
> And He is calling for manly workers,
> The strong of heart and unafraid.
> Ye men of purpose, arise and serve Him,
> The manly man of Galilee,
> That you may hasten the day of promise,
> The golden day that is to be.

The noise of battle, the clash of armies,
    The din of strife, will not be long;
For men are waking to high endeavor
    And soon shall swell the victor's song.
Then let our banner, the cross of Jesus,
    Be lifted high till all shall see
And hail as Saviour and King all-glorious
    The blessed Christ of Galilee.[118]

Such manly hymns did not appeal to musicologist H. Augustine Smith, who wrote, "In the reaction against Gospel hymns . . . we have jumped to the other extreme, to the hymns of the 'do and die' spirit, usually vague in thought, merely martial and exhilarating, with enough weapons, banners, conquests, and victories to go around."[119] Other musicologists, however, accepted manly hymns and celebrated their inclusion into mainline denominational hymnals.[120] In large part, this acceptance of manly hymns derived from their compatibility with the Social Gospel, which linked manly strength to social reform. But evidence indicates that the appeal of manly hymns was not entirely theological. That at least is the conclusion one draws from reading the work of YMCA historian John Gustav-Wrathall, who argues that Protestant celebrations of American manhood contained within them a strong element of homoeroticism.[121]

The validity of Gustav-Wrathall's assertion can easily be inferred by analyzing muscular Christian portraits of male Christian athletes. One such portrait, a 1922 YMCA painting entitled *His New Day*, features a scantily clad young Aryan and his hiking companion, both of whom are covered with sweat. Such raw male imagery (of which there was quite a lot in early-twentieth-century "Y" publications) arguably had homosexual connotations. But it is more than mere inference that ties homosexuality into the muscular Christian movement; it is also the fact that prominent muscular Christians such as YMCA International Committee Field Secretary Robert Weidensall valued male companionship to such a degree that they forswore marriage and spent their lives cultivating what Gustav-Wrathall refers to as "intense homosocial bonds."[122]

Whether these "homosocial bonds" among bachelors in the YMCA and other muscular Christian agencies included sexual intercourse is a difficult question to answer—at least with regard to the Victorian and Progressive Eras. In recent years, some gay men have made public the fact of their having found sexual partners in the YMCA, but such openness was hardly conceivable in the nineteenth century, and even Gustav-Wrathall's comprehensive study of male friendships in the "Y" stops short of proving that the love that bound together some early bachelor YMCA secretaries was anything more than chaste. What Gustav-Wrathall's study does reveal is that there were many lonely single men in Victorian America who may or may not have been gay, but who clearly found that male evangelical groups such as the "Y" offered benefits that cutthroat capitalism and the impersonal city did not: friendship, security, and a sense of belonging.[123]

Fulfilling emotional needs was of course but one of the muscular Christians' many goals. Their other aims included "defeminizing" the clergy, "masculinizing" religious imagery, and getting more men involved in the churches. Whether these goals were achieved is open to debate, largely because these goals are difficult to quantify. Figures kept by the Protestant brotherhoods and other muscular Christian agencies are unclear about the number of men who became lifelong church members as a result of the campaign to make religion more manly. The figures are equally unhelpful when it comes to determining how many pale and sensitive preachers lost their jobs in the push to hire ministers whose biceps outweighed their craniums. But this lack of hard numbers does not mean that the results of muscular Christianity were completely intangible. For as this chapter has shown, muscular Christians did succeed in forming religious men's groups, producing men's hymnals, and making Jesus more resemble what G. Stanley Hall referred to as the Christian equivalent of the Nietzschean superman: someone whom Protestant America could admire and who could lead in the crusade for social reform.[124]

CHAPTER FOUR

Fishers of Boys

The unpleasant sophistication of modern boys, and especially
of city boys, is a modifying fact of great moment. It takes a
week in tents to break the crust off a boy, and I fancy the
average Sunday school teacher never lifts a corner of it.

—THE REVEREND WILLIAM BYRON FORBUSH (1909)

The need to repopulate churches with men struck many within Progressive Era Protestantism as a matter of some urgency. But according to the Reverend William Forbush, a Congregationalist minister from Rhode Island and author of the best-selling jeremiad *The Boy Problem* (of which there were eight editions issued between 1901 and 1913), men's evangelism was "as salvage to salvation" when compared to work with boys. Forbush was not alone in this belief. Brotherhood of St. Andrew secretary Hubert Carleton, for one, concurred, calling boy evangelism "the hardest, highest, and holiest work in all the world."[1]

The Boy Problem

The conviction that there existed a "boy problem" in Progressive Era America was widespread. It was especially common among middle-class Anglo-Americans, who feared that their male offspring would be unable to compete in the changed world of female professionals and immigrant politicians.[2] Anglo parents also worried about the deleterious effect on boys of "congested city living," which in the opinion of two Boy Scout authorities led inevitably to profanity, flabbiness, and "contempt for decency and law."[3]

One of the most noteworthy aspects of the so-called boy problem was the absence of its obverse, a "girl problem." Whatever problem there was with girls certainly appeared "much less dramatic" than the problem with boys, admitted a female social worker in 1913, possibly because girls "do not organize gangs to turn pirates, fight Indians, or burglarize the corner store." As a result, observed boys and girls' club historian Herbert Gates in 1912, reformist "organizations for girls have not seemed to be so necessary to many" and were "few and . . . modest" compared with those for boys.[4]

But while girl problems were, according to one boys' club organizer, "easily taken care of," boy problems were more troublesome.[5] After all, reasoned a number of educators, wasn't the boy problem behind "the wave of juvenile vice that is sweeping the country"?[6] And wasn't it ultimately responsible for "the hideous reign of graft and crime that seems to devastate our land"?[7]

No matter how you looked at it, concluded Henry W. Gibson, an early apostle of organized camping, boys were the "key[s] to the future" and the "citizen[s] of tomorrow" upon whom depended the "political, social, commercial, and moral destiny" of the nation. Consequently, it made sense for America to ensure that its boys became "social asset[s]" rather than "social parasite[s]." And it made sense for America liberally to fund the nascent field of "boys' work."[8]

"Boys' work" as defined by Gibson aimed generally at all boys, but in particular its targets were two: boys from the streets and boys who were overly domesticated.[9] Dealing with both groups posed problems, acknowledged William Forbush. But the challenge posed by street boys was relatively straightforward, he concluded, since it obviously involved overcoming such antisocial tendencies as "clannishness" among Jews, Anglophobia among the Irish, and "ethical dualism" (dishonesty) among blacks.[10]

Heavily sheltered, native-born boys in contrast supposedly faced the less disruptive but far more insidious problem of what American Boy Scout co-founder Ernest T. Seton called "degeneracy": the transformation of "a large proportion of our robust, manly, self-reliant boyhood into a lot of flat-chested cigarette-smokers, with shaky nerves and doubtful vitality."[11] Bad enough in and of itself, degeneracy troubled reformers particularly for its incapacitating those very boys who ought optimally to "Americanize" others and carry moral values into the next generation.[12]

Of course, the extent to which lower-class boys were rebelling and upper-class ones degenerating remained open for debate. But conditions as they existed gave reformers cause to blame churches, schools, and other agents of boy socialization for failing in their duty. Some, including essayist Herman Scheffauer, went further, charging that traditional institutions were not merely incapable of handling boys; they themselves were often "source[s] of devitalizing weakness."[13]

A primary objection to conventional schooling arose from the fact that it was conducted exclusively indoors. Churches and schools were too "intellectual," too "bookish," and too much "under the roof," averred University of Chicago religion professor Allan Hoben. This was unfortunate, because city boys needed "strenuous [outdoor] experiences," the absence of which could lead to "tantalizing policemen, pilfering from fruit stands," and other "degenerate, urban forms of the old . . . game of forest and jungle."[14]

The prospect of American boyhood atrophying in the classroom was unsettling, acknowledged Clark University president G. Stanley Hall. But a far greater threat to youth was the "army of women teachers" whom he observed taking over the school system and treating boys with such "sugary benignity" as to deprive them of their manhood.[15] Women teachers were not ill-intentioned, explained Hall's friend, William Forbush, but "boy nature" was beyond them.[16] The truth was, confided a writer for *Popular Science Monthly,* that boys were not as "sympathetic" as women chose to see them; rather they were sadistic little "savages" who actually enjoyed pulling the wings off birds. Not that this was bad, he added; for "wholesome" boys were naturally cruel, whereas "good boy[s]" were "diseased."[17]

This notion of boy as savage differed quite a bit from the old Bushnellian view of him as an embryonic Christian wanting only careful nurturance to bloom. At the same time, it squared completely with the child development theories put forward by G. Stanley Hall in his massive 1904 work *Adolescence: Its Psychology and Its Relation to Physiology, Anthropology, Sociology, Sex, Crime, Religion, and Education.* In *Adolescence,* Hall laid particular stress on what Benjamin Rader calls "recapitulation theory": the idea that boys in their development move from savagery to civilization, repeating in essence "the history of the race." There were no shortcuts, Rader explains; rather the boy's failure to relive any one experience common to his race meant his never proceeding on to the next stage of development.[18]

One implication of recapitulation theory was the need for schools to rearrange their priorities. Instead of expanding boys' minds, argued Luther Gulick, physical education director of the New York City public schools from 1904 to 1907, educators ought first to condition their bodies. For as history and science showed, "physical reflexes" underlay "moral" ones, and bodily strength preceded mental acuity.[19]

Another consequence of recapitulation theory was a tendency among Progressive Era educators to view boys not as individuals but rather as members of "gangs." Boys acted *"en masse,"* explained William Forbush, just like "certain low orders of animal life." And the "feministic" idea that they might think independently and have certain inalienable rights was, in the words of moral educationist Charles K. Taylor, "excessively blind and stupid."[20]

Finally and most colorfully, recapitulation theorists urged educators to view boys as living representatives of premodern times. Why such concern for the foreign "heathen," wondered William Forbush, when heathenism flourished among American boys? What need of foreign missions, added Professor Allan Hoben, when "Africa and Borneo and Alaska come to you. The fire-worshipper of ancient times, the fierce tribesman, the savage hunter and fisher, the religion-making nomad, the daring pirate, the bedecked barbarian, the elemental fighter with nature and fellow and rival of every kind, the master of the world in making—comes before you in dramatic and often pathetic array in the unfolding life of the ordinary boy."[21]

Hoben's view of the boy as a savage in short pants seems ludicrous today. But such theories so clearly reflected the Progressive need for an antidote to overcivilization that they deserve to be taken seriously. Besides, notes boys' historian David Macleod, many of the issues raised by the recapitulationists were real: middle-class boys were more homebound than ever before; city boys did lack for manual labor; and schoolteaching was becoming a predominantly feminine profession.[22]

One recapitulationist theory of particular relevance for its time was adolescence: the idea that teenagers were neither boys nor men but instead "boymen."[23] Adolescence accurately describes youths who have reached puberty and who are still at home or school preparing for white-collar careers; hence Joseph Kett calls it a "middle-class" concept.[24] But it was a concept new to the Progressive Era, given the fact that in 1858 American boys were accused of being "premature men" whose immediate entry into business or farming precluded their ever passing through the English boy's "intermediate stage of football, cricket, and schoolboydom."[25]

The fact that antebellum boys preferred self-sufficiency to "schoolboydom" was often a source of national pride. But that self-sufficiency was harder to obtain after 1880 due to changes in the economy. Chief among these was the rise of corporations and their need for midlevel managers: workers with advanced education but little chance of reaching the top.[26] This professional-managerial revolution resulted in the desirability of more schooling and a devaluation of independent initiative. After all, notes David Riesman, corporations required team players as opposed to lone wolves, and this meant that the most valued employees tended to be other-directed rather than inner-directed, and friendly rather than reserved.[27]

Conformity in the workplace did not appeal to everyone. But those concerned with boys' training generally embraced the idea and held it up as a goal. One reason for this was scientific; for, as the "gang" theorists insisted, boys felt incomplete unless they were part of a gang.[28] Another reason was pragmatic; for, as playground reformer Joseph Lee observed, education ought to "fit our boys and girls to the industrial order as it exists."[29]

Fitting boys to meet the challenges of industrialism was a tall order, and the approaches by which boys' workers tried to accomplish this goal were at times contradictory. Thus while William Forbush concentrated primarily on forming Christian character, vocational training advocate Alfred Fletcher sought class harmony and the transformation of street boys into "privates in the industrial army."[30]

Boy Scout commissioner Ormond Loomis for his part believed that the chief end of boys' work was the saving of democracy. "Antidemocratic tendencies have appeared to an almost alarming degree in our social and political life," he warned in 1915; this made it imperative that "the coming generation of citizens should, through first hand experiments, realize the larger and common interests and social bonds before maturity is reached."[31]

Was Loomis right to stress the importance of boys' work for democracy? Or was Forbush right to view boys' work as an instrument for building Christian character? Boys' workers differed in their response to such questions, which has led one historian to describe their enterprise as "hopelessly muddled."[32] But David Macleod is right to point out that whatever their approach, the middle-class men who ran boys' work had one thing in common: fear that their own sons "had grown too soft for social leadership."[33]

This fear of lost leadership—more compelling even than the need for workplace conformity—caused the YMCA to emphasize the importance of instilling leadership qualities in middle-class boys. "The 'ward-heeler' did not learn to lead after he grew up," noted the YMCA. "He developed leadership in youth," just as "the good leader grew up by leading his gang in baseball, jumping fence posts, etc."[34]

To ensure that the middle class produced enough "good leaders" to undo the evils wrought by the lower-class "ward-heeler," the YMCA gradually turned away from mission work and focused its energies on boys in middle-class neighborhoods. That shift occurred during a forty-five-year period (1870–1915) that was marked, in the estimation of noted "boyologist" Henry Gibson, by two distinct stages of boys' work: work *for* boys and work *with* boys. As the popularity of the latter stage increased, explained Gibson, "the distinctly rescue and mission features [of boys' work] decreased and the constituency gradually changed from street boys to school boys of better homes."[35]

This shift from street- to schoolboys was a blow to women educators. In the early days of boys' work, women were highly influential. The first boys' club (the Wilson Mission of New York City) was founded by a woman in 1878.[36] And the YMCA, the first agency to engage in boys' work on a large scale, chose a woman to be its first salaried boys' secretary. But female "angels" ministering unto grimy street urchins was definitely not the image that Progressive Era boys' workers wished to project. Consequently, David Macleod has noted, "as [YMCA] boys' branches abandoned rescue work and took up gymnastics, the women quit or were forced out."[37]

Following the YMCA's switch to middle-class boys, Boy Scout leaders declared their intent never to hire women. They also made it clear that "No Miss Nancy[s] [effeminate men] need apply." Instead, what the Scouts wanted were "REAL, live men—red blooded and right-hearted men—BIG men" who were able to help the domesticated boy cope with "his own ingrowing effeminacy."[38]

The point of having "BIG" scoutmasters was not to coerce boys into becoming men, since that was something they had to accomplish on their own. But scoutmasters and other boys' workers could lead by example, noted the YMCA in 1918, considering that "character . . . is just as contagious as measles" and that it blossomed best under "masculine Christian leadership."[39]

In sum, no one was deemed better able to confront the boy problem than big men of character: men who understood the boy's nature and the importance of getting him out under the stars. Such men would ideally handle all boys, but would tackle middle- and upper-class ones first, as boys from these groups supposedly had graver problems and were at any rate closer to hand. As for what this process of improving boys should be called, most agreed on the term "character building," which one authority described as "the greatest means of salvation today, next to the power of Divinity."[40]

Building Character

Building character may have been akin to divinity, but one prominent scoutmaster admitted that it had a rather mundane goal: to "get the boy back to the old-fashioned spirit of courtesy, sturdiness of character, and respect for law and duly constituted authority" that had once made America great.[41] Such virtues in the past had been cultivated naturally, added another Scout leader, primarily through work on the farm or on the frontier. But modern city life made virtue (and correspondingly character) increasingly inaccessible except through "special guidance and training."[42] As a result, noted William Forbush, "artificial" environments had to be created wherein boys could learn manliness.[43] These environments could be gyms, playgrounds, or church recreation halls. But if well-roundedness was the goal, the best places were more often boys' schools, summer camps, or paramilitary nature organizations. Of the three, the last two were largely middle-class phenomena, while boys' schools catered primarily to the rich. Boys' schools were also the most venerable of the three, many having been in existence in America since the eighteenth century. In fact, until the late nineteenth century private boys' schools were the chief means whereby American boys got their secondary education.[44]

All of this changed, of course, with the advent of American public high schools, whose spread and influence in the last quarter of the nineteenth century was, in the words of one observer, "quite extraordinary."[45] Free of cost and open to all, public high schools gravely threatened private academies, forcing some to close, others to go public, and still others to become colleges or normal schools.[46]

The question confronting those academies that remained, observed educator Lawrence Hull in 1900, was whether "there [is] any longer a place for the public [that is, private] secondary school." The answer was yes, continued Hull, who thought private academies could survive if they stopped educating local yeomen and made themselves into what English "public" schools had become one hundred years earlier: places for the rich city boy whose "demoralizing . . . home life . . . make[s] it necessary for [him] . . . to leave his home if he is to grow up into sturdy, clean, effective manhood."[47]

Hull's belief that rich boys ought to be educated in the hinterlands may have surprised wealthy parents, who prior to the 1880s had tended to employ private tutors or patronize local day schools. William James had been educated in such a fashion, as had Theodore Roosevelt (who later enrolled all of his sons at Groton). But educating their boys in the city or at home became increasingly problematic for old-moneyed families as urban crime proliferated and as immigrant children began flooding city school systems.[48]

With wealthy people in the market for rural educational retreats, it was not long before the fortunes of country schools such as Phillips Andover and Phillips Exeter began to revive. Nor was it long before these schools began saying that they had more advantages than public schools—advantages that in the parlance of the time included all-male teaching staffs, relative freedom from bureaucracy, and (in many cases) definite church affiliation.[49]

Above all, boys' schools promised to instill what St. Paul's rector Henry Coit called "high-bred manliness": a combination of discipline, heartiness, and "freedom from the tendency to abnormal precocious vice."[50] Instilling "high-bred manliness" was not only something the schools did, noted Theodore Roosevelt in 1900; it was something they did well. For whereas rich boys had once been accused of being too "effeminate" and "luxurious," he wrote, "nowadays, whatever other faults the son of rich parents may tend to develop, he is at least forced by the opinion of all his associates of his own age to bear himself well in manly exercises and to develop his body—and therefore, to a certain extent, his character—in the rough sports which call for pluck, endurance, and physical address."[51]

Roosevelt's belief that school sports built character was common for its time. But not everyone agreed with it, as evidenced by the fact that many Catholic and Jewish schools continued to stress academics over athletics. One reason for their inattention to athletics may have been practical, since industrious working-class Jewish and Catholic boys probably had less need for artificial exercise than rich, sedentary WASP children. But the metaphysical applied here, too: many Catholic and Jewish educators simply failed to see how firm bodies strengthened souls.[52]

This reluctance on the part of Catholics and Jews to acknowledge the primacy of sports was by no means shared by the prestigious "St. Grottlesex" schools (the nation's top six Episcopalian academies) and their rectors.[53] One St. Grottlesex rector wrote that he viewed sports as a great way of saving boys from sloth, irreligion, and the worship of money.[54] Another rector who supported sports was Endicott Peabody, who founded the exclusive Groton School in 1884 and ran it for the next fifty-six years. A handsome, athletic man called the "Sun God" by schoolmates and "Old Peabo" by later contemporaries, Peabody descended from an old Massachusetts family, but was educated mainly in England, where he discovered the writings of Thomas Hughes and Charles Kingsley. These in turn led him to drop the bourgeois Unitarianism of his parents, to endorse Christian activism, and to pursue a career as an ordained minister in the American Episcopal Church.[55]

Peabody's first ministerial assignment was in a location that Theodore Roosevelt would surely have liked: Tombstone, Arizona. But Tombstone's cowboys turned out not to have much respect for their new pastor (whom some considered a "daisy"), so Peabody moved back east, intent upon helping members of his own social class, who, he observed, "[have] a tendency to overindulge their children, to wish to make life easy for them, a natural result of which is that the children sometimes lack intellectual and moral and physical fibre."[56]

Restoring "fibre" to the sons of the rich was a challenging task. But Peabody believed it could be done through an education similar to the one he had had at Cheltenham (an English school). Consequently, he began asking friends for funds with which to build a private boys' school, which ended up in rural Groton, Massachusetts.

Groton boys under Peabody's administration went without much that they had been accustomed to back home, including fancy meals, costly clothes, and hot showers. They were also subject to daily sports, chapel services, and Bible readings, all of which immunized them from Peabody's particular bête noire: "loafing."[57] One English public school practice Peabody did not wish to replicate was "fagging": the school-sanctioned servility (often sexual) of younger boys toward older ones. In fact, sexuality of any kind—homo or hetero—was considered at Groton to be corrupting of boyhood innocence.[58]

All this regimental strictness had mixed results. Boys who were bookish, bad at sports, or in other ways "misfits" often hated Groton. The young Averell Harriman, for example, confided to his father that Peabody "would be an awful bully, if he weren't such a terrible Christian."[59] And Dean Acheson, another prominent Grotonian, recalled how the school's prisonlike atmosphere (open rooms, constant policing, and the like) had "devoured my early freedom." "All was organized," he explained: "eating, studying, games, so-called free time, the whole thing. One could understand and accept rendering unto Caesar the things which were Caesar's, the control of one's external life. The mind and spirit were not Caesar's; yet these were demanded too. And I, for one, found it necessary to erect defenses for the last citadel of spiritual freedom."[60]

Still, for every Dean Acheson who complained, there were perhaps ten "Grotties" convinced of their rector's goodness and eager to pay him tribute. Parents such as the Theodore Roosevelts also generally approved of Peabody and spoke of him as if he were a latter-day Thomas Arnold.[61] One reason for all the enthusiasm, notes historian E. Digby Baltzell (himself a St. Paul's graduate), was the fact that Episcopal boarding schools like Groton actually made good on their promise to athleticize rich boys and to give them useful contacts. As a result, he concludes, graduates of these schools tended to excel in the corporate world of golf and networking, where their numbers gave rise to the term "Protestant establishment."[62]

Baltzell may be right that boarding schools contributed to increased Protestant power. But this contribution was mainly on behalf of the rich. Middle-class parents, who like rich parents were concerned about softness in their sons, generally could not afford private school educations. Consequently, they faced a dilemma: how to obtain the outdoor-oriented, physically rigorous training that Groton and its ilk provided, but at a reasonable price?

One answer was the boys' summer camp, which was of limited duration and whose physical plant cost less to maintain than the carefully groomed academies. Not that all boys' camps were cheap; far from it. Many were in fact expensive havens where rich boys spent their summers when not at prep school. But by far the greater number of camps were middle-class affairs, run by middle-class organizations like the "Y," that promised "the same opportunities for the formation of character as the boarding schools," only at lower rates.[63]

Low rates to make men of their boys? Middle-class parents leapt at the chance, and as a result the number of boys' camps grew impressively. The period between 1895 (when there were about sixty boys' camps) and 1905 was especially fruitful, with the YMCA alone increasing its camps from 167 in 1901 to 300 four years later.[64]

Many early boys' camps appeared in the Northeast, not far from that region's urban areas, and were either church- or YMCA-run. Still, their spread and ownership were sufficiently diverse by the turn of the century to convince Winthrop Talbot of Camp Asquam, New Hampshire, that there needed to be a national organization through which camp leaders could cooperate.[65]

Talbot's solution was to create the General Camp Association (GCA), whose first meeting was held in Boston in 1903. In attendance were a hundred of the most influential men in organized camping, including Edward H. Mays of the YMCA, G. L. Meylan of the Boys' Brigade, and the aged reformer Thomas Wentworth Higginson. Also in attendance were several women, including two who ran girls' camps in defiance of the fact that these "had not yet been generally accepted."[66]

GCA members may have represented different segments of the camping industry, but in general they agreed on one thing: the importance of getting boys (particularly those aged twelve to seventeen) away from "the tyranny of modern city life."[67] "We are finally learning from our English cousins that a city is no place in which to bring up a boy," explained two camping experts in 1910. And this "yearning for Nature" was at last prompting parents to provide their boys with those healthful, outdoor experiences that they themselves "were without."[68]

In addition to acquainting boys with nature, camps supposedly gave boys a chance to escape from their mothers, whose apron strings were widely viewed as a source of weakness.[69] Camps, of course, had no mothers (nor women of any kind) and thus seemed ideal places for learning "discipline" and "self-reliance." In fact, observed one enthusiast, it took only one summer at camp to transform a "typical . . . little, blasé, weary man of the world" into a real boy—one who "had had enough of dancing classes" and was in sum "done with women."[70]

Did this mean that boys at camp, freed from mothers and civilization, ran wild? Not at all, replied camp owners; for while camps were rough, they were not so rough as to be unsafe. Nor was their moral standard low, vouchsafed Winthrop Talbot, who wrote that "moral standards of boys' camps are generally as high as the home standards of the boys in camp, or higher; because, as the campers constantly live together night and day, there is no hiding-place secure from the searching eye of some small boy."[71]

If boy stoolies made camps safe, then so did camp counselors. These, as camping historian Henry Gibson explained, tended to be "well-bred" Christian college men. They were also "specialists," who in the estimation of one Brooklyn educator understood the boy better and could spend more time with him than either his "busy father" or his "tired mother."[72]

Placing camps under the supervision of trained Christian specialists seemingly conflicted with the idea that camps were refuges from civilization. But Progressive Era parents appeared not to mind the contradiction. In fact, they rather liked the idea of camps employing all the good in society and none of the bad. Some even viewed the camp, with its outdoor, masculine ambience, as a great place whereat to address issues with which society (particularly domesticated Victorian society) had difficulties.

One of these difficult issues was sex, the teaching of which G. Stanley Hall for one thought best left up to the YMCA.[73] Not that YMCA men devoted vast amounts of campfire time to sexual instruction; they did not. Nor did they approve of boys having sexual encounters before their late teens. Still, YMCA Boys' Secretary Edgar M. Robinson thought it important that boys' workers at least discuss sex openly with boys and that they emphasize in particular Christ's ire toward masturbators.[74]

Another difficult issue that camp directors often strove to address was social stratification, especially the widening gap between the very rich and the middle class. This gap was especially troubling to educational theorist Charles Taylor. Convinced that America was departing from time-tested, egalitarian truths, Taylor used his camp on the shores of Lake Champlain to teach boys from all classes (albeit mostly the richest class) that money did not matter, that "character" was the all-important determinant of human worth.[75]

Taylor's first lesson in character appreciation involved making his campers "strip to the last stitch" for a medical exam, regardless of whether they were "poorly set up" lads of "appalling wealth" or "well-set-up" sons of "factory foremen." Then came a bevy of competitive sports and "constructive hand-work" that was designed to promote "resourcefulness" and to eradicate "years of spoiling." Finally, at the end of the summer, Taylor's campers, now "brown and strong, were packed into Pullmans and shipped back home, very different in more ways than one than when they arrived."[76]

Admittedly, not all camp directors were as heavy-handed as Taylor in their attempts to build character or to improve society. Many, in fact, believed in the power of nature alone (supplemented by sports and camp counseling) to reclaim enervated boys and to "make them almost glow with vitality."[77] After all, reasoned two eminent camping authorities, the purpose of camp was not to militarize boys; rather it was "to keep the boys out of doors and engaged in some clean, healthful occupation, whether athletics, walking, fishing, trapping, in the meadows or the woods or on the water."[78]

Such an outdoor regimen, if adhered to, made boys inwardly more "kindly," observed Winthrop Talbot, and outwardly more "vital," with bodies that were "brown" and "muscular." It also made them less nervous, he concluded; for while the boy entered camp "talk-[ing]," "object[ing]," and "argu[ing]," wrote Talbot, "gradually he grows into harmony with the calm about him, and cheerful good nature replaces ill-temper and peevishness. He comes with a wrong conception of values; he has an idea that the land is dependent on its cities; he learns that all the wealth of nations comes first from the soil. Two summers usually suffice to make him a lover of Nature."[79]

Talbot's belief in the ability of camps to improve boys had few detractors. In fact, there was only one problem with camps as reformatory tools: they were open only during the summer. This meant (at least insofar as most character builders were concerned) that middle-class boys still needed supplements to their indoor, female-directed public school educations—supplements that could be year-round, economical, male-directed, and oriented toward nature.

One organization designed to meet these specifications was the Knights of King Arthur (about which more will be said in the next section). Another was the YMCA, a pioneer in the field of boys' work. But neither of these groups' reputations for character building surpassed that of the paramilitary nature organization, which made an appearance in the early 1900s and was an American fixture by World War I.

The forerunner to the paramilitary nature organization was the Boys' Brigade, which was given to parading about in church parlors and parish halls. Founded in 1883 by a Scots volunteer guardsman and Sunday school teacher named William Alexander, the Brigade was imported to America in 1890 by the Reverend John Quincy Adams of San Francisco. Three years later, it boasted an estimated 500 American companies, official recognition from the Baptist and Methodist Churches, and a national newsletter, the *Boys' Brigade Courier.*[80]

Henry Drummond, an enthusiastic supporter of the Boys' Brigade in Scotland, explained its potential benefits to Americans as follows: In the first place, he said, the Brigade was a religious organization, dedicated to "the advancement of Christ's Kingdom among Boys." But it was a religious organization cognizant of the fact that the "Old Process" by which boys learned religion was ineffective and that a "New Process" had superceded it. This "New Process," as practiced by the Brigade, drew heavily on boys' fascination with militarism and as a result was turning out Christian gentlemen "by the battalion."[81]

Foremost among the beneficiaries of the Boys' Brigade, in Drummond's opinion, were street boys. These boys, according to Drummond, were incorrigible in their natural state, but once they were given a cheap cap and sword they could be "order[ed] . . . about till midnight." Having such control over street boys struck Drummond as socially significant, even though he was forced to acknowledge that most British Brigaders came not from the lower class but from the middle class.[82]

If the Boys' Brigade was a middle-class phenomenon in Britain, it was even more so in America, where parents spent lots of money on Brigade uniforms and summer camps.[83] This sort of extravagance must have displeased Henry Drummond, who evidently felt that the Boys' Brigade could do more good controlling the lower orders than strengthening middle-class boys. But strengthening middle-class boys was an important goal for American character builders, many of whom criticized the Brigade for being hopelessly out of touch with modern-day methods of group socialization.[84] Such negative criticism of the Brigade obviously had a destructive effect on that organization, for in 1912 one religious educator observed that the Brigade had "served its day" and was fast being eclipsed by other boys' organizations.[85]

The groups that emerged to replace the Boys' Brigade included (Ernest Thompson) Seton's Woodcraft Indians (founded in 1901) and the Sons of Daniel Boone (founded in 1905). Both groups were less militaristic and more nature-loving than the Brigade. They also believed that the purpose of boys' work was not to enforce blind obedience; rather it was to rekindle in boys the virtues of the outdoorsman: ruggedness, self-mastery, and the "power of the savage."[86]

Seton's Woodcraft Indians and the Sons of Daniel Boone were not only more nature-oriented than the old Boys' Brigade; they were also more self-consciously American, as evidenced by their celebration of two icons from the American frontier: the Indian and Daniel Boone. These individuals towered over most European heroes, averred Seton and Sons of Daniel Boone founder Daniel C. Beard, especially when it came to outdoor prowess.[87] As for character, Beard added, no European had more grit than Boone, who was a "fighting Quaker," a patriot, and America's first conservationist.[88]

Believing that Boone and the Indian would make great role models for boys, notable Americans such as Theodore Roosevelt and naturalist John Burroughs expressed their support for the Woodcraft Indians and the Sons of Daniel Boone.[89] But those organizations did not only appeal to Americans; they also appealed—somewhat strangely, given their Americanism—to Englishmen such as Boer War hero Sir Robert (later Lord) Baden-Powell, who took the Seton-Beard emphasis on nature, combined it with militaristic elements from the old Boys' Brigade, and came up in 1908 with his own boys' group: the Boy Scouts.[90]

Baden-Powell's scouting idea caught hold immediately, first in England, then in America, where the Boy Scouts of America (BSA) was officially incorporated in 1910. The new group's popularity was such that it soon overwhelmed both the Woodcraft Indians and the Sons of Daniel Boone, leading to the demise of those groups and to the transfer of their leaders to high positions in the BSA, Seton becoming the "Chief Scout of America" and Beard becoming the "Chief Scout Commissioner."[91]

One reason for the BSA's success was its many powerful backers. Foremost among these was the YMCA, whose secretary for boys' work, Edgar M. Robinson, served on the BSA's governing board.

Convinced that non-Protestant boys would find the BSA more appealing than the YMCA, Robinson wanted the YMCA to take over the Scouts, thereby bringing more boys into the Association's sphere of influence. But as this takeover never occurred, Robinson had to content himself with rewriting the official Scout oath to read: "On my honor I will do my best . . . [t]o keep myself physically strong, mentally awake, and morally straight"—a promise that reflected the YMCA's body-mind-spirit ideal.[92]

In addition to enjoying YMCA support, the Boy Scouts garnered the support of Andrew Carnegie, John D. Rockefeller, Jr., and other wealthy businessmen. Such men were not necessarily outdoor enthusiasts: at a 1911 BSA fundraiser they dined sumptuously on such uncamplike fare as "punch de fantasie" while local Boy Scouts demonstrated various first-aid and teepee-building techniques. But business leaders appreciated the hardening influence of the outdoors and its potential benefits to society. William Randolph Hearst even foresaw the day when well-trained Scouts might act as strikebreakers; hence his support for a separate Scouting organization: the American Boy Scouts.[93]

Hearst's views generally conflicted with those of mainstream scoutmasters. But they are indicative of the fact that a number of issues divided scouting. One of those issues was religion. Scout troops were supposed to be open to all faiths, but Catholics maintained their own troops so as to avoid domination by liberal Protestant Scout leaders.[94] These leaders in turn were split by the issue of militarism. Many opposed it; but the BSA's honorary vice-president, Theodore Roosevelt, threatened to resign from the BSA in 1915 if pacifists were not purged from its ranks.[95]

Another issue that divided Progressive Era Scout leaders was racial integration. In Northern cities such as Buffalo and Philadelphia, some Boy Scout troops enrolled both black and white boys. But for the most part Scout troops remained racially segregated. And in the deep South white Scout leaders prevented black troops from forming at all. This situation changed somewhat in 1926, when the BSA executive board used Rockefeller money to promote the formation of black Southern troops. But until then BSA executives tacitly accepted the exclusion of blacks in the South. That they were willing to do so stemmed largely from what David Macleod calls their "heedless bigotry." Though hardly vicious racists by early-twentieth-century standards, BSA executives were nonetheless all too willing to denigrate blacks, as evidenced by their inclusion in the first American Boy Scout handbook of Lord Baden-Powell's odious mnemonic device for the letter "N" in Morse code: a cartoon of a "Nimble Nig" (the dot) chased by a crocodile (the dash).[96]

Boy Scout executives may have been terribly insensitive toward blacks. But they were passionate when talking about how to raise their own sons: middle- and upper-class white boys from the city. That such boys needed to be transformed struck most scoutmasters as obvious. But while some wanted to turn boys into citizen conformists, others wanted to turn them into outdoor adventurers. Supportive of the latter option were Ernest T. Seton and the YMCA's Edgar Robinson. In Seton's words, "*'city rot'* ha[d] worked evil in the nation," and boys needed to cut loose from society.[97] Not so, countered Chief Scout Executive James West, a man who Seton claimed had "never seen the blue sky in his life." With the nation about to enter World War I, it made sense to West for boys to uphold rather than to repudiate American civilization. Consequently, he strove successfully not only to infuse scouting with the spirit of militant patriotism but also to force Seton and Robinson off the BSA's governing board, effectively ending the organization's brief flirtation with romantic antimodernism.[98]

These philosophical disputes among scouting's leaders had not affected the movement's growth. Nine years after its founding the BSA counted 361,000 scouts and 32,000 scoutmasters. Its administration had expanded from a single office in a New York City YMCA to several departments, hundreds of employees, and a magazine, *Boys' Life*.[99]

One explanation for the Boy Scouts' growth was that despite (or perhaps because of) its internal inconsistencies, it promised something for everyone. For industrialists, it betokened order and a more obedient workforce. For progressives, it appeared to be "a new moral force" upon which "rest[ed] the future of this country."[100] And for the middle-class men who served as scoutmasters, it offered opportunities for leadership often denied them in their jobs.[101]

In addition, scouting promised succor to a variety of boys. For the country boy who might one day move to the city, it offered training in temptation resistance.[102] For those boys already "liv[ing] the unnatural life of the cities" it provided "opportunit[ies] to live through the race life" and to arrive in the twentieth century with "primitive" bodies and scientific minds.[103] Above all, commented Scout commissioner Ormond Loomis and Boston University School of Theology professor Norman Richardson, scouting provided a "controlled environment" wherein boys were kept "in ignorance of and without desires for those things that destroy character." Indeed, scouting kept boys so "busy forming good habits" that they had "little time for the formation of bad ones."[104]

This emphasis on protecting boys from vice (especially city vice) was, of course, something the Boy Scouts had in common with boys' schools and the camping movement. And while this characteristic belied all three groups' pretensions to rugged, independent manhood, it at least coincided with the ultimate aim of character building: the reinvention (using modern means) of old-fashioned, upright characters from the past.

But were character builders truly reasserting traditional notions of Christian virtue? Or were they instead promoting what today would be called secular humanism? These were questions of great import to the largest institutional backers of the character-building movement, the Protestant churches.

The Church and the Boy

Of all the organizations dedicated to improving boys' character, none were more important than the mainline Protestant churches. These were instrumental in the formation of boys' boarding schools, outdoor camping, and the Boys' Brigade. In 1915 they also sponsored 80 percent of all Boy Scout troops, 90 percent of whose members claimed in 1921 to be attending Sunday school.[105] Clearly, observed a Chicago Baptist minister in 1912, the church was striving to "face and meet its obligation to adolescent boys."[106]

The churches' entrance into the field of boys' work was hailed in 1913 by Men and Religion Forward movement leader Fred Smith as "the most hopeful sign upon the map for twentieth century Christianity."[107] But it might never have happened had not religious educators first grown frustrated with the old methods for improving boys. In particular, the Sunday school, with its "ultra-feminine atmosphere" and "goody-goody, wishy-washy, sissy, soft conception of religion" struck many pastors as a poor alternative to the Scouts, whose "practical" Christianity seemed comparatively "wholesome."[108] Scouting also appeared better suited for keeping boys in church than the Sunday school, whose attrition rate for boys aged twelve to eighteen was around 60 to 80 percent in the early 1900s.[109]

Of course, the main incentive for churches to involve themselves in boys' work had nothing to do with problems in the Sunday schools. It was related rather to growing secularization and to the belief that by helping out with boys, the church was finally proving itself useful. "The doubtful community" is looking for "more visible" evidence that the churches are worthwhile, warned University of Chicago religion professor Allan Hoben in 1911. And when it asks the minister, "'What do you do?[,]' it is well if . . . he can reply, 'We are saving your boys from vice and low ideals, from broken health and ruined or useless lives, by providing for wholesome self-expression under clean and inspiring auspices.'"[110]

Were churches primarily to be judged on their ministry to youth? Hoben thought so, but his was an attitude new to his generation. Before the 1880s, ministers took adolescents for granted. Or at least this was how it seemed to many character builders, who remembered their childhood churches as formidable places marked by "thou shalt nots" and "programme[s] of repression."[111]

The churches' attitude toward youth in the 1870s was very "discouraging," the Reverend John Beckley recalled in 1892. Churches tried to attract youths, but through "false methods" only succeeded in "repel[ling]" them. Then in the 1880s a discovery was made: youths did not want simply to be "amused" or tolerated; they wanted to be of "service" and to have their "soldier-like instincts" aroused on behalf of Christ's kingdom. This discovery led, said Beckley, to a "revolution[ary]" new "young people's movement," the "most effective and aggressive force for evangelism that the Church has yet seen." It also taught young people that "the Church is theirs," and as a result churches everywhere were experiencing "vigorous, buoyant, hopeful life."[112]

In the forefront of this youthful "uprising" was the Young People's Society of Christian Endeavor (YPSCE), an organization founded in 1881 by Francis ("Father Endeavor") Clark, a Congregationalist minister from Portland, Maine.[113] At first the organization was located mainly in New England. But within thirty-five years, the Society had captivated Protestant churches worldwide and could claim the allegiance (past and present) of around fifteen million young men and women.[114]

YPSCE founder Francis Clark attributed the success of his movement to its use of such modern-day business practices as the committee and the sales pitch.[115] Another Endeavorer praised instead the "solemn strenuousness" of the YPSCE pledge.[116] But the real reason YPSCEs succeeded, observed a Methodist bishop in 1892, had to do with their understanding of adolescent psychology: specifically their approach to teenagers not as children but as "straightforward, earnest, practical" individuals.[117]

YPSCEs may have been among the first church groups to treat teenagers with respect, but they were certainly not the last. By 1900 most denominations had founded young people's societies, all of which embodied YPSCE principles. These included the Methodists' Epworth League (1889), the United Presbyterian Young People's Union (1889), and the Baptist Young People's Union of America (1890). There was also a Junior Christian Endeavor Society, which enrolled boys and girls who were bored with the puerility of Sunday school.[118]

All of the these organizations were coeducational, which was a point of pride for Francis Clark, who felt that "each sex helps the other in religious work."[119] But increasingly boys' workers disagreed with Clark, some going so far as to call young people's societies "abnormal" and deserving of "eliminat[ion]."[120] William Forbush in particular believed YPSCEs to be fine for the young man, but terrible for the boy, who could not help but be embarrassed at having to pray in the presence of girls.[121]

Forbush's main objection to the YPSCE was its skewed ratio of women to men (almost three to one in the early 1900s).[122] "Everywhere . . . the movement is becoming predominantly feminine," complained Forbush in 1907.[123] There were boys in the YPSCE, he conceded, but those boys in his mind were either "unwholesome" or intent simply on flirting with girls.[124]

Another charge leveled against YPSCEs had to do with their reliance on women leaders.[125] This complaint applied also to the Sunday school, whose imbalance between male and female teachers was high (27 percent to 73 percent in a 1920 Indiana survey).[126] Not that female teachers were necessarily bad, explained Edwin Starbuck, a prominent psychologist. It was just that "the boy is a hero-worshipper, and his hero can not be found in a Sunday school which is manned by women."[127]

All in all, observed religious educator William McCormick in 1915, it almost appeared as if "the church does not want the boy." True, it accepted the "spiced, perfumed, blue-necktied and white-collared, bath-tubbed, manicured, slick-haired and dancing-school-mannered" type of boy. But it rejected the real boy, "the specific, concrete, individual boy, with his rough manners, his uncouth behavior, his rude attire, [and] his ungracious mien."[128]

Were the sons of middle-class churchgoers really as uncouth as McCormick depicted them? Probably not. Still, the conviction that rough-mannered boys were finding existing church youth groups too effeminate prompted most Protestant brotherhoods to form junior orders in the 1890s as part of what William Forbush called "the great masculine movement in the church."[129] The most significant of these orders were the Junior Brotherhood of Saint Andrew, the Junior Brotherhood of Andrew and Philip, and the Knights of St. Paul (an affiliate of the Brotherhood of St. Paul). Equally noteworthy, if somewhat less prominent, was the Anderson Boy Movement (a Christian Church phenomenon) which through its model community of Boyville attempted "to further good citizenship, clean athletics, [and] manly sports" among boys in and around Anderson, Indiana.[130]

Another church boys' group in revolt against Sunday school femininity was William Forbush's own Knights of King Arthur. Founded in 1893 when Forbush was ministering in Riverside, Rhode Island, the Knights heavily influenced the junior brotherhoods, mainly through its use of medieval imagery. The order also outstripped most junior brotherhoods in size, reaching (in combination with its sister organization, the Queens of Avalon) a membership of around 150,000 in 1925.[131]

One reason for the group's success lay in its appeal to chivalry, wrote "Mage Merlin" Forbush in his regular column for the YMCA's youth magazine, *Men of To-Morrow*. Boys aged twelve to eighteen were naturally chivalrous; hence it followed that they would like the Knights of King Arthur, with its castles (churches), its Anglo-Saxonism, and its three degrees of page, squire, and knight.[132]

The Knights also surpassed existing church youth groups, Forbush thought, in matters related to inclusivity, militarism, and sex. Unlike most junior brotherhoods, the group was interdenominational. Unlike the Boys' Brigade, it stood for chivalry rather than militarism. And unlike the Young People's Society of Christian Endeavor, its "ideal of personal religion" was neither "effeminate" nor "complicated by the presence of girls." Above all, wrote Forbush, the Knights of King Arthur had religion, something that even Scouting lacked. Scouting was merely "susceptible of a social-moral use," he explained. But the Knights of King Arthur was "definitely" religious (though not so religious as to be "repellent").[133]

Could boys really receive Christ "unobtrusively" while dressed as King Arthur? Today the idea seems unlikely. But ninety years ago, Forbush's organization made enough sense to inspire literally dozens of imitators, including the Knights of the Holy Grail, the Knights of the Triangle, and the Brotherhood of David (which prepared boys "for kingliness through hardship, discipline, and manly exercise").[134] There were also nonmedieval spinoffs such as George Walter Fiske's Pilgrim Fraternity, whose members undertook "a Pilgrimage toward ye goal of Christian Manliness, namely: ye winning of ye well-rounded life, in body, mind, and spirit."[135]

The total number of church-related boys' clubs probably peaked in 1911 at around forty-four. After this, boys' workers talked increasingly not of growth but of consolidation. "All agencies for boy saving will be federated," predicted the Boys' Work Commission of the Men and Religion Forward movement. In fact, there ought to be a "block plan" wherein "every block in the city will have some Christian man as supervisor whose business it shall be to know the boys in that block, discover the danger spots, find out who needs help and then organize 'leagues of friendship,' secretly perhaps, to keep those boys from going wrong."[136]

Unhappily for the Men and Religion Forward movement, its plan for placing all boys' work under Christian supervision never came to fruition. Instead of becoming integrated, church and secular boys' agencies became increasingly estranged during the 1910s, as patriotism surged and religious fervor waned. Illustrative of this estrangement was the push by executives of the Boy Scouts of America to reduce the number of clerical scoutmasters. Whereas 29 percent of all scoutmasters in 1912 were ministers, only 10 percent were thirteen years later.[137]

Ministers naturally resented being excluded from the BSA, and some in the 1920s even moved to ban scouting from the Church.[138]

But it was not the BSA alone that was responsible for clerical marginalization in boys' work; ministers had been undercutting their own authority for years by calling traditional Christianity incompatible with "a boy's religion."[139]

A Boy's Religion

What sort of religion best suited the boy? That issue sparked intense debate among character builders. Were gyms superior to churches? Was scouting more moral than Christianity? Was the boy even capable of religion? All of these questions and more received considerable attention in YMCA, brotherhood, and other muscular Christian publications.

Naturally, opinions on the boy-and-religion issue varied. But the consensus among liberals was that whatever else a boy's religion might be, it should at least correspond with Social Gospel principles. "Playing on harps and all that sort of thing . . . seldom appeals to the boy," explained the Reverend Dr. George Dawson in 1901. Instead, boys preferred their religion to be "practical," "wide awake," "social," and above all "active."[140]

Another characteristic of religion for boys, insofar as character builders were concerned, was its "naturalness." "The kind of religion that has to be put on . . . is repulsive" to the boy, explained Norman Richardson and Ormond Loomis. "A 'pulpit voice,' a 'whine,' falseness in religious devotion, all tend to set him against the religion advocated by that voice or contained in that devotion."[141]

Finally, boys demanded (or at least were perceived to demand) that their religious leaders be "masculine."[142] "Not until virile young men . . . enroll in Bible study and service in church and Sunday school may we with reason expect the fifteen-year-old boy to be attracted to and remain in the Bible school," predicted a YMCA director in 1912. For the boy's "hero-worshipping mind" affixed only on "strong, earnest . . . virile men."[143]

This tripartite emphasis on sociability, naturalness, and masculinity led many character builders to prescribe scouting. After all, reasoned the Reverend Cuthbert Guy, Jesus himself was a Boy Scout at heart, with his dislike for urban crowding. And what in truth was scouting but a more manly, outdoorsmanlike version of Christianity, with signals substituting for prayers and badges for baptism?[144]

Guy's equation of scouting and Christianity did not lack for supporters.[145] But others thought it rather excessive. This was particularly the case among those who objected to the BSA's growing anti-clericalism and to its practice of conducting Sunday morning outings (an issue only partially resolved in 1922 when the BSA agreed not to subtract merit points from boys who eschewed hiking for church).[146]

"The plain truth is," summed up the general secretary of the Religious Education Association in 1908, "that the boy needs his God."[147] He might not show it overtly; nonetheless, "deep within himself" he possessed "a strong . . . religious sense."[148] This sense could not be requited through scouting alone. Nor could it be ignored, given psychological studies by G. Stanley Hall and others that showed adolescence to be *the* period during which boyhood spirituality was either developed or buried forever.[149]

Compounding the need to develop boys religiously was the observation that schools and homes were becoming progressively secular. Of course, schools could no longer teach the Bible, one religious educator allowed; that was the price one paid for separation of church and state.[150] But homes—that was another story. "Many an American boy comes from a home that has been thoroughly commercialized," noted Norman Richardson and Ormond Loomis. And it was pitiful to watch his religious sensibilities dry up in "such a shrivelly atmosphere."[151]

Churches, too, were blamed for their spiritual dereliction towards boys, not because they were irreligious but because their religion failed to "harmonize with the masculinity of [boys'] nature."[152] "The Church is teaching the boy to-day a maimed religion, an imperfect religion, a religion with the heart left out of it," noted a spokesman for the Brotherhood of St. Andrew.[153] As a result, "many boys thoroughly believe that they cannot live a Christian life and have any fun."[154]

What was the answer? Many believed it lay in making church work more reflective of Hall's theories regarding "gang" psychology. The boy must not approach religion alone, urged the Men and Religion Forward movement; for "that will make him lonesome and morbid and no suitable saint for the twentieth century."[155] Instead, boys ought to be converted en masse by the church, which could become, in the words of one Union theologian, "the religious gang to the early adolescent."[156]

Another approach, employed chiefly by medievalists such as Forbush, entailed making churches more ritualistic. Modern-day Protestantism was much too aesthetically severe, argued University of Chicago professor of religion Clyde Votaw in 1909. This was unfortunate, because boys needed the "ancient ritual[s]" in order to be "stirred religiously."[157]

But were churches—even properly ritualized and psychologically aware churches—really the proper places wherein to evangelize boys? Many character builders had their doubts. W. H. Ball in particular believed gymnasia to be more effective than Sunday schools insofar as religious conversion was concerned.[158] And Lilburn Merrill agreed that boys could "pray more easily and effectively on the run than on their knees."[159]

Of course, the best places for converting boys were not gyms but camps. This at least was the thought of 112 YMCA employees who were quizzed in 1903 on why their organization ought to maintain camps.[160] The question prompted many to respond that camps were worthwhile because of their close proximity to nature, which according to William Gray was the one place where the boy might lead a "life as simple and unostentatious, as benevolent and unselfish, as our Lord."[161]

Nature may indeed have been morally superior to civilization, as character builders generally thought. But boys also learned religion best outdoors because they were "instinctively . . . nature worshipper[s]," wrote educator J. Adams Puffer, and inclined only to respect the "savage . . . red gods."[162]

Did this fondness for "savage red gods" preclude boys from receiving Christ? Not at all, wrote Lilburn Merrill; it simply argued for investing religion with as many "primitive" aspects as possible, since experience showed that "Old Testament stories never read so well as when you and the boys are in a cave around a boiling kettle of beans, or presumably lost in a forest and gathered around a crackling campfire."[163]

Merrill's case for religious primitivism found widespread support among character builders, many of whom also believed passionately in the sacredness of the campfire.[164] But Old Testament stories, however told, were not the best means of converting boys, argued Henry Gibson; hymns were, particularly when they avoided all reference to heaven and other "over-exaggerated sentiment[al]" subjects.[165]

"Real red-blooded boy[s]" were not religious sentimentalists, Gibson averred.[166] Nor did they want Jesus shown to them as "a weak, dejected victim of circumstances."[167] Instead, boys expected Christ to be *"clean, strong, manly, human"*—so human, in fact, that the YMCA's Camp Becket in the Berkshires portrayed Jesus more as a "chum" than a savior and celebrated him in a weekly "Chumship Service."[168]

The point of such revisionism was not simply to get boys to know Christ, Gibson explained. It was also to get them to do what he did. For the boy's religion was nothing if not active, making it imperative that camp religion be active as well. Could Gibson cite a specific example of manly, religious activism? Yes, he could. It all happened one lazy Sunday afternoon, he recalled. He was lecturing a group of campers on the perils of light reading when suddenly it occurred to him: why not burn all the dime novels in camp? The boys certainly liked the idea; hence

> the start was made for the place where the bonfires were usually held. By the time I reached the spot, the boys were coming from their tents with bundles of novels. Every boy was requested to tear each novel in half and throw it upon the heap. When everything was ready, the boys uncovered and in the silence that came upon the group, the match was struck and the flames began to leap upward, until finally, all that remained was the small pile of ashes. For the majority of boys it meant the burning up of the dross and the beginning of better and nobler thinking. I shall always remember this novel bonfire. This is what I mean by making Bible study and camp talks effective.[169]

Not all camp directors would have sanctioned Gibson's characterization of book burning as a religious event. Nonetheless, the incident does illustrate the anti-intellectualism inherent in much of the muscular Christians' conceptions of character building, and indeed in muscular Christianity as a whole. This anti-intellectualism was particularly evident with regard to ministers. Once, wrote a Baptist pastor, it had been true that the minister was valued for his theology and scholarship. But now that those skills were passé, it made sense for him to specialize in boys' work, where he might conceivably be of help.[170]

Of course, if the minister were truly to succeed with boys, he must first gain their approval. And this for boys' worker Eugene Foster raised the question of what boys respected in their minister. Was it scholarly achievement? he asked. No, it was not. Instead, boys liked clergymen who preached short sermons, who "play[ed] good basket-

ball," and who were "in every way unlike a minister generally is."
Naturally, the point of appealing to boys was not popularity, added
Foster; it was religious conversion.[171] But did the minister convert
boys, wondered Allan Hoben, or did they convert him?

The truth was, Hoben concluded, that boys "saved" the minister
more often then he saved them. After all, he reasoned, by associating
with boys the minister not only regained those qualities of youthfulness he had lost, he also

> retains his sense of fun, fights on in good humor, detects and saves him-
> self on the verge of pious caricature and solemn pathos; knows how to
> meet important committees on microscopic reforms as well as self-ap-
> pointed theological inquisitors and all the insistent cranks that waylay a
> busy pastor. Life cannot grow stale; and by letting the boys lead him
> forth by the streams of living water and into the whispering woods he
> catches again the wild charm of that all-possible past: the smell of the
> campfire, the joyous freedom and good health of God's great out-of-
> doors.[172]

Hoben was not the only writer to invest boys' work with therapeutic value. William Forbush also believed that boys' work possessed restorative power. "I was educated, as many boys are," he recalled, "to
the intent that I might become a perfect lady, and when I became a
man my desire to be of service to boys was pathetically thwarted by
my inability to have real points of contact with them." However,
"outdoor hardship and play" had overcome the problem, and as a result, "I returned last Tuesday from camping out for ten days with
twenty-two boys, who six weeks ago were listening to an address
from me with mild respect, but as a perfect stranger. Since then we
have swum together and played ball together and together built our
camp fire, and I have cooked for them and bound up their wounds.
To-day they have begun to know me and to like me, and they have
even given me a nickname, thus admitting me into their tribe."[173]

Forbush's eagerness to be thought a boy again (albeit one with superior temporal authority) may have reflected the yearnings of an aging population or the demand by corporations for youthful employees.[174] Beyond that, it clearly reveals changes in the liberal Protestant
worldview. For once people ceased talking of the afterlife (a subject
not in favor among character builders) and instead affixed all hope
for justice on the coming generation, it made sense for boys to be

thought more divine than their aging pastor, whose opportunities to do good were drawing to a close.

In the end, one wonders whether character builders truly made good on their promise to "reclaim" America's youth. Clearly, monumental efforts were made in this direction, efforts that in 1912 led the Knights of St. Paul to declare "the boy problem solved."[175] But was it solved in accordance with the goals of character building? That seems unlikely. For despite their stated intention of giving boys religious and ethical values from the past, boys' workers in essence preached the virtues of modernity: regulation, socialization, and reliance on oneself rather than God.

Theodore Roosevelt on a visit to Yellowstone in 1903. (Courtesy of the
Theodore Roosevelt Collection, Harvard College Library)

G. Stanley Hall, a pioneer
psychologist who wanted to stop
"old-stock" Americans from
committing "race suicide."
(Courtesy of Clark University)

Rustic chapel of St. Michaels Mission, an Episcopalian establishment on the
Wind River Reservation of central Wyoming. (Courtesy of the Grace Raymond
Hebard Collection, American Heritage Center, University of Wyoming)

The "stubby Christians" football team of the International YMCA Training School, Springfield, Massaachusetts, circa 1891. James Naismith, the inventor of basketball, is holding the ball. (Courtesy of the Kautz Family YMCA Archives, University of Minnesota Libraries)

African-American men exercising in a Chicago YMCA, circa 1916. (Courtesy of the Kautz Family YMCA Archives, University of Minnesota Libraries)

Hymn singing in the gymnasium of the International YMCA Training School, Springfield, Massachusetts, 1909. (Courtesy of the Kautz Family YMCA Archives, University of Minnesota Libraries)

His New Day by S. M. Palmer (1920). Subtitled *Youth Sees the Vision Splendid* in G. Walter Fiske, *Jesus' Ideals of Living* (New York: Abingdon Press, 1922), p. 3. The painting was commissioned by the Blue Ridge Assembly of the YMCA to honor Edgar M. Robinson, secretary of the YMCA Boys' Work Department from 1901 to 1922. (Courtesy of the Kautz Family YMCA Archives, University of Minnesota Libraries)

Boys in the Central YMCA of Rochester, New York, seated in the form of the YMCA triangle, which symbolizes the union of body, mind, and spirit. (Courtesy of the Kautz Family YMCA Archives, University of Minnesota Libraries)

Participants in the Far Eastern Championship Games, a YMCA-sponsored event, 1913. (Courtesy of the Kautz Family YMCA Archives, University of Minnesota Libraries)

Men and Religion Forward movement Conference on Religious Work, Atlantic City, April 1912. Movement leader Fred Smith (short, stocky, without a mustache) stands in the center of the second row, eighth from the left. (Courtesy of the Kautz Family YMCA Archives, University of Minnesota Libraries)

Hymn singing in the parlor of the Warrenton Street YWCA, Boston, Massachusetts (no date). (Courtesy of the Schlesinger Library, Radcliffe Institute for Advanced Study)

YMCA volleyball for women, circa 1925 (location unknown). (Courtesy of the
Kautz Family YMCA Archives, University of Minnesota Libraries)

Camp Fire Girls co-founder
Charlotte Gulick (aka Hiiteni,
or "Life More Abundant")
making a ceremonial fire, circa
1914. (Courtesy of the
Schlesinger Library, Radcliffe
Institute for Advanced Study)

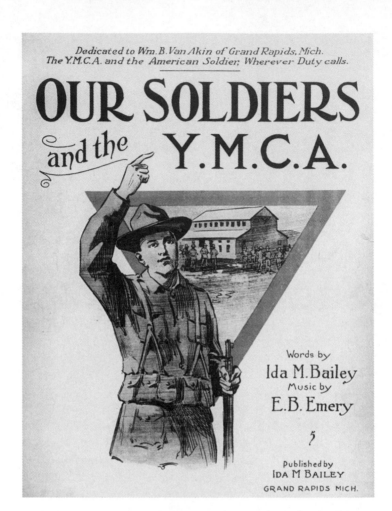

Cover of a YMCA-related song book, circa 1918. (Courtesy of the Sam DeVincent Collection of Illustrated American Sheet Music Covers, Archives Center, National Museum of American History)

Meeting of "the largest Bible class in the world," Great Cotton Palace Auditorium, Waco, Texas, 1918. Composed entirely of servicemen, the class was organized by the YMCA. (Courtesy of the Kautz Family YMCA Archives, University of Minnesota Libraries)

The Christian Student by Daniel Chester French, erected in 1913 on the campus of Princeton University. From *Association Men* 45, no. 6 (February 1920): 352. (Courtesy of the Kautz Family YMCA Archives, University of Minnesota Libraries)

CHAPTER FIVE

Worldwide Redemption

There is nothing effeminate in the modern missionary spirit.
Witness the Christian heroism which in recent years has
braved martyrdom in Turkey and suffered martyrdom in
China. Then look at the uprising of the student volunteers,
which is unequalled in all history. This splendid exhibition of
Christian zeal came in response to a call for service in the dark
places of the earth, a call to sacrifice, a call to "endure
hardness."

—JOSIAH STRONG (1901)

The Anglo-American boy was hardly the only target of Protestant
missionary endeavor at the beginning of the twentieth century. True,
his condition troubled reformers; but those reformers were also troubled by the condition of non-Anglos, who were repeatedly asked by
missionaries to accept both Christ and the accoutrements of Western
civilization. This missionary effort (illustrative of what H. Richard
Niebuhr called "aggressive" liberal Christianity)[1] affected natives in
the "foreign field" and immigrants in the "home field" alike. It also
drew strength from Anglo-American imperialism, which exposed the
globe to Western goods, government, and culture to an unparalleled
degree.

The early-twentieth-century Protestant missionary effort has recently begun to interest a number of women's historians, who have
written about the challenges faced by women missionaries.[2] But comparatively few historians have dealt with the influence of muscular
Christianity on Protestant missions. That influence is the subject of
this chapter.

Muscular Missionaries

Few authorities connected with American Protestantism at the turn of
the century doubted that it was their duty to carry the Gospel to peo-

ple recently brought within the sphere of Anglo-American influence. Nor did they doubt the worth of their message, or the likelihood of their message being accepted worldwide. In fact, leaders of the Student Volunteer Movement believed world reclamation to be not only possible but imminent. Hence their motto: "The evangelization of the world in this generation."[3]

In part, world evangelization meant Christian conversion. But it also meant cultural conformity, which one Baptist minister likened to human progress. Observe recent immigrants to the United States, he advised. Could they in their natural state be entrusted with "our cherished ideals"? Clearly not.[4] Nor apparently were they needful of anything quite so much as "the gospel of soap and water."[5]

The need to acquaint immigrants more thoroughly with Anglo-Saxon culture appeared to many missionaries more pressing even than evangelism. "To fuse a score of race stocks, with a half-dozen colors of skin, speaking forty languages, and inheriting the most diverse social and religious traditions, into a single homogeneous, democratic, and righteous nation, is the task that confronts us," declared the Home Missions Council, an interdenominational, assimilationist agency created in 1908.[6] Lest this seem overly difficult, Fred Rindge of the YMCA's Industrial Department hastened to add that science had contributed new weapons to the missionary arsenal, including improved techniques in the art of "human engineering."[7]

Americanizing immigrants was a challenging task. But John R. Mott of the Student Volunteer Movement believed world missions to be more important still. "Great as are the opportunities of the association movement on this continent," he told the assembled YMCA in 1901, "a far greater conflict awaits us at the ends of the earth." This was the "war against violence, bigotry, sensuality," and it was located

among the ten million young men of the Turkish Empire, Persia, Arabia, and Egypt . . . It is in that great continent of Africa, which has been unveiled within the memory of the delegates of this convention . . . It is in that great continent of India . . . It is in the islands of the Pacific . . . It is also in the Sunrise Kingdom of Japan . . . [and in] China and the countries which infringe upon her—Korea, Manchuria, and Tibet . . . And then I see another battlefield that we sometimes are prone to overlook— the ten million of young men of Mexico, Central America, and the South American republics—a warfare against immorality and gambling, against formalism and infidelity.[8]

Few in Mott's audience underestimated the severity of the conflict ahead. Nor was Mott alone in labeling it all-out war. In fact, missionaries were wont—particularly during the Spanish-American War—to fill their literature with military metaphors, in part because some considered themselves "the vanguard of imperialism," winning with Bibles what armies would later consolidate with force of arms.[9]

The main impetus, however, for missionary militarism sprung from the world's "staggering" indifference to Christ and the dire consequences of this indifference not being overcome. Unless "we . . . build such missionary fires of evangelization that . . . will send our best blood to the neglected places of the earth," warned Men and Religion Forward leader Fred Smith in 1913, "our descendants may witness the prophets of an eastern religion invading our centers of population and planting their banners in victory over places once claimed for Christ."[10]

Was Christianity truly endangered worldwide? Few believed this actually to be the case, provided measures were quickly taken to strengthen missionary forces and to increase their morale. Foremost among these measures would be the recruitment of more men to missionary service. As statistics showed, men comprised only 40 percent of America's missionary force in 1893 (as compared to 51 percent in 1830).[11] Male participation on missionary boards also lagged, causing the General Assembly of the Presbyterian Church (USA) to complain in 1895 that while female missionaries proliferated, "the men of our Church, as a class, are falling to the rear of the great host of God in both service and benevolence."[12]

One reason for Victorian men's lack of interest in the missionary enterprise stemmed from its impracticality. The missionary life gave men insufficient monetary incentive, explains historian Barbara Welter, while for women it provided opportunities for travel, service, and romance often denied them in normal bourgeois society. Missionary service also appeared more suited to women than men, given women's supposed "purifying influence" and the desirability of its being spread more generally abroad.[13]

Welter's arguments certainly help explain the predominance of female missionaries in the late nineteenth century. But they do not reflect men's increasing disenchantment with the doctrine of feminine sanctity and their doubts about the effectiveness of female missionaries. The truth was, declared Wilfred Grenfell, a missionary from Labrador, that "cut[ting] out a Kingdom for Jesus" was not easy. Rather it was "a tough job . . . a man's job," at which only the most "heroic" would succeed.[14]

That the world would one day capitulate not to saintly women but to manly men was also the belief of the Protestant brotherhoods and other men's groups formed in the 1890s to affirm male spirituality. In particular, it motivated members of the Laymen's Missionary Movement (LMM), an organization of the early twentieth century that endeavored "to enlist men in the interests of the kingdom."[15] The key to increasing male missionaries, the LMM believed, was heroism. More precisely, it was the young man's need to be heroic and to change the world that would make him a missionary. Hence the Laymen's Missionary Movement and other men's missionary publications emphasized hardship and battle. And Theodore Roosevelt asserted, upon hearing of a friend's son's desire to become a missionary, that that calling was in no way effeminate. In fact, said the President,

> the climax of [the minister's] calling is to go out in missionary service, as your son is doing. It takes mighty good stuff to be a missionary of the right type, the best stuff there is in the world. It takes a deal of courage to break the shell and go twelve thousand miles away to risk an unfriendly climate, to master a foreign language, perhaps the most difficult one on earth to learn; to adopt strange customs, to turn aside from earthly fame and emolument and the faces of the loved ones virtually forever.[16]

Roosevelt admired missionary hardness, and so did John R. Mott, who praised members of the Student Volunteer Movement for their eagerness to be shipped to the toughest, most remote missionary outposts.[17] There young men would find plenty of excitement, wrote Episcopal bishop Charles Brent of the Philippines, who in a book entitled *Adventure for God* described the missionary life as "full of romance . . . and pleasance," "daring and achievement."[18]

That missionary volunteers would wish to trade in the tedium of modern-day office work for adventure overseas is understandable. The romance of capitalism had ebbed with the advent of monopolies, and opportunities to advance financially on one's own were dimming. But missionaries fleeing from civilization brought into question the whole missionary enterprise. For how could missionaries impose that from which they had fled?

The irony of missionaries fleeing from industrial civilization only to impose it elsewhere was not completely lost on the Student Volunteers and other YMCA-related groups. These groups did not apologize for spreading civilization, but they were quick to point out that along with civilization they were spreading civilization's antidote: those sports and recreations that promised to correct neurasthenia, flabbiness, and other ills supposedly related to advanced corporate capitalism.

The need for "physical relaxation, recreation, and vitalization" had at one time been ignored by Western civilization, admitted John R. Mott. But thanks to the YMCA triangle idea, he told a group of YMCA physical educators, Christians had not only discovered "the sacredness of the body as a temple of the Holy Ghost"; they were also committed to spreading this truth among the less enlightened peoples of the world, whose religions allowed for the "mutilation, disfigurement, and the grossness of the body in comparison with the sacredness with which Christ dignified it."[19]

Not the least of those most needful of "this new gospel of physical salvation" were missionaries themselves, whom Luther Gulick accused in 1897 of overwork and neglect of their bodies. The idea that missionaries should be admired for overworking themselves to the point of breakdown would no longer do, he asserted, because God wished them to pursue every aspect of "the full-balanced life," including play, marriage and "all-round, regular, unexcited bodily exercise."[20]

Most missionaries granted that Gulick was right to uphold the importance of health. "When one is physically fit, the whole body tingles with the exuberance of that subtle something we call life," affirmed D. Willard Lyon of Shanghai. But when one was unfit, inefficiency, death, and disease were often the result. Consequently, observed J. R. Saunders of Canton, it behooved missionaries to take exercise, and to be "strong and ever aggressive for the Master."[21]

To improve their health and gain strength for the Master, a number of missionaries took up golf, the favorite sport of the Episcopal Missionary Bishop to the Philippines, Charles Brent, whose dexterity with a five iron once enabled him to save himself and his caddy from the depredations of a hooded cobra.[22] But golf was less popular among missionaries than tennis, "the national missionary outdoor game." Tennis generally attracted even the most hardened golfers, noted Edward Dodd of Persia, because "unless you happen to be one in a thousand who are located in some large and advanced city of many foreigners . . . you had better follow the scriptural injunction, and beat your brassies into tennis racquets and your golf balls into tennis balls, for the old prophecy of Tyre and Sidon applies to mission stations as a place for the 'spreading of nets.'"[23]

Did tennis and golf exist then for the benefit of missionaries alone? Not at all, explained George Pratt of the YMCA's Physical Department. For the whole point of missionary athleticism was not therapeutic; it was evangelical. Hence missionaries were obligated in Pratt's opinion to acquaint "ancient peoples" with "a new philosophy of life"—"a life of virility, of manliness, and joy [as opposed to] a life of repression and ultra-reserve."[24]

Whether ancient cultures were in fact repressive and unmanly or whether those terms really described the Victorian stereotypes against which muscular Christians were rebelling is open to debate. Most today would affirm the latter view, arguing that much of the missionary agenda derived less from foreign encounters than from home-based experience. But while this is a valid point, it fails adequately to explain the missionaries' success with regard to athletics.

The fact that non-Westerners eventually adopted the missionaries' sports is hard to dispute, given the participation of non-Westerners in the modern-day Olympics. But the non-Western adoption of Western sports did not occur without a hitch, since foreign assessments of these sports were at first largely negative. The Japanese, for example, thought that team sports such as basketball were inferior to their own individualized sports of karate and sumo wrestling. The Chinese viewed physical exertion as something that was appropriate only to the lower classes. And inhabitants of the tropics, where high heat and humidity prevailed, questioned the whole idea of strenuous, voluntary exercise.[25]

What finally convinced many foreigners to think positively about Western sports were the missionary efforts of the YMCA, which labored overseas as in America to show why healthy bodies were loved by God. As part of its missionary efforts, the YMCA created the first indoor heated swimming pool in Japan (1917), the first modern college physical fitness program in China (1917), and the first Filipino athletic meets (substitutes for the "disreputable" siesta). During the 1910s, the YMCA also internationalized basketball, volleyball, organized camping, and support for public playgrounds.[26]

The YMCA hoped that one day foreigners would take control of their own fitness destiny; so to help foreigners achieve self-sufficiency in the gym the Association brought foreign boys stateside to learn the latest health-care techniques.[27] The YMCA also helped convince foreign leaders to support the Far Eastern Championship Games (1913–1934), which was the first time the Chinese, Japanese, and Filipinos were brought "together for any purpose whatsoever."[28]

All this redounded obviously to the glory of sport and fitness. But whether it advanced Christ's kingdom is another matter. YMCA missionaries claimed that it did, and that health and religion were inextricable; but in the end their converts to Western sport outnumbered those to Christianity, leading one to suspect that many foreigners liked the "Y" less for its religion than for its progressivism: specifically its vision of hard-bodied, standardized young men working in tandem to better the world.

The Student Volunteer Movement

Enough has been said about YMCA missionaries to warrant closer inspection of their chief institutional backer, the Student Volunteer Movement (SVM). Hailed as "the most significant missionary uprising since Pentecost," the SVM garnered hundreds of recruits for the YM- and YWCAs.[29] It also assisted denominational missions and helped cast an aura of youthfulness over the whole late-nineteenth-century missionary enterprise.[30]

SVM leaders generally traced their roots back to the Haystack Revival of 1806 and the birth of American foreign missions.[31] But the movement's real impetus came from the state governments' postbellum expansion into higher education. This expansion not only helped phase out college Bible study, mandatory chapel, and denominational influence in curricular and personnel decisions; it also tended to alienate Christian students, many of whom responded by forming Bible studies and prayer groups.[32]

Another student response to the secularization of the academy was the formation of collegiate YMCAs (the first two of which appeared in 1858 at the Universities of Michigan and Virginia).[33] At first student "Y"s were largely informal and autonomous, and uncommunicative with one another. But in 1877 twenty-one local associations were organized into an Intercollegiate Department under the direction of the International YMCA. Thenceforth their numbers soared:

from twenty-six associations with a total of 1,300 members in 1877 to the point thirty years later where roughly one-third of all white male college students belonged to the YMCA.[34]

Many factors contributed to the growth of the student associations. One was their alliance with the national YMCA, which gave them both money and organization. "Y" backing also imbued student Christians with a manlier, more can-do image, ventured *Men* magazine in 1899, since none dared accuse "Y" men of being "timid and tender, pale and nervous, and afraid of being out after dark."[35] Another factor that accounted for student association growth was what two observers termed "denominational moulting."[36] By this they meant the postbellum gravitation among college Christians toward ecumenical groups such as the "Y," whose voluntarism and inclusivity seemed preferable to enforced prayers and strict religious credalism.[37] Finally, college association growth owed much to J. E. K. Studd, an English evangelist and world-renowned cricketeer who toured American campuses during the winter of 1886 at the behest of the YMCA. Studd frequently preached on "vital Christianity" and often made mention of his famous brother, C. T. Studd, whose group, the Cambridge Seven (seven athletes turned missionaries), were at that time evangelizing hundreds in China.[38]

An important stop on Studd's tour was Cornell University, whose student body included the young John R. Mott. An earnest Iowan possessed of "a phenomenal physique,"[39] Mott had been raised a Methodist, but was wrestling with his faith when he heard Studd quote Jeremiah 45:5: "Young man, seekest thou great things for thyself? Seek them not!" "These words," Mott later recalled,

> went straight to the springs of my motive life. I have forgotten all else he said. I went back to my room, not to study, but to fight. Next morning I went into the solitude of one of the gorges by the waterfall. At 2:30, I mustered courage to seek an interview with Studd, and found him in his sports clothes bent over his Bible. In a most discerning way he made me see the reasonableness of consulting for myself the source book of Christianity, the New Testament, and the wisdom of using my will to follow the gleam of light leading Christ's way. The great surrender to Christ as Lord came later.[40]

Mott's friend Sherwood Eddy once commented on the impossibility of modern men's understanding the intensity of the late-nineteenth-century conversion experience. Certainly its effect on Mott was transformative. After his conversion he took up morning Bible study and won election to the presidency of the Cornell University Christian Association. He also made an arduous trek to attend what was to be a momentous event: the 1886 summer gathering of religious workers at evangelist Dwight L. Moody's boys' school, Mt. Hermon, which was located in a town next to Northfield, Massachusetts.[41]

The 1886 gathering at Mt. Hermon was Moody's second Northfield conference (the first having been held in 1885). It was supposed to be unprogrammed, but unbeknownst to Moody a cadre of Princetonians had an agenda for the meeting. Led by the YMCA's college secretary, Luther Wishard, they lobbied hard on behalf of foreign missions. As a result of their efforts, one hundred men including Mott (a group later known as the "Mt. Hermon Hundred") agreed in late July to take the "Princeton pledge" and to commit themselves to a lifetime of missionary service.[42]

Not all members of the Mt. Hermon Hundred took up overseas work immediately. In particular, some stayed behind to tour American colleges and to interest youths in missionary service. This "Band" (modeled after the Cambridge Seven) soon managed to precipitate a missionary "gusher." It also found itself unable to handle that gusher, prompting urgent calls for YMCA intervention.[43]

Hitherto YMCA support for foreign missions had been mainly verbal. But at the third Northfield conference (1887) the Association was asked to help directly with missions, and in particular with student volunteers. One result of such lobbying was the creation in 1888 of the Student Volunteer Movement for Foreign Missions, whose executive committee was composed of representatives from the YMCA, the YWCA, the American Inter-Seminary Alliance, and the Canadian Intercollegiate Missionary Alliance.[44]

Of these four organizations, none had more influence over the SVM than the YMCA, whose representative to (and chairman of) the SVM executive committee was John R. Mott. At twenty-three, Mott was extraordinarily young to be entrusted with the governance of the SVM. But Association leaders, impressed by his one-year stint as traveling secretary for the Intercollegiate Department, deemed him fit for the task. Nor were they wrong. By the end of Mott's thirty-two-year reign, the SVM had fielded thousands of missionaries and was considered "a major force in American Protestantism."[45]

One of Mott's first tasks as SVM chairman involved defending organizational ties with the YWCA. Many Association members thought the SVM had best be an exclusively masculine phenomenon, but Mott argued instead for the inclusion of women as helpmates.[46] He also traveled extensively on behalf of the SVM and other ecumenical causes, fostering an international religious dialogue that led to the formation of the World's Student Christian Federation (1895), the International Missionary Council (1921), and the World Council of Churches (1948).

As a result of these endeavors, Mott was awarded the 1946 Nobel Peace Prize (which he shared with pacifist Emily Green Balch). Prior to this he had been offered the presidencies of Princeton and Oberlin, the deanship of Yale Divinity School, and an ambassadorship to China, all of which he turned down out of respect for his 1886 pledge: worldwide advancement of the Christian religion.[47]

But did Christian advancement mean the same thing for Mott at Stockholm as it had for him at Mt. Hermon? Judging from his writings, the answer is no. For whereas he had once envisioned missionary "war[s] of conquest," his Nobel Prize address stressed instead the importance of "fellowship" and worldwide religious "cooperation."[48]

Mott's changed view of missions was shared by the Student Volunteer Movement as a whole. Around 1900 SVM publications referred routinely to the "lower races" and to the need for uplifting them through aggressive missionary action.[49] But twenty years later, Movement emphasis lay instead on ameliorating the ill effects of colonialist expansion. This turnabout (especially evident in the 1920s disappearance of the famous SVM motto "The evangelization of the world in this generation") owed much to increased SVM acceptance of the Social Gospel, which dictated that the organization's aggressiveness be redirected toward social ends: namely, corporate as opposed to individual salvation, and cooperative as opposed to Western-led models of reform.[50]

Adherence to the Social Gospel also diverted SVM attention away from world affairs. At the 1912 SVM convention, for example, delegates were led for the first time to debate domestic issues. In 1920 they were upbraided by Methodist bishop Francis McConnell for placing world ahead of national reform. And in 1924, they willingly listened to an avowed supporter of the Socialist Party presidential candidate.[51]

The declining importance of foreign as opposed to domestic mission was especially pronounced following World War I. But Josiah Strong had anticipated it as early as 1901. After all, he reasoned in an address to prospective missionaries, "There is as real an opportunity for sacrifice in the United States as in Turkey or China. Right here, in the midst of ease and luxury and selfishness; here, in the midst of municipal corruption, and industrial hate, and social discontent, there is a call for the 'strenuous life,' a call for the 'living sacrifice' which 'dies daily.'"[52]

But were there men of sufficient "vigor" to heed Strong's call? Were there men sufficiently committed to "widening . . . the kingdom of our Lord in America?"[53] These were questions posed by the Protestant brotherhoods, many of which worked to Christianize American manhood through their participation in the Men and Religion Forward movement.

Men and Religion Forward

The Men and Religion Forward movement (MRFM) began in the spring of 1910. It existed for only two years and was not as historically significant as the Student Volunteer Movement. Still, Men and Religion Forward deserves mention for two reasons: it was the only countrywide religious revival in America ever to exclude women,[54] and it had the support of important figures such as Washington Gladden, who called it "the most salutary influence which has visited the churches of this country since my ministry began."[55]

Contributing to the rise of the Men and Religion Forward movement was men's adverse reaction to feminized Protestantism (discussed more fully in Chapter 3). This reaction found expression in the movement's official motto: "More religion for men, and more men for religion."[56] It was also reflected in the views of Laymen's Missionary Movement vice-president E. W. Halford, who attributed the success of Men and Religion Forward to its understanding that "men need an emphasis on the heroic and aggressive in Christianity."[57]

Another MRFM concern was church backwardness. For too long the churches had been the domain solely of ministers, women, and other nonbusiness types, observed MRFM publicity secretary Henry Rood.[58] As a result, the churches were plagued by "antiquated methods,"⁵⁹ "pestiferous parochialism,"⁶⁰ and an attitude toward commerce that was, in the words of one advertising executive, "sacredly stupid."⁶¹

The MRFM also faulted American religion for its social unresponsiveness and its inability to attract urban males. And this would continue to be a problem, predicted MRFM second-in-command Fayette L. Thompson, until the churches successfully forwarded "a program big enough, masterful enough, stalwart enough, comprehensive enough, far-reaching enough, to fit into the superb greatness of Jesus Christ, to fit into the marvelous wonders of this century, to appeal to the biggest man alive in this age of intellectual and commercial giants."⁶²

And what might such a program for Christian greatness be? One possibility widely discussed was a nationwide campaign to evangelize men, separate plans for which were made circa 1910 by Hubert Carleton of the Brotherhood of St. Andrew, Marion Lawrance of the International Sunday-School Association, and Harry Arnold of the YMCA.⁶³ Of these three, Arnold (a Christian athlete recently graduated from Otterbein University in Ohio) did the most to initiate what became the MRFM. His first step was to arrange a 1907 conference for Maine men's organizations. Its success prompted him to ask his superior, Fred Smith of the YMCA's Religious Work Department, to attempt something similar on a national scale.⁶⁴

At first Smith demurred, citing the enormous difficulties inherent in mounting so large a campaign. But when Arnold threatened to resign from the "Y" if no men's revival were forthcoming, Smith gave in and agreed to host a planning session to which delegates from the "Y," the International Sunday-School Association, and the various denominational brotherhoods were all invited.⁶⁵

Shortly before the meeting was to be held in New York City on May 18, 1910, Arnold collapsed from a perforated lung. This left responsibility for organizing the MRFM up to Smith, who might well have balked at the enormity of the task. But because he believed that the religious world already had, in his words, "too many cheap, silly, flabby, white-livered, jelly-spined, emasculated, sickly, cotton-tailed rabbit 'quitters' in it," he readily agreed to shoulder the burden.⁶⁶

Smith's intrepidness in the face of crisis contributed to his already solid reputation as a "great big he-man."⁶⁷ It also helped persuade the brotherhood men when they met in New York to endorse the MRFM idea and to reconvene several times to discuss particulars. From these meetings came the guiding principles of the MRFM. Known as the "Buffalo Resolutions" (after an important meeting held in Buffalo, New York, October 25–26, 1910), they set forth the movement's "five-fold method of attack": boys' work, Bible study, missions, individual evangelism, and social service.[68]

Another portion of the Buffalo Resolutions was a pledge to make religion more suited to men. "There will not be a trace of emotionalism or sensationalism in this entire campaign," explained Henry Rood. Instead, "The gospel of Jesus of Nazareth—and its practical application to our practical daily life—is presented calmly, sanely, logically, so that it will convince the average man, who is a man of sane, logical, common sense. Women have no part in this movement, the reason being that Mr. Smith believes that the manly gospel of Christ should be presented to men by men."[69]

Ensuring that this manly evangelism actually took place required organization; and toward this end the Buffalo Resolutions conferred upon Smith and ninety-six others (the "Committee of Ninety-Seven") responsibility for enlisting the help of one hundred of the "strongest" men in each of the seventy-six U.S. and Canadian cities the MRFM was to visit.[70] These "Committees of One Hundred" (composed for the most part of leading Protestant laymen) then pledged to ready their cities and satellite towns for the MRFM onslaught. They also received from MRFM headquarters in New York a complex set of survey questions, the answers to which were meant to apprise movement leaders of each city's educative, industrial, and moral situation.[71]

Meanwhile, as the committees completed their surveys and sent them back to New York to be converted into colorful graphs and charts, Fred Smith gathered to himself a group of thirty men, each of whom was an "expert" in at least one area of the MRFM program. These men (including "boy evangelist" John Dean, Social Gospel worker Charles Stelzle, and Alaskan goldminer turned millionaire philanthropist Raymond Robins)[72] were all "hearty meat eaters," observed a writer from *Collier's*. And they aimed to take hold of religion and "boost" it "with the fervor and publicity skill which a gang of salesmen would apply to soap that floats or suits that wear."[73]

But before Smith's experts commenced drumming, he asked that they attend a week-long retreat beginning September 21, 1911, at Bald Eagle Lake, Minnesota. There, in between bouts of "the hardest kind of exercise," he explained that the group was to break into three (later four) teams, each of which was to be composed of experts from all five of the MRFM program areas and each of which was to conduct eight-day city "sweeps," starting in the Midwest, then moving on to the West and East.[74]

The first city visited by the MRFM experts following their Bald Eagle Lake retreat was Minneapolis, Minnesota. The second (after which teams were formed) occurred in South Bend, Indiana. There Smith's group was met on October 9, 1911, taken to dine with hundreds of businessmen at Studebaker headquarters, and the next day (following "strenuous" morning exercise) shown a town

> decorated with banners strung across the principal streets, with hundreds of posters, smaller cards, and other advertising matter displayed at every available point. The three daily newspapers had started in to give several columns of space each day to the events, and this was rapidly increased to pages, including heavy display advertising. All this was done for a purpose which was most strongly emphasized that Tuesday evening, when three thousand men and boys took part in a parade—the purpose being to call attention to the belief of the men of South Bend and Mishawaka that the spirit of religion is not dead; that it is a vital thing in their lives—an actual, dynamic reality, and not mere ineffective sentimentality.[75]

South Bend's receptivity to the MRFM idea was by no means atypical, as evidenced by the fact that MRFM teams managed to hold seven thousand meetings and address 1.5 million men nationwide before their travels ended in the winter of 1912. Many attenders at MRFM events no doubt shared the organization's concern for the well-being of religion among men. Others probably showed up primarily in order to form potentially lucrative acquaintanceships with local church-going business elites. Whatever their motives, participants in MRFM activities were urged to reaffirm the manly element in religion and to attend the penultimate event of the MRFM campaign: a five-day "Christian Conservation Congress" at New York's Carnegie Hall.[76]

The Christian Conservation Congress, which began on April 19, 1912, and which attracted "an extraordinary proportion of the religious leadership in America," was heralded by a flurry of newspaper publicity, and even lighted billboards in Times Square. But despite the hoopla, the 1,338 delegates in attendance were in no mood for fun, partly because of the *Titanic* disaster of the week before and partly because they took their cause seriously. Indeed, noted MRFM publicity commissioner William Ellis, "the common concomitants of conventions, such as badges and buttons and noisy effervescing enthusiasm, were totally lacking," as delegates readied themselves instead "for the strongest utterances of the strongest men."[77]

Those paladins to whom Ellis referred included black rights advocate Booker T. Washington, statesman and prohibitionist William Jennings Bryan, and Hull House founder Jane Addams, who addressed the congress's only female gathering ("a monster mothers' meeting") on the evils of prostitution.[78] Other speakers no less luminous brought up additional topics current at the time, though none of the male religionists chose to discuss women's suffrage.[79]

On April 24, 1912, the speeches ended and the Christian Conservation Congress was declared officially adjourned. Subsequently, Fred Smith and a small coterie of followers began preparations for what was to be the final stage in the MRFM campaign: a round-the-world tour to advance the cause of men and religion.[80]

Meanwhile, journalists, academicians, and religious authorities fell to debating the effectiveness of the MRFM in America. On the down side, most agreed, the movement had produced a mere 7,000 converts—far fewer than anticipated.[81] Even worse, some exponents of the MRFM themselves chose not to stick with the church, but to emulate Fred Smith, who quit the "Y" in 1914 to become a "business evangelist" with the Johns-Manville Company.[82]

Another area in which the MRFM fell short was ecumenism. Ostensibly representative of all religious faiths (and eager to have Catholics and Jews address the Christian Conservation Congress),[83] MRFM leaders were nonetheless overwhelmingly Protestant, and mainstream, evangelical Protestant at that—Unitarians being excluded for their Monarchianism and conservatives such as the Missouri Synod Lutherans declining to join the MRFM on account of its troubling "go-as-you-please Christianity."[84]

Of course, assessments of the MRFM were not all negative. Many contemporaries praised the movement for its accomplishments, including its mastery (unprecedented in religious circles) of the mass media.[85] This mastery was particularly evident in the MRFM's ability to communicate stories of itself to the press and in its hiring of a pioneer advertising firm, N. W. Ayer, to help with publicity. As a result, in the estimation of one prominent newsweekly, religion finally was being "talked about at the table."[86]

Another success of the MRFM was the sociological survey used by Smith and his colleagues to advance the cause of religion. In one midwestern city, for instance, MRFM survey results forced the resignation of a corrupt chief of police. In other cities they led to the excommunication of prominent churchmen found to be the owners of brothels or saloons.[87] And in Chicago, MRFM-style polling was added to the curriculum of McCormick Theological Seminary.[88]

Finally and most importantly, the MRFM in the estimation of Walter Rauschenbusch did "more than any other single agency to lodge the social gospel in the common mind of the Church."[89] Not that this was its original intent; at first social service was to be "a minor feature" of the campaign, with the major focus on foreign missions.[90] Smith and other MRFM leaders even wondered whether social service ought to be featured at all, considering the likelihood of its antagonizing conservative churchmen.[91]

Such fears regarding the Social Gospel were not easily allayed. But over the course of time, Graham Taylor, Walter Rauschenbusch, Washington Gladden, Henry Sloan Coffin, Charles Stelzle, and Raymond Robins (the first four of whom served on the MRFM's Social Service Commission) helped demonstrate that manliness and the Social Gospel were nearly indivisible. As a result, observed William Ellis in 1912, masculinists within the MRFM who had once regarded social service as "a fad of the few" now considered it the duty of the many, and an important part of making religion "meet the test of practical efficiency."[92]

Proponents of the Social Gospel obviously succeeded in enabling the MRFM to see the value of social service. But did they also enable the MRFM to achieve its goal of making the churches more manly? To some degree, the answer is no, since it appears that the MRFM failed to achieve gender balance in the churches. Despite the movement's promise to reinstate "3,000,000 missing men," the proportion of men in the Protestant churches increased only 6.4 percent between 1906 and 1926 (going from 39.3 percent male to 41.8 percent male, according to U.S. census figures).[93]

But while the proportion of men in the Protestant churches may not have increased dramatically in the early twentieth century, it did increase, and this increase was especially pronounced in the ranks of the middle- and upper-class denominations that had been particularly favored by the MRFM. Those denominations included the Congregational Church (where the proportion of men grew by 10.9 percent between 1906 and 1926), the Northern Presbyterian Church (where male membership increased by 11.2 percent between 1906 and 1926) and the Episcopal Church (where the proportion of men grew by an impressive 20.8 percent between 1906 and 1926).[94]

As the proportion of men increased in the churches, the influence of men likewise increased, particularly with regard to missions. In that area of church work, Protestants not only witnessed aggressive efforts by the Student Volunteer Movement to recruit more male missionaries; they also witnessed the absorption of various female-run missionary societies into larger, male-run missionary boards.[95] Given this male expansion into missionary work, it seems fair to say that the SVM and the MRFM did in fact realize their dream of "masculinizing" the business of evangelism.

CHAPTER SIX

Muscular Women

Wanted, young women. What kind? Those to whom the Lord
can say, "Do this or that for me," and who can respond to the
hardest command, the carrying out of which will mean
endurance, a knowledge of the principles of the conservation
of energy and the putting forth of will power through bodily
power. It will mean the clear shining of a glowing soul
through a transparent medium, instead of the cloudy glass of
a dark lantern, an ill-used body.

—KANSAS CITY YWCA SECRETARY MARY S. DUNN (1895)

So far this study has underscored the aggressive, masculine aspects of
early-twentieth-century mainline Protestantism and the push by mid-
dle- and upper-class white male churchgoers to assert their virility. But
as the historian Margaret Marsh points out, Theodore Roosevelt's
"cult of manliness" (the ecclesiastical form of which was muscular
Christianity) did not lack for critics.[1] These included men such as the
Reverend Elmer Dent, who warned churches not to engage in "an
undignified scramble for men," and educator Joseph Rogers, who regretted the passage of "gentleness" from the public schools and its
replacement by "health" and "character-building."[2] Women also criticized the hypermasculinity inherent in much of Progressive Era culture. Especially critical of the Strenuous Life were women who turned
their backs on the muscular Christianity of the mainline churches in
order to join the newly formed Christian Science movement, whose
elevation of the "feminine principle" over the "masculine principle"
in religion will be discussed later in this chapter.

The fact that Christian Science women tended to view muscular
Christianity with disfavor is understandable. After all, muscular
Christians often lauded stereotypically male virtues while denigrating
female ones. But it would be a mistake to infer from the misogynous
statements of muscular Christian preachers that women were completely averse to the religion of the Strenuous Life. Many women did

not reject the Strenuous Life; they embraced it, or at least those aspects of it that advanced health instead of patriarchalism. Their enthusiasm was particularly evident in the Young Women's Christian Association (YWCA), the Girl Scouts, and the Camp Fire Girls. These female counterparts of the YMCA and the Boy Scouts denied that rugged outdoor experiences were meant for boys alone. They believed that girls also deserved to draw strength from nature and from strenuous outdoor games.

Women and the Strenuous Life

To understand more fully why the leaders of the YWCA, the Girl Scouts, and the Camp Fire Girls valued the Strenuous Life, it is necessary first to concede that the lives of these leaders were often less than ideal. Material deprivation was generally not the problem, since the middle- and upper-class white women who ran organizations such as the YWCA enjoyed a number of postbellum amenities. These included newly developed home appliances, which relieved women of many burdensome tasks. But were women freed from drudgery able to find alternative employment? Pioneer feminist Charlotte Perkins Gilman thought not. Instead of being emancipated by machines, women in Gilman's view were often forced by idleness into becoming "physically weak enough to be handed about like invalids; or mentally weak enough to pretend they are—and to like it."[3]

While some women may have benefited from enforced inactivity, others did not. Instead they experienced mental breakdowns and "nervousness," which doctors regarded as "peculiarly a disease of girls and women."[4] Symptoms such as nervousness were unfortunate, observed YWCA worker Jessie Holmes, but they were perfectly natural, considering that "the diaphragm wasn't made to be kept still, and sometimes, when its owner is sitting quietly in church, it rebels, and the poor girl weeps or giggles—a sad spectacle indeed!"[5]

Holmes's 1895 advice to "our nervous good girl" was that she "take her place frankly among the Christian workers where she belongs" and forget her "repress[ive]" notions of staid respectability.[6] But such advice was not always easy to follow, because it gainsaid traditional views of womanly decorum and because it clashed with the Victorian doctrine of "separate spheres": the idea that hard work was for men, and quiet home life for women.

The "separate spheres" doctrine was indeed a powerful force in

Victorian society. But it was a force whose constraints gave rise to a number of opponents, including female suffragists, who sought to exercise the same political rights as males. By questioning the legitimacy of certain gender stereotypes, the opponents of "separate spheres" helped to inaugurate what YMCA Education Secretary George Hodge called "[this] women's age": a period (1873–1898) during which the number of women college students rose sharply, the number of women professionals tripled, and the number of women trade and transportation workers increased fifteenfold.[7] Women were also advancing in church, observed a YWCA leader,[8] as evidenced by the formation of such aggressive reformatory bodies as the Daughters of the King (the female half of the Brotherhood of St. Andrew)[9] and by efforts on the part of over two dozen "women's training schools" to increase the number of salaried women church workers.[10]

Additional evidence that women were seeking new outlets for their pent-up energies can be found, interestingly enough, in the annals of the Young Men's Christian Association. Despite its commitment to men, the YMCA at first welcomed the formation of ladies' auxiliaries. These auxiliaries (which in 1890 numbered around 500) made a point of forgoing the usual YMCA privileges. Their purpose was not to produce women athletes, they averred; rather it was to "serve" the young man by cleaning his rooms, plying him with food, and in every way reminding him of his "dear Mother and her desire that he should become a follower of Christ."[11]

The fact that women claimed to be in the YMCA merely to serve seemed to justify their being kept on as associate members. But increasingly women argued that it behooved the "Y" to admit them as full voting members. After all, they pointed out, admitting women on an equal basis would not only enhance the Association's capacity for good; it would also attract men desirous of feminine guidance and companionship.[12]

Women's request that they be given a greater say in the YMCA was hotly debated. Indeed, it was a main topic of conversation at the 1868 Detroit and the 1869 Portland conventions. There it was duly noted that several YMCAs in Massachusetts alone had for some time been allowing women full voting rights, but this was judged to be a bad idea. The resulting ruling that women were not to be considered equal with men was to remain official "Y" policy for the next sixty-four years.[13]

One reason for this exclusionary policy was the Association's post-bellum swing into gym work. Women could be tolerated so long as YMCAs kept largely to Bible study; but once the organizations were filled with sweaty young men in gym suits, directors felt women's presence to be inviting of "scandal" and the depredations of "obnoxious mashers."[14] Besides, they argued, women belonged less in a YM- than in a YWCA, several of which had already been formed by the late 1860s.

Another reason YMCA officials gave for keeping the organization males-only was missiological. As New York secretary Robert McBurney (a leading opponent of women's admission) put it, the Association "has its work to do—to lead *young men* to the Lamb of God." Anything blocking that work—not excluding oversolicitous mothers—ought properly to be sidelined.[15]

McBurney's objections to women in the YMCA were not only missiological; they were also personal. That at any rate is the conclusion drawn by John Gustav-Wrathall, who argues that McBurney was but one of many "homosocial" (and probably homosexual) YMCA secretaries for whom the Association was a haven from enforced domesticity.[16] These men did not support coeducational policies aimed at making the "Y" a conduit toward marriage. Nor did they want it to become like the church, which one minister referred to as "the greatest mating institution in the world."[17]

The fact that most "Y" men wished their Association to retain its masculine edge did not result in the abolition of ladies' auxiliaries. But it did alienate those women whom one social worker described as leaning toward "organizations operated in accord with feminine taste and giving women full control." Such women, who evidently found limited satisfaction in ministering solely to the wants of young men, often left the YM- for the YWCA, an organization more responsive to feminine needs and concerns.[18]

Early YWCAs functioned much as the YMCA had—sheltering workers, converting them, and providing them with wholesome entertainments. Virtually the only YMCA program not adopted by the YWCA was gymnastics. Other women's organizations, such as Wellesley College (which hired Harvard's Dudley Allen Sargent to coach sports in the mid 1870s), had begun to encourage women to exercise.[19] But of twenty-eight YWCAs surveyed in 1875, none reported having gymnasiums.[20]

YWCA inattention to physical education did not last long. An early break came in 1884, when the Boston Association added a gymnasium. Three years later, "Philadelphia, Poughkeepsie, and New York City reported classes in light calisthenics accompanied by the piano."[21] Soon YWCAs everywhere had gyms; and by 1890 the Association had become the country's foremost purveyor of women's athletics.[22]

The YWCA's belated adoption of athletics was approved by Luther Gulick, who called the strengthening of women a defense against "spiritual disaster."[23] But other muscular Christians such as Lyman Abbott, the influential editor of *Outlook* magazine, considered the manufacture of strong, "cross-bear[ing]" women to be terribly unwise.[24] Abbott's chief objection to muscular womanhood involved the home. In particular, he thought it obvious that true women wished simply to be wives and "home builder[s]" and that activities aside from these appealed only to "virgin reformers who have never known the mystery of love."[25] Indeed, confirmed child-rearing expert William McKeever, training girls to become anything but mothers was not only futile; it was also immoral. For only girls victimized by "some unnatural process" declined motherhood. And the fate of these misfits was generally to become "coarse, unhappy animal[s]."[26]

But were nontraditional roles really that destructive of womanly character? Women leaders expressed doubt on this score, and some went so far as to praise their new freedoms as correctives to "nervousness, morbidity and too much introspection."[27] Women also wondered why their strength should be called decadent. Why all the talk of a "woman peril," one Seattle teacher wanted to know. "And after all of what does 'the woman peril' consist? That boys are being feminized . . . 'That abnormal families in which the mother's influence is too long continued and not sufficiently counteracted by masculine control are notoriously productive of decadence and degeneracy.' That is certainly a grave charge!"[28]

Grave, yes, but true? YWCA worker Abbie Mayhew thought not. After all, she reasoned, degeneracy applied more to "the limp anaemic maiden" of yesterday than it did to "the ruddy cheeked, full-limbed girl of to-day," since the former had allowed a "Draconian code of feminine decorum" to blight her life, whereas the latter was pursuing those paths to "physical betterment" wherein lay "the best hope for the future of our race."[29]

Mayhew's insistence that strong women constituted the hope of the world and not its bane was echoed by Mary Dunn, another YWCA physical director. In fact, wrote Dunn, women athletes and the "Y" gymnasia wherein they trained were not only healthful; they were also Christian, and pleasing "to Him that sitteth upon the throne."[30]

The question of why God should exhibit such an interest in women's athletics will be discussed more fully later in this chapter. Suffice it to say here that His disciples in the YWCA were great believers in "body as temple" theology: the "close relation," as the "Y" *Evangel* put it, "between good muscles and good health, and between good health and good morals."[31] Good health equals good morals. That was not only YWCA dogma; it was also a primary tenet of muscular Christianity. And this raises an interesting question: If YWCA women were muscular Christians concerning health, were they also muscular Christians concerning manliness?

Indeed they were, answered Harvard chaplain Francis Peabody, who believed that women revered Jesus largely for his "force, initiative and leadership" and that they harbored the same dislike for effeminacy in religion as men. Not so, countered Wellesley College professor Muriel Streibert. Girls admired Jesus most for his "friendship, thoughtfulness," and "trust." And they thought of him not as a Hercules, but as a lover of "flowers, birds, fields [and] winds."[32]

Not all women agreed with Streibert about Christ's feminine qualities being as admirable as his masculine ones. One dissenter was Jack London's friend, novelist Mary H. Austin, whose books portrayed Jesus as a rugged outdoorsman.[33] But while Austin strove to make Jesus appear more manly, other Progressive Era women questioned whether Christianity needed masculine reform.[34] One thirty-one-year-old Episcopalian woman in particular expressed her belief that the men's movement in religion had already gone too far. "I was a Radcliffe student," she told a male psychologist (who felt her to be illustrative "of the religious dyspeptic type"), and "have been taken everywhere travelling and sightseeing, but the ministers never talked about history or art or great men, but thought I must, of course, be interested in basket-ball, gymnasium work and Harvard men."[35]

What she wanted, the Radcliffe graduate explained, was for ministers to treat her as an intellectual equal. And this was what most YWCA women seemed to want as well: a religion reflective of muscular Christianity's physical side, but not of its hypermasculinity. Other women, however, opposed both manliness *and* physicality in religion. And these women (many of whom were devotees of Christian Science or New Thought) are notable not only for their rejection of muscular Christianity but also for their aversion to the whole idea of the Strenuous Life.

The Dissenters

Women who opposed the Strenuous Life and who objected to the masculinization of mainline Protestantism had several options. They could remain in the churches to fight for the retention of feminine iconography, or they could leave the establishment to join such newly founded, women-led religions as Christian Science (founded in 1875 by Mary Baker Eddy), Theosophy (founded in 1875 by Russian émigré Madame Blavatsky), and the Church of the Higher Life, a Boston organization headed by Helen Van Anderson that was instrumental in the spread of New Thought.[36]

Some of the new religionists, such as Mary Baker Eddy (a latter-day gnostic), denied physicality's very existence.[37] "The Christianly scientific real is the sensuous unreal," she explained in her book *Science and Health with Key to the Scriptures*. "Sin, disease, whatever seems real to material sense is unreal in divine Science."[38] Nor was this negation of grossness the only thing to distinguish "divine Science" from traditional Christianity, Eddy continued. For whereas traditional Christianity was patriarchal in nature, Christian Scientists prayed not to "Our Father," but to "Our Father-Mother God, all-harmonious."[39]

These were radical thoughts. But were they an adequate basis upon which to found an alternative religious faith? "Mother" Eddy thought so, and she set out to prove it, building her fledgling Christian Science Church into an organization described by *Harper's Weekly* in 1903 as "the most flourishing religious movement outside of the conventional churches that there is in this country."[40]

Indeed the growth of Christian Science (from one church with less then fifty members in 1882 to 711 churches with fifty thousand members in 1907) was remarkable.[41] Few could have predicted it back in the 1870s, when the organization consisted of a half-dozen shoe workers in Lynn, Massachusetts. Nor would greatness have seemed destined for the church's leader, an itinerant mentalist and onetime pupil of Maine sage and clockmaker Phineas P. Quimby.[42]

What catapulted Eddy into prominence was in large part her church's removal to Boston in the early 1880s. Following this move, the fortunes of Christian Science began to soar—a trend that was intensified by the founding in 1881 of the Massachusetts Metaphysical College (MCC), which gave degrees in Christian Science. Tuition at the college (actually Eddy's parlor) was not cheap: it cost $300, a "divinely inspired" figure.[43] Still, few complained, and no wonder, since MCC degrees were passports into the burgeoning field of Christian Science healing.[44]

Many (perhaps most) MCC degree recipients were women, whose inability to gain entry into the male-dominated medical profession led them to become Christian Science practitioners. Such women were welcomed by Mrs. Eddy and by female patients whose Victorian modesty and fear of harsh male doctors made them especially appreciative of Christian Science healers and their gentle, noninvasive techniques.[45]

But it was not just professional opportunities that drew women to Christian Science (a religion whose ratio of women to men was the highest in America);[46] it was also the church's theology, which praised feminine virtues, and which elevated Mrs. Eddy (the feminine principle) over Jesus (the masculine principle).[47] This theology caused many to venerate Eddy as they did God. But in a sensational and thoroughly documented exposé of Christian Science, Willa Cather (then a writer for *McClure's*) cautioned people against confusing the iconographic Mrs. Eddy with the real one, whom she called a tyrant, a paranoiac, and an arsonist.[48]

Cather's charges (distressing enough to the Christian Science Church for it to keep her book from circulating for decades) outraged Eddy loyalists.[49] But Christian Science dissidents already at odds with their "Mother" appeared more willing to listen. In particular, anti-Eddyism resonated with those who eventually left Christian Science to found what became known as New Thought, a loose collection of healers and mystics—mostly women—whose foremost family, the Dressers, had like Eddy been students of the redoubtable Phineas P. Quimby. But whereas Eddy had transformed Quimby's ideas regarding mind over matter into what detractors called a highly organized personality cult, the followers of New Thought considered themselves to be pure Quimbyites—resistant alike to creedalism, hierarchicalism, and anthropomorphism.[50]

This aversion to structure had its costs, of course; and many connected to New Thought ended up Buddhists, Bahais, or followers of the Swami Ramakrishna. But not all of New Thought was evanescent; its influence can be readily seen in the New Age, self-help, and positive-thinking movements of today.[51] Where New Thought mattered most, however, was arguably not outside the churches but within them. For in response to the growth of New Thought and Christian Science, many church groups such as the Emmanuel movement (named after Boston's Emmanuel Episcopal Church) strove hard to colonize mind cure, inner-healing, and other psychotherapeutic techniques.[52]

One reason churches had for becoming mental healers was philanthropic. After all, explained Emmanuel movement founder Elwood Worcester, hard-core neurasthenic cases, while impervious to President Roosevelt's "loud roar for the Strenuous Life," often succumbed to the "gentle voices" of caring church psychologists.[53] Nor was this all, observed Worcester's colleague, the Reverend Lyman Powell. For in addition to curing "queer" women of their neuroses, church psychology forestalled their desertion to Christian Science: "the Methodism of the Twentieth Century."[54]

Emulating Christian Science, however, was not universally thought to be the best means of keeping women in church. One fashionable New York minister wrote that the surest way whereby women might be kept from the "grotesque folly" of abandoning Christianity lay in convincing them that Jesus "has done more for woman than all the other men who have ever lived."[55] Another means of keeping women orthodox was not mental but physical, argued New York educator Frances Kellor. Sports cured women of the "nervousness, morbidity and . . . introspection" upon which "religious cults" were based.[56]

Finally (and most persuasively) those opposed to Eddy urged potential Christian Scientists not to forget social service. "If there is no such thing as poverty or sickness, then, of course, we are not called upon to give any of our money to maintain homes, hospitals, [or] relief societies," wrote the Reverend Charles Brown on the lack of Christian Science charities. "But it is untrue," he continued; "it is a 'false claim' which is leading scores of confused and undiscriminating people to become complacent, self-centered, self-satisfied, morally indifferent to the stern needs about them. Sin is a fact . . . Crime is a fact . . . Poverty is a fact; a hard, bitter, unyielding fact . . . [that we] cannot scare . . . away with big, unmeaning words, or by any silly pretense that it does not exist."[57]

Brown's critique of Eddy enjoyed considerable support among Social Gospel men. But female Progressives also questioned the compatibility of Christian Science and world reformation.[58] In particular, objections to gnostic "complacency" flourished within the Young Women's Christian Association, a body prepared not to sit but to serve.

The YWCA

To say that the YWCA and Christian Science were dissimilar is an understatement. The two not only differed with regard to the Social Gospel; they also had contrasting views of the body, Christ, and the existence of suffering. Still, Christian Science and the YWCA did have at least two things in common: a commitment to women and the time of their emergence, in the latter half of the nineteenth century.

The YWCA began in 1855. That year two Englishwomen, Miss Emma Robarts and the Hon. Mrs. Arthur Kinnaird, established two women's groups: Miss Robarts's "Prayer Union" and Mrs. Kinnaird's "General Female Training Institute." These groups were charitable in purpose and evangelical in theology; and in 1877 they merged, becoming the Young Women's Christian Association (a name first adopted in 1859 by the Prayer Union to complement the already existent Young Men's Christian Association).[59]

Meanwhile, independent steps were being taken toward the formation of an American YWCA. The first of these came in 1858 when Mrs. Marshall Roberts formed the Union Prayer Circle (later a YWCA) in New York City. Eight years later, the wife of Wellesley College founder Henry Durant started the Boston YWCA (the first in America to be so named). Soon there existed twenty-eight such groups in the United States and Canada (most of them in Eastern cities), and in 1877 they were brought under the governance of what later became the International Board of Womens' and Young Women's Christian Associations (W/YWCAs).[60]

Though founded by well-to-do philanthropists, the W/YWCA—with its boarding homes, libraries, and sewing schools—was an important force in the lives of working-class women. Such women brought its membership up to 8,604 in 1875.[61] At this point, the W/YWCA was almost entirely white. Philadelphians formed the first African-American Association in 1870, Daytonians formed the second African-American Association in 1893, and by World War I the

YWCA was the largest multiracial women's organization in America. But despite its strides toward racial inclusivity, the Association, like most other white-led institutions in America, excluded African-Americans from leadership positions and practiced racial segregation, especially in the South, until well after World War I.[62]

Like their city cousins in the W/YWCA, members of student YWCAs tolerated racial segregation in the decades before World War I. But unlike the first W/YWCAs, student YWCAs (the first of which appeared in 1873 at the state university at Normal, Illinois) were not the creations of wealthy women. Instead, they owed their birth largely to traveling YMCA secretaries, who believed it important that women collegians form prayer groups separate from men. As a result of this parentage, student YWCAs often resembled more the YMCA than the W/YWCA with regard to theology, membership requirements, and athletic policies.[63]

The main difference between the student YWCAs (which by 1885 had coalesced into seven midwestern state committees) and the larger W/YWCA was the fact that the student YWCAs were strictly evangelical whereas the W/YWCA admitted Unitarians and on occasion even Catholics. But other differences, such as age and geography, also split the two groups; and in 1885 these differences worked to derail a proposed W/YWCA–student YWCA merger.[64]

Prevented from joining the W/YWCA, student Associations voted in 1886 to create their own governing body: the American (later the International) Committee of YWCAs. This body grew quickly (from 129 Associations in 1887 to 307 in 1893) and in many ways its dynamism eclipsed that of the more genteel W/YWCA.[65] One area in which the students were especially active was missions. When John Mott took charge of the Student Volunteer Movement, for example, it was not the W/YWCA but the American YWCA whom he asked for help. And in 1898 it was the American YWCA that, in conjunction with various European YWCAs, arranged for the creation of a world YWCA.[66]

Such initiatives finally convinced the W/YWCA that it had better join forces with the students. And in 1908 it did, forming the 186,330-member YWCA of the USA: a group soon to be characterized less by personal evangelism than by attempts to Christianize the social order.[67] The united Association's first big project was the creation in 1908 of a women's professional institute: the National

Training School in New York City. This school, whose short-lived predecessors had included the International Association School and the Institute at Chicago, worked to train YWCA secretaries and to acquaint them with what Rebecca Morse (sister of YMCA General Secretary Richard Morse) called the four aspects of a woman's nature: physical, social, educational, and spiritual.[68] In addition, YWCA education covered a fifth aspect of female life, the "business" aspect. After all, Morse explained, women no longer had to stay at home. Instead, they faced unprecedented "business opportunities," opportunities that YWCA training would enable them to pursue.[69]

Many of these opportunities emanated from within the YWCA, which was one of the first institutions to employ salaried women professionals and to give women leadership roles in finance, religion, and management.[70] But the Association did not merely aim to hire women professionals; it also strove to improve such things as the female body. This "temple of the holy spirit" was always in need of maintenance, argued Minneapolis secretary Abbie Mayhew, who believed that it was the "high calling" of YWCA physical trainers to transform the body into "the willing servant . . . of the soul."[71]

Beliefs such as Mayhew's had not always been common. Most early YWCAs did not offer physical training at all. And of those that did, many regarded it simply as a "snare" whereby women were caught and made to take such comparatively "elevated" subjects as religion and Bible study.[72] Those were "dark" days, wrote Kansas City secretary Mary Dunn in 1895; but fortunately they had ended. And while many girls and women were still deaf to "the 'good tidings of great joy,' the gospel of the body," the YWCA at least understood that "city evangelization, home and foreign missions, teaching, business positions that young women hold, domestic duties (these are not put last because they are lowest, but just to cap the climax, as home is nearest heaven), all these demand thousands, yes, millions of women, with hearts physically strong, to pump pure blood through religiously cared-for bodies."[73]

Dunn's faith in the ability of strong women to effect change was widely shared among YWCA physical educators. But her wish that physical training apply to girls as well as to young women proved less popular. In fact, many YWCAs foreswore junior work on the grounds that their clientele resented "find[ing] the rooms full of little girls."[74]

Many women initially preferred that the "Y" not take up girls' work because they did not want the organization to make them mothers. Instead, they wanted it to give them careers. But this attitude, while prevalent, was wrong, argued M. Louise Slater of the Battle Creek YWCA. For without YWCA intervention, many girls would go astray and never "accept the Lord Jesus as Savior."[75]

Keeping girls from perdition was a powerful injunction, and in 1881 the Oakland, California, "Y" responded by forming the first YWCA junior branch. Thirty-two years later, a YWCA Girls' Department was formed; and in 1918 this was eclipsed by the Girl Reserve movement, the first "unified movement within the National YWCA for work with girls."[76] The YWCA's greatest contribution to girls' work, however, was arguably not the Girl Reserve movement. Instead it was their support for the Girl Scouts and the Camp Fire Girls, two organizations pledged to save the girl, if not from hell, at least from abnormality.

Saving the Girl

The story of the birth and spread of the Girl Scouts and the Camp Fire Girls (CFG) is complex, and it involves a colorful array of people and institutions. Yet in spite of their divergent backgrounds, both the Girl Scouts and the CFG drew strength from one simple premise: the idea that girls as well as boys needed to experience "the out-of-door habit, and the out-of-door spirit."[77]

The notion that girls deserved fully to participate in the Strenuous Life had not always been popular. In fact, girls' camps postdated boys' by almost thirty years. And while the first YWCA camp went up in 1874, it catered not to girls but to women, specifically "tired young women wearing out their lives in an almost endless drudgery for wages."[78]

Tired workers may have been obvious targets for female camping. But they did not long remain the only female campers. For around 1900 the Girls' Friendly Society (Episcopal), the YWCA, and other girls' workers began to ask whether camps might also uplift girls whose wealth had made them "cold-hearted . . . persons" prone to "vicious displays of vanity."[79]

Another justification for girls' camps derived from recapitulation theory (see Chapter 4), the belief that an individual's development paralleled that of the race. Just as boys' groups enabled boys to pass through their "primitive" period, explained one YWCA secretary, girls' groups enabled girls to pass through their "feudal" stage, the one during which they were most apt to learn marriage and mothering skills.[80]

Finally, girls' camps were linked to the betterment of humanity. "It was our [generation's] task to organize the great world of industry," explained Luther Gulick to the Camp Fire Girls in 1914. But it remained for girl campers "to develop wholesome social life so that it shall reach out and dominate the entire community."[81]

Gulick's rhetoric and that of other girls' workers was certainly expansive. But words alone did not build girls' camps; that took money, time, and effort. And here no one contributed more than the Gulicks and the Farnsworths, interrelated missionary families and pioneers in the field of girls' camping.

The first Gulick girls' camp (located in Fairlee, Vermont, and named Camp Aloha in honor of the Gulicks' missionary experience in Hawaii) was founded in 1905 by Luther Gulick's sister-in-law, Mrs. E. L. Gulick. The Farnsworth girls' camps (located in Thetford, Vermont, and named the Hanoum Camps in honor of the Farnsworths' missionary experience in Turkey) were founded in 1909 by Mrs. E. L. Gulick's brother and his wife, Dr. and Mrs. C. H. Farnsworth. But undoubtedly the most famous of the Gulick-related camps was Camp Sebago-Wohelo, the birthplace of the Camp Fire Girls.[82]

Founded in 1908 and located on Sebago Lake, Maine, Camp Sebago-Wohelo was the joint creation of Luther Gulick and his wife, Charlotte Vetter Gulick. Luther Gulick was highly enthusiastic about his family's new project. But since most of his time was spent directing the Child Hygiene Department of the Russell Sage Foundation, the actual administration of Camp Sebago-Wohelo fell to Charlotte Gulick, who later became the first president of the National Association of Directors of Girls' Camps.[83]

Charlotte Gulick was well prepared for camp management. Not only had she learned child psychology from G. Stanley Hall and fire-making from American Boy Scout co-founder Ernest Thompson Seton; she had also studied medicine back when it looked as if her husband would become an overseas missionary. These studies served Mrs. Gulick particularly well during the summer of 1910, when she drew on her knowledge of psychology and Indian lore to create the acronym "WoHeLo": the watchword of the Camp Fire Girls and the basis of their sacred Work-Health-Love ceremony.[84]

Another milestone from the summer of 1910 took place in Thetford, Vermont, the home of Charlotte Gulick's friend, Mrs. C. H. Farnsworth. Mrs. Farnsworth had asked William Langdon (the consultant on pageantry in Gulick's department at the Russell Sage Foundation) to organize the Thetford boys and girls in preparation for the town's 150th anniversary festival. But when Langdon arrived, he found that there was no girls' club with which he could work.

Chagrined by this absence, Langdon formed his own club, which he named the Camp Fire Girls. He also created the three CFG levels of achievement: Wood Gatherer (denoted by two crossed logs and a ring), Fire Maker (denoted by two crossed logs on fire and a bracelet), and Torch Bearer (denoted by two hotly flaming crossed logs and a pin).[85] Langdon believed his Camp Fire Girls idea to be a good one, and upon returning to New York City in the fall of 1910 he asked Luther Gulick to take charge of the plan. At first Gulick demurred, citing overwork. But then it occurred to him that the Camp Fire Girls might do "for the girls [nationally] what the Boy Scout movement is designed to do for boys."[86]

Aflame now with missionary zeal, Gulick petitioned for time off from the Russell Sage Foundation in order to work actively on behalf of the Camp Fire Girls. He also garnered support for the movement from such influentials as Mrs. Ernest T. Seton (wife of the "Chief Scout of America"), Boy Scout president James West, Playground Association of America secretary Howard Braucher, and YWCA secretaries Bertha Seely and Anna Brown. These individuals generally agreed with Gulick that girls' character needed help. On March 22, 1911, they were all in attendance at the Horace Mann School in New York City to hear him explain how the Camp Fire Girls could provide that help "and do it pretty quickly." The chief thing, Gulick averred, was for the Camp Fire Girls *not* to be like the Boy Scouts. For the Camp Fire Girls "to copy the Boy Scout movement would be utterly and fundamentally evil," he explained, "and would probably produce ultimately a moral and psychological involution which is the last thing in the world that any of us want."[87]

Gulick also urged the Camp Fire Girls to avoid an overtly Christian identity. "Some general recognition of the Great Spirit" was desirable, he allowed, but in order to have widespread appeal, "the national movement must not be religious."[88] Nor was the CFG fire a "wild fire," he asserted. Instead, it was a "domestic fire," signifying that the overall purpose of the Camp Fire Girls was to reacquaint girls with the duties of womanhood—marital, maternal, and domestic.[89]

Gulick's wish for the Camp Fire Girls ultimately to shore up the home did not appeal to Mrs. Ernest T. Seton. She feared that the new organization would end up simply giving out badges for cooking and cleaning; she wanted it to include more emphasis on competition and feats of strength. As a result, when illness temporarily forced Gulick to leave New York City and abandon the CFG idea during the summer of 1911, Mrs. Seton and her allies reworked his plans to create the short-lived Girl Pioneers of America, an organization dismissed by critics as "too masculine" and unreflective of essential boy-girl differences.[90]

The Girl Pioneers may not have succeeded, but the need to "get [girls] out of doors" remained too great to ignore.[91] Thus when Dr. and Mrs. Gulick—known by now to their campers as Timanous ("Guiding Spirit") and Hiiteni ("Life More Abundant")—returned to New York City in the fall of 1911, they sought, with the help of the YWCA, the Boy Scouts, and the Russell Sage Foundation, to revive the Camp Fire Girls and to make it into a national movement.[92] Their efforts paid off on March 15, 1912, when Charlotte Gulick signed the Camp Fire Girls' incorporation papers. Two years later the new club had 60,000 members, most of whom were white Protestants.[93] Blacks, Catholics, and Jews were invited to sit around some campfires, particularly northern ones, at an early date; but the Camp Fire Girls did not insist on racial and religious inclusivity nationwide until the 1940s.[94]

As soon as the Camp Fire Girls organization was formed, it faced competition from a rival girls' club, the Girl Scouts, the first troop of which was formed in Savannah, Georgia, on March 12, 1912. Like the Camp Fire Girls, the Girl Scouts at first catered mainly to middle-class white girls. An African-American Girl Scout troop was formed as early as 1917, but it was not until 1953 that the Girl Scouts stated definitively that "race, religion, national heritage, or economic status shall be no barrier to membership in the Girl Scout organization."[95] The fact that the Girl Scouts lagged behind the Camp Fire Girls in stressing inclusivity may be explained by regional differences. Unlike the Camp Fire Girls, whose roots were in the comparatively tolerant North, the Girl Scouts were founded in the Jim Crow South by Juliette ("Daisy") Gordon Low, a scion of the Confederacy.[96]

Juliette Low could boast of a colorful past. Twenty-six years before founding the Girl Scouts, she had become an American expatriate by moving from Georgia to England, where she married William Low, an intimate of the Prince of Wales. After much acrimony, The Lows' marriage failed in 1901, leaving Juliette "searching rather desperately," as her biographer put it, for something to do. That something turned out to be Girl Guiding, which Boy Scout founder General Sir Robert Baden-Powell and his sister Agnes Baden-Powell (both of whom were good friends of Mrs. Low) established in 1910.[97]

Juliette Low's first attempt at Girl Guiding occurred at her remote castle in Scotland, where she began in the summer of 1911 to coach the daughters of her neighbors in knot making, first aid, and other Girl Guide fundamentals. Later that year, after heading to London for the fall season, she started up several more Guide companies for the urban poor. These were well enough established by the winter of 1912 for Low to feel secure about visiting America, which she and her friend General Baden-Powell set out to do on January 6, 1912—he bound for New York to speak on behalf of the Boy Scouts, and she bound for her home town of Savannah to acquaint America with the Girl Guides.[98]

But would America accept the Girl Guides? That was the question uppermost in Low's mind, and with reason. After all, not only was Low herself a rather comedic figure (lampooned even by friends for her "ridiculous" Girl Guide hat, tin cup, and whistle);[99] she was also campaigning for an organization that strongly resembled the ill-fated Girl Pioneers, the club derided by developmentalists for its militarism and ignorance of girls' psychology.

Some YWCA secretaries also charged the Girl Guides (or Scouts, as they become known in America) with being too secular. The Girl Scout leader might well have been free, as one Scout official put it, "to meet the religious impulses of her girls by her reverent remarks during their Nature Study, or at any other time when allusion to the subject comes naturally."[100] But this indirect approach was insufficient, as far as many YWCA members were concerned. As a result, the YWCA became divided. Some expressed their enthusiasm for scouting, while the Association as a whole voted in 1918 not to affiliate with the Scouts in part because it believed their God-in-nature philosophy to be less religious than the Indianized Christianity of the Camp Fire Girls.[101]

The YWCA's reluctance fully to embrace Girl Scouts was undoubtedly a blow. But it was a blow from which the Scouts quickly recovered. For the Scouts could draw on assets such as their cheap and durable uniforms, garments far more practical than the Camp Fire Girls'

Indian squaw dress.[102] What really enabled Girl Scouts to succeed, however, was not practicality but World War I, which made the Scouts' militarism look patriotic rather than ungirlish. As a result, Scout troops were formed everywhere during the war, and Girl Scouts were asked to sell bonds, assist nurses, grow produce, entertain troops, and carry messages.[103]

The Girl Scouts' indispensability during World War I was not lost on either the YWCA or the Camp Fire Girls, both of which responded by founding their own girl militias: The CFG Minute Girls and the aforementioned YWCA Girl Reserves. Such militias had scant appeal for "girls who have headaches, tender feet, nerves, indigestion, or who are lazy and eat candy," wrote Luther Gulick. Instead, they attracted capable girls desirous of serving their country in time of war.[104]

Luther Gulick was not alone in viewing World War I as an important watershed for young women. Other advocates of strenuous womanhood agreed that the war was a test, and they wondered how their girls would respond. Would the demands of war prove too difficult, forcing women into a state of dependency and jangled nerves, or would years of hiking, canoeing, and outdoor camping with the YWCA, the Girl Scouts, and the Camp Fire Girls pay off, enabling women to provide efficient service in American factories and European hospitals? As it turned out, the character builders need not have worried. Women affiliated with the YWCA and other muscular Christian groups proved themselves vital to the war effort by driving ambulances, nursing soldiers, and doing their best in other ways to "make the world safe for democracy." Such services were rewarded at the end of the war by the ratification in 1920 of the Nineteenth Amendment, which gave women the right to vote nationally and acknowledged their substantial contributions to the Allied cause. But women alone were not responsible for toppling the German kaiser. That task required men as well as women, and it involved a host of Protestant wartime agencies, as described in the next chapter.

CHAPTER SEVEN

Christians in Khaki

Then it was that I saw Heaven opened and beheld One called
Faithful and True. He was no longer mounted on a white
horse, to be sure, nor arrayed in a white garment sprinkled
with blood nor was He armed with a sharp sword to smite.
Rather I discerned through clouds of gas and smoke One on
foot arrayed in a garb of olive drab which was stained with
blood and mire, and in His hands a bayonet sword attached
to a rifle.

—FROM A YMCA WAR WORK MANUAL (1918)

When America declared war against Germany on April 6, 1917, the
country's mainline Protestant groups by and large responded with
alacrity. Particularly eager to be of service were, in addition to the
YM- and YWCA, the Federal Council of Churches, the American Bible Society, the Home Missions Council, the Council of Women for
Home Missions, the Foreign Missions Conference of North America,
the Federation of Women's Boards of Foreign Missions in the United
States, and the World Alliance for Promoting International Friendship
through the Churches. These groups no doubt feared that the war
would be fraught with suffering. But when their representatives met
in Washington, D.C., on May 8, 1917, to coordinate Protestant
America's wartime activities, Oberlin president Henry Churchill King
urged the assembled delegates to have faith in the nation and its ability to create "a new epoch in the kingdom of God on earth."[1]

Most mainline Protestant leaders apparently joined King in viewing
the Great War as an opportunity to redeem the world by force. But
this stance fell out of favor in postwar religious circles to such an extent that even the YMCA (which had managed most of the U.S. Army
canteen) confessed to having been guilty during wartime of "shallow"
naïveté and "hopelessly unrealistic" optimism.[2] As YMCA General
Secretary Sherwood Eddy concluded in 1924, "the war to end war"

had not ended war after all. Instead, It had "settled nothing, made nothing safe, [and] achieved no lasting good commensurate with the awful sacrifices of the whole world."[3]

The Protestant establishment's disillusionment with the Great War paralleled its earlier disillusionment with the Spanish-American War (which Sydney Ahlstrom aptly called a "rehearsal" for the events of 1917–1918).[4] During both wars, ministers wrapped themselves in the flag and championed war as a cure for effeminacy in men. After each of these wars, however, ministers repudiated their support of war, embraced pacifism, and sought to cure effeminacy with "moral equivalents of war," such as boxing. These wild oscillations of opinion with regard to war may be explained in part by the fact that Progressive Era mainline clergymen were simply unable to separate themselves from their culture. Swept along by the spirit of mindless patriotism that prevailed during the Spanish-American War and World War I, ministers apparently forgot the Biblical injunction against equating God with Caesar (Mt. 22:21). As a result, they characterized America's cause as God's cause during wartime and repented of their wartime rhetorical excesses during peacetime, when they became as enthusiastic about peace as they had once been about war.

War and Peace

Clerical paeans to war were never more fulsome than they were during the Spanish-American War of 1898. Billed as an effort to free Spain's last remaining colonies from ignorance and oppression, the war, a "splendid little war" in the estimation of Secretary of State John Hay, appealed to idealistic clergymen and to their parishioners. Among the latter was "Battle Hymn of the Republic" author Julia Ward Howe, who viewed America as a force for good. "God has granted us as a people the supreme grace of rising up from our trade and money-getting at the call of our struggling and suffering neighbors," exclaimed the celebrated abolitionist in response to America's victory over Spain and subsequent expropriation of Puerto Rico, Cuba, and the Philippines; He wanted the nation "to make whole races free with the freedom of the nineteenth century, the freedom of intelligent thought, of just institutions, [and] of reasonable religion."[5]

Howe's vision of an enlightened America striving to promote world uplift enjoyed widespread support in the 1890s. It was especially appealing to a believer in Manifest Destiny and Anglo-Saxon pride like Luther Gulick's older brother, the Reverend Sidney Gulick, a Congregationalist missionary to Japan. "By the civilization which God has given and is still giving to those nations which have adopted Christianity . . . it is evident that He intends that these Christian nations shall have the predominant and moulding influence in the world," he reasoned. And since the foremost Christian powers happened to be "Protestant Germany," "Puritan England," and "Anglo America," it appeared as if God were uniquely fond of "the type of religion and civilization attained by the Anglo Saxon race."[6]

That God countenanced Anglo-Saxon Christian rule seemed clear to Sidney Gulick, who like many fin de siècle clerics viewed temporal power as divinely ordained. But while Gulick and other exponents of "imperial theology" celebrated Protestant expansionism, they generally refused (prior to the sinking of the Battleship *Maine,* at least) to advocate conversion by force. World uplift would not be achieved through conventional warfare, explained General Oliver Howard in 1896. Instead, it would be brought about by "spiritual contests" and by the use of "weapons [that] pierce the soul, yet shed no blood."[7]

Convinced like Howard that the Christian conquest of the world was to be achieved peaceably and through spiritual means, many Protestant journals at first upheld President McKinley in his efforts to avert war with Spain over Cuban independence. "The President should be sustained," declared the *Congregationalist* in an April 7, 1898, editorial. For there existed no glory in "defeating a nation [Spain] . . . with a splendid past, that more than once has befriended us, and is now so weak that its pride is all that is left for us to conquer."[8]

Protestant "Mugwumps" (antimilitarists) continued to voice objections to war despite attacks on their manhood by imperialists in Congress and the press. But following the country's declaration of war against Spain on April 25, 1898, most churchmen quickly joined the patriotic throng. "The churches have tried their best to avert war," declared the *Congregationalist* on May 5, 1898. But now that war was upon them, they were busily "drap[ing flags] from pulpits and float[ing them] from steeples" in order to prove that "the Church of God is not emasculated as some would have us think."[9]

Belief that the war would revive the strength of Anglo Christian manhood was particularly prevalent among critics of "overcivilization" such as the *Outlook,* which declared that men needed the "high adventure" of "splendid combat" in order to avoid being "diverted into narrow channels and directed to mean ambitions." Also struck by the restorative power of war was YMCA columnist the Reverend Dr. Frank Crane, who regarded "the sudden growth of the tremendous war spirit in America" with glee. "It's been a generation since we let blood," wrote Crane (who, like many ultramilitarists, was too young to have experienced the horrors of Civil War combat); and "now we feel the old Anglo Saxon passion to go out and kill somebody."[10]

Crane's celebration of the war as an Anglo-Saxon revival was not, of course, reflective of American Protestants as a whole, most of whom viewed the war not as a blood fest but as a chance, as one missionary journal put it, to extend the Gospel and to save "the non-Christian world from the oppression and death which everywhere accompany the tyrannical rule of the devil and his subjects."[11] Even black ministers (a majority of whom were suspicious of the war's Anglophilic overtones) occasionally praised imperialism's missionary potential, reasoning as did African Methodist Episcopal Bishop W. J. Gaines that Spanish colonists "are like us a colored people" and therefore likely to welcome American black missionaries and settlers."[12]

But were Cubans, Puerto Ricans, and Filipinos in fact "heathens" who represented, as one Methodist missionary put it, "a field ripe unto harvest for direct evangelism"?[13] The Catholic Church thought not. After all, it argued, Spanish friars had worked among the islanders for centuries and had already successfully converted large numbers to Christianity. Protestant reformers acknowledged Spanish missionary efforts, but argued that the Old World type of Christianity imposed by Spain was too "rotten" and "fanatic[al]" to attract nonbelievers.[14] Some went further, seeing war against Spain as a chance to rid the hemisphere of Roman Catholic influence. "It was a fight between the American school house against the Spanish monastery," explained one Presbyterian minister, the goal being to overcome "the medievalism of a decayed and dying despotism."[15]

Talk of saving blacks and Latinos from papal domination was nothing new. But missionary historian Andrew Ross argues that the beliefs underlying such talk had changed considerably since the mid-1800s. Whereas early Victorian missionaries had expressed faith in the power of reason alone to transform nonwhites into full-fledged liberal Protestants, he avers, late Victorian missionaries often gathered from the scientific racism that they were exposed to in college that nonwhites were innately inferior and therefore incapable of adjudging advanced ideas.[16]

Accompanying this rise in scientific racism among missionaries (not to mention academics and other professionals) came a strong sense of paternalism. Where reformers had once encouraged Asians and Latin Americans to establish independent democracies, they now talked of "the white man's burden" and the incapacity of nonwhites for self-government. "God has put us in the Philippine Islands in order that, with England, we may become the world's peace keepers, and the protectors and guardians of the awakening Oriental nations," explained the Reverend George Pentecost in response to America's 1898 conquest of the Philippines. For the Filipinos "are no more fit to govern themselves than at present the Cubans are to govern themselves; than the negroes of the South are fit to govern the Southern States."[17]

The idea that white Americans should aid in the uplift of those whom Theodore Roosevelt called "our little brown brothers" had few detractors.[18] But some ministers questioned whether this uplift should come at the point of a gun. Broadway Tabernacle Congregationalist minister Charles Jefferson, for example, lamented in 1898 that "the spirit of conquest is in the air" and that many formerly peace-loving Americans had adopted "that proud and fatal phrase, 'Imperial America.'"[19]

Doubts such as Jefferson's regarding the purity of America's wartime aims were highly controversial. Most ministers hastened to combine whatever criticism they had of the war with praise for the military's altruistic goals. Even Washington Gladden (who was widely censured later for his opposition to World War I) expressed confidence that "the Nation can be trusted to distinguish between philanthropy and piracy" and that the United States wished only "to lift [the Cubans] up and lead them on into larger liberty and more abundant life."[20]

Reports from the Philippines, however, suggested that America's military operations were not quite as beneficent as Gladden supposed. Especially troubling to reformers were tales (later proved true) that in response to Emilio Aguinaldo's anti-American Filipino independence movement, certain U.S. officers were ordering the burning of villages and the killing and torturing of villagers in an attempt to crush Aguinaldo and his insurrectionary troops.[21]

That U.S. soldiers could be guilty of barbarism supposedly restricted to the "lower races" was an appalling thought. And many such as *Outlook* editor the Reverend Lyman Abbott (who kept military atrocity stories from appearing in his journal) simply refused to believe it. Besides, argued the *Advance* (a Congregationalist organ), even if individual U.S. soldiers had committed acts of cruelty in the Philippines, it was clear from the Boxer rebels' massacre of U.S. missionaries in China that "a show of force is the only argument which appeals to an Oriental mind."[22]

Taking the Filipino mind by force may have appealed to the *Advance* and the *Outlook* (whose editor, Lyman Abbott, had informed the 1899 International Congregational Council meeting in Boston that armies representing force must precede the establishment of Christian peace in foreign lands). But to an interdenominational group of Boston ministers meeting in 1902 to protest violence in the Philippines, the argument that progress excused carnage was anathema. "A war begun in the interests of humanity has passed into a war of conquest," summed up one meeting speaker, largely because "of a fancied race superiority that it is imagined gives us a right to ride rough-shod over men and women as truly the children of one Eternal Father as we ourselves."[23]

Doubts about the morality of war did not emanate from Boston's clergy alone. Other intellectuals also began to question imperialism, and with it the belief in war as a corrective for "overcivilization."[24] Especially dubious with regard to the supposed moral and therapeutic benefits of war was Harvard philosopher William James, who in an open letter dated April 15, 1899, speculated that arch-imperialist Theodore Roosevelt viewed war as "the ideal condition of human society" simply because he was "still mentally in the Sturm and Drang period of early adolescence."[25]

The fact that militarists such as Roosevelt viewed war as an essential part of the Strenuous Life was certainly regrettable, agreed *Atlantic* writer Goldwin Smith. But it was not only militarists who glorified war; it was also those pastors who in their haste to reverse "the softening of manners made during the century" had forgotten "the religion of mild and philanthropic virtue" and were instead preaching "the use of war as a moral medicine for the state."[26]

In response to such criticism, many clergymen conceded that they had indeed been wrong to view America's victory over Spain as an expression of Anglo-Saxon cultural vitality. Sidney Gulick, in particular, ceased to preach crusading Anglo-Saxonism during the early 1900s, and instead became one of the country's foremost exponents of peace and racial tolerance. "The scourge of war has disclosed the brutal, degrading character of militarism," he declared in his 1915 work, *The Fight for Peace*. And "in proportion as militarism prospers do civilization and religion vanish and human values disappear."[27]

Gulick's conversion to pacifism, while especially dramatic, was hardly unique. According to John Dewey, the "bad aftertaste" left over from the Spanish-American War gave people a deep hunger for peace. Indeed, added the philosopher, "I doubt if any propaganda has ever been carried on with greater persistence or with greater success— so far as affecting feelings was concerned—than that for peace during the decade prior to 1914. The times were so ripe that the movement hardly had to be pushed."[28]

Evidence of the country's shift toward pacifism came in a variety of forms. These included U.S. participation in the two Hague peace conferences of 1899 and 1907, the public schools' observance of "Peace Day" on May 18 (the date of the first Hague conference), the churches' observance of "Peace Sunday" on the Sunday nearest May 18,[29] and the 1912 inclusion within Theodore Roosevelt's Bull Moose Party of a peace plank, which lamented "the survival in our civilization of the barbaric system of warfare among nations" and called for the settling of disputes by civil means.[30]

Pacifism also flourished within the thirty-odd peace societies that either sprang up or gained new life in the years between the Spanish-American War and World War I. Chief among these groups was the Church Peace Union (CPU), which Andrew Carnegie founded in 1914 with a gift of $2 million. Composed of religious notables such as John R. Mott of the YMCA, the CPU was asked by Carnegie to encourage the arbitration of international disputes, with the aim of preventing the barbaric "killing of man by man in battle." Carnegie also stipulated with the confidence of a true Progressive that after war had been "abolished," the CPU's money should be used "to relieve the deserving poor."[31]

Carnegie's generosity enabled the CPU to become a force in the peace movement. But it was not just the CPU that led in that movement; it was also the Protestant churches, most of which declared before World War I that they were in favor of international arbitration. Among the first churches to endorse peace (aside from historic peace churches such as the Quakers) were the Congregationalists, who called in 1904 for the establishment of a regular international congress, or league of nations. The Northern Presbyterians also came out early in support of peace, declaring in 1907 that "the forces of this world should be organized for and in the interest of peace, and not for and in the interests of war."[32]

With various Protestant denominations calling for peace, it was not long before their representative body, the Federal Council of Churches (FCC), did so as well. At its first meeting, in 1908, the FCC voted to "awaken the public conscience and create a universal demand for the abolition of war." Three years later, the council again acted in the interest of peace by establishing a Commission on Peace and Arbitration, one of whose members, the Reverend Frederick Lynch, went on to become the first head of the Church Peace Union.[33]

The FCC's commitment to international peace (which some, including John Dewey, cynically viewed as an avoidance of national economic problems)[34] was intense. But even at the height of the peace movement, neither the FCC nor the CPU entirely forgot the old muscular Christian adage that war begat manly character. As a result, at least one CPU trustee felt compelled to explain that pacifists were no less manly than militarists, as evidenced by the fact that Jesus had been both a "pacifist" and a "man of the out-of-doors."[35]

That pacifists were as manly as militarists seemed clear not only to churchmen but also to William James. Pacifists did not condemn war for its "manly" and valorous qualities, confirmed the veteran anti-imperialist in his famous 1910 essay, "The Moral Equivalent of War." Instead, they objected to its senseless "monstrosity."[36]

As for whether "manliness" and "discipline" could be achieved without resorting to war, James believed that they could, but only if America instituted some type of universal peacetime service. After all, he argued, sending all young men

to coal and iron mines, to freight trains, to fishing fleets in December, to dishwashing, clothes-washing, and window-washing, to road-building and tunnel-making, to foundries and stoke-holes, and to the frames of skyscrapers, would . . . get the childishness knocked out of them, and [would enable them] to come back into society with healthier sympathies and soberer ideas. They would have paid their blood-tax, done their own part in the immemorial human warfare against nature, they would tread the earth more proudly, the women would value them more highly, they would be better fathers and teachers of the following generation.[37]

The fact that such an eminent philosopher as James could seriously envision the achievement of strength through peaceful means encouraged other pacifists to propose their own "moral equivalents of war." These included Boy Scouting (as ennobling as universal service but eminently more practical),[38] settlement house work, physical education, and even pugilism, which one YMCA official described as "positive righteousness physically expressed."[39]

Another morally superior alternative to war was the playground, averred Pittsburgh Playground Association superintendent George Johnson, and in particular the "manly" sports and games that were played there. For "play preserves, purifies, perpetuates, the martial capacities, while it diminishes the belligerent spirit," he explained. "For pure achievement of endurance, for plucky continuation in fatigue, I do not know that war can surpass the foot races."[40]

Not all pacifists, of course, were as optimistic as Johnson about the possibility of transferring human aggression from the battlefield to the playground. But the near universality of pro-peace sentiment coupled with an eruption of international treaties of arbitration (ninety-six of which were signed between 1900 and 1910)[41] convinced many that the abolition of war was finally at hand. "It looks as though this were going to be the age of treaties rather than the age of wars, the century of reason rather than the century of force," exclaimed the Reverend Dr. Frederick Lynch in 1911. And "the one word that is upon all men's lips today is the brotherhood of man."[42]

To celebrate the imminence of "a warless world," Lynch and his colleagues in the CPU and the FCC arranged with church leaders worldwide to hold an international church peace conference in Constance, Switzerland. The conference was scheduled for August 1914 (the hundredth anniversary of the Treaty of Ghent); but as this date approached, European and American conferees began debating whether it ought to be postponed. For many of the Europeans, it seemed advisable to reschedule the conference in light of rising international tensions. But to the Americans, whose arguments in favor of going ahead with the conference ultimately won out, the gravity of the international situation was vastly overrated. Besides, argued FCC secretary Charles Macfarland (a conference delegate), "we followed the tenets of the liberal school, which counted on moral progress and the essential goodness of human nature to help us overcome any serious difficulties that might threaten."[43]

War against War

When the Constance Peace Conference convened on the evening of August 1, 1914, the world stood poised on the brink of war. That very morning Germany had declared war on Russia over events in the Balkans, and it appeared likely that other countries would soon join the fray. But despite the deepening crisis, many of the ninety-odd delegates (thirty-five Americans, sixteen Britons, and representatives from eleven other nations) who managed to attend the Constance Conference still clung to the belief that peace could be restored and that "war could not be carried on in the Twentieth Century."[44]

The peacemakers' hopes, however, were dashed on August 3, 1914. That was the day when Germany (with complete disregard for the Constance conferees' August 2 call for the "Christian rulers" of Europe and America "to avert war between millions of men amongst whom friendship and common interest have been steadily growing") declared war on France and prepared to invade Belgium. It was also the day when the peace delegates, yielding finally to entreaties from the mayor of Constance for them to disband, began an arduous trek across war-torn Europe to London, where they reassembled to form what later became the World Alliance for Promoting International Friendship through the Churches.[45]

After helping to create the Alliance, the CPU delegates to the Constance Conference returned home, confident that in America at least peace and neutrality would be maintained. But although they were right about most Americans wanting peace, they soon encountered stiff opposition from advocates of "preparedness" such as the American Defense Society, the National Security League, and the American Legion, all of which argued that America had best be prepared to help England and France in their fight against Germany.[46]

At the head of the preparedness movement was American Legion president Theodore Roosevelt, who by 1916 was referring to pacifists as "active agents of the devil." "Professional pacifists [think they are] serving God," fumed the aging Rough Rider. But in fact their "silly resolutions" not only kept the United States from waging "righteous" war against the kaiser; they also gave comfort to "Pro-German" immigrants, selfish industrialists, effete intellectuals, and other "Anti-American[s]" whom Roosevelt considered "not fit to cumber the world."[47]

As for the commonly held view that Jesus himself had been a pacifist, Roosevelt denied it utterly. "When the Saviour saw the money-changers in the Temple [he did not keep] quiet in the presence of wrong," the ex-President declared. Instead, "the Saviour armed himself with a scourge of cords and drove the money-changers from the Temple," illustrating for all time that peace could not be maintained "at the expense of righteousness."[48]

Roosevelt's call to arms did not have much effect on committed pacifists within the FCC and the CPU. But other ministers (particularly those belonging to denominations of English descent) began increasingly to sanction preparedness.[49] It was not only the need to relieve Belgium that made war attractive, they argued; it was also war's nobility and romance, qualities that were especially evident in Donald Hankey's *A Student in Arms,* a 1915 British account of army chaplaincy that was highly popular on both sides of the Atlantic.

The fact that even clergymen were beginning to endorse war caused the peace community to react in different ways. For some, such as Unitarian minister John Haynes Holmes (a founder of the NAACP and the ACLU), the imminence of war called for an ever more militant pacifism. America had no need to defend itself militarily even if "Germany came here to-day as she came to Belgium yesterday," declared Holmes in 1916. For America's "faith in brotherhood and democracy" was stronger than "the sword and shield" and would inevitably "conquer" the German invaders.[50]

Holmes's touching faith in the transformative power of American liberalism was common among pacifists. But many had doubts about Germany's succumbing to liberalism alone. Among such doubters were Washington Gladden, Shailer Mathews, and Alexander Graham Bell, all of whom joined together on June 17, 1915, with militarists such as Lyman Abbott and William Howard Taft (the group's leader) to form the League to Enforce Peace: a bipartisan organization committed, as one member put it, to "the enthronement of reason, if necessary, by force."[51]

But was peace through force the only answer? A majority of religious pacifists thought not. Nor did they countenance Holmes's notion of complete nonresistance. Instead, these mainstream pacifists tried various means of simply keeping America out of the war. These included getting President Wilson to set aside Sunday, October 14, 1914, as a day of prayer for peace; and conducting antiwar polls, one of which revealed that out of 10,000 ministers questioned in January 1915, fully 95 percent opposed an increase in U.S. armaments.[52]

The pacifists' efforts on behalf of neutrality were not without success, as evidenced by the fact that President Wilson won reelection to the presidency with the slogan "He kept us out of war." But despite such triumphs, the public was becoming increasingly incensed by Germany's behavior in Belgium and by its sinking of English passenger liners. These and similar atrocities weakened people's commitment to pacifism. By the winter of 1916, 151 of the 165 ministers who responded to a poll conducted by the New York Federation of Churches expressed support for preparedness.[53]

The move toward war received an additional boost on January 17, 1917, when Germany declared certain waters off-limits to American shipping. Six weeks later, the public learned of the Zimmermann note, which revealed Germany's plans for a German-Mexican alliance against the United States. These developments finally resulted in a congressional declaration of war against Germany. And the fact that this declaration occurred on Good Friday led many ministers to liken America's war against Germany on behalf of humanity with Christ's suffering for humanity and death on the cross.[54]

That the clergy's acquiescence in World War I made sense politically would be hard to deny. But it is equally clear that this acquiescence placed Protestant leaders in an awkward position. For years they had argued in accordance with liberal theology that original sin could be expunged, that moral equivalents such as playgrounds could easily be found for war, and that the mission of the churches was to extend God's kingdom on earth. Now, however, they were faced with having to admit that sin—at least on the part of Germany—was deeply ingrained, that strenuous sports were only "temporary schemes for checking the passion of militarism,"[55] and that the churches were unable to legislate human suffering out of existence.

To make such admissions was far from easy. Indeed, it came perilously close to declaring that liberal Protestantism was intellectually
bankrupt. And while intellectuals such as President Emeritus Charles
W. Eliot of Harvard had no problem with viewing the war as indicative of Christianity's failure,[56] most clergymen shrank from abandoning the notion of Christian perfectionism. The war did not disprove
the feasibility of endless peace, they argued; rather it was the means
whereby endless peace would be achieved. Or as President Robert
Speer of the General War-Time Commission of the Churches put it,
the Great War was not a war per se, but a "war against war"—a determined assault against nonprogressive thinking.[57]

By defining World War I as a "war against war," Protestant theologians not only justified the conflict; they also helped turn it into a
Christian crusade. As George Williams noted, it was the last war in
which most Americans believed themselves to be acting in complete
accordance with God's will;[58] prominent ministers variously described
the conflict as "America's holy war,"[59] "a truly holy war,"[60] and a
"twentieth century crusade."[61]

The mainline Protestant belief in the holiness of World War I did
have its detractors, of course. One of the most important of these was
the Catholic Church. Catholics ought not to suppose that they were
fighting to establish a social "utopia" or to "solve every problem of
heaven and earth," declared Boston's William Cardinal O'Connell.
Instead, their wartime service should be "founded on duty and not on
emotion."[62]

The Catholic view of military service as a necessary duty obviously
differed from the Protestant view of it as an uplifting opportunity to
missionize the world. But this did not mean that Catholics overall
were significantly less supportive of the war than Protestants. Indeed,
many Catholics believed that their military service records would
demonstrate conclusively their loyalty to America and the groundless-
ness of anti-Catholic nativism.[63] One priest, Father T. A. Nummey of
Richmond Hill, New York, went so far as to assert that conservative
Catholicism was of more value to America than liberal Protestantism,
considering that "when degenerate men and unnatural women were
preaching race suicide, birth control and other nasty, pernicious doctrines detrimental to the State, our people were fulfilling the sacred
duties of married life; and when you called for soldiers to fight your
battles—whereas these people had nothing to offer you but poodle

dogs, our Catholics are to-day proudly wearing service flags on their breasts with one, two—yes, even four or more stars upon them."[64]

Nummey's praise for Catholic soldiers (who comprised 35 to 40 percent of the U.S. Army)[65] was well founded. But his intimation that liberal reformers contributed nothing to the state but "poodle dogs" was patently unfair, as evidenced by the wartime activities of the Church Peace Union. This organization had initially viewed the Great War as a menace to civilization. But when America entered the war in 1917, the CPU abandoned neutrality and agreed to assist the Creel Commission in distributing pro-war propaganda. It also chose to downplay its name—to operate not as the CPU but as the National Committee on the Churches and the Moral Aims of the War, an organization that declared itself "absolutely loyal to our Government in its prosecution of the war as a righteous effort to make the world safe for democracy."[66]

The CPU's belated acceptance of the war prompted a mixed response. Some welcomed the organization's help in elevating public opinion, while others questioned its trustworthiness. Chief among this latter group was the famous baseball-playing evangelist Billy Sunday. An inveterate foe of pacifism in all its forms, Sunday once got into a fistfight over his characterization of the Germans as "a dirty bunch that would stand aside and allow a Turk to outrage a woman." He also traveled throughout the war preaching patriotism and declaring that "if you turn hell upside down you will find 'Made in Germany' stamped on the bottom."[67]

Not all antipacifists were as colorful as Sunday; nor were they as theologically conservative. Some of pacifism's severest critics were, in fact, religious leftists such as Christian socialist Mercer Green Johnston, who referred to opponents of World War I as "paxomaniacs: or pacifists run mad." He continued, "Of course the ultra-pacifist or paxomaniac will say that it is before the Prince of Peace, and not Pax, that he prostrates himself." But this was clearly nonsense, considering that "the paxomaniac is too lacking in masculinity and veraciousness to be inspired by, and too overloaded with femininity and freakishness to be very acceptable to, the Prince of Peace."[68]

With virulent attacks on pacifism emanating from both left and right, several trustees of the Church Peace Union confessed to having been wrong about preparedness and about the virtues of war. One penitent was Shailer Mathews, the dean of Chicago Divinity School and a former president of the Federal Council of Churches. Before the war "we thought [patriotic] sentiment beneath our dignity," Mathews wrote. But since then it had become clear "that we were not only overcomplacent, but that we were being led astray by an active propaganda conducted by those who wished to keep us in a state of military unpreparedness."[69]

Mathews's repudiation of his peace movement colleagues appears rather craven today. But his stance is understandable in light of what happened to such unrepentant pacifists as Washington Gladden, Jenken Lloyd Jones, and Walter Rauchenbusch, all of whom according to Jane Addams were hounded to death as a result of their continued opposition to World War I.[70] Other, less prominent ministers also suffered for their pacifism and for disobeying Theodore Roosevelt's injunction that "the clergyman who does not put the flag above the church had better close his church and keep it closed."[71]

While clerical pacifists faced the loss of a job or a brief stint in jail, other iconoclasts also paid for their opposition to "the war against war." Chief among these were the conscientious objectors: young men whose religious and/or political beliefs precluded their killing German soldiers. Conscientious objection in the form of alternative service was allowed under the Selective Training Act of 1917, but the government actively discouraged it by placing conscientious objectors in army training camps, where they were often subjected to beatings, torture, and imprisonment.[72] As a result of such treatment (described by one army officer as "good-natured hazing . . . undertaken in a spirit of fun"),[73] many conscientious objectors abandoned their scruples and agreed to fight after all.

For those who persisted, and who would not serve in the army as noncombatants, the government created the Board of Inquiry. The task of this board was to separate true conscientious objectors from false, a task made exceptionally difficult by the hostility of board chairman Major Walter Kellogg toward pacifists in general. According to Kellogg, most of the Mennonites, Pentecostalists, and other dissidents whom he had to interview were not true Christians. Instead, they were "maliciously annoying" fanatics whose "strange and unAmerican beliefs" threatened the peace of society and the whole trend toward "social uplift."[74]

Kellogg was hardly alone in his dislike of conscientious objectors. Other establishment figures also vilified the noncombatants, and

Clark University president G. Stanley Hall went so far as to declare that many had "sex abnormalities."[75] But while the preponderance of newspaper editors, college professors, and elected officials condemned "slackerdom" in the harshest possible terms, the Federal Council of Churches publicly affirmed "freedom of conscience" (a move whose heroism was tempered considerably by the council's failure to assist conscientious objectors or to protest against their treatment in prison).[76]

The FCC also warned at the outset of the war against the suppression of freedom of speech.[77] And while it later backed down from this position (to the point where one of its committees insisted that it was the sacred duty of every pastor to stifle antiwar criticism), individual council members continued gingerly to caution against an overabundance of pro-war enthusiasm. Chief among such Cassandras was the chairman of the FCC's General War-Time Commission of the Churches, Robert Speer, who on February 18, 1918, spoke at Columbia University under the auspices of the Intercollegiate YMCA of New York City on the pros and cons of American democracy. On the pro side, Speer foresaw the day when American democracy would transform the world. But he also stressed that American democracy as it existed was far from perfect and that America retained too much of the "German" penchant for racism, militarism, and intolerant nationalism.[78]

Speer's attempt to define tolerance as a patriotic duty was well intentioned. But his suggestion that America's sins vaguely resembled those of Germany outraged such prominent individuals as the editor of the *New York Times* (who accused Speer of doing as much harm as one of "the Kaiser's secret agents")[79] and Professor Charles Fagnani of Union Theological Seminary, who despite his 1903 prediction that "Quaker principles" would one day conquer the world[80] was quick to condemn Speer for exhibiting "Teutonic susceptibilities."[81]

To understand why Speer's remarks generated such controversy and why he had to spend much of the remainder of the war defending himself against charges of pro-Germanism, it helps to recall that many Americans viewed their wartime conduct as beyond reproach. This was especially true of ministers such as the Reverend Dr. Isaac J. Lansing, who spoke before gatherings of New York City lawyers, clergymen, and Rotarians on the sanctity of America's wartime aims. "Beyond all question we are on God's side," Lansing assured the civic boosters. And in all honesty, he continued, "even God Himself, we say with profoundest reverence, has prescribed no higher aims for human welfare than we have literally claimed and undertaken to realize in the interests of mankind."[82]

The notion that America's wartime conduct was more godlike than God had a variety of adherents, including popular poet, minister, and newspaper columnist Frank Crane, who in 1917 advised readers of the YMCA journal, *Association Men,* not to be ashamed of their patriotism. "Of all the signs and symbols since the world began there is never another so full of meaning as the flag of this country," he declared. "That flag is the cream of all religions, the concentrated essence of the best impulses of the human race; reverence it as you would reverence the signature of the Deity."[83]

With apostles of American divinity such as Crane dominating the newspapers, many Americans must have been tempted to view themselves as world saviors. Many must have also concluded that if the Allied powers were divine, the Central powers were satanic, a charge considered by Theodore Roosevelt to be beyond dispute. After all, explained the former President in a letter written to American troops on behalf of the New York Bible Society, the Bible itself sanctioned the fight "against the armies of Germany and Turkey, for these nations in this crisis stand for the reign of Moloch and Beelzebub on this earth."[84]

When Roosevelt referred to German perfidy, he meant the nation rather than its people. But this distinction between corporate and individual guilt was far too subtle for the Reverend Dr. Newell Dwight Hillis, a successor to Henry Ward Beecher at Brooklyn's Plymouth Congregational Church and a man who traversed the country advocating that the entire German race be forcibly sterilized.[85] Arguments for distinguishing individual Germans from Germany also failed to sway the War Committee of the misaptly named Chapel of the Comforter in New York City, which in a series of "war papers" (recommended by *The North American Review* for distribution throughout the land)[86] declared that the Germans were "monsters of cruelty" who ought to be made to "suffer for their sins in every way you can devise."[87]

Killing Germans was not only a righteous act, continued the War Committee; it was also a "religious duty." And while Christ preached love of one's enemies (Luke 6:32–36), the Committee argued in Orwellian fashion that "to love is to hate," since "those who do not hate do not love."[88] As for Christ's warning against militarism in Matthew 26:52, Unitarian scholar Abraham Rihbany dismissed it as an obvious mistranslation. Christ could not have said simply that "all who take the sword shall perish by the sword," argued Rihbany. Instead, He had undoubtedly declared that "they who take the sword (for aggression) shall perish with the sword; arise, ye brave, and check the tide of lust for worldly power and domination."[89]

Attempts such as Rihbany's to prove that Christ was no "big, fat, blubbering non-resister" were numerous.[90] But a few ministers, such as Frederick Lynch and Charles Jefferson, had the courage to fault these attempts and to speak up on behalf of decency, tolerance, and moderation even in war.[91] Walter Rauschenbush also took American church leaders to task for German-bashing and for offering "a Utopian scheme as a justification for emasculating and hog-tying one of the great parts of humanity."[92]

The fact that the clergy had permitted the country's "moral indignation" to mutate into a "spirit of hate" was appalling, agreed Professor Daniel Evans of Andover Theological School. Also appalling in his view was the clerical tendency to share in this hate, one result of which was the decision of some people to become irreligious "for the sake of religion itself."[93]

Evans was right to chastise the clergy for failing to speak out against the excesses of war and for becoming caught up in the prevailing spirit of bigotry and intolerance. But it would be wrong to assume that all patriotic pastors were bigots. Evidence suggests that many of the pastors who refrained from criticizing the ill treatment of dissidents did so not out of hatred but because they viewed the war's curtailment of individual liberties as an acceptable price to pay for its reformation of society and promise of world peace.

Proof that the clergy had inordinately high hopes for the war came in a variety of forms. One was their faith in the blessings of an American victory, a faith amply illustrated by YMCA secretary George Perkins's speech to the soldiers of Camp Madison, New Jersey. According to Perkins, the familiar world of labor strife and inefficient government would be "almost obsolete when this war is over." In its place would be a "great new world," the benefits of which were wonderful to contemplate.[94]

The likelihood of the war's resulting in a new world order was beyond dispute, agreed Professor Henry Hallam Tweedy of Yale Divinity School. But it was not only the war's rosy aftermath that excited him; it was also the war's more immediate benefits. Chief among these, according to Tweedy, was the war's bracing effect on professional men lately grown soft and "effeminate" and its ability "to lift them above a great danger in peace times, that of living a 'ghastly, smooth life, dead at heart.'"[95]

Tweedy was not alone in praising the war's more "virile" qualities. Other writers also commented on the invigorating atmosphere of wartime and how superior it was to the "soft, easy, adipose" air of peacetime.[96] As for the beneficent influence of war on manhood, G. Stanley Hall considered this to be almost beyond measure. After all, he argued, "war is, in a sense, the acme of what some now call the manly protest. In peace women have invaded nearly all the occupations of man, but in war male virtues come to the fore, for women cannot go 'over the top.'"[97]

Talk such as Hall's regarding the moral manliness of war was widespread, especially among older Progressives. As a result, the Reverend Richard Boynton of the First Unitarian Church in Buffalo, New York, concluded that the United States was rediscovering the virtues of *Tom Brown at Rugby* and experiencing a revival of "muscular Christianity."[98] But while Boynton was right to draw parallels between 1918 and the 1890s, the muscular Christianity of World War I differed from the muscular Christianity of the Spanish-American War in several important respects, one of which was its decreased emphasis on the superiority of Anglo-Saxonism.

Anglo-Saxon triumphalism was not entirely absent during World War I. But as the Reverend Joseph Odell of the First Presbyterian Church in Troy, New York, pointed out in a highly influential *Atlantic Monthly* article, such triumphalism was no longer realistic in light of the country's growing religious and ethnic diversity. As a result, he urged mainline clergymen to concede that "the day of the Pilgrim Fathers is over" and that the war was less about Anglo-Saxon pride than about pride in "the New Americanism."[99]

The willingness of young clergymen such as Odell to abandon talk of Anglo-Saxon superiority was matched by their willingness to cut back on that other muscular Christian staple theme, the degeneracy of urban-dwelling youth. For years it had been customary for ministers to condemn such youth, explained the Reverend Dr. John Kelman to a gathering of Yale Divinity School faculty, and to rail against "the pleasure-loving softness, luxuriousness, and self-indulgence" that were everywhere rampant during the Edwardian Age. But now, he pointed out, even the most dissolute lads had been swept off to war, where they were conducting themselves in an irreproachable manner.[100]

The power of the U.S. Army to effect what G. Stanley Hall called the transformation of the average "flab" into someone whose "hair [grew] on the chest not only of his body but of his very soul"[101] did more than quiet talk of rampant American degeneracy. It also forced many muscular Christians to question their old emphasis on individual initiative. After all, reasoned the FCC-sponsored Committee on the War and the Religious Outlook, while the incompatibility of army life and individual freedom was disturbing, it was more than offset by the fact that "thousands of men have gained mentally and physically from the comradeship and discipline of the army" and that "'soft' men" in particular "have gained in healthy physical and spiritual readiness to 'endure hardness.'"[102]

Of course, men were not the only beneficiaries of military discipline, observed Brown University president the Reverend William H. P. Faunce; women also seemed to thrive under wartime conditions. Especially encouraging for Faunce were the numbers of women who had abandoned their prewar "parasitic" life of endless consumption and bridge parties and who had opted instead to join the Red Cross and "cooperate with the great leaders of humanity in ushering in a finer and nobler era for the world."[103]

With women subordinating their wills to that of the federal government, and with men being transformed through compulsory military service into models of Christian manhood, it seemed to many muscular Christians as if the ultimate solution to the problem of character building was government coercion. But other muscular Christians pointed out that while Progressive governmental influence on the formation of individual character was undoubtedly beneficent, it paled in significance when compared to the government's power in time of war to correct hitherto intractable social ills. One such ill, according to the Reverend Charles Jefferson, was the consumption of alcohol, which the government made illegal for soldiers three years before the passage of Prohibition. Another problem tackled by the government was the "Americanization" of foreign immigrants at army training camps, where according to the Reverend George Fiske "nondescript squads of heterogeneous 'butchers and bakers and candlestick makers'" were converted after "a few strenuous weeks" into "soldierly men" whose "spirit of utter loyalty, instant obedience, [and] absolute devotion to the cause" boded well for the future.[104]

What enabled military trainers to succeed where so many reformers had hitherto failed was the newness of their approach, averred Luther Gulick, who in 1917 left the Camp Fire Girls to work as a wartime consultant for the YMCA. Old-style reformers had attempted "to defeat evil by converting one man at a time," he explained. But the military aimed instead at "capturing the entire force," signifying (for Gulick at least) that "the day of collective righteousness is here."[105]

The possibility that the state might one day forcibly ensure universal public morality elicited a mixed response from Protestant leaders. On the one hand, many agreed with Gulick that "chang[ing] the moral tone of the world" justified the loss of traditional democratic freedoms. But others questioned his assertion that the state needed the church in order "to lift the world to a new moral level."[106] After all, they wondered, if the tasks of socialization and civic betterment were best handled by the state, what need was there for the Christian religion?

The Religion of the Trenches

The thought that Christianity had outlived its usefulness as a tool for socialization was disturbing. But it did not (for the moment at least) spark a mass exodus of muscular Christian character builders out of the church and into psychiatric wards, psychology faculties, and other emerging centers of social control. Instead, character builders such as Luther Gulick strove during the war to demonstrate that religious commitment and national vitality remained intimately linked and that there was (as one YMCA war manual put it) "no power like that in a blow from one who knows that he is in the right."[107]

Proving that American "morale" still depended largely on religion not only concerned individuals such as Gulick; it also concerned organizations such as the Federal Council of Churches, which in September 1917 created the General War-Time Commission of the Churches (GWTCC) to address issues raised by the war. Composed of 104 Protestant leaders (many of whom either were or had at one time been members of the Church Peace Union),[108] the GWTCC moved to increase America's military effectiveness by fostering cooperation among the various denominational war boards, by advocating the passage of Prohibition as a means of enhancing combat readiness, and by working in conjunction with the YMCA, the YWCA, the Red Cross, and other military service organizations.[109]

While the GWTCC worked to coordinate Protestant energies on a national level, church pastors made various contributions toward heightening the war consciousness of their local communities. One such contribution was patriotic oratory, which a number of ministers delivered in their capacity as "four-minute men" (government-sponsored volunteer speakers whose lectures on patriotic themes were often scheduled during theater intermissions).[110] Another wartime pastoral contribution was fund-raising, the greatest instance of which was the United War Work Campaign: a nationwide effort spearheaded by John R. Mott that raised $200 million to aid in the war work of the YMCA and other charitable organizations.[111]

These ministerial efforts on behalf of the war generally pleased government officials (though George Creel sometimes chided his "four-minute men" for overindulging in "hymns of hate").[112] But other patriots thought that in addition to covering the domestic front, ministers ought to be located "over there." One such supporter of overseas service was theology professor Henry Hallam Tweedy of Yale Divinity School, who praised military chaplains for overcoming the "heavy burdens" and class antagonisms of army camp life. "Such men," he declared,

will increasingly merit and possess the respect of laymen and soldiers. Their lives have been knit together in the fellowship of suffering. Their bodies are inured to the same hardships, their faces lined with the same grim marks of dangers laughed at and of conquered pain. In the democracy of the trenches the sons of the Pilgrims and the immigrant sons of the slums have come to know and to understand one another. The pagan, illiterate dock-hand has fought shoulder to shoulder with the teacher of religion, trained in the first universities of our own and other lands. When such laymen attend plays like "The Hypocrites" or read novels like "The Pastor's Wife," they will never be persuaded that the clerical cartoons represent reality. Each will recall days in the dugouts and nights in the hospitals, when they came to know a different type of minister, a "beloved captain," who marched through the mire with song and laughter, and crept with them through the darkness and shadow of death in No Man's Land. An almost irresistible attraction will draw them to the churches of such ministers. To their leadership they will be inclined to render obedience; to their messages they will listen with respect.[113]

Tweedy's position on military chaplaincy is an excellent illustration of the link between muscular Christianity and the struggle of old-stock Americans to retain social control, and it had a number of adherents. One was Harvard chaplain Francis Peabody, who argued that the benefits of military life were such as to warrant the drafting of ministers.[114] But while Protestant leaders such as Peabody viewed drafting clergymen as an excellent idea (and fully consistent with the Social Gospel conflation of sacred and secular), Catholic leaders disagreed. Their clergy would not fight in any but the holiest of crusades, they argued. And since the Great War was (in their view at least) not holy but simply just, drafting clergymen made no sense.[115]

The dispute between Catholics and Protestants over whether or not to draft clergymen came to an end in 1917, when Congress bowed to the increasing political influence of the Catholic clergy and voted for the first time in its history to exempt ordained ministers and divinity school students from military service.[116] This decision, however, did little to diminish mainline Protestant respect for the virtues of clerical combativeness. Nor did it stop ministers from participating voluntarily in the war as military chaplains, relief specialists, and welfare workers.

Of these three groups, military chaplains (referred to by an admirer as "splendid soldiers of the Lord")[117] were probably the least numerous. Estimates are that at the outset of World War I there were only 74 chaplains in the Army, 72 in the National Guard, and 40 in the Navy. These numbers had not changed much since the end of the Civil War. Nor were they reflective of America's growing religious diversity, since there were no Jewish chaplains until 1918, and of the 146 chaplains in the Army and National Guard circa 1916, only 25 were Catholic.[118]

The chaplaincy's low numbers denoted its marginal status. Nineteenth-century chaplains were often ill-paid, assigned to isolated posts, required to serve as schoolteachers and librarians, and ridiculed for their opposition to profanity and alcohol.[119] As a result, when Army Commander-in-Chief William T. Sherman was asked in 1882 to recommend a candidate for chaplaincy, he urged reconsideration. "Our frontier posts . . . are ill adapted for raising a large family of small children," he wrote. But "if your brother wants to join in this scramble to become a martyr, let him send me his papers, and I will see they are filed."[120]

Sherman's warning about the inadequacies of military chaplaincy went largely unheeded through the Spanish-American War. But in the five years following that conflict, Congress enacted a series of laws designed to upgrade the chaplaincy. These laws allowed for pay raises and promotions, placed chaplains on parity with other staff officers, and reduced the problem of patronage by requiring that all chaplains be endorsed by their respective denominations. Congress also listened respectfully to chaplains opposed to intemperance and in 1901 forbade the sale of liquor on all military bases.[121]

Additional changes in chaplaincy occurred around the time of World War I. These included the abolition in 1916 of 141-year-old rules (largely ignored for a century) against swearing and absence from worship services in the army; the establishment in 1918 of the first army chaplains' school at Fort Monroe, Virginia; the induction of twenty-five Jewish chaplains (who successfully fought for permission to wear the Star of David instead of the Latin Cross); the impaneling of a "Committee of Six" (four Protestants, one Catholic, and one Jew) to advise the government on chaplaincy issues during the war; and the long-sought appointment of two head chaplains: Navy Chief of Chaplains John Frazier (a Southern Methodist) and Army Senior Chaplain Charles H. Brent (former Episcopal missionary bishop to the Philippines and a close friend of General John J. Pershing).[122]

As a result of such reforms, military chaplains enjoyed heightened prestige. They also experienced a huge wartime increase in numbers. During World War I the Navy went from having 40 chaplains to having 203, and the Army went from having 74 chaplains to having 2,363.[123] But despite these improvements (which, according to Chaplain S. Parkes Cadman, better enabled chaplains to toughen "the moral and physical fibre" of lads formerly "petted and spoiled"),[124] the young Reinhold Niebuhr privately confessed after touring various army camps on behalf of the Federal Council of Churches that he still viewed chaplains as little more than "priests of the great god Mars." "What I dislike about most of the chaplains," he wrote in his private journal,

> is that they assume a very officious and also a very masculine attitude. Ministers are not used to authority and revel in it when acquired. The rather too obvious masculinity which they try to suggest by word and action is meant to remove any possible taint which their Christian faith might be suspected to have left upon them in the minds of the he-men in the army. H—— is right. He tells me that he wants to go into the army as a private and not as a chaplain. He believes that war is inevitable but he is not inclined to reconcile its necessities with the Christian ethic. He will merely forget about this difficulty during the war.[125]

The fact that ministers such as Niebuhr viewed chaplaincy as too militant may account for why the number of World War I chaplains fell short by half of the one army chaplain per 1,200 men ordained by Congress in 1917.[126] It may also explain why many of the ministers who served overseas did so not as chaplains, but as stretcher bearers, medical attendants, and ambulance drivers for the American Red Cross, which undertook responsibility for relief work in the field according to international Red Cross rules first established by the 1864 Geneva Convention.[127]

Caring for the entire U.S. Army did not come easily for the American Red Cross, which was only thirty-six years old in 1917 and therefore lacked the Civil War relief work experience of older, more overtly religious agencies such as the YMCA. Nor did the Red Cross have enough funds for its work (despite a June 1917 fund drive that netted $115 million).[128] As a result, observed war correspondent Elizabeth Sergeant in 1918, "the front line work of the Red Cross is negligible as yet in quantity as compared with that of the YMCA" (even though soldiers had more respect for the Red Cross flag—the Swiss flag with colors reversed—than they did for the YMCA red triangle).[129]

Sergeant may have been right about the Red Cross providing fewer relief services than the YMCA, which raised a staggering $170 million for its wartime activities and served between four and five million U.S. servicemen (not including prisoners of war). But relief work was not the Association's chief wartime focus. Instead, YMCA secretaries strove primarily to upgrade the servicemen's welfare and to provide "those social, recreational, educational, and religious activities that are lacking in the routine of army and navy life."[130]

The YMCA's distinction between welfare and relief work was nothing new. It dated back to 1861, when fifteen northern associations formed the United States Christian Commission, an organization ultimately responsible for fielding 5,000 assistant chaplains, building 140 chapels, and distributing 4 million pieces of edifying literature to Civil War soldiers.[131] Thirty-seven years later, the YMCA (by now widely known for "represent[ing] American civilization, *AMERICAN CHRISTIANITY* and American institutions, wherever American soldiers have gone") again came to the aid of U.S. soldiers, this time those fighting the Spanish-American War.[132] And when President Roosevelt undertook to build the Panama Canal, he asked the YMCA to provide "moral sanitation" at seven points along the twenty-eight-mile line of operations.[133]

As a result of such services, the YMCA (whose Christian commissioners became known as welfare secretaries circa 1909) gradually assumed jurisdiction over welfare work throughout the military. The Association was also given permission by a special 1902 Act of Congress to erect buildings on government property (subject to approval from the Secretary of War). But while these were significant accomplishments, Association head John R. Mott believed his organization was capable of performing even greater feats. As a result, he was quick to telephone President Wilson on the day America entered World War I in order to offer "the service of the Associations in whatever ways might be found useful."[134]

In response to Mott's offer, Raymond Fosdick, a War Department official and brother of famous theologian and preacher Harry Emerson Fosdick, invited the YMCA to join his Commission on Training Camp Activities (CTCA). He also persuaded the commission (which was formed in April 1917 to oversee welfare work in the camps) to place the "Y" in direct control of all camp recreational activities. But this arrangement greatly upset the Roman Catholic Church, which objected to the YMCA's having a monopoly on service to non-Protestant soldiers.[135]

Anxious to quell such criticism, Fosdick (who eventually came to regret not having the government simply take charge of its own welfare work) invited the Knights of Columbus to join the CTCA. He also later extended this invitation to include the YWCA, the Salvation Army, the Jewish Welfare Board, the American Library Association, and the War Camp Community Service (a subset of the Playground and Recreation Association).[136] But when the Allies expressed alarm at the prospect of so many civilians accompanying U.S. troops overseas,[137] Fosdick stopped issuing CTCA memberships—much to the chagrin of groups such as the Brotherhood of St. Andrew, which had to content itself with visiting servicemen and sending them letters.[138]

With Fosdick refusing to expand the CTCA any further, membership in that body stood at seven groups, each of which had a primary function. For the American Library Association and the War Camp Community Service, that function was largely informational: they distributed books and other documents.[139] For the Salvation Army (whose smiling "lassies" made it the most popular of the service groups) camp work meant serving hot coffee and doughnuts. And for the Jewish Welfare Board and the Knights of Columbus, the challenge lay in meeting the religious and recreational needs of non-Protestant soldiers.[140]

While most of the above-mentioned groups mainly endeavored to meet the needs of male servicemen, the YWCA sought to protect and entertain the thousands of women working overseas in the army as nurses, telephone operators, and "signal corps girls." It also built eighty French and American "Hostess Houses" (places of wholesome, as opposed to naughty, recreation) for the benefit of servicemen and their girlfriends.[141] These services equaled or eclipsed those of the American Library Association, the War Camp Community Service, the Salvation Army, the Jewish Welfare Board, and the Knights of Columbus, but they fell far short of the tremendous wartime contributions of the YMCA, which according to General Pershing "conducted nine-tenths of the welfare work among the American forces in Europe."[142]

Evidence for the YMCA's preeminence among CTCA members came in a variety of forms. One was the use made of YMCA facilities by CTCA workers (especially Jewish Welfare Board workers, who generally relied on Association buildings). Another was the YMCA's vast personnel force, which included 25,926 paid workers recruited specifically for the war. These workers (who were divided almost equally between home and overseas service) came from an applicant pool of 200,000 individuals, all of whom were scrutinized by YMCA review boards—patriotic tribunals that favored applicants endowed with Christian character, staunch Americanism, and evangelical church membership, but that did not accept immigrants from enemy countries, their children, and other "high risk" ethnic types.[143]

As a result of this selection process, the YMCA ended up hiring 22,426 mostly WASP men of nondraftable age and 3,500 mostly WASP women (although a small number of blacks were hired to work with black troops).[144] Of the men, around 25 percent were ministers.[145] And of these ministers, many, such as inventor of basketball James Naismith (who headed the YMCA's wartime Bureau of Hygiene),[146] were athletes, a fact not lost on Daniel Poling, who toured the front on behalf of the United Society of Christian Endeavor and a variety of temperance groups. Indeed, commented Poling, it was heartening to see YMCA facilities staffed by men such as "'Heints,' a strong-bodied, big-hearted young Methodist preacher [and] a 'North-western' man of football fame."[117]

Of course, there were plenty of YMCA secretaries who in no way resembled "Heints," and who were instead "of the 'pale young cu-rate' type."[148] But such men generally did not appeal to YMCA of-ficials, who preferred hiring "husky saints" such as "Gyp the Blood" (a California preacher famous on the front for physically squelching an irreverent rowdy)[149] to handle their strenuous wartime program, each element of which reflected one of the three aspects of the Associ-ation's "body-mind-spirit" ideal.

For servicemen's bodies, the "Y" ran clubs, operated hotels, and oversaw "holiday areas."[150] It also became the military's chief sup-plier of luxury items such as stationery, cigarettes, and cookies (these last emanating from special YMCA-run French factories). But the greatest material comfort provided by the Association was undoubt-edly its camp "hut," an all-purpose "club, theater, gymnasium, church, school, post-office, express agency, information bureau and general store"[151] where soldiers often gathered (according to Poling) to "talk and muse" amidst an atmosphere of "manly decency."[152]

When soldiers were not resting inside an Association hut, they were often outside participating in Association-led sports such as basket-ball, football, and "mass athletics" (games meant to include nonath-letes).[153] These sports (for which the Association furnished all requi-site personnel and equipment) were at first discouraged by some older officers, who preferred military drill; but YMCA physical education workers quickly overcame such opposition by likening sports such as boxing to bayonet practice[154] and by insisting that "athletics stimu-lated the fighting spirit."[155] YMCA workers also praised wholesome, vigorous games for keeping men's minds off sex and for preventing the war from becoming a venereal-disease–ridden "sex festival."[156]

Ensuring that men's bodies stayed wholesome was a challenging task. But it did not cause the Association to overlook men's minds, as evidenced by its various wartime educational programs. One such was the YMCA/government-run post school, which served illiterates (whose attendance was mandatory) and collegians alike, and which taught courses ranging from psychology to engineering.[157] Another noteworthy (albeit macabre) educational enterprise was the YMCA's Honey Bee Club, which encouraged black stevedores and grave-diggers to view themselves as hard-working honeybees, and which awarded 21,550 Honey Bee badges (possession of which often enabled the wearer to escape military police persecution).[158]

On the lighter side of the educational spectrum, various Association agencies presented edifying shows and skits. Particularly active in this regard were the Overseas Entertainment Bureau, the Speakers' Bureau, the Sacred Music Bureau, and the Over There Theater League, all of which provided servicemen with a variety of entertainments, some live, others not. In the latter category were YMCA movie shows (127,000 of which were held in stateside camps); live entertainment included the Association's speaking and performance tours, which featured statesmen such as William H. Taft, entertainers such as Harry Houdini, industrialists such as John D. Rockefeller, Jr., preachers such as James and Joseph Vance, and choirs such as the Columbia University Glee Club.[159]

Many of these wartime entertainments were entirely secular. But others quickly segued into religious activities such as hymn-singing, group prayer, and Bible study (the last of which enrolled upwards of 250,000 students).[160] As a result, Elizabeth Sergeant accused the YMCA of concealing religion in its shows "like a pill in strawberry jam."[161] The Association defended itself on the grounds that "religion and life are bound together" and that Christian witness remained an important part of its historic red triangle.[162] The Association also remained true to its evangelical heritage by distributing over a million "Khaki Testaments,"[163] by maintaining a "War Roll" of Christian conversions (more than 260,000 by war's end),[164] and by encouraging soldiers to sign up for careers in ministry (an effort whose rather disappointing outcome was 1,000 signed cards and only 300 actual applications).[165]

Although committed to the old-time religion, the YMCA was equally committed to making that religion as attractive as possible. To this end, it preached a religion it thought soldiers would like, a "Religion of the Trenches" whose god was a "God with guts."[166] It also specialized in performing "bright and snappy" church services replete with vaudeville singing and jazz band music.[167]

In response to the Association's religious activities, and in recognition of its work on behalf of servicemen's bodies and minds, many prominent individuals issued encouraging words of praise. One especially noteworthy fan was ex-President Taft, who called YMCA welfare work "one of the greatest achievements of peace in all the history of human warfare."[168] Another enthusiast was the Reverend Dr. Joseph Odell, who considered the YMCA's wartime program to be "just as startling as the Crusades, the Franciscan movement, the Reformation, or the rise of Puritanism."[169]

But while establishment figures such as Taft and Odell extolled the Association, servicemen often attacked it for employing too many "Holier-than-thou's,"[170] for refusing to deliver religion "straight,"[171] and for overcharging on cigarettes (which were given away free by the Knights of Columbus).[172] Servicemen also expressed disrespect for the Association in front of Judge Ben Lindsey (a frontline observer sympathetic to the "Y"), who recalled that "when the Y was mentioned, both men and officers either criticized or fell silent, and most of the soldiers' criticisms were so violent as to be unprintable."[173]

When soldiers did speak of the YMCA worker without cursing, Lindsey added, they generally faulted him for cowardice. And while the judge believed this charge to be entirely untrue in view of the many YMCA men who had died during the war or been decorated for bravery, he confessed that "over and over, the boys would say [of the YMCA worker], 'That sissyfied son of a gun is using up gasolene over here to warn us fellows against the skirts, when he ought to be down in the trenches where he belongs or get the blazes out 'o here.'"[174]

Such recalcitrance on the part of those whom they were trying so hard to serve caused some YMCA men to despair.[175] But others expressed confidence that servicemen would come around once they realized that the Associaton's reputation for hypocrisy and preachiness was largely undeserved. One such optimist was future advertising mogul Bruce Barton (a member of the YMCA's wartime activities governing board), who pointed out in 1918 that while the Association had begun the war by quizzing workers on their evangelicalism, it had since stopped that practice and was instead hiring "big men and women" regardless of their theology.[176]

Additional ways whereby the Association sought to improve its image included ceasing to ask workers for conversion statistics;[177] hiring "Hut Mothers" (who could not be called slackers);[178] and developing a certain tolerance toward cigarettes, condoms, and other items formerly regarded as sinful.[179] YMCA workers also stressed that their religious activities did not detract from but were instead essential to the war effort. After all, explained a YMCA war workers' manual, many a pious draftee had refrained from shooting to kill until told by some trusted chaplain or religious worker, "Lad, I would not enter this work until I could see Jesus Himself sighting down a gun barrel and running a bayonet through an enemy's body."[180]

The ability of some "Y" men to position Christ in the trenches may have impressed army headquarters. But enlisted men remained skeptical of the Association's efforts to reconcile religion with modern warfare, as evidenced by the fact that an entire transport ship returning from France broke into boos when asked to cheer for the "Y." Soldiers also continued to give Association workers names such as "Old Wine, Women, and Song," a fact which led more than one officer to comment, "Heaven help the Y after this war! How the fellows will hate it!"[181]

The soldiers' disenchantment with the YMCA and its "religion of the trenches" was undoubtedly profound. But it was not only soldiers who disliked deifying war; it was also some religious workers. Robert Veach, a chaplain in the U.S. Air Service, for example, confessed that "when the first trainload of six hundred and fifty-two wounded men arrived at the hospital from Chateau-Thierry, the glamour of war vanished and we realized what a hellish thing it all was. I thought my heart would break those first few days. Fifty-six of the men had been so badly burned with mustard gas that they looked like boiled lobsters. There were deep burns on their bodies as big as a plate, leaving the quivering flesh exposed to the air."[182]

The sight of "men with bowels dropping out, lungs shot away, with blinded, smashed faces, or limbs blown into space" certainly stripped the romance off war, agreed Sherwood Eddy, a leader of the YMCA forces in France. It also made him think that he had been wrong to write *The Right to Fight, With Our Soldiers in France,* and other pro-war volumes. "I believed that it was a war to end war, to protect womanhood, to destroy militarism and autocracy and to make a new world 'fit for heroes to live in,'" he later wrote. But the sight of the carnage soon filled him with "grave doubts and misgivings" concerning the war and its supporters.[183]

Eddy's wartime thoughts concerning the immorality of battle were atypical; most Allied churchmen apparently viewed Germany's defeat in 1918 as divinely ordained. But in the years following 1918, many conscientious clergymen came to regret their wartime behavior and their submission to what University of Chicago Divinity School professor Ozora Davis called "a kind of shrieking and hysterical patriotism."[184] This postwar disenchantment with militarism (a disenchantment even more extensive than what had followed the Spanish-American War) was caused in part by the horrors of war and the discovery that many anti-German atrocity stories had been faked. But the churches' greatest cause for disillusionment may have been the federal government's refusal in 1919 to join the newly created League of Nations—an action that belied clerical assurances that the United States would emerge from the "war against war" as the world's chief insurer of international peace.[185]

With progressive justifications for World War I being undermined by congressional hostility to the League of Nations, many liberal clerics concluded that the war had been meaningless and that their support for it had been wrong. One such penitent was the Reverend Harry Emerson Fosdick, who during the war had heartily endorsed Christian combat,[186] but who afterward wrote that "the more I consider war, its sources, methods, and results, its debasing welter of lies and brutality, its unspeakable horror while it is here and its utter futility in the end to achieve any good thing mankind could wish, the more difficult I find it to imagine any situation in which I shall feel justified in sanctioning or participating in another war."[187]

Nouveau pacifists such as Fosdick did not impress veteran antiwar activist John Haynes Holmes, who charged postwar peacemakers with being "guilty of the final indecency—that of doing late and in security . . . what they refused to do at some cost, when the honor and lives of men were hanging in the balance."[188] But most people appeared more accepting of nouveau pacifism than Holmes, and soon the churches were awash with declarations for peace. Among the most notable of these antiwar declarations, hundreds of which were penned in 1924 alone,[189] were those emanating from the Chicago Federation of Churches, which voiced its opposition to "the entire war system"; the Student Volunteer Movement, which resolved "not to sanction or participate in any future war";[190] and the Federal Council of Churches, which urged Christians everywhere to work toward the creation of a "warless world."[191]

The Protestant churches' post–World War I campaign to create a "warless world" obviously did not succeed, since it failed to prevent later wars, such as World War II. But while post–World War I church pacifism did not vanquish war, it did at least reflect America's growing disenchantment with ultramilitant muscular Christianity, which had been embraced by many Protestants during the Spanish-American War and World War I. In the aftermath of both those wars, there was a retreat from the idea of uplifting the world by force; this retreat was especially precipitous in the years following World War I. During that period, muscular Christians such as Sherwood Eddy came to regret their support for the war, and their disillusionment was shared by *Christian Century* magazine, which in 1935 condemned "the blind servility with which the Christian Church gave itself to the government of the United States in 1917 and 1918."[192]

Conclusion

I've paddled my canoe across this broad lake, I have threaded
the waters of the winding treacherous River Songo, I have
paddled on up Long Lake and lugged and tugged and carried
my burden and finally hiked it up hill and down dale and
climbed the rocky summit of Mount Washington. In other
words I have made a good fight, finished my life's work and
attained the zenith of my ambition. What more in sight is
there for me to accomplish? Lord, if it is thy will, I am ready
and happy to go.

—LUTHER GULICK'S LAST WORDS
(AS IMAGINED BY DUDLEY ALLEN SARGENT)

Americans in the decade following World War I greeted the return to
what Warren G. Harding called peaceful "normalcy" with celebration
and relief.[1] But while the Roaring Twenties may have benefited many
Americans, they did not benefit the muscular Christians, who were attacked by a number of critics in the postwar period. These critics
blamed muscular Christianity for fanning the flames of World War I,
and they worked to bring down muscular Christian idols such as
Daniel Chester French's statue *The Christian Student,* a bronzed em-
bodiment of "manly character, athletic prowess, intellectual force and
fine spiritual fellowship" that was erected at Princeton in 1913 to
commemorate Princeton's historic involvement with the Student Volunteer Movement, the intercollegiate YMCA movement, and the
World's Student Christian Federation.[2]

The Christian Student survived World War I and remained standing
at Princeton throughout the 1920s. During that decade, however, the
statue and the muscular Christian ideals that it represented fell out of
favor with students, who repeatedly vandalized it and referred to it
jokingly as "Earl." Such irreverent behavior finally forced Princeton
authorities to remove "Earl" in 1931, thus symbolizing the postwar
decline of muscular Christianity not only at Princeton but also in
Protestant institutions nationwide.[3]

If muscular Christian ideas were on the decline in the 1920s, so were their chief institutional backers, the mainline Protestant churches. These guardians of Anglo-Christian culture had long fought to retain their influence over leading academic centers such as Princeton. But their efforts to maintain cultural uniformity met with increasing resistance in the 1920s, when demographic changes, cultural diversification, and scientific skepticism combined to produce what Robert Handy calls "the second disestablishment" of the Protestant churches in America.[4] Unlike the disestablishment that followed the Revolution, the second disestablishment did not deprive the churches of tax money. Instead, it deprived them of cultural and political influence. As a result, Sydney Ahlstrom viewed the postwar period in which the second disestablishment occurred as "the critical epoch when the Puritan heritage lost its hold on the leaders of public life."[5]

Ahlstrom and Handy were right to call the 1920s a time of "crisis" for Protestant leaders.[6] But those leaders generally did not anticipate the fact that their churches would emerge from the 1920s in a state described by Harry Emerson Fosdick as "intellectually chaotic, ethically confused [and] organizationally challenged."[7] Instead of dreading the future, most Protestant leaders appeared confident immediately following World War I that despite the church's waning idealism and loss of "moral tone," it still had sufficient energy to engage in what the Committee on the War and the Religious Outlook called "a new war against vice, disease, poverty [and] death."[8]

Enthusiasm to fight in this new war against evil was especially strong in the ranks of the muscular Christians, many of whom emerged from World War I with confidence in the future and pride in the past. Their confidence in the future may not have been warranted, but their pride in the past was firmly based on a number of achievements in various fields. In the field of sports, muscular Christians had reduced mind-body dualism, broken down evangelical Protestant resistance to sports, invented "character-building" games such as basketball, and acquainted the world with Western athleticism. They had also made headway in the field of education, which was transformed during the Progressive Era by the spread of physical education programs, outdoor camps, nature-oriented clubs, boys' preparatory schools, and other educational entities in which muscular Christianity was highly visible.

While some muscular Christians achieved success in the fields of sport and education, others managed in some ways to "defeminize" the Protestant churches. These churches continued to have more female members than male ones, but their reliance on women leaders, sentimental hymns, and maternal imagery came under heavy attack from muscular Christians, who bombarded the churches with manly hymns, masculine images of Jesus, and complaints about feminine leadership and effeminate ministers. As a result of this antifeminine bombardment, noted Leonard Sweet, women lost some of their power and authority in church during the Progressive Era.[9] Men, in contrast, were encouraged to become more active in church by the Protestant brotherhoods. These muscular Christian groups worked to infuse the churches with men, and their efforts apparently paid off, since religious census figures compiled in 1916 by the Department of Commerce revealed that there had been "an advance in the proportion of males in the total membership of all the churches."[10]

Having successfully promoted manliness and health in America, muscular Christians felt ready following World War I to aid Protestant churches in their new antivice and antipoverty campaign, which was described by one Methodist leader as so "strenuous" that it would make even "the most ardent scrapper . . . sit up and take notice."[11] To finance this new campaign, the churches initiated ambitious fund-raising drives, among the most notable of which were the Disciples' Men and Millions movement, the Presbyterians' New Era movement, and the Congregationalists' Pilgrim Memorial Fund (begun in 1920 to commemorate the three hundredth anniversary of the Pilgrims' landing on Plymouth Rock). These denominational "forward movements" were designed to emulate the churches' wartime fund-raising successes, and their goals were high, with the Congregationalists aiming to raise $5 million and the Disciples actually netting over $7 million.[12]

The greatest church fund-raisers, however, were neither the Congregationalists nor the Disciples but the Methodists, who organized a centenary in 1919 that eventually raised over $166 million. As part of this celebration, the Methodists staged a huge exhibition of Methodist world missions at the Ohio State Fairgrounds in Columbus from June 20 to July 13, 1919. Billed as "the most remarkable meeting in Methodist history," this exhibition showcased a giant blimp, wherefrom issued the world's first "aeroplane sermons." The exhibition also featured nightly pageants, orchestral music, athletic contests, military drills, bucking bronco contests, open air preaching, speeches by some of the nation's top military and political leaders, and an eight-story picture screen (upon which were shown slides from the world's largest stereopticon machine).[13]

The overall purpose of the Columbus Exhibition was to direct attention to Methodist missions (in honor of which a siren went off daily at noon, calling everyone to one minute of silent prayer). But in many ways the event served to illustrate the takeover of genteel Protestantism by muscular Christianity, whose most obvious proponents at the exhibition were the Centenary Cadets: 1,000 "soldierly" teenage boys ("the best product of Methodism") recruited from around the country to police the fairgrounds and to demonstrate that religion was "manly, muscular and attractive to boy life."[14]

The Columbus Exhibition constituted a high-water mark for muscular Christianity. At the same time, however, the event signaled the height of postwar Protestant optimism. For in the years that followed, the mainline churches experienced a series of organizational setbacks and setbacks in morale that were of unprecedented severity.

Among the churches' postwar tribulations was the collapse of the Interchurch World Movement (IWM), a campaign to gather all the churches' missionary activities under one roof. Described by its chairman, John R. Mott, as "the greatest program undertaken by Christians since the days of the Apostles," the IWM (which lasted from 1919 to 1921) spent millions of dollars annually and even produced a Broadway musical about the inevitability of progress. Called *The Wayfarer,* the show mixed popular show tunes with passages from *The Messiah,* sung by an all-Methodist choir of three thousand singers.[15]

These outward signs of prosperity, however, were largely deceptive, since the IWM suffered from a host of internal difficulties, some of which were financial, others ideological. On the financial front, the IWM's predominantly liberal leadership came up with a series of completely unrealistic fund-raising goals ($1 billion at one point); on the ideological level the IWM encountered stiff opposition from religious conservatives, who rejoiced when it failed to raise its own operating costs, lost its denominational support, and had to close its doors.[16]

The failure of the IWM to consolidate church missions frustrated progressive church leaders, who had to concede that denominational unification was a more daunting task than they had thought. But an even greater trial for religious liberals than the collapse of the IWM was the great fundamentalist-modernist controversy, which erupted immediately following World War I. In the course of this dispute (which raged with special fierceness among Baptists, Methodists, Disciples, and Presbyterians), religious conservatives accused theological liberals of abandoning historic Christianity and of promulgating what J. Gresham Machen described as an atheistic cult of progress. To halt the spread of this cult, conservatives endeavored to wrest denominational control away from the liberals and to stop modernists from teaching in seminaries.[17]

In response to these efforts, religious liberals fought hard and (as it turned out) successfully to block fundamentalism and to retain their place in the churches. They also managed with the help of the secular press to portray their fundamentalist opponents as backwoods rubes (an image heavily reinforced by William Jennings Bryan's pitiful performance during the infamous Scopes Trial).[18] But before the liberals could exult in their triumph over the fundamentalists, they faced a new challenge from feminists such as Charlotte Perkins Gilman, who accused the churches' male leadership of clinging to outmoded and "ultra-masculine" concepts such as the virtuousness of pain, the unavoidability of sorrow, and the importance of an afterlife.[19]

So long as these "death-based" concepts remained in place, Gilman explained, events such as "our shameful World War" would be inevitable. But if these concepts and the male priests who espoused them were replaced by a "birth-based religion" led by mothers and scientists, the world would experience "the most glorious hope ever opened to us—the hope of a race growing better in geometrical progression, faster and faster as each new generation gives us children better born, circumstances which lift us further, and education spreading wider with every year that we live in a regenerate world."[20]

Gilman's plea for more womanliness in religion obviously clashed with muscular Christianity. But it failed to arouse much of a response from America's most prominent muscular Christians, largely because many were dead. Among the first to go was Thomas Wentworth Higginson, who died in 1911, fifty-three years after writing the muscular Christian manifesto "Saints, and Their Bodies" (see Chapter 1). He was followed by Josiah Strong in 1916, Theodore Roosevelt in 1919, and Luther Gulick, who died of sudden heart failure at Camp Sebago-Wohelo in 1918, hours after organizing a water carnival.[21]

Another group of muscular Christian pioneers survived the 1910s, but died shortly thereafter. Foremost among them were *Outlook* editor Lyman Abbott (who died in 1922), Francis "Father Endeavor" Clark (who died in 1927), and G. Stanley Hall, whose death in 1924 undoubtedly disheartened muscular Christians, even though Hall had some years previously given up hope of reinvigorating Protestant denominations such as Unitarianism, which he declared to be in irreversible decline "because it is uneugenic and does not make good by adding proselytes to make up for its losses from race suicide" (that is, nonreproduction).[22]

With the passage of academic leaders such as Hall, muscular Christianity lost much of its intellectual viability. But while the movement declined as an intellectual force, paeans to health and manliness continued to emanate both from the mainline churches and from bestselling authors such as Bruce Barton, whose 1925 biography of Jesus, *The Man Nobody Knows,* portrayed the Savior not as a "sissified . . . physical weakling" but as someone whose "muscles were so strong that when He drove the moneychangers out, nobody dared oppose Him!"[23]

The fact that such spiritual hardihood persisted through the 1920s indicates that whatever intellectuals thought, strenuous Christianity was by no means dead. But what survived World War I was, as David Macleod points out, a "mindless strenuosity" tied not to social reform but to what cereal king J. H. Kellogg called the "new religion . . . *of being good to yourself.*"[24]

Being good to yourself (a practice termed "therapeuticism" by T. J. Jackson Lears)[25] meant exercising for health, of course; and in that it resembled the muscular Christianity of the 1880s. But while old-style muscular Christians put healthy bodies in the service of reform, new-style therapeutic Christians often praised healthfulness alone. After all, the Reverend John T. Stone explained, indications that "happiness and pleasure are business interests to-day" made it imperative that the Gospel be billed as "a joy-filling . . . happy-hearted piece of goods."[26]

The fact that ministers such as Stone preached a gospel that was more personally fulfilling than socially transformative owed much to their disillusionment with wartime ideals. It also reflected what Arthur S. Link described as the country's "extraordinary [postwar] reaction against idealism and reform."[27] Examples of this reaction included the decline of the Progressive Party, congressional opposition to the League of Nations, and attacks on Prohibition from writers such as J. P. McEvoy, who made known his opinion of Progressives by declaring in verse:

> Reformers, they are noble men,
>   I hate 'em,
> Most necessary too, but then,
>   I hate 'em,
> They snoop around upon the scene
> And sanctimonious is their mien,
> I'd like to bam them on the bean,
>   I hate 'em.[28]

McEvoy's low opinion of crusading reformers was hardly unique in America's postwar literary community. Nor did this community have much regard for the Christian manliness of Ben-Hur and other literary heroes of an older generation. Instead, its heroes tended to resemble Ernest Hemingway's soldier-narrator in *A Farewell to Arms,* a rugged stoic who confessed to having seen "nothing sacred" in the Great War, and who wanted nothing more to do with "the words sacred, glorious, and sacrifice and the expression in vain."[29]

Such expressions of disdain for the ideals of Christian chivalry abounded in the work of postwar writers. But it was not only writers who emerged from the Great War with an open aversion to muscular Christian rhetoric; it was also the general public. The postwar crowd was not receptive to "world-saving, civic cleanups, and personal salvation," wrote William McLoughlin. Instead, it was excited by such newly accessible leisure-time pursuits as automobiling and listening to the radio.[30]

With the country more interested in escapist entertainment than saving the world, evangelists such as Billy Sunday lost much of their prewar audience.[31] Protestant churches also experienced a decline, as much of their membership forsook Sunday morning worship for recreational activities such as golf. But as distressing as these developments were, there was nothing more symptomatic of waning evangelical fervor than the decline of foreign missionary enterprises such as the once great Student Volunteer Movement, which went from 2,700 volunteers in 1920 to only 252 in 1928.[32]

Presbyterian leader Robert Speer noted these setbacks for the Protestant establishment with dismay. To him, they were evidence of the country's "moral relaxation."[33] H. L. Mencken, however, had a different interpretation. He associated Protestant decline with broad demographic trends such as the spread of American Catholics, who in his words built a new church every day that "another Methodist or Presbyterian church is turned into a garage."[34] Mencken's disagreement with Speer over Protestant reversals highlights an important point: the mainline Protestant churches were in decline for a number of reasons. But however diverse the reasons, the consequences of that decline were clear; and nowhere were they more apparent than in the pulpit, whose occupants found it increasingly difficult in the 1920s to retain the regard of the nation's power elite.[35]

In view of the clergy's diminishing power, many religious commentators concluded that the country was bereft of moral leadership. But this verdict failed to reflect the growing authority of professional psychologists, who had emerged from the academy during World War I to sort, classify, and test army servicemen on behalf of the U.S. government. As a result of these efforts (whose aura of scientific efficiency contrasted markedly with the YMCA's wartime attempts to inculcate character through the distribution of Bibles and basketballs), psychology gained the attention of government and industrial leaders.[36] After the war, these leaders invited psychologists to enter the workplace and assist in the improvement of people's behavior.[37]

In response to this invitation, the psychological profession (which was increasingly led not by ex-theology students such as G. Stanley Hall but by individuals whose education and outlook were entirely secular) worked to make its discipline an applied science, and to divorce character building from its muscular Christian past.[38] Psychology also did much to popularize the language of therapeutic healing, which according to Bernie Zilbergeld has since displaced the Bible as the nation's "common reference point."[39] But as impressive as these accomplishments were, they did not make psychology the beau ideal of the 1920s; that title belonged to the American businessman.

Explanations for the high prominence of businessmen during what G. K. Chesterton described as "this Rotarian age" are numerous.[40] But none is more compelling than that provided by Earnest E. Calkins (co-founder of the pioneer advertising firm of Calkins and Holden), who viewed the business craze as an outgrowth of people's disillusionment with the exponents of "religion, government, and war." These "priests," "kings," and "generals" had clearly "failed" to make the world a better place, Calkins declared. As a result, people were seeking guidance from the formerly "despised businessman," who alone among the world's leaders understood that the basis for civilization was not arms or idealism but "selfish, huckstering trade."[41]

That the world's future peace and prosperity depended largely on businessmen was undeniable, agreed Rotary founder Paul Harris. For businessmen generally did not hold with the sort of "militant religion" and "extremist" politics that had caused the Great War. Nor did they engage in pointless and potentially divisive religious and political discussions (both of which were banned from Rotary). Instead businessmen, according to Harris, were "ambassadors of good will" whose broad-minded leadership style made it possible even for "Catholic priests, Jewish rabbis, and Protestant ministers [to] sit together at Rotary meetings, singing songs and indulging in happy fellowship."[42]

Harris's vision of a peaceful businessman's world utterly devoid of religious and philosophical debate appalled Episcopal Church bishop Charles Fiske, who complained of the nation's mounting urge to view God as "a sort of Magnified Rotarian."[43] But other church leaders agreed with Harris that the clergyman ought to be more "efficient" and that he ought to trade in his "militancy" for the breezy, uncritical spirit of the congenial businessman. As a result, observed Babson College founder Roger Babson, the churches were hiring pastors who were "of the salesman type rather than of the academic type" and who understood that the best religion was that which made people "healthy, happy, and prosperous."[44]

The churches' quest for a more businesslike workforce had many supporters, the staunchest of which was undoubtedly the YMCA, which urged its employees to adopt new and more efficient techniques. Association secretaries could no longer rely on the "disappointing" muscular Christian emphases of the past, explained one YMCA official. Instead, their attempts at "character-building" would have to involve "the critical examination, testing, and measuring of all processes to see if they are producing the expected results and are in harmony with our best knowledge."[45]

As part of their postwar modernization and professionalization efforts, YMCA leaders dropped their old evangelical church membership requirement and scaled back on their celebration of intense male friendships (which psychologists and the popular press were

beginning to associate with homosexuality).[46] "Y" leaders also de-
emphasized Bible study, stopped keeping conversion statistics, and
spoke less about God than about "moral hygiene": the idea that practices such as sport, exercise, and teeth-cleaning ought to be encouraged not because they strengthened reformers, but because they possessed an "ethical significance" all their own.[47]

These changes helped make the "Y" what it is today: a largely secular health-care organization specializing in "personal wellness."[48] But
they hardly pacified inveterate YMCA-haters such as H. L. Mencken,
who had been forced as a round-shouldered, atheistic teenager to
undergo physical training at the Baltimore YMCA and who retaliated
in later life by condemning "Y" war work.[49] "Whether or not the
YMCA has decorated its chocolate peddlars and soul snatchers I do
not know," wrote the irascible journalist in 1920.

> If not, then there should be some governmental recognition of these
> highly characteristic heroes of the war for democracy. The veterans of
> the line, true enough, dislike them excessively, and have a habit of de-
> nouncing them obscenely when the corn-juice flows. They charged too
> much for cigarettes; they tried to discourage the amiability of the ladies
> of France; they had a habit of being absent when the shells burst in the
> air. Well, some say this and some say that. A few, at least, of the pale and
> oleaginous brethren must have gone into the Master's work because
> they thirsted to save souls, and not simply because they desired to escape
> the trenches. And a few, I am told, were anything but unpleasantly righ-
> teous, as a round of Wassermanns would show. If, as may be plausibly
> argued, these Soldiers of the Double Cross deserve to live at all, then
> they surely deserve to be hung with white enameled stars of the third
> class, with gilt dollar marks superimposed. Motto: "Glory, glory, halle-
> lujah!"[50]

Mencken's animosity toward the YMCA reflected his aversion to
all "high-powered uplifter[s]," whom he relentlessly parodied with
devastating effect in his avant-garde journal *The American Mercury*.
But despite his genius for deriding Protestant evangelical culture, the
cosmopolitan, beer-drinking, Germanophilic Mencken had never really moved within that culture or learned its inner workings. As a result, his parody of the churches was in some ways less cutting than
that of his friend and protégé Sinclair Lewis, whose firsthand experiences of evangelicalism included membership in the Congregational
Church and the Young People's Society of Christian Endeavor of Sauk

Centre, Minnesota, college membership in the Student Volunteer Movement (which Lewis joined in hopes of becoming a foreign missionary), and membership in the Oberlin College YMCA (which Lewis praised in 1903 for its "positive earnest muscular Christianity").[51]

As a result of these experiences, Lewis gained an intimate knowledge of bourgeois Protestant culture. And while he later repudiated this culture following his transferal to Yale and exposure to Eastern sophistication, he remembered enough of his youthful affiliations to parody them effectively in novels such as *Elmer Gantry*, wherein a "red-blooded" YMCA secretary named Judson Roberts ("the Praying Fullback") urges the hulking Gantry (representative of the Reverend William Stidger—"Gyp the Blood"—and the Reverend John Roach Straton of New York City) to view religion as an alternative to reading dirty books. "I've got a swell plan, old boy," Roberts tells his muscular pupil:

> "Make a study of missions, and think how clean and pure and manly you'd want to be if you were going to carry the joys of Christianity to a lot of poor gazebos that are under the evil spell of Buddhism and a lot of these heathen religions. Wouldn't you want to be able to look 'em in the eye, and shame 'em? Next thing to do is to get a lot of exercise. Get out and run like hell! And then cold baths. Darn' cold. There now!" Rising, with ever so manly a handshake: "Now skip along and remember"— with a tremendous and fetching and virile laugh—"just run like hell!"[52]

The fact that writers such as Lewis and Mencken could draw laughs (and sell books) by pillorying muscular Christianity and the "Y" forced Association leaders to concede that in their push to make religion "bright and snappy" they had sometimes neglected to make room for "services of dignity and beauty."[53] But the rush by "irresponsible literary desperadoes" to parody "all forms of 'uplift'" was too much for the YMCA's *Home Work Bulletin*, which objected in 1928 to "the virulent criticism of our work which appears everywhere now." "This is a sophisticated crowd we are up against today," complained the *Bulletin*. And it was "discouraging" to watch "Flaming Youth," "Exploding Age," and "even those who should be our friends line up in the ranks of the scornful."[54]

The YMCA's concern for the future of muscular Christian character building was well founded. For the demographic and cultural diversification that had lessened the influence of Anglo-Saxon Christian ideals did not abate with the passage of time. Nor did the mainline churches remain committed to their prewar policy of achieving utopia through manly exertion. Instead, their leaders increasingly sided with Reinhold Niebuhr and other neo-orthodox theologians, who argued in the 1930s, 1940s, and 1950s that divinity resided not in men's muscles, but with God.

Seeing neo-orthodoxy replace muscular Christianity in the mainline churches might lead some to conclude that muscular Christianity died out and is no more. It certainly did fade away in its most strident form from liberal seminaries and mainline churches. But while muscular Christianity declined in mainline Protestant circles, it remained very much alive in fundamentalist churches, particularly those that lay far outside northeastern centers of influence. Such churches were at first inclined to regard sports as sinful.[55] But by the third decade of the twentieth century, they were not only using muscular Christianity's athletic metaphors; they were also using muscular Christianity's masculine rhetoric against theological liberals, who were portrayed by many fundamentalists as soft and effeminate.[56]

The survival of muscular Christianity within fundamentalist circles went largely unnoticed by much of the academic establishment during fundamentalism's separatist phase, which lasted roughly from the aftermath of the Scopes Trial until the dramatic rise to prominence of right-wing Christian groups such as the Moral Majority in the 1970s.[57] But the fact that fundamentalists did not receive a lot of serious scholarly attention during their separatist phase does not mean that they were inactive. While scholars highlighted mainline Protestant developments such as "Death of God" theology, fundamentalists, emulating the old YMCA, encouraged the development of manly Christian athletes by supporting sports-oriented organizations such as Youth for Christ (est. 1945), the Fellowship of Christian Athletes (est. 1954), and Athletes in Action (est. ca. 1966).[58] Fundamentalists also struggled, as had the Men and Religion Forward movement, to promote more manliness in religion; hence their participation in Christian men's groups such as Oral Roberts's Full Gospel Businessmen's Fellowship (est. 1951) and Promise Keepers, which was created by University of Colorado football coach Bill McCartney in 1990.[59]

With athletic Christian Promise Keepers such as McCartney envisioning "men coming together in huge numbers in the name of Jesus," it is obvious that muscular Christianity is alive in America today.[60] It is arguably a different strain of muscular Christianity from the type that permeated the late-nineteenth-century YMCA, many of whose members (unlike the Promise Keepers) openly aimed to halt the alleged decline of the "Anglo-Saxon race."[61] But while the muscular Christians of today generally avoid talk of racial strengthening, they, like their nineteenth-century counterparts, are committed to injecting health and manliness into America's churches.

Notes

Introduction

The epigraph is from G[ranville] Stanley Hall, "Christianity and Physical Culture," *Pedagogical Seminary* 9, no. 3 (September 1902): 377.

1. Thomas W. Higginson, "Saints, and Their Bodies," *Atlantic Monthly* 1, no. 5 (1858): 583–588.
2. Randy Balmer, "Introduction," in Dane S. Claussen, ed., *The Promise Keepers: Essays on Masculinity and Christianity* (London: MacFarland & Co., 2000), p. 3.
3. Christine Heyrman, *Southern Cross: The Beginnings of the Bible Belt* (New York: Alfred A. Knopf, 1997), pp. 212–243.
4. Tony Ladd and James Mathisen, *Muscular Christianity: Evangelical Protestants and the Development of American Sport* (Grand Rapids, Mich.: Baker Books, 1999), p. 34.
5. Margaret Bendroth, *Fundamentalism and Gender, 1875 to the Present* (New Haven: Yale University Press, 1993), p. 13.
6. Ladd and Mathisen, *Muscular Christianity*, pp. 52–53.
7. Ibid., p. 32.
8. Dane Claussen, "What the Media Missed about the Promise Keepers," in Dane Claussen, ed., *Standing on the Promises: The Promise Keepers and the Revival of Manhood* (Cleveland, Ohio: Pilgrim Press, 1999), p. 20.
9. Bendroth, *Fundamentalism and Gender*, p. 26.
10. Ann Douglas, *The Feminization of American Culture* (New York: Doubleday, 1988), pp. 121–256.
11. Benjamin Rader, *American Sports: From the Age of Folk Games to the Age of Spectators* (Englewood Cliffs: Prentice-Hall, 1983), pp. 150–151.

12. Douglas, *The Feminization of American Culture,* pp. 80–256.
13. See Mark Carnes, *Secret Ritual and Manhood in Victorian America* (New Haven: Yale University Press, 1989); and Clifford Putney, "Service over Secrecy: How Lodgestyle Fraternalism Yielded Popularity to Men's Service Clubs," *Journal of Popular Culture* 27, no. 1 (1993): 179–190.
14. Gail Bederman, *Manliness and Civilization: A Cultural History of Gender and Race in the United States, 1880–1917* (Chicago: University of Chicago Press, 1995), p. 18.
15. E. Anthony Rotundo, *American Manhood: Transformations in Masculinity from the Revolution to the Modern Era* (New York: BasicBooks, 1993), p. 5.
16. Bederman, *Manliness and Civilization,* pp. 88–120.
17. Not all men's historians are mute with regard to muscular Christianity. Gail Bederman talks about it in "'The Women Have Had Charge of the Church Work Long Enough': The Men and Religion Forward Movement of 1911–1912 and the Masculinization of Middle-Class Protestantism," *American Quarterly* 41, no. 3 (September 1989): 434–459; and Michael Kimmel has a section entitled "The Manly Church" in *Manhood in America: A Cultural History* (New York: Free Press, 1996), pp. 175–181.
18. Rotundo, *American Manhood,* p. 224.
19. James Turner, *Without God, Without Creed: The Origins of Unbelief in America* (Baltimore: Johns Hopkins University Press, 1985), p. 235.
20. The phrase "surprisingly underexploited" comes from Leonard Sweet, who uses it to describe the topic of muscular Christianity. Leonard Sweet, *The Minister's Wife: Her Role in Nineteenth-Century American Evangelicalism* (Philadelphia: Temple University Press, 1983), p. 232.
21. Nina Mjagkij, "True Manhood: The YMCA and Racial Advancement, 1890–1930," in Nina Mjagkij and Margaret Spratt, eds., *Men and Women Adrift: The YMCA and the YWCA in the City* (New York: New York University Press, 1997), p. 146. For a fuller treatment of the history of African-Americans in the YMCA, see Mjagkij, *Light in the Darkness: African-Americans and the YMCA, 1852–1946* (Lexington: University Press of Kentucky, 1994).
22. Mjagkij, "True Manhood," p. 152.
23. Evelyn Brooks Higginbotham, *Righteous Discontent: the Women's Movement in the Black Baptist Church, 1880–1920* (Cambridge: Harvard University Press, 1993), pp. 142–146.
24. Kimmel, *Manhood in America,* p. 443. The 92nd Street Young Men's Hebrew Association in New York City is the nation's oldest Jewish community center in continuous existence. It was founded in 1874. Twenty-eight years later, an independent Young Women's Hebrew Association was organized in New York City. For more on the YMHA and the YWHA and their parallels with the YMCA and the YWCA, see David Kaufman, *Shul with a Pool:*

The "Synagogue-Center" in American Jewish History (Waltham, Mass.: Brandeis University Press, 1999).

25. Patrick Kelly, "The Sacramental Imagination, Culture, and Play" (Licentiate's thesis, Weston Jesuit School of Theology, 1999), pp. 86, 67.

26. Christa Klein, "The Jesuits and Catholic Boyhood in Nineteenth-Century New York City: A Study of St. John's College and the College of St. Francis Xavier, 1846–1912" (Ph.D. diss., University of Pennsylvania, 1976), pp. 318–322.

27. Ibid., p. 321.

28. E. Digby Baltzell, *The Protestant Establishment: Aristocracy and Caste in America* (New York: Random House, 1964).

29. Bendroth, *Fundamentalism and Gender*, pp. 3–9, 19, 64–65. Bendroth writes that conservative churchmen adopted muscular Christian rhetoric during the fundamentalist-modernist controversy of the 1920s in order to combat not only the "woman peril" in religion but also theological liberalism, which many conservatives viewed as an effeminate doctrine.

30. Clifford Putney, "From Character to Body Building: The YMCA and the Suburban Metropolis, 1950–1980," in Mjagkij and Spratt, *Men and Women Adrift*, pp. 231–249.

31. For information on the Fellowship of Christian Athletes, see Shirl Hoffman, ed., *Sport and Religion* (Champaign, Ill.: Human Kinetics Books, 1992). For information on the Promise Keepers, see Claussen, *The Promise Keepers*; and Claussen, *Standing on the Promises*.

1. The Birth of a Movement

The epigraph is from Theodore Roosevelt, "Manliness and Decency," *Men* 22, no. 39 (Feb. 6, 1897): 704–705.

1. "Two Years Ago," *Saturday Review* 3 (Feb. 21, 1857): 176.

2. "Muscular Christianity," *Tait's Edinburgh Magazine* 25 (February 1858): 100–102.

3. More has been written about English muscular Christianity than about the American strain. Those interested in English muscular Christianity might consider engaging in the lively debate on Hughes and Kingsley that has recently sprung up between Norman Vance, Sean Gill, Peter Gay, and Donald Hall. Hall is particularly struck, as am I, by the straightforwardness of Hughes and Kingsley. They were undoubtedly complex people, as Vance, Gill, and Gay insist, but they delivered unambiguous messages in their novels, and they clearly viewed male aggression as a praiseworthy element in Christianity. See Peter Gay, "The Manliness of Christ," in R. W. Davis and R. J. Helmstadter, eds., *Religion and Irreligion in Victorian Society* (London: Routledge, 1992), pp. 102–116; Sean Gill, "How Muscular Was Vic-

torian Christianity? Thomas Hughes and the Cult of Christian Manliness Reconsidered," in R. N. Swanson, ed., *Gender and Christian Religion* (Woodbridge, England: Boydell Press, 1998), pp. 421–430; Donald Hall, ed., *Muscular Christianity: Embodying the Victorian Age* (Cambridge: Cambridge University Press, 1994); and Norman Vance, *The Sinews of the Spirit: The Ideal of Christian Manliness in Victorian Literature and Religious Thought* (Cambridge: Cambridge University Press, 1985).

4. Norman Vance, *Sinews of the Spirit,* p. 3.

5. William Winn, "Tom Brown's School-Days and the Development of Muscular Christianity," *Church History* 29 (March 1960): 65–66.

6. Thomas Hughes, *The Manliness of Christ* (Boston, 1880), p. 77.

7. Henry R. Harrington, "Muscular Christianity: A Study of the Development of a Victorian Idea" (Ph.D. diss., Stanford University, 1971), p. 178.

8. See F. E. Kingsley, ed., *Charles Kingsley: His Letters and Memories of His Life,* vol. 1 (London, 1877), p. 249; and Charles Kingsley, "What, Then, Does Dr. Newman Mean?" in John Henry Newman, *Apologia Pro Vita Sua: Being a History of His Religious Opinions,* ed. Martin J. Svaglic (Oxford: Clarendon Press, 1990), p. 363.

9. Quoted in Harold Nicolson, *Good Behaviour: Being a Study of Certain Types of Civility* (London: Constable & Co., 1955), p. 231.

10. Harrington, "Muscular Christianity," p. 28.

11. Quoted in Phillip Goodhart and Christopher Chataway, *War without Weapons* (London: W. H. Allen, 1968), p. 42.

12. Charles Kingsley, *Sanitary and Social Lectures and Essays* (London, 1880), p. 265.

13. David Newsome, *Godliness and Good Learning* (London: John Murray, 1961), p. 211.

14. Charles Kingsley, *True Words for Brave Men* (New York, 1886), p. 45.

15. Norman Vance, *Sinews of the Spirit,* p. 109.

16. Harrington, "Muscular Christianity," p. 130.

17. Ibid., p. 177.

18. Charles Kingsley, "Froude's History of England, Vols. 7 and 8," *Macmillan's Magazine* (January 1864): 211–224.

19. Quoted in James Hastings, ed., *Encyclopedia of Religion and Ethics,* vol. 9 (New York, 1928), p. 357.

20. Frederic Harrison, *Studies in Early Victorian Literature* (London, 1895), p. 180.

21. For more about Thomas Hughes and the muscular Christian movement, see George Worth, "Of Muscles and Manliness: Some Reflections on Thomas Hughes," in J. R. Kincaid and A. J. Kuhn, eds., *Victorian Literature and Society: Essays Presented to Richard Altick* (Columbus: Ohio State University Press, 1984), pp. 300–314.

22. Quoted in Gill, "How Muscular Was Victorian Christianity?" p. 425.

23. Hughes, *Tom Brown at Oxford* (Philadelphia, [1861]), p. 121.

24. *Tom Brown's School Days* was well known not only in England but also in France, where the Baron de Coubertin (founder of the modern Olympic games) quoted liberally from the book when pushing athletics for Frenchmen as a moral corrective to the humiliations of the Franco-Prussian War. Pierre de Coubertin, *L'Education en Angleterre* (Paris, 1888), pp. 63–71.

25. Hughes, *The Manliness of Christ*, p. 5.

26. Harrington, "Muscular Christianity," p. 72.

27. Hughes, *Tom Brown's School Days* (Boston, 1868), p. 35.

28. Quoted in E[mma] E. Brown, ed., *True Manliness: From the Writings of Thomas Hughes* (Boston, 1880), p. x.

29. Nicolson, *Good Behaviour*, pp. 258–259.

30. Thomas Arnold, *The Miscellaneous Works* (New York, 1845), p. 411.

31. Edward Bellasis, *Notes for Boys (and Their Fathers) on Morals, Mind, and Manners* (Chicago, 1888), p. 73. "The deadly habit" is Bellasis's euphemism for masturbation.

32. Hughes, *Tom Brown's School Days*, pp. 157–158. Russell quoted in Nicolson, *Good Behaviour*, p. 256.

33. E. M. Forster, *Abinger Harvest* (New York: Harcourt, Brace & Co., 1936), p. 5. Alec Waugh, *The Loom of Youth* (London, 1921), p. 141.

34. An anonymous reviewer wrote with regard to Lawrence's work, "If we are to have a rattling novel about dogs . . . and Byronic ferocity, perhaps it might be as well to leave the Christianity alone." "Guy Livingston," *Edinburgh Review* 18 (July–October 1858): 540.

35. David Newsome, *On the Edge of Paradise: A. C. Benson, the Diarist* (Chicago: University of Chicago Press, 1980), p. 212.

36. See Tony Ladd and James A. Mathisen, *Muscular Christianity: Evangelical Protestants and the Development of American Sport* (Grand Rapids, Mich.: Baker Books, 1999), pp. 45–46; and Mathisen, "From Muscular Christianity to Jocks for Jesus," *Christian Century* 109, no. 1 (Jan. 1–8, 1992): 12.

37. Quoted in Norman Vance, *Sinews of the Spirit*, p. 173.

38. Arnold Lunn, *The Harrovians* (London, 1913), pp. 138–142.

39. Bellasis, *Notes for Boys*, p. 164.

40. Hughes, *The Manliness of Christ*, p. 2.

41. Harrington, "Muscular Christianity," p. 232.

42. For a brief history of muscular Christianity in mid-nineteenth-century America, see Guy Lewis, "The Muscular Christianity Movement," *Journal of Health, Physical Education, and Recreation* 37 (May 1966): 27–28, 42.

43. "Mr. Thomas Hughes and His Address," *Harvard Advocate Supplement* 10, no. 1 (Oct. 14, 1870): i–ii.

44. Margaret McGehee, "A Castle in the Wilderness: Rugby Colony, Tennessee, 1880–1887, *Journal of East Tennessee History* 70 (1998): 62–89.

45. David J. Burrell, *For Christ's Crown and Other Sermons* (New York, 1896), pp. 244–253. Jenkin L. Jones, "The Manliness of Christ," *Unity Short Tracts*, no. 12 [1903], pp. 1–3.

46. Theodore Roosevelt, "What We Can Expect of the American Boy," *St. Nicholas* 27 (1900): 573. The other book recommended by Roosevelt was Nelson Aldrich's *Story of a Bad Boy.*

47. Edward Everett Hale, *Public Amusement for Poor and Rich* (Boston, 1857), p. 20. I was directed to this work and several others by Patrick Kelly, "The Sacramental Imagination, Culture, and Play" (Licentiate's thesis, Weston Jesuit School of Theology, 1999).

48. Washington Gladden, *Amusements: Their Uses and Abuses* (North Adams, Mass., 1866), p. 6.

49. Hale, *Public Amusement for Poor and Rich,* pp. 5–6, 20–23; and Hale, *A New England Boyhood* (New York, 1893), pp. 177–179.

50. Quoted in Clyde Griffen, "Reconstructing Masculinity from the Evangelical Revival to the Waning of Progressivism: A Speculative Synthesis," in Mark Carnes and Clyde Griffen, eds., *Meanings for Manhood* (Chicago: University of Chicago Press, 1990), p. 189.

51. Horace Bushnell, *Christian Nurture* (New York, 1861), pp. 340–341, 356–357.

52. John Sterling, *A Correspondence between John Sterling and Ralph Waldo Emerson,* ed. E. W. Emerson (Boston, 1897), p. 67.

53. Ralph Waldo Emerson, *English Traits* (Boston, 1857), p. 76.

54. Ibid., pp. 215–227. Charles Kingsley, who had little use for Emerson's Transcendentalism (thinking it productive not of labor but of loafing), naturally took exception to his anti-Anglican remarks. Reviewing *English Traits* in 1856, Kingsley wondered how Emerson could congratulate the English on their materialism while abhorring that quality in the English Church. After all, he argued, Anglicanism's "Judaism" (i.e., its sanctification of "family life, law, politics, and nationality") "has been for centuries the kindly foster-mother of those very virtues which he [Emerson] most admires in us." Kingsley, review of *English Traits, Saturday Review* (Oct. 4, 1856): 509–510.

55. John A. Lucas, "Thomas W. Higginson: Early Apostle of Health and Fitness," *Journal of Health, Physical Education, and Recreation* 42 (1971): 30–33. For additional commentary on Higginson's ideas, see Linda J. Borish, "The Robust Woman and the Muscular Christian: Catharine Beecher, Thomas Higginson, and Their Vision of American Society, Health, and Physical Activities," *International Journal of the History of Sport* 4, no. 2 (September 1987): 139–154.

56. Thomas W. Higginson, "Saints, and Their Bodies," *Atlantic Monthly* 1, no. 5 (1858): 584, 588. Higginson returned to the theme of muscular Christianity in "Barbarism and Civilization," *Atlantic Monthly* 7 (1861): 51–61.

57. Higginson, "Saints, and Their Bodies," pp. 583–587. Higginson did concede that there were promising signs of health on the horizon, including the recent decision of the Harvard Divinity School to organize a boat club and the transparent manliness of America's three most popular preachers:

Beecher with his "sinewy arm," Parker with his "great strength," and Chapin with his "burly frame."

58. During the Civil War, Beecher observed that "[t]here ought to be gymnastic grounds and good bowling-alleys, in connection with reading-rooms . . . under judicious management, where, for a small fee, every young man might find various wholesome exercises, and with all good society, without the temptations which surround all the alleys and rooms of the city, kept for bowling and billiards. It seems surprising, while so many young men's associations are organized, whose main trouble it is to find *something to do*, that some Christian association should not undertake this important reformation, and give to the young men of our cities the means of physical vigor and health, separated from temptations to vice. It would be a very gospel." Henry Ward Beecher, *Eyes and Ears* (Boston, 1863), pp. 205–206, quoted in Ladd and Mathisen, *Muscular Christianity*, p. 31.

59. Moses Coit Tyler, *The Brawnville Papers* (Boston, 1869), p. 20.

60. James Whorton, *Crusaders for Fitness: The History of American Health Reformers* (Princeton, N.J.: Princeton University Press, 1982), p. 280.

61. See Moses Tyler, *The Brawnville Papers,* p. 162; and Ladd and Mathisen, *Muscular Christianity,* p. 24.

62. *New York Times,* July 18, 1869, p. 5, quoted in Ladd and Mathisen, *Muscular Christianity,* pp. 24–25.

63. J. C. Pollock, *Moody without Sankey: A New Biographical Portrait* (Bungay, Suffolk: Hodder & Stoughton, 1963), p. 176. The writer for the *Sunday Times* has been mistakenly identified by some as Walt Whitman.

64. "Muscular Christianity and UnChristian Muscularity," *The Friend* 47, no. 9 (September 1889): 78.

65. John M. Tyler, "The Physical Education of Girls and Women," *American Physical Education Review* 16, no. 8 (November 1911): 487.

66. "Charles Kingsley," *Illustrated Christian Weekly* 5 (March 6, 1875): 113–114.

67. Envious of the manly status that their forefathers had achieved by participating in the Civil War, some members of Congress supported the Spanish-American War because they thought that fighting the Spaniards would spark a revival of Civil War–era heroism. Kristin Hoganson, *Fighting for American Manhood: How Gender Politics Provoked the Spanish-American and Philippine-American Wars* (New Haven: Yale University Press, 1998), pp. 140–141.

68. Hale, *Public Amusement for Poor and Rich,* p. 21.

69. Ann Douglas, *The Feminization of American Culture* (New York: Doubleday, 1988). Douglas's "feminization" thesis is not without critics, most of whom fault her for overemphasizing the power of women in antebellum America. See David Reynolds, "The Feminization Controversy: Sexual Stereotypes and the Paradoxes of Piety in Nineteenth-Century America," *New England Quarterly* 53, no. 1 (1980): 96–106.

70. Barbara Welter, "The Feminization of American Religion, 1800–1860," in William L. O'Neill, ed., *Insights and Parallels* (Minneapolis: Burgess Publishing Co., 1973), p. 307. For a more comprehensive view of women in antebellum American religion, see Leonard I. Sweet, *The Minister's Wife: Her Role in Nineteenth-Century American Evangelicalism* (Philadelphia: Temple University Press, 1983).

71. Quoted in Milton Powell, ed., *The Voluntary Church: American Religious Life, 1740–1865, Seen through the Eyes of European Visitors* (New York: Macmillan, 1967), pp. 68–69.

72. Quoted in Douglas, *The Feminization of American Culture,* p. 251.

73. For more on the subject of antebellum Protestant attitudes toward death, see ibid., pp. 200–226; and (for a humorous view of morbidity) Mark Twain, "Ode to Stephen Dowling Bots, Dec'd," in *The Adventures of Huckleberry Finn* (New York, 1896), p. 137.

74. Henry C. Merwin, "On Being Civilized Too Much," *Atlantic Monthly* 79 (June 1897): 838–839. Theodore Roosevelt, "Machine Politics in New York City," *Century Magazine* 23 (November 1886): 76.

75. Henry James, *The Bostonians* (New York, 1945), p. 283.

76. See George Beard, *American Nervousness, Its Causes and Consequences* (New York, 1881).

77. H. Addington Bruce, "Insanity and the Nation," *North American Review* 187 (January 1908): 70–79.

78. Tom Lutz, *American Nervousness* (Ithaca: Cornell University Press, 1991), p. 19.

79. Christian F. Reisner, *Roosevelt's Religion* (New York, 1922), p. 75.

80. Luther Gulick, "Neurasthenia," *Physical Training* 2, no. 4 (January 1903): 148–152.

81. T. J. Jackson Lears, *No Place of Grace: Antimodernism and the Transformation of American Culture, 1880–1920* (New York: Pantheon Books, 1981), p. 47.

82. Robert M. Crunden, "Essay," in John D. Buenker et al., *Progressivism* (Cambridge: Schenkman Books, 1977), pp. 71–103.

83. See Charlotte P. Gilman, *The Yellow Wall Paper* (Boston, 1899).

84. Lears, *No Place of Grace,* p. 25.

85. Lutz, *American Nervousness,* pp. 6–7.

86. See Richard Hofstadter, *The Age of Reform: From Bryan to FDR* (New York: Knopf, 1955).

87. Aaron Abell, *The Urban Impact on American Protestantism, 1865–1900* (Cambridge: Harvard University Press, 1943), p. 57.

88. Fred Smith, *A Man's Religion* (New York, 1913), pp. 46–47.

89. Myron T. Scudder, "The Value of Recreation in Rural Communities," in *The Rural Church,* vol. 6 of *Messages of the Men and Religion Forward Movement* (New York, 1912), pp. 228–229.

90. Edward Hitchcock, Jr., "The Physical Condition of the American People," *Chautaquan* 23 (April–September 1896): 151–153.

91. Quoted in Peter Roberts, "The Association and the Immigrant," *Association Men* 32, no. 10 (July 1907): 426–427.

92. Henry T. Finck, "Are Womanly Women Doomed?" *Independent* 53 (Jan. 31, 1901): 267–268.

93. Goldwin Smith, "Woman's Place in the State," *Forum* 8 (January 1890): 524.

94. David I. Macleod, *Building Character in the American Boy: The Boy Scouts, YMCA, and Their Forerunners, 1870–1920* (Madison: University of Wisconsin Press, 1983), p. 46.

95. G. Stanley Hall, *Morale: The Supreme Standard of Life and Conduct* (New York, 1920), pp. 248–249. Lilburn Merrill, *Winning the Boy* (New York, 1908), p. 35.

96. Henry C. Potter, "The Message of Christ to the Family," in A. V. G. Allen et al., *The Message of Christ to Manhood* (Boston, 1899), p. 195.

97. William Blaikie, "Is American Stamina Declining?" *Harper's* 79 (July 1889): 241.

98. William James, *On Vital Reserves* (New York, 1911), p. 53. G. Stanley Hall, *Youth: Its Education, Regimen, and Hygiene* (New York, 1906), p. 326.

99. Holmes quoted in H. W. Foster, "Physical Education vs. Degeneracy," *Independent* 52 (Aug. 2, 1900): 1835. J. F. A. Adams, "Neglect of Physical Training," *Educational Review* 11 (March 1896): 273–276. Luther Gulick, "Fundamental Basis of the Young Men's Christian Association" [typescript, ca. 1890], Archives, Babson Library, Springfield College, Springfield, Mass., pp. 1–2.

100. Macleod, *Building Character in the American Boy,* p. 46.

101. Earl Barnes, "The Feminizing of Culture," *Atlantic Monthly* 109 (June 1912): 775.

102. G. Stanley Hall, "Feminization in School and Home," *World's Work* 16 (1908): 10239.

103. "Race Suicide in the United States," *American Physical Education Review* 20, no. 7 (October 1915): 463–464.

104. F. E. Chadwick, "The Woman Peril in American Education," *Educational Review* 47 (February 1914): 116.

105. Mitchell quoted in Lears, *No Place of Grace,* p. 104. James Lane Allen, "Two Principles in Recent American Fiction," *Atlantic Monthly* 80 (October 1897): 438.

106. Roosevelt, *Theodore Roosevelt: An Autobiography* (New York, 1920), pp. 86–87. The unmanliness of the Victorian intelligentsia was also the subject of a 1883 Union College address, wherein the speaker regretted how "[i]t is the want of . . . virile energy which often makes diligent students and dextrous writers entirely ineffective when great interests are at stake, and

sharp issues are being decided, as their walking sticks would be in the rush and clash of a cavalry charge." Richard Storrs, *Manliness in the Scholar* (New York, 1883), p. 22.

107. Alfred T. Mahan, *The Interest of America in Sea Power, Present and Future* (Boston, 1897), p. 121.

108. Charles S. Macfarland, *Spiritual Culture and Social Service* (New York, 1912), pp. 50, 52.

109. Ibid., p. 48.

110. Storrs, *Manliness in the Scholar,* p. 22.

111. See Paul A. Carter, *The Spiritual Crisis of the Gilded Age* (DeKalb: Northern Illinois University Press, 1971).

112. For a fuller discussion of late-nineteenth-century Protestant liberalism, see William R. Hutchison, *The Modernist Impulse in American Protestantism* (Cambridge: Harvard University Press, 1976).

113. Lears, *No Place of Grace,* pp. 5, 32.

114. William Forbush, *The Boy Problem: A Study in Social Pedagogy* (Boston, 1907), p. 54.

115. See "The Great Moral Upheaval Now Taking Place in America," *Current Literature* 40 (May 1906): 535–536; and Gerald F. Roberts, "The Strenuous Life: The Cult of Manliness in the Era of Theodore Roosevelt" (Ph.D. diss., Michigan State University, 1970).

116. Reisner, *Roosevelt's Religion,* p. 75. Though more of a hagiography than a biography, Reisner's book is useful for its emphasis on Roosevelt's religious views. For a more critical treatment of Roosevelt, see Edmund Morris, *The Rise of Theodore Roosevelt* (New York: Coward, McCann and Geoghegan, 1979).

117. Reisner, *Roosevelt's Religion,* p. 86.

118. Quoted in Richard Hofstadter, *Anti-Intellectualism in American Life* (New York: Vintage Books, 1966), p. 194.

119. Reisner, *Roosevelt's Religion,* p. 72.

120. Hofstadter, *Anti-Intellectualism in American Life,* pp. 192–193.

121. Reisner, *Roosevelt's Religion,* p. 72.

122. Ibid., p. 46.

123. Gerald F. Linderman, *The Mirror of War* (Ann Arbor: University of Michigan Press, 1974), p. 93.

124. Quoted in John Blum et al., *The National Experience,* vol. 2 (New York: Harcourt Brace Jovanovich, 1989), p. 490.

125. Linderman, *The Mirror of War,* p. 92.

126. "Great Moral Upheaval Now Taking Place in America," p. 535.

127. Macleod, *Building Character in the American Boy,* p. 57.

128. Quoted in Reisner, *Roosevelt's Religion,* p. 245.

129. "Back to Nature," *Outlook* 74 (June 8, 1903): 305–306.

130. When both the Harvard and Yale football teams showed up clean-shaven in

1889, it appeared as if the venerable beard was out (Benjamin Harrison was the last U.S. president to wear one). And when historian Theodore Greene did a study on turn-of-the-century heroes, he found that they were more valued for their physicality than their counterparts had been one hundred years earlier. See Gerald Carson, "Hair Today, Gone Tomorrow," *American Heritage* 17, no. 2 (February 1966): 45; and Theodore Greene, *America's Heroes: The Changing Models of Success in American Magazines* (New York: Oxford University Press, 1970), pp. 127–131.

131. Henry W. Gibson, *Camping for Boys* (New York, 1911), p. 7.

132. H[enry] W. Gibson, "The History of Organized Camping," *Camping Magazine* [7], January 1936: 26; February 1936: 26; March 1936: 18–19.

133. Gibson, *Camping for Boys*, p. 7.

134. Henry S. Curtis, *The Play Movement and Its Significance* (New York, 1917), pp. 6–15. For a comprehensive history of the organized playground movement, see Dominick Cavallo, *Muscles and Morals: Organized Playgrounds and Urban Reform, 1880–1920* (Philadelphia: University of Pennsylvania Press, 1981).

135. Joseph Lee, "Play as an Antidote to Civilization," *Playground* 5, no. 4 (July 1911): 110–120.

136. Luther H. Gulick, *Popular Recreation and Public Morality* (New York, 1909), pp. 3–6.

137. E. Anthony Rotundo, *American Manhood: Transformations in Masculinity from the Revolution to the Modern Era* (New York: Basic Books, 1993), p. 226.

138. Austin Lewis, "Kipling and Women," *Overland Monthly* 42 (October 1903): 357–358.

139. Hall, "Feminization in School and Home," p. 10241.

140. See Eugene S. Talbot, *Degeneracy: Its Causes, Signs, and Results* (New York, 1898).

141. Merrill, *Winning the Boy*, p. 51.

142. W. W. Hastings, "Racial Hygiene and Vigor," *American Physical Education Review* 15 (1910): 516.

143. G. Stanley Hall, "Eugenics: Its Ideals and What It Is Going to Do," *Religious Education* 6, no. 2 (June 1911): 156. Hall allowed that for Christianity truly to be wedded to science, it first had to be rid of such outmoded appendages as miracles ("surds injected into the lower plexi of thought"), "botanical impossibilities" such as the crown of thorns, the asceticism of "pathological saints and anchorites," and "all the contorted scrupulosities of the New England conscience." Hall, *Jesus, the Christ, in the Light of Psychology* (Garden City, N.Y., 1917), pp. 24, xiii, ix; and Hall, *Morale*, p. 4.

144. John C. Burnham, "The Progressive Era Revolution in American Attitudes toward Sex," *Journal of American History* 59, no. 4 (March 1973): 886 and passim.

145. Hastings, "Racial Hygiene and Vigor," pp. 524–525.

146. The 1880s and 1890s also witnessed the self-conscious professionalization of physical education, which was aided by the establishment of the Association for the Advancement of Physical Education (later the American Physical Education Association) in 1885, the Boston Physical Education Society in 1896, and the Society of College Gym Directors in 1897. A primary goal of these societies was the implementation of physical education in the public schools, which occurred with great rapidity in the late nineteenth century. An 1892 study revealed that of 272 leading cities in the United States, 164 possessed identifiable programs for physical education, only 10 percent of which had been in place before 1887. Emmett A. A. Rice, *A Brief History of Physical Education* (New York, 1929), pp. 238–239.

147. Dudley Allen Sargent, "The Hemenway Gymnasium: An Educational Experiment," *Harvard Graduates' Magazine* 3 (December 1894): 172.

148. Charles K. Taylor, *Character Development* (Philadelphia, 1913), pp. 1, 206, 12.

149. Taylor, "Better Boys," *American Magazine* 77 (June 1914): 50–51.

150. Elwood Worcester et al., *Religion and Medicine: The Moral Control of Nervous Disorders* (New York, 1908), p. 309.

151. Eugene L. Richards, "The Physical Element in Education," *Popular Science Monthly* 47 (1895): 476, 472.

152. Frances A. Walker, "College Athletics," *Harvard Graduates' Magazine* 2 (1893): 11.

153. Eliot's belief that the "well-rounded" student should be neither a "bookworm" nor a "monk" helped to effect changes in the Harvard curriculum, including a minimization of Greek and Latin and the introduction of courses presumably of some relevance to young men's lives. Eliot's support for school sports ("under modern stresses . . . an indispensable part of young life") likewise influenced Harvard's foray into intercollegiate athletics and its building of athletic facilities, such as Soldiers Field. Alar Lipping, "Charles W. Eliot's View of Education, Physical Education, and Intercollegiate Athletics" (Ph.D. diss., Ohio State Univ., 1980), pp. 169–174.

154. Ibid., pp. 242, 176.

155. Quoted in Rotundo, *American Manhood*, p. 224.

156. See Ladd and Mathisen, *Muscular Christianity*, p. 30; and Henry Churchill King, *The Moral and Religious Challenge of Our Times* (New York, 1911), pp. 240–248.

157. Edward I. Bosworth, "How Can the Association in the Future Render the Largest Service to the Church?" *Association Men* 33, no. 3 (December 1907): 118.

158. Henry King, *How to Make a Rational Fight for Character* (New York, 1902), p. 39.

159. Abell, *The Urban Impact on American Protestantism*, p. 56.

160. Josiah Strong, *The New Era; or, The Coming Kingdom* (New York, 1893), p. 314.

161. See Janet Fishburn, *The Fatherhood of God and the Victorian Family: A Study of the Social Gospel* (Philadelphia: Fortress Press, 1981), p. 164; and Susan Curtis, "The Son of Man and God the Father: The Social Gospel and Victorian Masculinity," in Carnes and Griffen, eds., *Meanings for Manhood*, p. 74. The words "almost exclusively" come from Fishburn.

162. Courtland Myers, *Why Men Do Not Go to Church* (New York, 1899), pp. x–xi.

163. Josiah Strong, *The Times and Young Men* (New York, 1901), p. 179–180. Strong viewed the churches of his day as "weak, effeminate."

164. Carl Case, *The Masculine in Religion* (Philadelphia, 1906), p. 21. For more on the attitudes of Social Gospel ministers toward women, see Ronald Huff, "Social Christian Clergymen and Feminism during the Progressive Era" (Ph.D. diss., Union Theological Seminary, 1974).

165. James I. Vance, *Royal Manhood* (New York, 1899), pp. 229, 200.

166. G. Walter Fiske, *Finding the Comrade God* (New York, 1918), p. 1. "Men despise a weak religion," a "religion of mere millinery," Fiske averred. "But a religion of power gets men."

167. Rauschenbusch quoted in Curtis, "The Son of Man and God the Father," p. 73. Strong, *The Times and Young Men*, p. 182.

168. Josiah Strong, *Religious Movements for Social Betterment* (New York, 1900), pp. 29–30.

169. See Strong, *The New Era*, p. 32; and Strong, *The Times and Young Men*, pp. 125, 222. James I. Vance, *Royal Manhood*, pp. 66–68.

170. Washington Gladden, *Straight Shots at Young Men* (New York, 1900), p. 42. George J. Fisher, "Character Development through Social and Personal Hygiene," *Religious Education* 4 (December 1909): 339–401.

171. T. J. Jackson Lears, "From Salvation to Self-Realization: Advertising and the Therapeutic Roots of the Consumer Culture, 1880–1930," in Lears and Richard W. Fox, eds., *The Culture of Consumption: Critical Essays in American History, 1880–1980* (New York: Pantheon Books, 1983), pp. 1–17. Baptist minister George B. Cutten would have agreed with Lears about the Social Gospellers wanting to eliminate the boundaries between sacred and secular. "The Church of to-day has eliminated the distinction between sacred and secular," wrote Cutten, "and recognizes that all things are sacred." George B. Cutten, "The Ministry of Mental Healing," in Charles S. Macfarland, ed., *The Christian Ministry and the Social Order* (New Haven, 1909), pp. 266–267.

172. Robert T. Handy, *A Christian America: Protestant Hopes and Historical Realities* (New York: Oxford University Press, 1984), p. 139. The phrase "right body keeping" comes from G. Stanley Hall, "Christianity and Physical Culture," *Pedagogical Seminary* 9, no. 3 (September 1902): 378.

173. King, *How to Make a Rational Fight for Character,* pp. 8, 16–17. Francis Peabody, *Jesus Christ and the Christian Character* (New York, 1905), p. 175. Strong, *The New Era,* p. 32.

2. God in the Gym

The Munger epigraph is from William G. Anderson, *Anderson's Physical Education* (New York, 1897), p. 25. Munger believed that nothing but physical strength would ever effect positive changes in the world, though he also rather inexplicably warned against letting "the revival of interest in our physical nature" end in "paganism." Theodore Munger, "Message of Christ to the Will," in A. V. G. Allen et al., *The Message of Christ to Manhood* (Boston, 1899), pp. 109–112.

1. Roberta J. Park, "Physiologists, Physicians, and Physical Educators: Nineteenth Century Biology and Exercise, Hygienic and Educative," *Journal of Sport History* 14, no. 1 (Spring 1987): 28. Robert K. Barney, "Physical Education and Sport in North America," in Earle Zeigler, ed., *History of Physical Education and Sport* (Englewood Cliffs, N.J.: Prentice-Hall, 1979), p. 186. Elmer Johnson, *The History of YMCA Physical Education* (Chicago: Association Press, 1979), p. 47.
2. Burges Johnson, "'Old Doc' Hitchcock, Creator of a System of Physical Education," *Outlook* 85 (April 27, 1907): 958.
3. John Higham, "The Reorientation of American Culture in the 1890s," in John Higham, ed., *Writing American History: Essays on Modern Scholarship* (Bloomington: Indiana University Press, 1970), p. 79. While intercollegiate sports gained widespread acceptance in the liberal Protestant schools of the Northeast, they were opposed in the West and South by more conservative Baptist and Methodist schools, many of which remained morally opposed to sports until the twentieth century. Hal Sears, "The Moral Threat of Intercollegiate Sports: An 1893 Poll of Ten College Presidents, and the End of 'The Champion Football Team of the Great West,'" *Journal of Sport History* 19, no. 3 (Winter 1992): 211–226.
4. Higham, "The Reorientation of American Culture," p. 79.
5. Luther H. Gulick, "Notes Relating to Physical Training in Brooklyn, Chicago, and Harrisburg YMCAs, 1854–?" typescript, Archives, Babson Library, Springfield College, Springfield, Mass., pp. 1–3.
6. Barney, "Physical Education and Sport," pp. 188–191.
7. C. E. Patterson, "Muscular Christianity," *Men* 26, no. 5 (May 1899): 264.
8. Gerald F. Roberts, "The Strenuous Life: The Cult of Manliness in the Era of Theodore Roosevelt" (Ph.D. diss., Michigan State University, 1970), p. 96.
9. Richard Harding Davis, "A Day with the Yale Team," *Harper's Weekly* 37 (Nov. 18, 1893): 1110.
10. See, for example, Maurice Thompson, "Vigorous Men, a Vigorous Nation," *Independent* 50 (Sept. 1, 1898): 609–611.

11. See Daniel Rodgers, *The Work Ethic in Industrial America* (Chicago: University of Chicago Press, 1978).

12. John Paul Bocock, "The Foot-Ball Heroes," *Leslie's Weekly* 88 (Jan. 5, 1899): 7.

13. "Last Will and Testament of Miss Sophia Smith Late of Hatfield, Mass.," *Official Circular of Smith College,* no. 4 (Oct. 1877), p. 7. For an extensive treatment of women's athletics in the nineteenth century, see Jan Todd, *Physical Culture and the Body Beautiful: Purposive Exercise in the Lives of American Women, 1800–1870* (Macon, Ga.: Mercer University Press, 1998).

14. John M. Tyler, "The Physical Education of Girls and Women," *American Physical Education Review* 16, no. 8 (November 1911): 491. G. Stanley Hall, *Morale: The Supreme Standard of Life and Conduct* (New York, 1920), pp. 248–250. Helen M. McKinstry, "Athletics for Girls," *Playground* 3, no. 4 (July 1909): 6–7.

15. Luther Gulick, "Athletics from the Biologic Viewpoint," *American Physical Education Review* 11 (1906): 159–160. Frances A. Kellor, "Ethical Value of Sports for Women," *American Physical Education Review* 11 (1906): 162.

16. Dudley Allen Sargent, "What Athletic Games, If Any, Are Injurious for Women in the Form in Which They Are Played by Men?" *American Physical Education Review* 11 (1906): 179–181.

17. McKinstry, "Athletics for Girls," pp. 3–5. Gulick, "Athletics from the Biologic Viewpoint," p. 160. Sargent, "What Athletic Games, If Any, Are Injurious for Women?" p. 180.

18. Henry Smith Williams, "The Educational Value and Health-Giving Value of Athletics," *Harper's Weekly* 39 (Feb. 16, 1895): 165.

19. Isaac B. Potter, "The Bicycle Outlook," *Century Magazine* 52 (September 1896): 786.

20. A. O. Downs, "Clergymen and the Bicycle," *Wheelman* 1, no. 3 (December 1882): 218.

21. Thorstein Veblen, *The Theory of the Leisure Class* (New York: New American Library, 1953), pp. 170–180.

22. Ibid., pp. 170–180.

23. Charles D. Lanier, "The World's Sporting Impulse," *Review of Reviews* 14 (July 1896): 58.

24. "The Confessions of a Clergyman," *Wheelman* 1, no. 3 (December 1882): 201.

25. A. Holmes, "The Soul and the Body in Physical Training," *American Physical Education Review,* v. 14 (1909), p. 480.

26. Kenneth G. Vanderpool, "The Attitude of Selected Nineteenth-Century Disciples of Christ Leaders Regarding Physical Activity" (Ph.D. diss., Temple University, 1973), p. 12. Earle Zeigler and Harold Vanderswaag credit "Christian religious idealism" with having had "detrimental effects on physical education." Their colleague, Robert Barney, goes further, calling

the rise of sport a triumph over "its former antagonist and suppressant, religion." See Earle F. Zeigler and Harold J. Vanderswaag, *Physical Education: Progressivism or Essentialism?* (Champaign, Ill.: Stipes Publishing Co., 1966), p. 21; and Barney, "Physical Education and Sport," p. 197.

27. Edward M. Hartwell, "Physical Training and Character," *Physical Training* 4, no. 1 (November 1906): 5.

28. John R. Faris, "The Influence of Plato and Platonism on the Development of Physical Education in Western Culture," *Quest,* monograph 11 (Dec. 1968), p. 22.

29. Deobold B. Van Dalen et al., *A World History of Physical Education* (Englewood Cliffs, N.J.: Prentice Hall, 1971), pp. 97–98.

30. Bruce L. Bennett, "The Curious Relationship of Religion and Physical Education," *Journal of the History of Physical Education Review* 41, no. 7 (September 1970): 69–70. Bennett notes that it was an ordained Lutheran minister, Charles Beck, who served as the first physical education instructor in the United States (ca. 1825) at the Round Hill School in Northampton, Massachusetts.

31. See Harold M. Barrow, *Man and His Movements: Principles of His Physical Education* (Philadelphia: Lea & Febiger, 1971), pp. 52–53; and John R. Betts, "Mind and Body in Early American Thought," *Journal of American History* 54, no. 4 (March 1968): 788. For a lengthier discourse on the relationship between Protestantism and sports in early America, see Steven J. Overman, *The Influence of the Protestant Ethic on Sports and Recreation* (Brookfield, Vt.: Avebury Press, 1997).

32. Robert Higgs, *God in the Stadium: Sports and Religion in America* (Lexington: University Press of Kentucky, 1995), p. 9. In Chapter 2, Higgs argues that even though the Calvinistic Puritans regulated sports, they were not completely averse to recreational activities.

33. See Ann Douglas, "Clerical Disestablishment," Chapter 1 in *The Feminization of American Culture* (New York: Doubleday, 1988), pp. 17–43.

34. Holmes, "The Soul and the Body," p. 486. The quotation is from Benjamin Rush.

35. Theodore L. Cuyler, *Sermons on Christian Recreation and UnChristian Amusement* (New York, 1858), pp. 9, 13.

36. Richard A. Swanson, "The Acceptance and Influence of Play in American Protestantism," *Quest,* Monograph 11 (December 1968): 59–70.

37. See Harold Bloom, "American Original: The Mormons," pt. II in *The American Religion: The Emergence of the Post-Christian Nation* (New York: Simon & Schuster, 1992), pp. 79–128.

38. Louis J. Kern, *An Ordered Love: Sex Roles and Sexuality in Victorian Utopias—the Shakers, the Mormons, and the Oneida Community* (Chapel Hill: University of North Carolina Press, 1981), pp. 151–152.

39. Bennett, "Religion and Physical Education," *The Physical Educator,* v. 19, no. 3 (Oct. 1962), pp. 83–86.

40. Holmes, "The Soul and the Body," p. 188.
41. Vanderpool, "The Attitude of Selected Nineteenth-Century Disciples of Christ Leaders," pp. 51, 100–101, 136–137.
42. Ibid., p. 115. Stone's plea for ministerial dignity was made ca. 1829.
43. Andrew Doyle, "Foolish and Useless Sport: The Southern Evangelical Crusade against Intercollegiate Football," *Journal of Sport History* 24, no. 3 (Fall 1997): 317–340.
44. Martin I. Foss and G. A. Cornell, "Vitality, Mortality, Temperment, and Efficiency," *Physical Training* 6, no. 5 (March 1909): 8.
45. Robert J. Roberts, "The Saints' Bodies," *Men* 23 (March 19, 1898): 513.
46. William W. Hastings, "A Christian and an Athlete," *Men* 23 (April 2, 1898): 553.
47. Henry C. King, *How to Make a Rational Fight for Character* (New York, 1902), p. 31.
48. Park, "Physiologists, Physicians, and Physical Educators," p. 36.
49. T. J. Jackson Lears, "American Advertising and the Reconstruction of the Body, 1880–1930," in Kathryn Grover, ed., *Fitness in American Culture* (Amherst: University of Massachusetts Press, 1989), p. 47.
50. "Athletics and Religion," *Outlook* 107 (May 23, 1914): 151–152.
51. See William Hutchison, *The Modernist Impulse in American Protestantism, 1865–1915* (Cambridge: Harvard University Press, 1976).
52. "Play as a Means of Realizing the Universal Brotherhood of Man," *Current Opinion* 57 (1914): 122.
53. Herbert W. Gates, *Recreation and the Church* (Chicago, 1917), p. 21.
54. Charles F. Thwing, "The Ethical Function of Football," *North American Review* 173 (November 1901): 631, 628. Charles Eliot Norton, "Some Aspects of Civilization in America," *Forum* 20 (February 1896): 645–646. In response to abuses within college athletics, Dr. Edward Hartwell of the YMCA argued that religious monitoring of sports was needed to stop "rampant athletics" from producing "immoral athletes." Edward M. Hartwell, "Physical Training and Character II," *Physical Training* 4, no. 2 (December 1906), p. 7.
55. Clifford J. Waugh, "Bernarr Macfadden: The Muscular Prophet" (Ph.D. diss., Sate University of New York at Buffalo, 1979), pp. 35, 55, 81. For more on the life of Bernarr Macfadden, see Clement Wood, *Bernarr Macfadden: A Study in Success* (New York: Beckman Publishers, 1974); and Robert Ernst, *Weakness Is a Crime: The Life of Bernarr Macfadden* (Syracuse, N.Y.: Syracuse University Press, 1991).
56. Allen A. Stockdale, "Pitching and Preaching," *Association Men* 38, no. 9 (January 1913): 467.
57. "Eight-Minute's Common-Sense Exercise for the Busy Man," *Outlook* 27 (June 1914): 470.
58. Young Men's Christian Association, International Committee, *The American Standard Program for Boys* (New York, 1918), p. 31.

59. "Strength," *Men* 22 (Oct. 10, 1898): 360.

60. William H. Ridgway, "God in the Gym," *Association Men* 40, no. 6 (March 1915): 296.

61. William R. Richards, "An Extraordinary Saint," in William H. Sallmon, ed., *The Culture of Christian Manhood* (New York, 1897), p. 125.

62. Andrew Lipscomb, "Christ's Education of His Body," *Methodist Review* 67 (1885): 692.

63. William A. McKeever, *Training the Boy* (New York, 1913), p. 147.

64. Francis G. Peabody, *Mornings in the College Chapel* (Boston, 1907), p. 159.

65. C. H. Brent, *The Splendor of the Human Body* (New York, 1908), pp. 42, 33.

66. "Reasons Why a Christian Man Should Take Regular Physical Exercise," *Men* 23 (April 2, 1898): 555.

67. W. A. Harper, *The Making of Men* (Dayton, Ohio, 1915), p. 19.

68. Tyler, "The Physical Education of Girls and Women," p. 488. Hall, *Morale*, p. 1. Frank Crane, "The Last Punch," *Association Men* 46, no. 4 (December 1920): 151.

69. "The Recreative Life and Health," in *Social Service,* vol. 2 of *Messages of the Men and Religion Forward Movement* (New York, 1912), p. 58.

70. George J. Fisher, "Character Development through Social and Personal Hygiene," *Religious Education* 4 (December 1909): 399.

71. "The Recreative Life and Health," p. 55.

72. Quoted in Joe D. Willis and Richard G. Wettan, "Religion and Sport in America: The Case for the Sports Bay in the Cathedral Church of Saint John the Divine," *Journal of Sport History* 4, no. 2 (1977): 192.

73. S. D. McConnell, "The Moral Side of Golf," *Outlook* 65 (June 2, 1900): 300. For more on the easing of Sabbath restrictions on sport and play, see Alexis McCrossen, *Holy Day, Holiday: The American Sunday* (Ithaca, N.Y.: Cornell University Press, 2000).

74. Silas E. Persons, "Rural Recreation through the Church," *Playground* 6, no. 12 (March 1913): 464. Alfred T. Mahan, *The Harvest Within: Thoughts on the Life of the Christian* (Boston, 1909), p. 145. James Vance, *Royal Manhood* (New York, 1899), p. 41.

75. John L. Scudder, "The Pulpit and the Wheel," *Wheelman* 1, no. 1 (October 1882): 47.

76. "The People's Palace of Jersey City," *Charities Review* 1 (December 1890): 90–91.

77. Scudder, "The Pulpit and the Wheel," p. 48.

78. S. L. Gracey, "The Minister—Mental and Muscular," *Wheelman* 1, no. 3 (December 1882): 213–214.

79. For more on the life of Billy Sunday, see William G. McLoughlin, *Billy Sunday Was His Real Name* (Chicago: University of Chicago Press, 1955). More recent biographies of Sunday include Lyle Dorsett, *Billy Sunday and the Redemption of Urban America* (Grand Rapids, Mich.: William B.

Ferdman's Publishing Co., 1991); and Roger Bruns, *Preacher: Billy Sunday and Big Time American Evangelism* (New York: Norton, 1992).

80. Quoted in Richard Hofstadter, *Anti-Intellectualism in American Life* (New York: Vintage Books, 1966), pp. 114–115.
81. For more information on Stagg see his autobiography: *Touchdown!* (New York, 1927).
82. James A. Mathisen, "From Muscular Christians to Jocks for Jesus," *Christian Century* 109, no. 1 (Jan. 1–8, 1992): 13.
83. Roberts, "The Strenuous Life," p. 92.
84. John A. Garraty, ed., *Dictionary of American Biography* (New York: Charles Scribners Sons, 1981), s.v. "Amos Alonzo Stagg" by Horton W. Emerson, Jr.
85. Robert E. Speer, *Young Men Who Overcame* (New York, 1905), p. 21.
86. Theodore Munger, "Message of Christ to the Will," in A. V. G. Allen et al., *The Message of Christ to Manhood* (Boston, 1899], p. 108.
87. C. Howard Hopkins, *History of the YMCA in North America* (New York: Association Press, 1951), p. 259.
88. Richard Harding Davis, "The Thanksgiving-Day Game," *Harper's Weekly* 37 (Dec. 9, 1893): 1171.
89. George Fisher, "The Association's Contribution to the Physical Life of the Nation," *Association Men* 41, no. 1 (December 1915): 2.
90. Charles Gillkey, "Recreation and the Church," *Playground* 17, no. 9 (December 1923): 497–498.
91. Quoted in George W. Knox, "Recreation and the Higher Life," *Playground* 4, no. 9 (December 1911): 296.
92. Fisher, "The Association's Contribution to the Physical Life of the Nation," p. 2.
93. Josiah Strong, *Religious Movements for Social Betterment* (New York, 1900), p. 28.
94. Carl H. Barnett, "The Church and Recreation Programs," *Playground* 17, no. 9 (December 1923): 500.
95. "For a Muscular Ministry," *Men* 22 (Mar. 20, 1897): 834–835.
96. Another church to experiment with athletics was the Fort Street Presbyterian Church of Detroit, Michigan, which played games on its athletic field during the summer and offered classes in its gym during the winter. The Brick Presbyterian Church of Rochester, New York, likewise offered gymnastics and swimming classes, all of which were held in its "Brick Institute," a building kept open every day of the week. Gates, *Recreation and the Church*, pp. 135, 126, 131.
97. "Play at Trinity Church," *Playground* 3, no. 12 (March 1910): 1–23.
98. Barnett, "The Church and Recreation Programs," p. 500.
99. Myron T. Scudder, "The Value of Recreation in Rural Communities," in *The Rural Church*, vol. 6 of *Messages of the Men and Religion Forward Movement* (New York, 1912), pp. 240, 233.
100. Gates, *Recreation and the Church*, pp. 134, 129, 125.

101. See Francis Couvares, *The Remaking of Pittsburgh: Class and Culture in an Industrializing City, 1877–1919* (Albany: State University of New York Press, 1984).

102. Lebert H. Weir, "Recreational Phases," in William T. Foster, ed., *The Social Emergency: Studies in Sex Hygiene and Morals* (Boston, 1914), p. 81.

103. Gates, *Recreation and the Church,* p. 134. The minister quoted was the Reverend William R. Taylor.

104. Willis and Wettan, "Religion and Sport in America," p. 196.

105. Quoted in Frank G. Cressey, *The Church and Young Men* (Chicago, 1903), p. 155.

106. James H. Ross, "Fifty Years of the Young Men's Christian Assocation in America," *New England Magazine* 24 (1901): 375–377.

107. Clifford Putney, "From Character to Body Building: The YMCA and the Suburban Metropolis, 1950–1980," in Nina Mjagkij and Margaret Spratt, eds., *Men and Women Adrift: The YMCA and the YWCA in the City* (New York: New York University Press, 1997), p. 237.

108. Cressey, *The Church and Young Men,* p. 164.

109. Hopkins, *History of the YMCA in North America,* pp. 239–242.

110. Paul Super, *Formative Ideas in the YMCA* (New York, 1929), p. 5.

111. "Young Men's Christian Associations," *Harper's Monthly Magazine* 64 (1882): 264.

112. Laurence L. Doggett, "Jubilee of the Young Men's Christian Association," *North American Review* 172 (1901): 889–891.

113. "YMCA Introduced Sex Education in the 1880s via White Cross Army and Started a Furor," *YMCA Bulletin* (April 1968): 15.

114. Wiley Winsor, ed., *The Leaders' Handbook for the Young Men's Christian Associations of North America* (New York, 1922), p. 105.

115. Sherwood Eddy, *A Century with Youth: A History of the YMCA from 1844 to 1944* (New York: Association Press, 1944), p. 25.

116. Holmes, "The Soul and the Body," p. 488.

117. *Physical Education in the YMCAs of North America* (New York, 1914), p. 3.

118. George Fisher, "The Relation of the Young Men's Christian Association to Public Recreation," *American Physical Education Review* 8 (1908): 391.

119. Patterson, "Muscular Christianity," p. 262.

120. Hastings, "A Christian and an Athlete," p. 553.

121. Hopkins, *History of the YMCA in North America,* pp. 107–109.

122. Elmer Johnson, *History of YMCA Physical Education,* pp. 39–40.

123. *Physical Education in the YMCAs of North America,* p. 4.

124. Luther H. Gulick, "Fundamental Basis of the Young Men's Christian Association," typescript [ca. 1890], Archives, Babson Library, Springfield College, Springfield, Mass., pp. 1–3.

125. Ethel J. Dorgan, *Luther Halsey Gulick* (Washington, D.C.: McGrath Publishing Co., 1976), pp. 4–5. For a less adulatory treatment of Gulick, see

Stephanie Wallach, "Luther Halsey Gulick and the Salvation of the American Adolescent" (Ph.D. diss., Columbia University, 1989).

126. Dorgan, *Luther Halsey Gulick*, pp. 13–14.

127. See Gulick, *The Efficient Life* (New York, 1907).

128. Luther H. Gulick, "Some Psychical Aspects of Muscular Exercise," *Popular Science Monthly* 531, no. 6 (October 1898): 804.

129. Dorgan, *Luther Halsey Gulick*, pp. 36–37.

130. Hopkins, *History of the YMCA in North America*, p. 260.

131. Luther H. Gulick, "Revised Clean Sport Roll," *Men* 22 (Dec. 19, 1896): 564.

132. Hopkins, *History of the YMCA in North America*, p. 266.

133. Fred S. Goodman, "Religious Efficiency in the Physical Department," *Physical Training* 12, no. 9 (September 1915): 302.

134. George J. Fisher and Martin I. Foss, eds., *Physical Work: Management and Methods* (New York, 1913), p. 11.

135. R. C. Cubbon, "The Physical Department's Religious Opportunities," *Association Men*, v. 38, no. 1 (Oct. 1912), pp. 28–29. There was also much talk following Gulick about "upbuilding the kingdom of God through physical education"—an ambitious goal perhaps, but not unapproachable, given that in 1915 fully 70% of all United States physical education instructors were men of Association experience or training. (See Fisher and Foss, eds., *Physical Work: Management and Methods*, p. 185; and Fisher, "The Association's Contribution to the Physical Life of the Nation," p. 1.)

136. President MacCracken (of Vassar College), "Address at the Funeral Services," *American Physical Education Review* 23, no. 7 (October 1918): 424.

137. "The New Crusade," in Clarence Barbour, ed., *Fellowship Hymns* (New York, 1918), pasted on inside cover.

3. Men and Religion

The epigraph is from a poem entitled "For the Man of Galilee" in I. H. Meredith and Grant Colfax Tullar, eds., *Manly Songs for Christian Men: A Collection of Sacred Songs Adapted to the Needs of Male Singers* (New York, 1910), p. 1.

1. Theodore Roosevelt to John R. Mott, Oct. 12, 1908, TDS (photostat), Theodore Roosevelt Collection, Widener Library, Harvard University, n.p.

2. See Susan Curtis, "The Son of Man and God the Father," in Mark C. Carnes and Clyde Griffen, eds., *Meanings for Manhood* (Chicago: University of Chicago Press, 1990), pp. 67, 77; and Janet Fishburn, *The Fatherhood of God and the Victorian Family: A Study of the Social Gospel in America* (Philadelphia: Fortress Press, 1981), p. 32.

3. Jasper C. Massee, *Men and the Kingdom* (New York, 1912), pp. 134, 140.

4. Fred S. Goodman, "A Survey of Typical Church Bible Classes for Boys and

Men," *Religious Education* 5, no. 4 (October 1910): 363–365. Social Gospel leader Washington Gladden agreed with the "Y" that the female-to-male church membership ratio was about three to one, and he urged Congregational brotherhoods to balance it. "We have none too many women," he allowed, "and no words can tell the debt we owe to them, but a preponderance of female influence in the Church or anywhere else in society is unnatural and injurious." Gladden quoted in Frederick D. Leete, *Christian Brotherhoods* (New York, 1912), p. 382.

5. Howard A. Bridgman, "Have We a Religion for Men?" *Andover Review* 13 (April 1890): 390–391.

6. Fayette L. Thompson, "The Church's Lost Asset: Men," in Norman E. Richardson, ed., *The Religion of Modern Manhood: or, Masculine Topics for Men's Bible Classes* (New York, 1911), p. 40.

7. Bridgman, "Have We a Religion for Men?" p. 390.

8. Ann Douglas, *The Feminization of American Culture* (New York: Doubleday, 1988), p. 111.

9. Charles R. Brown, *The Making of a Minister* (New York, 1927), p. 129.

10. Douglas, *The Feminization of American Culture,* p. 91.

11. Brown, *The Making of a Minister,* p. 130.

12. "A Christian and a Man," *Men* 25 (September 1899): 468.

13. "Religion for Men," *Century* 58 (1910): 154.

14. Bridgman, "Have We a Religion for Men?" p. 396.

15. Fred B. Smith, *A Man's Religion* (New York, 1913), p. 70.

16. Carl D. Case, *The Masculine in Religion* (Philadelphia, 1906), pp. 28, 50–51.

17. Ibid., pp. 29, 88.

18. Ibid., pp. 89–99.

19. Mary Ann Clawson, *Constructing Brotherhood: Class, Gender, and Fraternalism* (Princeton: Princeton University Press, 1989), p. 185.

20. Mark C. Carnes, *Secret Ritual and Manhood in Victorian America* (New Haven: Yale University Press, 1989), pp. 65, 76.

21. "Why Men Don't Go to Church," *Outlook* 96 (Sept. 3, 1910): 10–10a.

22. Quoted in T. J. Jackson Lears, *No Place of Grace: Antimodernism and the Transformation of American Culture, 1880–1920* (New York: Pantheon Books, 1981), p. 46.

23. John Kelman, "The Manhood for Which Christ Stood and Stands," *Association Men* 39, no. 1 (October 1913): 5.

24. Benjamin Young, "Common Sense," in Richardson, ed., *The Religion of Modern Manhood,* p. 122.

25. Bridgman, "Have We a Religion for Men?" p. 392.

26. G. Stanley Hall, "The Efficiency of the Religious Work of the Young Men's Christian Association," *Pedagogical Seminary* 12, no. 4 (December 1905): 479–489.

27. Archdeacon Cody, "The Church and Young Men of America," *Association Men* 41, no. 9 (June 1916): 491–492.

28. "Be Men, Every Inch of You," *St. Andrew's Cross* 5, no. 7 (April 1891): 331.

29. In 1909 Roosevelt privately confided to a friend, Archie Butt, that the two denominations best suited to America were Methodism and Episcopalianism. Methodism represented "the great middle class," he said, and Episcopalianism the lower and upper classes; but despite their differences, both were solidly "American," and both encapsulated American ideals. Catholicism, in contrast, seemed to Roosevelt "in no way suited to this country . . . for its thought is Latin and entirely at variance with the dominant thought of our country and institutions." Quoted in "Theodore Roosevelt: Exactly What He Thought of American Churches," *American Standard* 1, no. 5 (March 8, 1924), p. 1.

30. Christian Reisner, *Roosevelt's Religion* (New York, 1922), pp. 344, 34, 345, 191.

31. Riis quoted in ibid., pp. 257, 260–261.

32. Jacob Riis, "Roosevelt's Creed," *Cosmopolitan* 32 (February 1902): 410.

33. Reisner, *Roosevelt's Religion*, p. 324.

34. Ferdinand C. Iglehart, *Theodore Roosevelt: The Man as I Knew Him* (New York, 1919), p. 56.

35. John D. Rockefeller, Jr., "Every Christian Man at Work for His Fellow Men—How Shall This Be Accomplished?" *Association Men* 41, no. 9 (June 1916): 493.

36. Douglas, *The Feminization of American Culture*, pp. 93–99.

37. Henry C. King, *How to Make a Rational Fight for Character* (New York, 1902), p. 27. James I. Vance, *Royal Manhood* (New York, 1899), p. 28.

38. Jenkin L. Jones, "The Decline of the Ministry," *Outlook* 80 (May 13, 1905): 124–125.

39. John R. Mott, *The Future Leadership of the Church* (New York, 1908), p. 61.

40. George A. Gordon, *The Claims of the Ministry on Strong Men*, Claims and Opportunities of the Christian Ministry [Series], ed. John R. Mott (New York, 1909), p. 18.

41. Jones, "The Decline of the Ministry," p. 125.

42. David S. Hill, "The Education and Problems of the Protestant Ministry III," *American Journal of Religious Psychology* 3, no. 1 (May 1908): 65.

43. Edward I. Bosworth, *The Weak Church and the Strong Man*, Claims and Opportunities of the Christian Ministry [Series], ed. Mott, pp. 5–6.

44. Ibid., p. 6.

45. Brown, *The Making of a Minister*, p. 130.

46. Case, *The Masculine in Religion*, p. 80.

47. See Hill, "The Education and Problems III," p. 35; and Catherine F.

Hitchings, "Universalist and Unitarian Women Ministers," *Journal of the Universalist Historical Society* 10 (1975): 3, 6.

48. See Cynthia Grant Tucker, *Prophetic Sisterhood: Liberal Women Ministers of the Frontier* (Boston: Beacon, 1990); and Barbara Brown Zikmund, "Winning Ordination for Women in Mainstream Protestant Churches," in Rosemary Radford Ruether and Rosemary Skinner Keller, eds., *Women and Religion in America,* vol. 3 (San Francisco: Harper & Row, 1981), pp. 339–347.

49. Samuel J. Niccolls, "Woman's Position and Work in the Church," *Presbyterian Review* (April 1889), reprinted in Ruether and Keller, *Women and Religion in America,* vol. 1 (San Francisco: Harper & Row, 1981), pp. 229–238.

50. Mott, *The Future Leadership of the Church,* p. 10.

51. Bridgman, "Have We a Religion for Men?" p. 395.

52. William C. Covert, "Jesus 100% Masculine—*and* His Men," *Association Men* 45, no. 4 (December 1920): 162.

53. Gordon, *The Claims of the Ministry on Strong Men,* pp. 10–11.

54. William F. McDowell, *The Right Sort of Men for the Ministry,* Claims and Opportunities of the Christian Ministry [Series], ed. Mott, p. 19.

55. Hill, "The Education and Problems III," pp. 67, 56–57, 62.

56. Ibid., pp. 58, 42, 37, 65, 63.

57. Case, *The Masculine in Religion,* pp. 83, 88.

58. David S. Hill, "The Education and Problems of the Protestant Ministry I," *American Journal of Religious Psychology* 1, no. 2 (November 1906): 213–215, 219, 221.

59. Joshua Levering, "For a Muscular Ministry," *Men* 22 (March 20, 1897): 834–835.

60. William H. Scott, *Men in the Church: An Address Delivered Before the [Presbyterian] Synod of Pennsylvania* (Philadelphia, 1909), p. 9.

61. World War I did not bring about the extinction of church brotherhoods, but they did "disappear from view." Daniel W. Martin, "The United Presbyterian Church—Policy on the Men's Movement—An Historical Overview," *Journal of Presbyterian History* 59, no. 3 (Fall 1981): 410.

62. Edwin J. Gardiner, "Church Work among Young Men," *Church Review* 49 (May 1887): 484–485, 489–491.

63. Ibid., pp. 485, 490, 500, 488.

64. Frank Graves Cressey, *The Church and Young Men* (Chicago, 1903), pp. 137–139.

65. Ibid., pp. 131–137. The Baraca movement was founded ca. 1890.

66. Rima Lunin Schultz, *The Church and the City: A Social History of 150 Years at Saint James, Chicago* (Chicago: Cathedral of Saint James, 1986), pp. 135–139.

67. Gardiner, "Church Work among Young Men," p. 494.

68. Cressey, *The Church and Young Men*, pp. 116–118.
69. See, for example, T. N. Morrison, "Christian Manliness," *St. Andrew's Cross* 5, no. 11 (1891): 400; and Frederick A. Atkins, "What Is It Makes a Man," *St. Andrew's Cross* 6, no. 9 (1892): 166–167.
70. Congregational Church, Executive Council, *Brotherhood of Andrew and Philip?* [Boston, 1901], p. 1.
71. Quoted in Cressey, *The Church and Young Men*, p. 122.
72. Ibid., pp. 123–128.
73. Martin, "United Presbyterian Church Policy," pp. 408–418.
74. Cressey, *The Church and Young Men*, pp. 128–131.
75. Ibid., p. 221.
76. See Peter McDonough, *Men Astutely Trained: A History of the Jesuits in the American Century* (New York: Free Press, 1992).
77. Cressey, *The Church and Young Men*, pp. 221–225.
78. See Will Herberg, *Protestant, Catholic, Jew: An Essay in American Religious Sociology* (Garden City, N.Y.: Doubleday, 1955).
79. Frederick Siedenburg, "The Recreational Value of Religion," *American Journal of Sociology* 25 (January 1920): 448.
80. Martin, "United Presbyterian Church Policy," p. 410.
81. Leete, *Christian Brotherhoods*, pp. 388–392.
82. Quoted in Gardiner, "Church Work Among Young Men," p. 495.
83. Leete, *Christian Brotherhoods*, pp. 387–388.
84. Ian Maclaren, *Men* 22 (Oct. 31, 1896): 1.
85. King, *How to Make a Rational Fight for Character*, pp. 37, 25.
86. Frank E. Wilson, *Contrasts in the Character of Christ* (New York, 1916), pp. 113–114.
87. Cressey, *The Church and Young Men*, pp. 211–215.
88. Edward H. McKinley, *Marching to Glory: The History of the Salvation Army in the United States of America, 1880–1980* (San Francisco: Harper & Row, 1980), pp. 6–12, 37.
89. Ibid., pp. 39–42.
90. Ibid., p. 35.
91. Cressey, *The Church and Young Men*, p. 218.
92. Clifford Putney, "Character Building in the YMCA, 1880–1930," *Mid-America* 73, no. 1 (1991): 49–70.
93. Charles E. Jefferson, *The Character of Jesus* (New York, 1908), p. 45.
94. Robert Handy, *A Christian America: Protestant Hopes and Historical Realities* (New York: Oxford University Press, 1984), p. 143.
95. Francis G. Peabody, "The Character of Jesus Christ," *Hibbert Journal* 1 (July 1903): 642.
96. Jason W. Pierce, *The Masculine Power of Christ* (Boston, 1912), p. 1.
97. G. Stanley Hall, *Jesus, the Christ, in the Light of Psychology* (Garden City, N.Y., 1917), pp. 36–37.

98. Case, *The Masculine in Religion,* p. 120.
99. Frederick A. Atkins, "Superfluous Young Men," *St. Andrew's Cross* 6, no. 7 (April 1892): 127.
100. Kelman, "The Manhood for Which Christ Stood and Stands," p. 3.
101. See Walter Rauschenbusch, "Jesus as an Organizer of Men," *Biblical World* 11 (January 1898): 102–111; and Jefferson, *The Character of Jesus,* pp. 47–48, 88 and passim.
102. Francis G. Peabody, *Jesus Christ and the Christian Character* (New York, 1905), pp. 53–54.
103. Peabody, "The Character of Jesus Christ," p. 656.
104. Brown, *The Making of a Minister,* p. 132.
105. Jefferson, *The Character of Jesus,* pp. 46–47.
106. Hall, *Jesus, the Christ, in the Light of Psychology,* pp. 28–29.
107. "New Portrayals of Christ by American Painters," *Current Literature* 40 (May 1906): 537–540. The Lauber portrait was entitled *In Him Was Life: And the Life Was the Light of Men.*
108. Lears, *No Place of Grace,* p. 133.
109. C. M. Smart, *Muscular Churches: Ecclesiastical Architecture of the High Victorian Period* (Fayetteville: University of Arkansas Press, 1989), pp. 2–4.
110. John A. Garraty, ed., *Dictionary of American Biography* (New York: Chas. Scribners Sons, 1981), s.v. "Leopold Eidlitz," by Montgomery Schuyler.
111. Charles H. Richards, "Evolution in Hymnology," *Forum* 54, no. 6 (December 1915): 757.
112. H. Augustine Smith, "The Music of the Sunday-School and Its Value in the Religious Development of the Child," *Religious Education* 5, no. 3 (August 1910): 255.
113. Richards, "Evolution in Hymnology," pp. 757–758.
114. A. A. Pfanstiehl, "The Manliness of Jesus—II," *Men* 23 (July 30, 1898): 887.
115. Frederick Gates, "The Change of the Hymn Books," *Independent* 63 (Aug. 15, 1907): 412.
116. Richards, "Evolution in Hymnology," pp. 757, 760.
117. See Henry Wilder Foote, *Three Centuries of American Hymnody* (Cambridge: Harvard University Press, 1940), p. 264; and the YMCA International Committee, *Association Hymn Book* (New York, 1907), foreword.
118. I. H. Meredith and Grant Colfax Tullar, eds., *Manly Songs for Christian Men: A Collection of Sacred Songs Adapted to the Needs of Male Singers* (New York, 1910), p. 27.
119. Smith, "The Music of the Sunday-School," p. 255.
120. Foote, *Three Centuries of American Hymnody,* p. 307.
121. John Gustav-Wrathall, *Take the Young Stranger by the Hand: Same-Sex Relations and the YMCA* (Chicago: University of Chicago Press, 1998).
122. Ibid., p. 46.

123. Ibid., pp. 46–63.
124. Hall, *Jesus, the Christ, in the Light of Psychology,* pp. 33, 183–185.

4. Fishers of Boys

The epigraph is from William B. Forbush, "Boys' Clubs," *Pedagogical Seminary* 16, no. 3 (September 1909): 342.

1. William B. Forbush, *The Boy Problem: A Study in Social Pedagogy* (Boston, 1907), p. 169; Carleton quoted on p. 98.
2. This chapter focuses mainly on adult constructions of boyhood. For a boy's-eye view of boys' life see E. Anthony Rotundo's book *American Manhood,* which contains highly illuminating chapters entitled "Boy Culture" and "Male Youth Culture." E. Anthony Rotundo, *American Manhood: Transformations in Masculinity from the Revolution to the Modern Era* (New York: BasicBooks, 1993).
3. Norman Richardson and Ormond Loomis, *The Boy Scout Movement Applied by the Church* (New York, 1915), p. 26.
4. Mrs. Charles F. Weller, "Life for Girls," *Playground* 7, no. 5 (August 1913): 201. Herbert W. Gates, "The History, Scope, and Success of Organizations for Boys and Girls," *Religious Education* 7, no. 2 (June 1912): 223.
5. Frances Maule, "Getting at the Boys," *Outlook* 81 (Dec. 2, 1905): 826.
6. Charles K. Taylor, "Moral Training of Private-School Boys," *Education* 31, no. 8 (April 1911): 541.
7. Herman Scheffauer, "The Moulding of Men," *Lippincott's* 82 (September 1908): 383.
8. Henry W. Gibson, *Twenty-Five Years of Organized Boys' Work in Massachusetts and Rhode Island, 1891–1915* (Boston, 1915), pp. 7–8.
9. Ibid., p. 10.
10. Forbush, *The Boy Problem,* pp. 43–44.
11. Ernest T. Seton, "The Boy Scouts in America," *Outlook* 95 (July 23, 1910): 630.
12. Forbush, *The Boy Problem,* p. 43.
13. Scheffauer, "The Moulding of Men," p. 382.
14. Allan Hoben, "The Minister and the Boy II: An Approach to Boyhood," *Biblical World* 38 (November 1911): 308.
15. G. Stanley Hall, "Feminization in School and Home," *World's Work* 16 (1908): 10238. In 1900 70 percent of America's public school teachers were women. By 1925 that number had risen to 83 percent. James McLaclan, *American Boarding Schools: An Historical Study* (New York: Scribner's, 1970), p. 278.
16. Forbush, *The Boy Problem,* p. 126. The fact that there existed a widespread fear of women teachers is confirmed in Victoria Bissell Brown, "The Fear of

Feminization: Los Angeles High Schools in the Progressive Era," *Feminist Studies* 16, no. 3 (1990): 493–518.

17. John Johnson, "The Savagery of Boyhood," *Popular Science Monthly* 31 (1887): 796–800.

18. Benjamin Rader, "The Recapitulation Theory of Play: Motor Behavior, Moral Reflexes, and Manly Attitudes in Urban America, 1880–1920," in J. A. Mangen and James Walvin, eds., *Manliness and Morality: Middle-Class Masculinity in Britain and America, 1880–1940* (Manchester, England: Manchester University Press, 1987), pp. 123–134. Another excellent analysis of recapitulation theory can be found in Gail Bederman, *Manliness and Civilization: A Cultural History of Gender and Race in the United States, 1880–1917* (Chicago: University of Chicago Press, 1995), pp. 92–96.

19. Quoted in Rader, "The Recapitulation Theory of Play," p. 124.

20. William B. Forbush, "Boys' Clubs," *Pedagogical Seminary* 16, no. 3 (September 1909): 341. Charles K. Taylor, "Boys and Men: One or Two Training Problems," *Outlook* 129 (Oct. 26, 1921): 292.

21. Forbush, *The Boy Problem*, p. 169. Hoben, "The Minister and the Boy II," p. 307.

22. David I. Macleod, *Building Character in the American Boy: The Boy Scouts, YMCA, and Their Forerunners, 1870–1920* (Madison: University of Wisconsin Press, 1983), pp. 46–48, 67–68, and passim.

23. See Hanford M. Burr, *The Calling of Boyman* (New York, 1916).

24. See Joseph F. Kett, *Rites of Passage: Adolescence in America, 1790 to the Present* (New York: Basic Books, 1977).

25. A. K. Boyd, *History of Ridley College* (1948), quoted in Macleod, *Building Character in the American Boy*, p. 53.

26. See Robert H. Wiebe, *The Search for Order, 1877–1920* (New York: Hill and Wang, 1967), pp. 111–132; and Olivier Zunz, *Making America Corporate, 1870–1920* (Chicago: University of Chicago Press, 1990).

27. David Riesman et al., *The Lonely Crowd: A Study of the Changing American Character* (New York: Doubleday, 1953), pp. 28, 32, and passim.

28. Forbush, *The Boy Problem*, p. 23.

29. Quoted in Rader, "The Recapitulation Theory of Play," p. 130.

30. Alfred P. Fletcher, "An Experiment in Industrial Education," *Elementary School Teacher* 11 (September 1910): 8, quoted in William Jordan, "Making Men Out of Boys: Educators and Masculinity, 1910–1915" (paper, University of New Hampshire, 1991), p. 7.

31. Richardson and Loomis, *The Boy Scout Movement Applied by the Church*, pp. 43–44.

32. Jordan, "Making Men Out of Boys," p. 8.

33. Macleod, *Building Character in the American Boy*, p. 79.

34. Wiley Winsor, ed., *The Leaders' Handbook for the Young Men's Christian Associations of North America* (New York, 1922), p. 105.

35. Gibson, *Twenty-Five Years of Organized Boys' Work,* p. 10.

36. Barrett P. Tyler, "The Boys' Club in Its Relation to the Church," *Yale Divinity Quarterly* 3 (June 1906): 7.

37. Macleod, *Building Character in the American Boy,* p. 79.

38. The first two quotations are from Jeffrey P. Hantover, "The Boy Scouts and the Validation of Masculinity," *Journal of Social Issues* 34, no. 1 (1978): 191. The remark about "ingrowing effeminacy" was made by G. Walter Fiske, quoted in Carolyn D. Wagner, "The Boy Scouts of America: A Model and a Mirror of American Society" (Ph.D. diss., Johns Hopkins University, 1978), p. 80.

39. YMCA International Committee, *American Standard Program for Boys* (New York, 1918), p. 13.

40. William A. McKeever, *Training the Boy* (New York, 1913), p. viii.

41. Richardson and Loomis, *The Boy Scout Movement as Applied by the Church,* p. 25.

42. Quoted from a Boy Scout pamphlet in Gerald F. Roberts, "The Strenuous Life: The Cult of Manliness in the Era of Theodore Roosevelt" (Ph.D. diss., Michigan State University, 1970), p. 114.

43. Forbush, *The Boy Problem,* p. 168.

44. Steven B. Levine, "The Rise of American Boarding Schools and the Development of a National Upper Class," *Social Problems* 28, no. 1 (October 1980): 65.

45. Lawrence C. Hull, "Private Schools for Boys," *Educational Review* 20 (November 1900): 366.

46. McLaclan, *American Boarding Schools,* p. 220.

47. Hull, "Private Schools for Boys," pp. 366–367. Hull followed the English tradition of calling private schools "public" ones.

48. Levine, "The Rise of American Boarding Schools," pp. 63, 70.

49. McLaclan, *American Boarding Schools,* pp. 278, 289.

50. Henry A. Coit, "An American Boys' School—What It Should Be," *Forum* 12 (September 1891): 3–4.

51. Theodore Roosevelt, "What We Can Expect of the American Boy," *St. Nicholas* 27, no. 7 (May 1900): 571–572.

52. See Sister Ildgerhonse Wyseman, "The Catholic High School and Education for Leisure" (master's thesis, Catholic University of America, 1932); and Sandra P. Dorfman, "Attitudes toward Physical Activity as a Function of Religious Identification, with Particular Reference to Judaism" (master's thesis, University of Wisconsin, 1968). See also Christa R. Klein, "The Jesuits and Catholic Boyhood in Nineteenth-Century New York City" (Ph.D. diss., University of Pennsylvania, 1976) for a discussion of how Catholic educators, hoping to foster obedience to authority, initially neglected team sports in favor of military drill.

53. The "St. Grottlesex" schools, in order of age, were: St. Paul's School, Concord, New Hampshire (1856); St. Mark's School, Southborough, Massa-

chusetts (1865); Groton School, Groton, Massachusetts (1884); St. George's School, Newport, Rhode Island (1896); Middlesex School, Concord, Massachusetts (1901); and Kent School, Kent, Connecticut (1906).

54. Coit, "An American Boys' School—What It Should Be," pp. 7–11. Coit was the first rector of St. Paul's School, serving from 1856 until his death in 1895.

55. See McLaclan, *American Boarding Schools,* pp. 245–247; and Frank Kintrea, "'Old Peabo' and the School," *American Heritage* 31, no. 6 (October–November 1980): 98–99.

56. Quoted in McLaclan, *American Boarding Schools,* pp. 250, 277.

57. Kintrea, "'Old Peabo' and the School," p. 98.

58. McLaclan, *American Boarding Schools,* pp. 267, 281.

59. Quoted in Kintrea, "'Old Peabo' and the School," p. 102.

60. Quoted in McLaclan, *American Boarding Schools,* p. 276.

61. Ibid., pp. 257–258, 276, 278–279.

62. See E. Digby Baltzell, *The Philadelphia Gentlemen* (Glencoe: Free Press, 1958); and Baltzell, *The Protestant Establishment* (New York: Random House, 1964).

63. W. W. Mulford and R. J. Mulford, "The Call of the Camp," *Outlook* 95 (May 1910): 185. Boys' camps were not the only things that were seen as economical; rather, camping as a whole was billed as an activity appropriate for those "who cannot afford yachting trips and the like, and whose ideas of summer recreation are not attuned to the string band of a 'summer hotel.'" Ernest Ingersoll, "Practical Camping," *Outlook* 56 (1897): 324.

64. Winthrop T. Talbot, "Summer Camps for Boys," *World's Work* 10 (1905): 6169. These early-day camps were, in the main, Protestant-run or -affiliated. The first Catholic camp for boys was established in 1892 by the Marist Brothers of St. Ann's Academy, New York City. It was located on Lake Champlain. Henry W. Gibson, "The History of Organized Camping," *Camping Magazine* [7] (April 1936): 19.

65. Henry W. Gibson, "The History of Organized Camping," *Camping Magazine* [7] (May 1936): 18.

66. Ibid., pp. 18–19. The two women were Elizabeth F. Holt and "a Mrs. Barrows" from New York. Holt abandoned girls' camping shortly after the GCA meeting, changing her camp into a boys' camp and giving its direction over to Alcott F. Elwell.

67. Talbot, "Summer Camps for Boys," pp. 6170, 6173.

68. Mulford and Mulford, "The Call of the Camp," pp. 181, 186.

69. Ibid., p. 182.

70. Thomas Foster, "Making Men: How a Student of Psychology Deals with the Sons of the Rich in a Camp for Boys," *Outing* 67 (January 1916): 390, 398.

71. Talbot, "Summer Camps for Boys," p. 6171.

72. Calvin L. Lewis, "Summer Camps for Boys," *Outlook* 80 (June 10, 1905): 379–380.
73. G. Stanley Hall, "The Bible Is a Love Story," *Association Men* 39, no. 1 (October 1913): 9.
74. Edgar M. Robinson, "Six Things to Be Recognized in Dealing with Adolescent Boys," *Christian Student* 8, no. 3 (August 1907): 11.
75. See Charles Taylor, "Training Young America," *Outlook* 119 (May 15, 1918): 107–110; and Thomas Foster, "Making Men," pp. 389–398. The name of Taylor's camp was Camp Penn.
76. Taylor, "Training Young America," pp. 107–110.
77. Talbot, "Summer Camps for Boys," p. 6169.
78. Mulford and Mulford, "The Call of the Camp," pp. 184–185.
79. Talbot, "Summer Camps for Boys," p. 6172.
80. See Boys' Brigade, *The Boys' Brigade in the United States of America* (San Francisco, 1891); and Henry Drummond, "Manliness in Boys—by a New Process," *McClure's Magazine* 2 (1893): 77.
81. Drummond, "Manliness in Boys," pp. 68–72.
82. Ibid., pp. 70–72.
83. William B. Forbush, *Church Work with Boys* (Boston, 1910), pp. 65–66.
84. Macleod, *Building Character in the American Boy*, pp. 104–105.
85. F. A. Crosby, "Boy Scouts and the Sunday School," *Religious Education* 7, no. 2 (June 1912): 241.
86. Seton, "The Boy Scouts in America," p. 630. For more on the life of Ernest Thompson Seton, see Betty Keller, *Blackwolf: The Life of Ernest Thompson Seton* (Vancouver: Douglas and McIntyre, 1984).
87. See Seton, "The Boy Scouts in America," p. 630; and Daniel C. Beard, *Hardly a Man Is Now Alive* (New York: Doubleday, Doran & Co., 1939), pp. 353–354.
88. Daniel C. Beard, *The Boy Pioneers, Sons of Daniel Boone* (New York, 1909), pp. 12, 15.
89. David E. Shi, "Ernest Thompson Seton and the Boy Scouts: A Moral Equivalent of War?" *South Atlantic Quarterly* 84, no. 4 (1985): 384.
90. Wagner, "The Boy Scouts of America," pp. 9–39. For more on the life of Lord Baden-Powell, see Michael Rosenthal, *The Character Factory: Baden-Powell and the Origins of the Boy Scout Movement* (New York: Pantheon, 1986); and Tim Jeal, *The Boy-Man: The Life of Lord Baden-Powell* (New York: William Morrow, 1990).
91. Shi, "Ernest Thompson Seton and the Boy Scouts," p. 386.
92. Wagner, "The Boy Scouts of America," pp. 63–65, 101.
93. Ibid., pp. 104, 112–113.
94. Macleod, *Building Character in the American Boy*, pp. 197–198.
95. Shi, "Ernest Thompson Seton and the Boy Scouts," p. 389.
96. Macleod, *Building Character in the American Boy*, pp. 212–214.

97. Quoted in Wagner, "The Boy Scouts of America," p. 74.

98. Macleod, *Building Character in the American Boy,* pp. 156, 181.

99. Ibid., p. xi.

100. Ashley Piper, "A New Moral Force," *Outlook* 121 (Feb. 12, 1919): 265–266.

101. Richardson and Loomis, *The Boy Scout Movement Applied by the Church,* p. 38. Not all the reasons scoutmasters had for joining the Scouts met with the organization's approval. As Cincinnati Scout executive Arthur Roberts explained, "The mistake sometimes made is that of choosing as a leader some anaemic, sanctimonious person who has no real qualifications for leadership of boys. In this context," he added, "a note of warning should be sounded against the 'enthusiastic volunteer' [i.e., pederast]—avoid him." Arthur E. Roberts, "Scouting and the Church," *Religious Education* 18 (April 1923): 132.

102. Macleod, *Building Character in the American Boy,* p. 37.

103. Henry S. Curtis, "The Boy Scouts," in *The Play Movement and Its Significance* (New York, 1917), pp. 245, 252.

104. Richardson and Loomis, *The Boy Scout Movement Applied by the Church,* pp. 42, 378.

105. Richardson and Loomis, *The Boy Scout Movement Applied by the Church,* p. 57; Macleod, *Building Character in the American Boy,* p. 192.

106. Charles W. Gilkey, "What Can the Church Do in the Field of Work with Boys?" *Religious Education* 7, no. 2 (June 1912): 218.

107. Fred B. Smith, *A Man's Religion* (New York, 1913), p. 264.

108. "The Sunday-School Boy Problem," *Literary Digest* 47 (Aug. 9, 1913): 214; Franklin D. Elmer, "The Scouts and the Church," *Religious Education* 11, no. 4 (August 1916): 366.

109. Macleod, *Building Character in the American Boy,* p. 42.

110. Allan Hoben, "The Minister and the Boy I: The Call of Boyhood," *Biblical World* 38 (October 1911): 231.

111. Richardson and Loomis, *The Boy Scout Movement Applied by the Church,* p. 61.

112. John T. Beckley, "The Young People's Movement No Menace to the Church," *Independent* 44 (July 7, 1892): 7.

113. James L. Hill, "The Leaders of the Christian Endeavor Movement," *New England Magazine* 12 (1895): 586.

114. Francis E. Clark, "The Christian Endeavor Movement," *Hibbert Journal* 13 (April 1915): 630.

115. Ibid., p. 632; and W. F. McCauley, *Why: Reasons for the Christian Endeavor Movement* (Cincinnati, Ohio, 1894), p. 45.

116. Wayland Hoyt, "The Power of the Pledge," *Independent* 44, no. 2275 (July 7, 1892): 4. The YPSCE pledge read in part as follows: "Trusting in the Lord Jesus Christ for strength, I promise Him that I will strive to do whatever He would like to have me do; that I will make it the rule of my life to

pray and to read the Bible every day, and to support my own church in every way, especially by attending all her regular Sunday and mid-week services, unless prevented by some reason which I can conscientiously give to my Savior, and that, just so far as I know how, throughout my whole life, I will endeavor to lead a Christian life."

117. John H. Vincent, "The Coming Church," *Independent* 44, no. 2275 (July 7, 1892): 1.
118. Alice May Scudder, "The Junior Christian Endeavor Society," *Independent* 44, no. 2275 (July 7, 1892): 4.
119. See Clark, "The Christian Endeavor Movement," p. 642; and McCauley, *Why*, pp. 34–36.
120. Frederick T. Galpin, "The Normal Religion of a Boy," *Religious Education* 4 (August 1909): 276.
121. Forbush, *The Boy Problem*, pp. 93–94.
122. Macleod, *Building Character in the American Boy*, p. 44.
123. Forbush, *The Boy Problem*, p. 94.
124. Forbush, *Church Work with Boys*, pp. 70–71.
125. McCauley, *Why*, pp. 34–36.
126. Walter S. Athearn et al., *The Religious Education of Protestants in an American Commonwealth* (New York, 1923), pp. 359–365.
127. "The Sunday-School Boy Problem," p. 214.
128. William McCormick, *Fishers of Boys* (New York, 1915), p. 63.
129. Forbush, *Church Work with Boys*, pp. 63–64.
130. Gates, "The History, Scope, and Success of Organizations for Boys and Girls," pp. 229–230.
131. Forbush, *The New Round Table: The Order of the Knights of King Arthur* (Taunton, Mass., 1925), p. 12.
132. William Forbush and Frank L. Masseck, "Knights of King Arthur," *Men of To-Morrow* 35 (November 1902): 672–673.
133. Forbush, *The New Round Table*, pp. 9, 11, 18–19.
134. Forbush, *Church Work with Boys*, p. 67.
135. Gates, "The History, Scope, and Success of Organizations for Boys and Girls," p. 227.
136. Men and Religion Forward Movement, Boys' Work Commission, *Boys' Work in the Local Church*, vol. 5 of *Messages of the Men and Religion Forward Movement* (New York, 1912), pp. 154–155, 92.
137. Macleod, *Building Character in the American Boy*, pp. 190–191.
138. Ibid., p. 192.
139. George E. Dawson, "A Boy's Religion," in YMCA International Committee, *The Jubilee of Work for Young Men in North America* (New York, 1901), pp. 176–179.
140. Ibid., pp. 176–181.
141. Richardson and Loomis, *The Boy Scout Movement Applied by the Church*, p. 380.

142. "Sunday-School Boy Problem," p. 215.
143. Crosby, "Boy Scouts and the Sunday School," pp. 240, 237, 240.
144. Cuthbert A. Guy, *Scouting and Religion* (New York, 1924), pp. 21–38.
145. See Elmer, "The Scouts and the Church," p. 366, for a full discussion on why Jesus ought to be considered the "Master Scout."
146. Macleod, *Building Character in the American Boy,* p. 192.
147. Henry F. Cope, "The Character Training of the High School Boy," *Association Boys* 7, no. 4 (1908): 145.
148. "A Boy's Ideas on Religion," *Atlantic Monthly* 133 (May 1924): 632–633.
149. McKeever, *Training the Boy,* pp. 349–353.
150. Cope, "The Character Training of the High School Boy," p. 145.
151. Richardson and Loomis, *The Boy Scout Movement Applied by the Church,* p. 387.
152. Lilburn Merrill, *Winning the Boy* (New York, 1908), p. 42.
153. Forbush, *The Boy Problem,* p. 97 (quotation from Hubert Carleton).
154. Edgar Robinson, "Boys' Camps," *Association Boys* 5, no. 3 (1906): 175.
155. Men and Religion Forward Movement, *Boys' Work in the Local Church,* p. 14.
156. Forbush, *The Boy Problem,* p. 178 (quotation from George A. Coe).
157. Clyde W. Votaw, "The Religious Life of Boys," *Physical Training* 6, no. 10 (October 1909): 8.
158. W. H. Ball, "Religious Possibilities of a Gymnasium," *Association Boys* 6, no. 4 (1907): 164–165.
159. Merrill, *Winning the Boy,* p. 132.
160. Edgar Robinson, "What Some Prominent Men Think about the Boys' Camp," *Association Boys* 2, no. 3 (1903): 65–75.
161. William C. Gray, *Musings by Camp-fire and Wayside* (New York, 1902), p. 298, quoted in Shi, "Ernest Thompson Seton and the Boy Scouts," p. 383.
162. J. Adams Puffer, *The Boy and His Gang* (Boston, 1912), pp. 163–164.
163. Merrill, *Winning the Boy,* p. 134.
164. Talbot, "Summer Camps for Boys," p. 6170.
165. Gibson, *Services of Worship for Boys* (New York, 1914), p. 11.
166. Ibid., p. 12.
167. "The Manly Side of the Life of Christ," *Association Boys* 2, no. 4 (1903): 188.
168. See Albert H. Gage, *Evangelism of Youth* (Philadelphia, 1922), p. 44; and Kenneth M. Clampit, "Religious Subculture of a YMCA Camp" (Ph.D. diss., Harvard University, 1969), p. 55.
169. Henry W. Gibson, *Camping for Boys* (New York, 1911), pp. 87–100.
170. Galpin, "The Normal Religion of a Boy," pp. 272–275.
171. Eugene C. Foster, *The Boy and the Church* (Philadelphia, 1909), pp. 88–93.
172. Hoben, "The Minister and the Boy I," pp. 229–230.
173. Forbush, "Boys' Clubs," pp. 340–341.

174. Andrew W. Achenbaum, "The Obsolescence of Old Age in America, 1865–1914," *Journal of Social History* 8, no. 1 (Fall 1974): 52–59.

175. Gates, "The History, Scope, and Success of Organizations for Boys and Girls," p. 224.

5. Worldwide Redemption

The epigraph is from Josiah Strong, *The Times and Young Men* (New York, 1901), p. 180.

1. H. Richard Niebuhr, *The Kingdom of God in America* (Hamden, Conn.: Shoe String Press, 1956), p. 198.

2. The subject of women in missions has been addressed recently, for example, by Patricia Grimshaw, Patricia Hill, Dana Robert, Susan Yohn, and Jane Hunter.

3. This phrase likely made its first appearance at the 1886 Northfield–Mt. Hermon missionary conference. It is attributed to evangelist Arthur T. Pierson. C. Howard Hopkins, *History of the YMCA in North America* (New York: Association Press, 1951), p. 297.

4. Howard B. Grose, "Association Men and Immigration," *Association Men* 33, no. 1 (October 1907): 6.

5. Peter Roberts, "America's Foreign Born Men and the Association's Duty to Them," *Association Men* 32, no. 7 (April 1907): 293.

6. Home Missions Council, *New Americans for a New America* (New York, 1913), p. 2.

7. Fred H. Rindge, "Human Engineering: How the Young Men's Christian Association Is Reaching Industrial Workers," *American City* 16, no. 6 (June 1917): 584–586.

8. John R. Mott, "The Great Conflict before the Young Men's Christian Associations," in YMCA International Committee, *The Jubilee of Work for Young Men in North America* (New York, 1901), pp. 238–240.

9. "'The Army Follows the Missionary': Yes!" *Independent* 52 (June 28, 1900): 1571.

10. Fred Smith, "Will Christianity Win?" *Missionary Review of the World* 38 (January 1915): 29; and Fred Smith, *A Man's Religion* (New York, 1913), p. 231.

11. Barbara Welter, "She Hath Done What She Could: Protestant Women's Missionary Careers in Nineteenth-Century America," in Janet W. James, ed., *Women in American Religion* (Philadelphia: University of Pennsylvania Press, 1980), p. 119.

12. Daniel W. Martin, "The United Presbyterian Church Policy on the Men's Movement—An Historical Overview," *Journal of Presbyterian History* 59, no. 3 (Fall 1981): 410–411.

13. Welter, "She Hath Done What She Could," pp. 111–125.

14. Wilfred T. Grenfell, "The Romance of a Missionary's Life," in *Christian Unity; Missions,* vol. 4 of Men and Religion Forward Movement, *Messages of the Men and Religion Forward Movement* (New York, 1912), pp. 295, 312.

15. William H. Scott, *Men in the Church: An Address Delivered before the [Presbyterian] Synod of Pennsylvania* (Philadelphia, 1909), p. 15. The quotation is from J. Campbell White.

16. Ferdinand C. Iglehart, *Theodore Roosevelt: The Man as I Knew Him* (New York, 1919), p. 297.

17. John R. Mott, *The Future Leadership of the Church* (New York, 1908), p. 191.

18. Charles H. Brent, *Adventure for God* (New York, 1905), pp. 17, 83.

19. John R. Mott, "The Contribution of Physical Education to the Kingdom of God in the World," in *Addresses and Papers,* vol. 3 (New York, 1947), pp. 655–656.

20. George D. Pratt, "Breaking the Spell and Shell of Centuries," *Association Men* 41, no. 4 (January 1916): 212; and Luther Gulick, "Missionary Efficiency and Service," *Student Volunteer* 5, no. 7 (April 1897) [n.p.].

21. D. Willard Lyon, "The Marks of a Spiritual Man," *Student World* 10 (October 1917): 294. J. R. Saunders, *Men and Methods that Win in the Foreign Fields* (New York, 1921), pp. 34–35.

22. Alexander Zabriskie, *Bishop Brent: Crusader for Christian Unity* (Philadelphia: Westminster Press, 1948), p. 94.

23. Edward M. Dodd, "Hobbies and Recreations," *Student Volunteer Movement Bulletin* 5, no. 7 (November 1924): 6.

24. Pratt, "Breaking the Spell and Shell of Centuries," p. 212.

25. Elmer Johnson, *The History of YMCA Physical Education* (Chicago: Association Press, 1979), pp. 151, 146, 99. The Japanese objection to team sports was that they would impede individual initiative.

26. Ibid., pp. 148–167; and Henry W. Gibson, "The History of Organized Camping," *Camping Magazine* [7] (December 1936): 190.

27. Johnson, *The History of YMCA Physical Education,* p. 169.

28. Pratt, "Breaking the Spell and Shell of Centuries," p. 212.

29. C. M. Hobbs, "Practical Christianity," *Men* 24 (November 1898): 14.

30. For a comprehensive history of the Student Volunteer Movement, see Michael Parker, *The Kingdom of Character: The Student Volunteer Movement for Foreign Missions, 1886–1926* (Lanham, Md.: University Press of America and the American Society of Missiology, 1998); and Dwayne Ramsey, "College Evangelists and Foreign Missions: The Student Volunteer Movement, 1886–1920" (Ph.D. diss., University of California, Davis, 1988).

31. Harlan P. Beach, "Historical Sketch of the Student Volunteer Movement for Foreign Missions," *Student Volunteer* 6, no. 3 (December 1897): 35.

32. George Marsden, "The Soul of the American University: An Historical Overview," in George Marsden and Bradley Longfield, eds., *The Secularization of the Academy* (New York: Oxford University Press, 1992), pp. 9–45.

33. John R. Mott, "Beginnings of the International Student Movement," in *Ad dresses and Papers,* vol. 3, p. 27.

34. See Ibid., p. 27; and "The Coming Four Years in Student Work," *Association Men,* v. 33, no. 4 (Jan. 1908), p. 164.

35. "A Christian and a Man," *Men* 25 (September 1899): 468.

36. Josiah Morse and James Allan, "The Religion of One Hundred and Twenty-Six College Students," *Journal of Religious Psychology* 6, no. 12 (April 1913): 186.

37. Bradley Longfield, "From Evangelicalism to Liberalism: Public Midwestern Universities in Nineteenth-Century America," in Marsden and Longfield, *The Secularization of the Academy,* p. 53.

38. Charles K. Ober, "The Beginnings of the North American Student Movement," *Student World* 6 (January 1913): 10–11.

39. Bruce Barton, "The Greatest 'Y' Man," *American Magazine* 86 (October 1918): 9.

40. Quoted in Ruth Rouse, *The World's Student Christian Federation* (London: Student Christian Movement Press, 1948), p. 48.

41. Howard Hopkins, *John R. Mott, 1865–1955: A Biography* (Grand Rapids, Mich.: William B. Eerdmans Publishing Co., 1979), pp. 20–24. Mt. Hermon is located in Gill, Massachusetts. Next to Gill is Northfield, the site of Moody's home.

42. Ibid., pp. 25–27. The Princeton pledge read simply: "I am willing and desirous, God permitting, to become a foreign missionary."

43. Ibid., pp. 26–28, 60; and Ober, "The Beginnings of the North American Student Movement," p. 13.

44. The SVM also had an advisory committee composed of members from eight of the leading Protestant mission boards.

45. Clifton J. Phillips, "Changing Attitudes in the Student Volunteer Movement of Great Britain and North America, 1880–1920," in Torben Christensen and William R. Hutchison, eds., *Missionary Ideologies in the Imperialist Era, 1880–1920: Reports for the Durham Consultation, 1981* (Arhus, Denmark: Forlaget Aros, 1982), p. 135.

46. Hopkins, *John R. Mott,* pp. 61–62.

47. Rouse, *The World's Student Christian Federation,* pp. 49–50.

48. See John R. Mott, "The Two Hundred Million Young Men in Non-Christian Lands," speech given May 28, 1899, in *Addresses and Papers,* vol. 3, p. 222; and Hopkins, *John R. Mott,* p. 696.

49. See for example Frederick P. Noble, "Africa's Claims," *Student Volunteer* 4, no. 7 (April 1896): 121.

50. Phillips, "Changing Attitudes in the Student Volunteer Movement of Great Britain and North America, 1880–1920," pp. 136–140.

51. Ibid., pp. 138–140.

52. Josiah Strong, *The Times and Young Men* (New York, 1901), pp. 182–183.

53. Don O. Shelton, *Men and the Christian Conquest of America* (New York, 1906), p. 28.

54. Gail Bederman, "'The Women Have Had Charge of the Church Work Long Enough': The Men and Religion Forward Movement of 1911–1912 and the Masculinization of Middle-Class Protestantism," *American Quarterly* 41, no. 3 (September 1989): 434, 459.

55. Washington Gladden, "As It Has Never Been Done in My Day," *Association Men* 37, no. 7 (April 1912): 323.

56. "A Permanent Awakening?" *Outlook* 101 (May 4, 1912): 9.

57. E. W. Halford, "Men and Religion Forward Movement," *Missionary Review* 34 (October 1911): 754.

58. Henry Rood, "Men and Religion," *Independent* 71 (Dec. 21, 1911): 1362.

59. Henry Rood, "On the March with the New Crusaders," *Everybody's* 26 (May 1912): 638.

60. William T. Ellis, "A Movement: A Message: A Method," *Independent* 72 (May 9, 1912): 987.

61. George Coleman, "The Advertising Man's Great Moral Revival," *Association Men* 38, no. 12 (September 1913): 625.

62. Fayette L. Thompson, "Men and Religion: The Program," in Fayette L. Thompson et al., *Men and Religion* (New York, 1911), pp. 1–13.

63. Rood, "On the March," p. 638.

64. Allyn K. Foster, "The Dream Come True," in Clarence A. Barbour, ed., *Making Religion Efficient* (New York, 1912), pp. 9–10.

65. The brotherhoods most supportive of the MRFM included the Baptist Brotherhood, the Brotherhood of Andrew and Philip, the Brotherhood of Disciples of Christ, the Brotherhood of St. Andrew, the Congregational Brotherhood of America, the Gideons, the Lutheran Brotherhood, the Methodist Brotherhood, the Otterbein Brotherhood (United Brethren Church), the Presbyterian Brotherhood of America, and the United Presbyterian Brotherhood. James G. Cannon, "Report of the Committee of Ninety-Seven of the Men and Religion Forward Movement," in *Congress Addresses,* vol. 1 of Men and Religion Forward Movement, *Messages of the Men and Religion Forward Movement,* pp. 19–20.

66. Fred B. Smith, "God Almighty Hates a Quitter," *Association Men* 34, no. 8 (May 1909): 358.

67. Arthur H. Gleason, "Going after Souls on a Business Basis," *Collier's* 48, no. 14 (Dec. 23, 1911): 13.

68. Orrin G. Cocks, "The Scope and Value of the Local Surveys of the Men and Religion Movement," *Proceedings of the Academy of Political Science* 2, no. 4 (July 1912): 537.

69. Rood, "Men and Religion," p. 1364.

70. Bederman, "'The Women Have Had Charge of the Church Work Long Enough,'" p. 441.

71. "Men and Religion," *Outlook* 99 (Dec. 16, 1911): 892.

72. Arthur P. Kellogg, "In Hartford as It Is in Heaven: Campaigning with a Men and Religion Team," *Survey* 27 (Feb. 3, 1912): 1673–1675.

73. Gleason, "Going after Souls," p. 13.
74. Rood, "On the March," pp. 639–640.
75. Ibid., pp. 644–645.
76. William T. Ellis, "The Christian Conservation Congress," in *Congress Addresses,* p. 4.
77. Ibid., p. 2.
78. "Closing Strides in the Men and Religion Movement," *Survey* 27 (March 30, 1912): 1993.
79. Gail Bederman notes that while suffrage may not have been an issue at the Christian Conservation Congress, elsewhere MRFM leaders condemned women's rights "in no uncertain terms." Others in the MRFM, however, evinced sympathy toward suffrage, and some, such as Raymond Robins (whose wife was the national labor reformer and suffragette Margaret Dreier Robins), firmly supported women's advancement. Bederman, "'The Women Have Had Charge of the Church Work Long Enough,'" p. 451.
80. "A World Tour on Behalf of Men and Religion," *Outlook* 103 (Jan. 11, 1913): 56–57.
81. "Net Results for Men and Religion," *Literary Digest* 44 (April 27, 1912): 886.
82. "An Evangelist in Business with Men of Business," *Association Men* 39, no. 5 (February 1914): 240. Smith's change of employers did not signal his abandonment of Christianity; he remained a committed layman throughout his career. See Fred Smith, *I Remember* (New York: Fleming H. Revell, 1936).
83. "Closing Strides," p. 1993.
84. "A Rebuff to the Men and Religion Movement," *Literary Digest* 44 (March 9, 1912): 486.
85. "Men and Religion Publicity," in *The Church and the Press,* vol. 7 of Men and Religion Forward Movement, *Messages of the Men and Religion Forward Movement,* p. 99. While mass media publications such as newspapers and magazines may have been the chief means whereby MRFM leaders disseminated their ideas, books also played a role—particularly a seven-volume set of books published by the "Y" in 1912 and collectively entitled *Messages of the Men and Religion Forward Movement.*
86. "A Year of Men and Religion," *Literary Digest* 46 (March 1, 1913): 461.
87. "Men and Religion: A Review," *Outlook* 100 (April 27, 1912): 891.
88. Ellis, "A Movement: A Message: A Method," p. 987.
89. Walter Rauschenbusch, *Christianizing the Social Order* (New York, 1912), p. 20.
90. See Smith, *I Remember,* p. 97; and Ellis, "A Movement: A Message: A Method," p. 986.
91. Bederman, "'The Women Have Had Charge of the Church Work Long Enough,'" p. 448.
92. Ellis, "A Movement: A Message: A Method," pp. 987–988. For more on

why leaders of the MRFM viewed themselves as social progressives, see Gary Scott Smith, "The Men and Religion Forward Movement of 1911–1912: New Perspectives on Evangelical Social Concern and the Relationship between Christianity and Progressivism," *Westminster Theological Journal* 49, no. 1 (Spring 1987): 91–118.

93. See "For Men," *Christian Advocate* 86 (August 1911): 1026; and Bederman, "'The Women Have Had Charge of the Church Work Long Enough,'" p. 454.

94. Bederman, "'The Women Have Had Charge of the Church Work Long Enough,'" p. 454.

95. The Southern Baptists consolidated their female-run missionary societies into a single, male-run missionary board in 1906. A similar consolidation occurred within the Disciples Church in 1919, the Northern Presbyterian Church in 1923, and the Congregational Church in 1925. These consolidations took place for a variety of reasons, including financial ones. But Virginia Brereton and Christa Klein are right to point out that however "practical" the missionary society consolidations may have been, they certainly had the effect of reducing women's influence within the churches. Virginia Brereton and Christa Klein, "American Women in Ministry," in James, *Women in American Religion,* p. 181.

6. Muscular Women

The epigraph is from Mary S. Dunn, "The Gospel of the Body," *Evangel* 8 (October 1895): 5.

1. Margaret Marsh, "Suburban Men and Masculine Domesticity, 1870–1915," *American Quarterly* 40, no. 2 (June 1988): 165–186.

2. See Elmer Dent, "Analysis of Why Young Men Are Not Church Members," *Association Men* 33, no. 5 (February 1908): 212; and Joseph Rogers, "Educating Our Boys," *Lippincott's* 81 (May 1908): 632–642.

3. Charlotte P. Gilman, *The Man-Made World* (New York, 1911), p. 55.

4. Elwood Worcester et al., *Religion and Medicine: The Moral Control of Nervous Disorders* (New York, 1908), p. 137.

5. Jessie R. Holmes, "The Vices of Good Girls," *Evangel* 9 (March 1895): 3.

6. Ibid., pp. 3–4.

7. George B. Hodge, "Educational Work in the Young Women's Christian Association," *Evangel* 10 (April 1898): 8.

8. Margaret Sangster, "The Present Opportunity of the Christian Woman," *Evangel* 10 (April 1898): 5.

9. The Daughters of the King was (and is) an Episcopal order founded in 1885. Its original aim was to furnish women with more than just Bible study, and its motto is "Magnanimiter Crucem Sustine" ("Bear forward almost aggressively the Cross with great mind"). Helen T. Birney, "The His-

tory of the Daughters of the King," *Royal Cross* 32, no. 1 (February 1935); 16 17.

10. According to Dean Agnes Taylor of the Congregational Training School for Women in Chicago, the women's training school movement (which began around 1910) existed partly to help churches cope with a shortage of volunteer labor. Taylor also believed that as of 1917 there were thirty-four such schools in the United States and Canada, though this number was to decline sharply after World War I, thanks largely to the absorbtion of such programs into the orthodox seminary curriculum. See Agnes Mabel Taylor, "Standards of Preparation of Women Church Assistants," *Religious Education* 12, no. 6 (December 1917): 438–441; and Virginia Brereton and Christa Klein, "American Women in Ministry," in Janet James, ed., *Women in American Religion* (University of Pennsylvania Press, 1980), pp. 181–182.

11. Mary Hall and Helen Sweet, *Women in the YMCA Record* (New York: Association Press, 1947), p. 50. The quotation is from a speech that was delivered to the first convention of YMCA women's auxiliaries in 1889.

12. Ibid., pp. 29, 32.

13. See ibid., pp. 31, 34–35; and C. Howard Hopkins, *The History of the YMCA in North America* (New York: Association Press, 1951), pp. 564–565.

14. Quoted in Elmer Johnson, *The History of YMCA Physical Education* (Chicago: Association Press, 1979), p. 66.

15. Hall and Sweet, *Women in the YMCA Record,* p. 30. The quotation is from a speech given by McBurney to the International YMCA Convention of 1866.

16. John Gustav-Wrathall, "'Many of Our Brightest and Best': The Problem of Unmarried Secretaries in the YMCA, 1868–1920" (paper, University of Minnesota, 1993), pp. 1–21. Gustav-Wrathall bases his conclusion regarding the homosexuality of several important YMCA secretaries largely upon his reading of these men's private correspondence. In particular, he cites the exchange of homoerotic love poems as evidence that some YMCA correspondents were more than just friends.

17. Carl H. Barnett, "The Church and Recreation Programs," *Playground* 17, no. 9 (December 1923): 500.

18. Hall and Sweet, *Women in the YMCA Record,* pp. 39–43.

19. Virginia Stimpson, "Healthy Body, Healthy Mind, Healthy Womanhood: The Changing Role of Physical Education for Students at Wellesley College, 1870–1930" (BA thesis, Harvard College, 1989), p. 32.

20. Mary S. Sims, *The YWCA—an Unfolding Purpose* (New York: Woman's Press, 1950), p. 1.

21. Elizabeth Wilson, *Fifty Years of Association Work among Young Women, 1866–1916* (New York: Columbia University Teachers College, 1916), p. 100.

22. Emmett Rice, *A Brief History of Physical Education* (New York, 1921), p. 201.

23. Quoted in Helen Buckler et al., *Wo-He-Lo: The Story of Camp Fire Girls, 1910–1960* (New York: Holt, Rinehart and Winston, 1961), p. 7.

24. Lyman Abbott, *Christianity and Social Problems* (Boston, 1896), pp. 150–151.

25. Lyman Abbott, *The Home Builder* (Boston, 1908), p. 25.

26. William McKeever, *Training the Girl* (New York, 1916), p. 242.

27. Frances A. Kellor, "Ethical Value of Sports for Women," *American Physical Education Review* 11 (1906): 168.

28. Anne B. Stewart, "The 'Woman Peril' Again," *Educational Review* 48 (November 1914): 383.

29. Abbie Mayhew, "Shall Delicate Girls Take Physical Training," *Evangel* 5 (November 1892): 6.

30. Mary S. Dunn, "The Gospel of the Body," *Evangel* 8 (October 1895): 4.

31. "A Sermonette," *Evangel* 8 (July 1896): 15.

32. Francis Peabody, *Jesus and the Christian Character* (New York, 1905), p. 54. Muriel Streibert, "The Life of Jesus and the Lives of Girls," *Religious Education* 9 (December 1914): 536.

33. See, for example, Mary H. Austin, *Christ in Italy; Being the Adventures of a Maverick among Masterpieces* (New York, 1912); and Austin, *A Small Town Man* (New York, 1925).

34. Occasionally women religious writers conceded, as did a MRFM-inspired "Minister's wife," that "women have had charge [of the churches] long enough." But more often they averred that men's irreligion, while a problem, was as likely due to insufficient mothering as to any excess of femininity within the churches. See Gail Bederman, "'The Women Have Had Charge of the Church Work Long Enough': The Men and Religion Forward Movement of 1911–1912 and the Masculinization of Middle-Class Protestantism," *American Quarterly* 41, no. 3 (September 1989): 453; and "Have Women Robbed Men of Their Religion?" *Ladies Home Journal* 17 (February 1900): 17.

35. David Spence Hill, "Education and Problems of the Protestant Ministry," *American Journal of Religious Psychology* 1, no. 2 (November 1904): 216–217.

36. The fact that Christian Science, Theosophy, New Thought, and other "mind cure" religions were characterized by a "ubiquity of women" is confirmed by Donald Meyer. "Not only was [Mind Cure's] most famous exponent [Mary Baker Eddy] a woman," he writes; "scores of its lesser exponents were women, as founders, writers, preachers, teachers, healers." Donald Meyer, *The Positive Thinkers: A Study of the American Quest for Health, Wealth, and Personal Power from Mary Baker Eddy to Norman Vincent Peale* (Garden City, N.Y.: Anchor Books, 1966), p. 28.

37. My portrayal of Eddy is not terribly flattering. For a more sympathetic yet

still scholarly portrait of the founder of Christian Science, see Robert D. Thomas, *"With Bleeding Footsteps": Mary Baker Eddy's Path to Religious Leadership* (New York: Alfred A. Knopf, 1994).

38. Mary Baker Eddy, *Science and Health with Key to the Scriptures* (Boston, 1918), p. 353. Eddy may have declared evil to be unreal, but she did confess to being afraid of what she called "malicious animal magnetism." In fact, it was in order to combat MAM (or more precisely, a Christian Scientist whom she accused of practicing it) that Eddy in 1878 brought to Salem Court the case of Brown vs. Spofford, the last trial for witchcraft to be held in the United States. See Willa Cather and Georgine Milmine, *The Life of Mary Baker G. Eddy and the History of Christian Science* (Lincoln: University of Nebraska Press, 1993), p. 241; and Gaius Glenn Atkins, *Modern Religious Cults and Movements* (New York, 1923), p. 133.

39. Eddy, *Science and Health with Key to the Scriptures,* pp. 57, 16.

40. "Woman and the Religion of the Future," *Harper's Weekly* 47 (Dec. 5, 1903): 1934.

41. Cather and Milmine, *The Life of Mary Baker G. Eddy,* pp. 364, 480.

42. Eddy generally claimed not to have been influenced by Quimby, but evidence suggests that it was really he who invented the term "Christian Science," together with much of its philosophy. Atkins, *Modern Religious Cults and Movements,* pp. 116–118.

43. Cather and Milmine, *The Life of Mary Baker G. Eddy,* p. 283.

44. Mark Twain once dryly observed that the Christian Science Church believed nothing "to be real, except the Dollar. But all through and through its advertisements," he added, "that reality is eagerly and persistently recognized." Mark Twain, *Christian Science* (Buffalo, N.Y.: Prometheus Books, 1986), p. 41.

45. Meyer, *The Positive Thinkers,* pp. 53–54.

46. "Religion for Men," *Century* 58 (May 1910): 153.

47. See Eddy, *Science and Health with Key to the Scriptures,* pp. 562–565; and Cather and Milmine, *The Life of Mary Baker G. Eddy,* pp. 188–189, 343–346.

48. Cather and Milmine, *The Life of Mary Baker G. Eddy,* pp. 125, 259, 384, 387, 451–452. Cather based her charges on the research of journalist Georgine Milmine.

49. Christian Science officials objected to Cather's work from the start. But though they were unable to stop its appearance either in serial form or as a book, they did buy the copyright so as to prevent further publication. In addition, individual Christian Scientists over time sought out and destroyed most copies of the work, making it extremely difficult for scholars to find. David Stouck, afterword to Cather and Milmine, *The Life of Mary Baker G. Eddy,* pp. 497–498.

50. See Horatio W. Dresser, *A History of the New Thought Movement* (New York, 1919), pp. 41, 309; and Beryl Satter, *Each Mind a Kingdom: Ameri-*

can Women, Sexual Purity, and the New Thought Movement, 1875–1920 (Berkeley: University of California Press, 1999).

51. See Meyer, *The Positive Thinkers,* pp. 18–19; and Charles Braden, *Spirits in Rebellion: The Rise and Development of New Thought* (Dallas: Southern Methodist Univ. Press, 1963), pp. 236–263, 386–391.

52. For a historical account of the Emmanuel movement, see Ralph Adams, "The Emmanuel Movement: An Antecedent to Occupational Therapy" (master's thesis, Rush University, 1986); and John Greene, "The Emmanuel Movement, 1906–1929," *New England Quarterly* 7, no. 3 (1934): 494–532.

53. Worcester et al., *Religion and Medicine,* p. 145.

54. Lyman Powell, *The Emmanuel Movement in a New England Town* (New York, 1909), pp. 91–92, 166.

55. Charles Jefferson, *The Character of Jesus* (New York, 1908), pp. 100, 181.

56. Frances Kellor, "Ethical Value of Sports for Women," *American Physical Education Review* 11 (1906), p. 168. Dr. James Rogers agreed with Kellor that the attractions of the new religions were mainly pathological, considering that the weak and unproductive "are often aware of their shortcomings and seek relief in Christian Science, which may help them to imagine that they are not physically inferior, or in the New Thought cults which assuage the misery a little by reducing the friction from worry and discontent,—attitudes of mind their physical state makes spontaneous." James Rogers, "Physical and Moral Training," *Pedagogical Seminary* 16, no. 3 (September 1909): 302.

57. Charles R. Brown, *Faith and Health* (New York, 1910), pp. 195–197.

58. As evidence that not all women were supportive of the new faiths, Dean Agnes Taylor of the Congregational Training School for Women noted how "earnest" women church assistants were especially good at dealing "with people who are caught in the partial truths of New Thought and Christian Science." Taylor, "Standards of Preparation of Women Church Assistants," p. 444.

59. See Mary S. Sims, *The Natural History of a Social Institution—the Young Women's Christian Association* (New York: Woman's Press, 1936), pp. 2–3; and Sims, *The YWCA—an Unfolding Purpose,* p. 1.

60. Anna Rice, *A History of the World's Young Women's Christian Association* (New York: Woman's Press, 1947), pp. 36–38.

61. Sims, *The YWCA—an Unfolding Purpose,* pp. 4, 7.

62. See Adrienne Lash Jones, "Struggle among Saints: African American Women and the YWCA, 1870–1920," in Nina Mjagkij and Margaret Spratt, eds., *Men and Women Adrift: The YMCA and the YWCA in the City* (New York: New York University Press, 1997), pp. 160–184; and Judith Weisenfeld, *African American Women and Christian Activism: New York's Black YWCA, 1905–1945* (Cambridge: Harvard University Press, 1997).

63. Rice, *A History of the World's Young Women's Christian Association,* p. 40.

64. Ibid., pp. 38, 40–41.

65. Ibid., p. 42.

66. The fact that student YWCAs were especially active in the 1890s does not mean that city Associations were inactive. In fact, two city Associations, Topeka and Dayton, were among the first YWCAs to work with racial minorities: Topeka with American Indians in the early 1890s, and Dayton with African-Americans in 1893. Sims, *The Natural History of a Social Institution*, pp. 25–26, 34, 204.

67. Grace Wilson, *The Religious and Educational Philosophy of the Young Women's Christian Association* (New York, 1933), pp. 16, 41–44. The student YWCAs supported the 1906 merger on the condition that the W/YWCA adopt an evangelical basis for membership. Nine years later, however, the students agreed to drop this stance.

68. See Rebecca Morse, "The Young Women's Christian Association: Its Five Departments," *Evangel* 5 (April 1893): 10; and Nancy Boyd, *Emissaries: The Overseas Work of the American YWCA, 1895–1970* (New York: Woman's Press, 1986), pp. 17, 23. Boyd points out that in addition to Miss Morse, many other YWCA leaders had male relatives who were prominent in the YMCA. These women included Mrs. Luther Wishard (wife of YMCA College Secretary Luther Wishard), Leila Mott (wife of John Mott), and Emma Bailey Speer (wife of Presbyterian missionary Robert Speer).

69. Morse, "The Young Women's Christian Association," p. 11.

70. Rice, *A History of the World's Young Women's Christian Association*, pp. 43–44.

71. Abbie Mayhew, "Physical Training a Christian Profession," *Evangel* 7 (September 1894): 11–12.

72. Sims, *The Natural History of a Social Institution*, pp. 7, 12.

73. Dunn, "The Gospel of the Body," pp. 4–5.

74. Catherine Vance, *The Girl Reserve Movement of the Young Women's Christian Association* (New York: Columbia University Teachers College, 1937), p. 8.

75. M. Louise Slater, "Junior Work," *Evangel* 3 (December 1890): 12–13.

76. Vance, *The Girl Reserve Movement*, pp. 7, 15, 35.

77. From the Camp Fire Girl Constitution, quoted in Henry Curtis, *The Play Movement and Its Significance* (New York, 1917), p. 272.

78. Henry W. Gibson, "The History of Organized Camping," *Camping Magazine* [7], January 1936: 14; March 1936: 28; April 1936: 19. Boys' camping took off in the 1880s, girls' camping in the 1910s. The first recognizable boys' camp, the Gunnery Camp near New Haven, Connecticut, was founded in 1861. The first camp to admit girls, Camp Arey in Arey, New York, did so in 1892.

79. McKeever, *Training the Girl*, pp. 263, 266.

80. Mary Moxcey, "The Sunday School and the Young Women's Christian Association in Relation to the Moral and Religious Education of the Girl," *Religious Education* 6, no. 2 (June 1911): 204.

81. See Curtis, *The Play Movement and Its Significance,* p. 273; and Luther Gulick, "Team Work in Social Life: An Address to the Girls of America," *Journal of Education* 60 (July 9, 1914): 27.
82. See Gibson, "The History of Organized Camping," *Camping Magazine* [7], April 1936: 31–32; and Buckler et al., *Wo-He-Lo,* pp. 4–5.
83. Gibson, "The History of Organized Camping," p. 31.
84. Buckler et al., *Wo-He-Lo,* pp. 11–12, 15, 47–48. The Work-Health-Love ceremony (performed nationally by the Gulicks as a CFG fund-raiser) proceeds as follows: First, a fire is made with sticks. Then three girls dressed as Indians ascertain that "WoHeLo means work . . . WoHeLo means health . . . WoHeLo means love."
85. Ibid., pp. 9–10; and Camp Fire Girls, *The Book of the Camp Fire Girls* (New York, 1915), p. 14.
86. Buckler et al., *Wo-He-Lo,* p. 20.
87. Ibid., pp. 20–22.
88. Ibid., p. 24. Gulick may not have wished for the Camp Fire Girls to be overtly Christian, but he did concede the movement "to have spiritual vision and purpose for our practical endeavors." Luther Gulick, "Annual Report of the President," *Wohelo* 4 (August 1916): 6–7, quoted in Ethel Dorgan, *Luther Halsey Gulick, 1865–1918* (Washington, D.C.: McGrath Publishing Co., 1976), p. 119.
89. Buckler et al., *Wo-He-Lo,* pp. 22–23, 39. While Gulick conceded that much of women's work was "monotonous," he also expected Camp Fire Girls "to take drudgery and make of it a game; to strip the dull gray covering of the commonplace from the significant acts of daily life and reveal their real beauty and romantic form."
90. Ibid., pp. 26–32.
91. Mary Roberts Rinehart, *Why I Believe in Scouting for Girls,* Girl Scout Series, no. 10 (New York, [1921]), n.p.
92. Dorgan, *Luther Halsey Gulick,* pp. 123–124.
93. Curtis, *The Play Movement and Its Significance,* pp. 271, 279.
94. Buckler et al., *Wo-He-Lo,* pp. 196–197.
95. Lillian S. Williams, *A Bridge to the Future: The History of Diversity in Girl Scouting* (New York: Girl Scouts of America, 1996), pp. 10–11, 21.
96. For a comprehensive history of the Girl Scouts, see Margaret Rogers, "From True to New Womanhood: The Rise of the Girl Scouts, 1912–1930" (Ph.D. diss., Stanford Univ., 1992); and Wendy Sterne, "The Formation of the Scouting Movement and the Gendering of Citizenship" (Ph.D. diss., Univ. of Wisconsin, Madison, 1993).
97. Gladys Shultz and Daisy Lawrence, *Lady from Savannah: The Life of Juliette Low* (Philadelphia: J. B. Lippincott Co., 1958), p. 299 and passim. For a more critical look at Juliette Low, see Melissa Ann Biegert, "Woman Scout: The Empowerment of Juliette Gordon Low, 1860–1927" (Ph.D. diss., University of Texas, Austin, 1998).

98. Rose Kerr, "Juliette Low Meets Sir Robert Baden-Powell and the Girl Guides of England," in Anne Choate and Helen Ferris, eds., *Juliette Low and the Girl Scouts: The Story of an American Woman, 1860–1927* (New York, 1928), pp. 82–86.

99. Shultz and Lawrence, *Lady from Savannah*, p. 351.

100. Helen Ferris, *Girls' Clubs: Their Organization and Management* (New York, 1918), p. 269.

101. Vance, *The Girl Reserve Movement*, pp. 27–28.

102. Curtis, *The Play Movement and Its Significance*, p. 284. The Camp Fire Girls' Indian dress is today used only for ceremonial occasions.

103. Shultz and Lawrence, *Lady from Savannah*, pp. 349–351. During World War I, Mrs. Woodrow Wilson served as honorary president of the Girl Scouts while her husband served as honorary president of the Camp Fire Girls.

104. Dorgan, *Luther Halsey Gulick*, p. 121.

7. Christians in Khaki

The epigraph is from George Stewart and Henry B. Wright, *The Practice of Friendship: Studies in Personal Evangelism with Men of the United States Army and Navy in American Training Camps* (New York, 1918), p. 23.

1. Charles Macfarland, ed., *The Churches of Christ in Time of War* (New York, 1917), p. 32.

2. William Overholt, "The YMCA and the Christian Mission on Campus," *Christian Century* 75 (Dec. 31, 1958): 1508.

3. Sherwood Eddy and Kirby Page, *The Abolition of War* (New York, 1924), pp. 15, 23.

4. Sydney Ahlstrom, *A Religious History of the American People* (New Haven: Yale University Press, 1972), p. 877.

5. Julia Ward Howe, "The Uses of Victory," *Christian Register* 77 (Sept. 22, 1898): 1071.

6. Sidney Gulick, *The Growth of the Kingdom of God* (New York, 1897), pp. 307, 316, quoted in Robert Handy, *A Christian America: Protestant Hopes and Historical Realities* (New York: Oxford University Press, 1984), p. 106.

7. Oliver Howard, "The Warfare of the Future," *Men* 22 (Sept. 19, 1896): 300–301.

8. "The President Should Be Sustained," *Congregationalist* 83 (April 7, 1898): 486.

9. "The Churches Have Tried Their Best," *Congregationalist* 83 (May 5, 1898): 645.

10. "Some Advantages of War," *Outlook* 59, no. 8 (June 25, 1898): 461. Frank Crane, "The Bubbling of Anglo-Saxon Blood," *Men* 23 (May 7, 1898):

651. For more on how the Spanish-American War was supposed to enhance the manliness of American men, see Kristin L. Hoganson, *Fighting for American Manhood: How Gender Politics Provoked the Spanish-American and the Philippine-American Wars* (New Haven: Yale University Press, 1998).

11. "The War with Spain," *Missionary Review of the World* 11 (June 1898): 462–463. Missionary support for American expansionism undercuts Richard Welch's assertion that the most distinguishing characteristic of the pro-expansionist churches was a Calvinist theological heritage. For while some Puritan-based bodies, such as the Congregationalists (a strong missionary church), generally supported expansionism, others, such as the Unitarians (a weak missionary church), had their doubts, leading one to conclude that the pro-expansionist churches were distinguished less by Calvinism than by a strong commitment to foreign missions. Richard Welch, *Response to Imperialism: The United States and the Philippine American War, 1899–1902* (Chapel Hill: University of North Carolina Press, 1979), p. 94.

12. Welch, *Response to Imperialism,* p. 109.

13. John Bushingham, American Protestantism and Expansion," *Methodist Review* 81 (July 1899): 592.

14. F. De P. Castells, "The Friars in the Philippines," *Missionary Review of the World* 11 (July 1898): 517.

15. George Pentecost, *The Coming Age of America: A Retrospect and a Forecast* (New York, 1898), p. 8.

16. Andrew Ross, "Whose History? Historiographical Issues in Writing African Church History," lecture, Episcopal Divinity School, March 4, 1994. According to Ross, scientific racism was particularly endemic among educated liberal missionaries. Uneducated conservative missionaries, in contrast, continued throughout the imperialist period to preach unfashionable notions such as equality under God and the pervasiveness of sin.

17. Pentecost, *The Coming Age of America,* pp. 24, 14.

18. J. Gordon Stapleton, "Theodore Roosevelt: Theologian of America's New Israel Concept" (Ph.D. diss., Temple University, 1972), p. 70.

19. Charles Jefferson, "Temptation from the Mountain Top," in Robert Fulton and Thomas Trueblood, eds., *Patriotic Eloquence Relating to The Spanish-American War and Its Issues* (New York, 1900), pp. 176–177.

20. Washington Gladden, "The Issues of the War," *Outlook* 59, no. 11 (July 16, 1898): 674–675.

21. E. Winchester Donald et al., *Ministers' Meeting of Protest against the Atrocities in the Philippines* (Boston, 1902), pp. 15–17.

22. Welch, *Response to Imperialism,* pp. 100, 97. The position of the *Advance* with regard to the Philippines is based on a series of editorials (dated May 8, May 15, and July 10, 1902) quoted by Welch. The reference to "an Oriental mind" appears in the journal's November 8, 1900, issue.

23. Donald et al., *Ministers' Meeting of Protest,* pp. 26, 10–11. The quotation is from an address by the Reverend Francis H. Rowley of the First Baptist Church in Boston.

24. See, for example, Joseph Dana Miller, "Militarism or Manhood," *Arena* 25 (October 1900): 384; and Ernest Crosby, "The Military Idea of Manliness," *Independent* 53 (April 18, 1901): 873–875.

25. Quoted in Robert Beisner, *Twelve against Empire: The Anti-Imperialists, 1898–1900* (New York: McGraw-Hill Book Co., 1968), pp. 42–43.

26. Goldwin Smith, "War as Moral Medicine," *Atlantic Monthly* 86 (December 1900): 735–737.

27. Sidney Gulick, *The Fight for Peace: An Aggressive Campaign for the American Churches* (New York, 1915), p. 189.

28. John Dewey, "Conscience and Compulsion," *New Republic* 11, no. 141 (July 14, 1917): 297.

29. In an April 30, 1914, letter mailed to 50,000 pastors, Federal Council of Churches secretary Charles Macfarland estimated that 25,000 peace sermons had been preached on Peace Sunday 1913, and he expressed hope that that number would be raised to 75,000 in 1914. Macfarland, *The Churches of Christ in America and International Peace* (New York, 1914), p. 17.

30. Ray Abrams, *Preachers Present Arms* (New York: Round Table Press, 1933), p. 10.

31. Charles Macfarland, *Pioneers of Peace through Religion* (New York: Fleming H. Revell, 1946), pp. 17–22.

32. Macfarland, *The Churches of Christ in America,* pp. 30–31.

33. Ibid., pp. 4–9.

34. Dewey, "Conscience and Compulsion," p. 297.

35. Jenkin Lloyd Jones, "Jesus the Founder of Christianity and the Master of Men," *Unity* (August 30, 1915): 422–423.

36. William James, "The Moral Equivalent of War," *International Conciliation,* no. 27 (February 1910): 18, 15.

37. Ibid., pp. 17–18.

38. David Shi, "Ernest Thompson Seton and the Boy Scouts: A Moral Equivalent of War?" *South Atlantic Quarterly* 84, no. 4 (Autumn 1985): 391.

39. Edgar Robinson, "Six Things to Be Recognized in Dealing with Adolescent Boys," *Christian Student* 8, no. 3 (August 1907): 9.

40. George Johnson, "Play as a Moral Equivalent of War," *Playground* 5, no. 4 (July 1912): 116–120.

41. Harry Emerson Fosdick, *Shall We End War?* (New York, 1921), p. 4.

42. Frederick Lynch, *The Peace Problem* (New York, 1911), pp. 30, 96.

43. Macfarland, *Pioneers of Peace,* pp. 42–43.

44. Ibid, p. 43; and The Church Peace Union, *The Church Peace Union: Record of Twenty Years, 1914–1934* (New York: The Union, 1935), p. 7.

45. Macfarland, *Pioneers of Peace,* pp. 44, 114. The World Alliance for Pro-

moting International Friendship through the Churches was a group whose American Council consisted in 1916 of forty-one Protestant denominations, the YMCA, the Laymen's Missionary Movement, the Missionary Education Movement, the Student Volunteer Movement, the International Sunday-School Association, the World's Sunday School Association, and the United Society for Christian Endeavor.

46. David Kennedy, *Over Here: The First World War and American Society* (New York: Oxford University Press, 1980), pp. 217–218. The American Legion came into existence during the pre–World War I preparedness campaign. It was officially incorporated in 1919.
47. Theodore Roosevelt, *Fear God and Take Your Own Part* (New York, 1916), pp. 22–29.
48. Ibid., p. 26.
49. Abrams, *Preachers Present Arms,* pp. 27–31.
50. John Haynes Holmes, *New Wars for Old* (New York, 1916), p. 346.
51. Samuel Elder, "The League to Enforce Peace," in George Blakeslee, ed., *The Problems and Lessons of the War* (New York, 1916), pp. 214–215; and Abrams, *Preachers Present Arms,* p. 164.
52. Abrams, *Preachers Present Arms,* pp. 22, 26.
53. Ibid., p. 37.
54. Eddy and Page, *The Abolition of War,* p. 16.
55. Francis Peabody, *The Religious Education of an American Citizen* (New York, 1917), p. 177.
56. "Eliot Sees No Road to Peace in Religion," *New York Times,* Dec. 28, 1914, p. 8.
57. Robert Speer, *The Christian Man, the Church, and the War* (New York, 1918), p. 17.
58. George Williams, "The Chaplaincy in the Armed Forces of the United States of America in Historical and Ecclesiastical Perspective," in Harvey Cox, ed., *Military Chaplaincy: From Religious Military to a Military Religion* (New York: American Report Press, [1971]), pp. 15–16.
59. Austen Kennedy De Blois, "America's Holy War—The Fight for the Future of the Human Race," in Samuel Batten, ed., *The Moral Meaning of the War* (Philadelphia, [1918]), p. 57.
60. Henry Churchill King, quoted in Abrams, *Preachers Present Arms,* p. 50.
61. Lyman Abbott, *The Twentieth Century Crusade* (New York, 1918).
62. William Cardinal O'Connell, "Addresses," in *War Addresses from Catholic Pulpit and Platform* (New York, n.d.), pp. 37–61.
63. Elizabeth McKeown, *War and Welfare: American Catholics and World War I* (New York: Garland Publishing Co., 1988), pp. 50–51 and passim.
64. T. A. Nummey, "Patriotic Address at Raising of Service Flag at Richmond Hill, N.Y.," in *War Addresses from Catholic Pulpit,* p. 263.
65. McKeown, *War and Welfare,* pp. 72, 144.

66. Macfarland, *Pioneers of Peace*, pp. 68–72.
67. Quoted in Horace Peterson and Gilbert Fite, *Opponents of War, 1917–1918* (Seattle: University of Washington Press, 1968), pp. 113–114.
68. Mercer Green Johnston, *Patriotism and Radicalism* (Boston, 1917), p. 52.
69. Shailer Mathews, *Patriotism and Religion* (New York, 1918), pp. 3, 78.
70. Jane Addams, *Peace and Bread in Time of War* (New York, 1922), p. 148.
71. Peterson and Fite, *Opponents of War, 1917–1918*, p. 115.
72. Albert Keim and Grant Stoltzfus, *The Politics of Conscience: The Historic Peace Churches and America at War, 1917–1955* (Scottsdale, Pa.: Herald Press, 1988), pp. 42, 46–47.
73. Walter Kellogg, *The Conscientious Objector* (New York, 1919), pp. 84–85.
74. Ibid., pp. 84, 106, 38.
75. G. Stanley Hall, *Morale: The Supreme Standard of Life and Conduct* (New York, 1920), p. 136.
76. Abrams, *Preachers Present Arms*, pp. 147–152.
77. Ibid., p. 146.
78. John F. Piper, Jr., *The American Churches in World War I* (Athens: Ohio University Press, 1985), p. 137, 51–52. The FCC committee that wanted to stifle antiwar criticism was the Committee on War-Time Work in the Local Church and Cooperation with the American Red Cross.
79. Quoted in ibid., p. 53.
80. Abrams, *Preachers Present Arms*, p. 111. Fagnani made his remarks concerning Quakerism at the ninth annual meeting of the Lake Mohonk Conference on International Arbitration.
81. Piper, *American Churches*, p. 53.
82. Isaac Lansing, *Why Christianity Did Not Prevent the War* (New York, 1918), pp. 248, 242.
83. Frank Crane, "The Flag," *Association Men* 42, no. 10 (July 1917): 541.
84. Quoted in Robert W. Veach, *The Meaning of the War for Religious Education* (New York, 1920), p. 168.
85. Abrams, *Preachers Present Arms*, p. 109.
86. *North American Review* 206 (September 1917): 483.
87. Chapel of the Comforter War Committee, *The Causes of the War*, War Paper No. 3 (Brooklyn, 1918), pp. 5, 38.
88. Ibid., pp. 36–37.
89. Abraham Rihbany, *Militant America and Jesus Christ* (Boston, 1917), p. 30.
90. See for example Edward Leigh Pell, *What Did Jesus Really Teach About War?* (New York, 1917). This author not only called Christ the antithesis of "the big, fat, blubbering non-resister" (p. 47); he also described Him as "a tremendous fighter" (p. 34).
91. Frederick Lynch et al., *The Christian in War Time* (New York, 1917), pp. 12–17, 54–55, and passim.

92. Quoted in Ahlstrom, *A Religious History,* p. 888.

93. Daniel Evans, *Some Religious Problems Created by the War* (Boston, 1917), pp. 6, 9.

94. George Perkins, "The Supreme Test of a Man," *Association Men* 42, no. 10 (July 1917): 554.

95. Henry Hallam Tweedy, "The Ministry and the War," in E. Hershey Sneath, ed., *Religion and the War* (New Haven, 1918), pp. 86, 95.

96. Abbott, *The Twentieth Century Crusade,* p. 55.

97. Hall, *Morale,* p. 102.

98. Richard Boynton, *The Vital Issues of the War* (Boston, 1918), pp. 119–120.

99. Joseph Odell, "Peter Sat by the Fire Warming Himself," *Atlantic Monthly* 121 (February 1918): 152–153.

100. John Kelman, *The War and Preaching* (New Haven, 1919), p. 57.

101. Hall, *Morale,* pp. 30, 147.

102. Committee on the War and the Religious Outlook, *Religion among American Men* (New York, 1920), pp. 108–109. The Committee on the War and the Religious Outlook was created in 1918 by joint action of the FCC and the General War-Time Commission of the Churches. Its first president was the Reverend Henry Churchill King of Oberlin College; its purpose was "to consider the state of religion as revealed or affected by the war, with special reference to the duty and opportunity of the Churches." Committee on the War and the Religious Outlook, *The Missionary Outlook in the Light of the War* (New York, 1920), p. v.

103. William H. P. Faunce, *Religion and War* (New York and Cincinnati, 1918), pp. 139–140.

104. Charles E. Jefferson, *What the War Has Taught Us* (New York, 1919), p. 184. G[eorge] Walter Fiske, *Finding the Comrade God: The Essentials of a Soldierly Faith* (New York, 1918), p. 210.

105. Luther Gulick, *Morals and Morale* (New York, 1919), pp. 3, 97.

106. Ibid., pp. 92, 98.

107. George Stewart and Henry B. Wright, *The Practice of Friendship: Studies in Personal Evangelism with Men of the United States Army and Navy in American Training Camps* (New York, 1918), p. 14.

108. The list of men associated with both the Church Peace Union (CPU) and the General War-Time Commission of the Churches (GWTCC) included the Rev. Frederick Lynch (chairman of the CPU), the Rev. Dr. Robert Speer (chairman of the GWTCC), Dr. John R. Mott of the YMCA, President William H. P. Faunce of Brown University, Dean Shailer Mathews of Chicago Divinity School, Prof. William Adams Brown of Union Seminary, and Bishop William Lawrence of the Massachusetts Episcopal Church.

109. See William A. Brown, *General War-Time Commission of the Churches: Its Organization and Its Purpose* (New York, 1917), pp. 3–11; and Piper, *American Churches,* pp. 110, 116–117. The GWTCC also influenced the selection of all Protestant military chaplains through its General Committee

on Army and Navy Chaplains, which recommended chaplains for consideration by the War Department.

110. Abrams, *Preachers Present Arms,* pp. 111.

111. Ahlstrom, *A Religious History,* p. 896. The first version of the United War Work Campaign was crafted principally by the YMCA. It called (largely out of deference to Southern Protestants) for two separate fund drives: the first for mainline Protestant wartime activities and the second for the Salvation Army, the Jewish Welfare Board, and the Knights of Columbus. But these latter groups (which did not approve of the segregation) convinced President Wilson to drop the two-drive scheme in favor of a more unified plan. McKeown, *War and Welfare,* pp. 146–149.

112. Abrams, *Preachers Present Arms,* p. 112.

113. Tweedy, "The Ministry and the War," pp. 96–97.

114. Abrams, *Preachers Present Arms,* p. 70.

115. Williams, "The Chaplaincy in the Armed Forces," pp. 48–49.

116. Ibid. The decision to exempt clergymen from military service was part of the Selective Service Act of 1917.

117. Macfarland, *The Churches of Christ in Time of War,* p. 124. Quotation from the Reverend John Henry Jowett.

118. See Williams, "The Chaplaincy in the Armed Forces," pp. 48–49, for statistics on the Navy chaplaincy; and Roy Honeywell, *Chaplains of the United States Army* (Washington, D.C.: Office of the Chief of [U.S. Army] Chaplains, 1958), p. 171, for statistics on the Army and National Guard chaplaincies.

119. Eugene Klug, "The Chaplaincy in American Public Life," in A. Ray Appelquist, ed., *Church State and Chaplaincy* (Washington, D.C.: General Commission on Chaplains and Armed Services Personnel, [1969]), p. 79.

120. Honeywell, *Chaplains of the United States Army,* p. 155.

121. Ibid., pp. 166–169.

122. Ibid., pp. 168–171; and Williams, "The Chaplaincy in the Armed Forces," pp. 45–48.

123. Klug, "The Chaplaincy in American Public Life," p. 80.

124. S. Parkes Cadman, "Toughening Moral and Physical Fibre," *Association Men* 42, no. 6 (March 1917): 320–321.

125. Reinhold Niebuhr, *Leaves from the Notebook of a Tamed Cynic* (San Francisco, 1980), pp. 15–16.

126. Klug, "The Chaplaincy in American Public Life," p. 80.

127. William H. Taft et al., eds., *Service with Fighting Men: An Account of the American Young Men's Christian Associations in the World War* (New York, 1922), vol. 1, pp. 46–47.

128. Henry Davidson, *The American Red Cross in the Great War* (New York, 1919), pp. 6–11.

129. Elizabeth Sergeant, "Men for the YMCA," *New Republic* 16 (August 17, 1918): 68.

130. Taft et al., *Service with Fighting Men,* vol. 1, pp. 243, vii, 26.
131. Williams, "The Chaplaincy in the Armed Forces," p. 38.
132. YMCA, Philadelphia Association, *War and Peace: A Quaker City Narrative* (Philadelphia, 1899), p. 9.
133. Lewis Theiss, "The YMCA—Maker of Men," *World's Work* 26 (June 1913): 208.
134. Taft et al., *Service with Fighting Men,* vol. 1, pp. 54, 213.
135. Piper, *American Churches,* pp. 24–25.
136. McKeown, *War and Welfare,* pp. 144–147, 153–154.
137. Taft et al., *Service with Fighting Men,* vol. 1, p. 269.
138. Bernard Bell, *The Church's Work for Men at War,* Hale Memorial Sermon no. 11 (Milwaukee, Wisc., 1919), pp. 25–29.
139. Taft et al., *Service with Fighting Men,* vol. 1, pp. 95, 347. The War Camp Community Service was also known for providing facilities for U.S.-based soldiers on leave.
140. Worth Tippy, *The Church and the Great War* (New York, 1918), pp. 24–25, 51.
141. Anna Rice, *A History of the World's Young Women's Christian Associations* (New York: Woman's Press, 1947), pp. 161–162.
142. Taft et al., *Service with Fighting Men,* vol. 1, p. vii.
143. Ibid., vol. 1, pp. 298, 249, 269.
144. Ibid., vol. 1, p. 258 (statistics on women), and vol. 2, p. 410 (for mention of "colored secretaries").
145. Fred Goodman, "Religious Education in Camps," *Religious Education* 13 (December 1918): 417.
146. Taft et al., *Service with Fighting Men,* vol. 2, p. 27.
147. Daniel Poling, *Huts in Hell* (Boston, 1918), pp. 49–50. Poling was pleased to note that in addition to the strong presence of the YMCA, there were 140,000 graduates of Christian Endeavor serving in the army (pp. 138–139).
148. Veach, *The Meaning of the War,* p. 99.
149. For a description of "Gyp the Blood," see Poling, *Huts in Hell,* pp. 155–156, 165, 162 (for "husky saints" quote); and "Educating Our Ministers at the Front," *Literary Digest* 58 (August 17, 1918): 29. Blood's real name was William Stidger. He was the pastor of the the the First Methodist Episcopal Church of San José, California, and the author of *Soldier Silhouettes* and *Star Dust from the Dugouts.*
150. "The YMCA Reinterprets Religion," *Outlook* 120 (Oct. 16, 1918): 248.
151. Taft et al., *Service with Fighting Men,* vol. 1, pp. 146, 31.
152. Poling, *Huts in Hell,* p. 87.
153. Taft et al., *Service with Fighting Men,* vol. 2, pp. 324–325.
154. Abrams, *Preachers Present Arms,* p. 172.
155. Taft et al., *Service with Fighting Men,* vol. 2, p. 321.
156. Ibid., vol. 1, p. 118.

157. Ibid., vol. 2, pp. 13–14.
158. Ibid., vol. 1, p. 610.
159. Ibid., vol. 1, pp. 613, 175, 341–342.
160. Goodman, "Religious Education in Camps," p. 418.
161. Sergeant, "Men for the YMCA," p. 67.
162. Abrams, *Preachers Present Arms,* p. 174.
163. Taft et al., *Service with Fighting Men,* vol. 1, p. 303. The number of Bibles distributed by the YMCA during the war totaled 4,558,871 (Committee on the War and the Religious Outlook, *Religion among American Men,* p. 88).
164. Goodman, "Religious Education in Camps," p. 419.
165. Taft et al., *Service with Fighting Men,* vol. 1, p. 611. '
166. Abrams, *Preachers Present Arms,* pp. 61, 174.
167. Committee on the War and the Religious Outlook, *Religion among American Men,* p. 102.
168. Taft et al., *Service with Fighting Men,* vol. 1, p. vii.
169. Fiske, *Finding the Comrade God,* p. 229.
170. Ben Lindsey and Harvey O'Higgins, *The Doughboy's Religion and Other Aspects of Our Day* (New York, [1920]), p. 13.
171. Committee on the War and the Religious Outlook, *Religion among American Men,* p. 102.
172. McKeown, *War and Welfare,* pp. 141, 148. The Knights rightly viewed their canteen policy of giving cigarettes away for free as a public relations triumph over the YMCA. But they were eventually forced to abandon this policy by order of the Secretary of War, who wished to keep CTCA members from engaging in popularity contests.
173. Lindsey and O'Higgins, *The Doughboy's Religion,* pp. 5–6.
174. Ibid., pp. 4, 6.
175. Ibid., p. 7.
176. Bruce Barton, "Out of the 'Y' and in Again," *Outlook* 120 (Oct. 16, 1918): 258.
177. Sergeant, "Men for the YMCA," p. 67.
178. Taft et al., *Service with Fighting Men,* vol. 1, pp. 257, 597. The YMCA began the practice of hiring women for overseas service in the late summer of 1917.
179. James McCurdy to John Pershing, "Recreation Recommendations from the American YMCA to the American Army General Staff in France," Dec. 22, 1917, Archives, Babson Library, Springfield College, Springfield, Mass.
180. Stewart and Wright, *The Practice of Friendship,* p. 23.
181. Lindsey and O'Higgins, *The Doughboy's Religion,* pp. 19, 6.
182. Veach, *The Meaning of the War,* p. 151.
183. Eddy and Page, *The Abolition of War,* pp. 15–19.
184. Ozora Davis, *The Gospel in the Light of the Great War* (Chicago, 1919), p. 60.
185. Eldon Ernst, *Moment of Truth for Protestant America: Interchurch Cam-*

paigns Following World War I (Missoula, Mont.: Scholars' Press, 1974), p. 139.

186. Fosdick, *The Challenge of the Present Crisis* (New York, 1917). This treatise on the necessity of war was the only book Fosdick ever regretted having written. Piper, *American Churches*, p. 63.

187. Quoted in Kirby Page, *War: Its Causes, Consequences, and Cure* (New York, 1923), p. vii.

188. John Haynes Holmes, "Belated Aid for Objectors," *New Republic* 18, no. 228 (March 15, 1919): 217.

189. Abrams, *Preachers Present Arms*, p. 234.

190. Eddy and Page, *The Abolition of War*, pp. 192–194.

191. Federal Council of Churches, Commission on International Justice and Good-Will, *The Church and a Warless World* (New York, 1921), p. 14 and passim.

192. "The Chaplaincy Question," *Christian Century* 52 (Jan. 16, 1935): 70–72.

Conclusion

The epigraph is from Dudley Allen Sargent, "The Life and Work of Dr. Gulick," *American Physical Education Review* 23, no. 7 (October 1918): 421–422.

1. Randolph Downes, *The Rise of Warren Gamaliel Harding, 1865–1920* ([Columbus]: Ohio State University Press, 1970), p. 411. Harding delivered his famous "Back to Normal" speech to the Home Market Club in Boston on May 14, 1920.

2. "The Christian Student," *Association Men* 45, no. 6 (February 1920): 352.

3. "A Cast of Sculptures," *Princeton Alumni Weekly* (Jan. 17, 1970): 15. *The Christian Student* has recently been taken out of storage and renamed *The Student*. It now stands in the Princeton gymnasium.

4. Robert T. Handy, *A Christian America: Protestant Hopes and Historical Realities* (New York: Oxford University Press, 1984), pp. 171–181.

5. Sydney Ahlstrom, *A Religious History of the American People* (New Haven: Yale University Press, 1972), p. 899.

6. Ibid.

7. Harry Emerson Fosdick, "Recent Gains in Religion," in Kirby Page, ed., *Recent Gains in American Civilization* (New York, 1928), p. 238.

8. See Robert Speer, *The New Opportunity of the Church* (New York, 1919), pp. 4–5; and Committee on the War and the Religious Outlook, *The Missionary Outlook in the Light of the War* (New York, 1920), p. 208.

9. Leonard Sweet, *The Minister's Wife: Her Role in Nineteenth-Century American Evangelicalism* (Philadelphia: Temple University Press, 1983), pp. 232–233.

10. Department of Commerce, Bureau of the Census, *Religious Bodies: 1916*

(Washington, D.C.: Government Printing Office, 1919), pp. 1, 41, cited in Sweet, *The Minister's Wife,* p. 234.

11. S. Earl Taylor, "Stand Up and Fight, You Red-Blooded Men!" *Association Men* 45, no. 7 (1920): 409.
12. Eldon Ernst, *Moment of Truth for Protestant America: Interchurch Campaigns Following World War I* (Missoula, Mont.: Scholars' Press, 1974), pp. 43–44.
13. Ibid., pp. 57, 98–99.
14. Ibid., pp. 99–100. The quotations used are from promotional literature pertaining to the missionary exhibition.
15. Ibid., pp. 58, 73, 91, 101, 142–144.
16. Ahlstrom, *A Religious History of the American People,* p. 898.
17. George Marsden, *Fundamentalism and American Culture: The Shaping of Twentieth-Century Evangelicalism, 1870–1925* (New York: Oxford University Press, 1980), pp. 153–175.
18. Ibid., pp. 176–187.
19. Charlotte Perkins Gilman, "His Religion and Hers I: What His Religion Has Done to the World," *Century* 105 (March 1923): 676–683.
20. Gilman, "His Religion and Hers II: What Her Religion Will Do for the World," *Century* 105 (April 1923): 855–861.
21. Ethel Dorgan, *Luther Halsey Gulick, 1865–1918* (Washington, D.C.: McGrath Publishing Co., 1976), p. 147.
22. G[ranville] Stanley Hall, *Morale: The Supreme Standard of Life and Conduct* (New York, 1920), pp. 342–343.
23. Bruce Barton, *The Man and the Book Nobody Knows* (Indianapolis: Bobbs-Merrill, 1956), p. 12.
24. See David Macleod, *Building Character in the American Boy: The Boy Scouts, YMCA, and Their Forerunners, 1870–1920* (Madison: University of Wisconsin Press, 1983), p. 45; and J. H. Kellogg, "The Decay of American Manhood," *Association Men* 43 (October 1917): 115.
25. T. J. Jackson Lears, "From Salvation to Self-Realization: Advertising and the Therapeutic Roots of Consumer Culture, 1880–1930," in T. J. Jackson Lears and Richard Wightman Fox, eds., *The Culture of Consumption: Critical Essays in American History, 1880–1930* (New York: Pantheon Books, 1983), pp. 3–38.
26. John T. Stone, "The Selling Power of the Gospel," *Association Men* 45, no. 1 (September 1919): 10.
27. Arthur S. Link, "What Happened to the Progressive Movement in the 1920s?" *American Historical Review* 64, no. 4 (July 1959): 833, quoted in Handy, *A Christian America,* p. 166.
28. J. P. McEvoy, "Reformers," in *The Sweet Dry and Dry* (Chicago, 1919), n.p.
29. See Gerald Roberts, "The Strenuous Life: The Cult of Manliness in the

Era of Theodore Roosevelt" (Ph.D. diss., Michigan State University, 1970), p. 236; and Ernest Hemingway, *A Farewell to Arms* (New York: Charles Scribner's Sons, 1957), pp. 184–185.

30. William McLoughlin, *Billy Sunday Was His Real Name* (Chicago: University of Chicago Press, 1955), p. 260.

31. Ibid., p. 260.

32. Ahlstrom, *A Religious History of the American People*, p. 899. The lassitude of the Student Volunteer Movement in the 1920s differed sharply from the organization's crusading spirit in World War I. Nathan Showalter, *The End of a Crusade: The Student Volunteer Movement for Foreign Missions and the Great War* (Lanham, Md.: Scarecrow Press, 1998).

33. Speer, *The New Opportunity of the Church*, p. 3.

34. H[enry] L. Mencken, "The New Barbarians," in *Prejudices*, 5th ser. (New York, 1926), p. 157, quoted in Ahlstrom, *A Religious History of the American People*, p. 915.

35. E. Digby Baltzell, *The Protestant Establishment: Aristocracy and Caste in America* (New York: Random House, 1964), p. 198.

36. Henry Misiak and Virginia Staudt Sexton, *History of Psychology: An Overview* (New York: Grune & Stratton, 1966), pp. 153–154.

37. Charles Anderson and L. D. Travis, *Psychology and the Liberal Consensus* (Waterloo, Ont.: Wilfred Laurier University Press, 1983), pp. 1–9.

38. Misiak and Sexton, *History of Psychology*, pp. 137–145, 154–158.

39. Bernie Zilbergeld, *The Shrinking of America: Myths of Psychological Change* (Boston: Little, Brown and Co., 1983), p. 5. Additional arguments for the increasing influence of psychology in American life are contained in Ellen Herman, *The Romance of Psychology: Political Culture in the Age of Experts* (Berkeley: Univ. of California Press, 1995).

40. Paul Harris, *This Rotarian Age* (Chicago: Rotary International, 1935), p. 7.

41. Earnest E. Calkins, *Business the Civilizer* (Boston, 1928), pp. 293–295.

42. Harris, *This Rotarian Age*, pp. 14, 58, 65, 160–162, 220, 257.

43. Charles Fiske, *The Confessions of a Puzzled Parson and Other Pleas for Reality* (New York, 1928), quoted in Handy, *A Christian America*, p. 173.

44. See Roger Babson, *New Tasks for Old Churches: Studies of the Industrial City as the New Frontier of the Church* (New York, 1922), pp. 164–166; and Babson, *Religion and Business* (New York, 1921), p. 83. For a thumbnail sketch of Babson and his ideas, see "An Engineer of Commerce Discovers in Religion a Vitalizing Force," *World Outlook* 6 (May 1920): 37.

45. Paul Super, *Formative Ideas in the YMCA* (New York, 1929), pp. 7–9.

46. Joanna Bourke, *Dismembering the Male: Men's Bodies, Britain, and the Great War* (Chicago: University of Chicago Press, 1996), p. 25. The rule that YMCA members had to belong to an evangelical Protestant church was dropped in 1925.

47. See Clifford Putney, "Character Building in the YMCA, 1880–1930," *Mid-America* 73, no. 1 (January 1991): 64–67; and Enrique Mattia, "Phys-

ical Education and the Boy" (master's thesis, Springfield College, 1932), pp. 38–39.

48. See Clifford Putney, "Going Upscale: The YMCA and Postwar America, 1950–1990," *Journal of Sport History* 20, no. 2 (Summer 1993): 151–166; and Mayer Zald and Patricia Denton, "From Evangelism to General Service: The Transformation of the YMCA," *Administrative Sciences Quarterly* 8, no. 2 (September 1963): 214–234.

49. H. L. Mencken, "Adventures of a YMCA Lad [1894]," in *The Vintage Mencken,* ed. Alistair Cooke (New York: Vintage Books, 1990), pp. 18–25.

50. H. L. Mencken, "Star-Spangled Men," in *The Vintage Mencken,* p. 114.

51. Mark Schorer, *Sinclair Lewis: An American Life* (New York: McGraw-Hill Book Co., 1961), pp. 482, 48–51.

52. Ibid., p. 481; and Sinclair Lewis, *Elmer Gantry* (New York, 1927), pp. 36–37. A more sympathetic fictional muscular Christian than Judson Roberts is George Santayana's Oliver Alden: a scrupulously conscientious Christian athlete who struggles against idleness and materialism and who is killed (symbolically) toward the end of World War I. See George Santayana, *The Last Puritan* (New York: Scribner & Sons, 1936).

53. Committee on the War and the Religious Outlook, *Religion among American Men* (New York, 1920), p. 102.

54. "The Developing Association in a Changing World," *Home Work Bulletin* (January 1928): 4–7.

55. See Andrew Doyle, "Foolish and Useless Sports: The Southern Evangelical Crusade against Intercollegiate Football," *Journal of Sport History* 24, no. 3 (Fall 1997): 317–340; and Hal Sears, "The Moral Threat of Intercollegiate Sports: An 1893 Poll of Ten College Presidents, and the End of 'The Champion Football Team of the Great West,'" *Journal of Sport History* 19, no. 3 (Winter 1992): 211–226.

56. See Margaret Bendroth, *Fundamentalism and Gender, 1875 to the Present* (New Haven: Yale University Press, 1993), pp. 64–65; and Betty DeBerg, *Ungodly Women: Gender and the First Wave of American Fundamentalism* (Minneapolis: Fortress Press, 1990), p. 91.

57. Lloyd Averill, *Religious Right, Religious Wrong* (New York: Pilgrim Press, 1989), pp. xiii–xv. While Averill writes that fundamentalism reemerged in the 1970s, Joel Carpenter contends that it reemerged in the 1950s with the rise of "Neo-fundamentalists" such as Billy Graham. Fundamentalist authors Ed Dobson and Ed Hindson, however, are quick to distinguish themselves from Graham, who in their eyes is not a fundamentalist but an evangelical. See Joel Carpenter, *Revive Us Again: The Reawakening of American Fundamentalism* (New York: Oxford University Press, 1997), p. xi; and Ed Dobson and Ed Hindson, "The Resurgence of Fundamentalism," in Jerry Falwell, ed., *The Fundamentalist Phenomenon* (Garden City, N.Y.: Doubleday, 1981), pp. 143–155.

58. Tony Ladd and James Mathisen, *Muscular Christianity: Evangelical Protes-*

tants and the Development of American Sport (Grand Rapids, Mich.: Baker Books, 1999), pp. 106, 130, 133.

59. See David E. Harrell, *Oral Roberts: An American Life* (Bloomington: Indiana University Press, 1985), pp. 153–154; and Dane Claussen, "What the Media Missed about the Promise Keepers," in Dane Claussen, ed., *Standing on the Promises: The Promise Keepers and the Revival of Manhood* (Cleveland, Ohio: Pilgrim Press, 1999), p. 17.

60. Claussen, *Standing on the Promises,* p. 17. The quotation is from Bill McCartney.

61. Charles Lippy makes an interesting comparison between the muscular Christians of yesteryear and the muscular Christians of today in Charles Lippy, "Miles to Go: Promise Keepers in Historical and Cultural Context," *Soundings* 80, nos. 2–3 (Summer–Fall 1997): 289–304. According to Lippy, the Promise Keepers are less concerned about physical strength than were their counterparts in the Men and Religion Forward movement.

Selected Bibliography

The following is a bibliography of the most important primary sources upon which this study was based. It does not list articles, dissertations, archival materials, and modern books (which can all be located in the notes); it does include published monographic works that were written before 1930.

Abbott, Lyman. *Christianity and Social Problems.* Boston: Houghton, Mifflin, 1896.

———. *The Home Builder.* Boston and New York: Houghton Mifflin Co., 1908.

———. *The Twentieth Century Crusade.* New York: Macmillan Co., 1918.

Adams, Henry. *The Education of Henry Adams.* Boston: Houghton Mifflin Co., 1918.

Addams, Jane. *Peace and Bread in Time of War.* New York: Macmillan Co., 1922.

Alexander, John L. *The Boy and the Sunday School.* New York: Association Press, 1913.

Allen, A. V. G., et al. *The Message of Christ to Manhood.* Boston: Houghton, Mifflin & Co., 1899.

Anderson, William G. *Anderson's Physical Education.* New York: A. D. Dana, 1897.

Arnold, Thomas. *The Miscellaneous Works.* New York: D. Appleton & Co., 1845.

Athearn, Walter S., et al. *The Religious Education of Protestants in an American Commonwealth.* New York: Doran, 1923.

Atkins, Gaius G. *Modern Religious Cults and Movements.* New York: Fleming H. Revell Co., 1923.

Austin, Mary H. *Christ in Italy; Being the Adventures of a Maverick among Masterpieces.* New York: Duffield & Co., 1912.

———. *A Small Town Man.* New York: Harper & Bros., 1925.

Babson, Roger. *New Tasks for Old Churches: Studies of the Industrial City as the New Frontier of the Church.* New York: Fleming H. Revell Co., 1922.

———. *Religion and Business.* New York: Macmillan, 1921.

Barbour, Clarence A., ed. *Fellowship Hymns.* New York: Association Press, 1918.

———. *Making Religion Efficient.* New York: Association Press, 1912.

Barton, Bruce. *The Man and the Book Nobody Knows.* Indianapolis: Bobbs-Merrill, 1956.

———. *A Young Man's Jesus.* Boston: Pilgrim Press, 1914.

Batten, Samuel, ed. *The Moral Meaning of the War.* Philadelphia: American Baptist Publication Society, [1918].

Beard, Daniel C. *The Boy Pioneers, Sons of Daniel Boone.* New York: Scribner's Sons, 1909.

Beard, George. *American Nervousness, Its Causes and Consequences.* New York: Putnam, 1881.

Beecher, Henry Ward. *Eyes and Ears.* Boston: Ticknor and Fields, 1863.

Bell, Bernard. *The Church's Work for Men at War.* Hale Memorial Sermon no. 11. Milwaukee, Wisc.: Morehouse Publishing Co., 1919.

Bellasis, Edward. *Notes for Boys (and Their Fathers) on Morals, Mind, and Manners.* Chicago: A. C. McClurg & Co., 1888.

Blakeslee, George, ed. *The Problems and Lessons of the War.* New York: G. P. Putnam's Sons, 1916.

Bok, Edward. *Young Man and the Church.* Philadelphia: Altemus, 1896.

Bosworth, Edward I. *The Weak Church and the Strong Man.* Ed. John R. Mott. The Claims and Opportunities of the Christian Ministry [Series]. New York: Student Dept. of the YMCA, 1909.

Boynton, Richard. *The Vital Issues of the War.* Boston: Beacon Press, 1918.

Boy Scouts of America. *Handbook for Scout Masters.* New York: BSA, 1914.

———. *The Official Handbook for Boys.* New York: BSA, 1914.

Boy Scouts of America and the Catholic Committee on Scouting. *Scouting for Catholics.* New York: BSA and CCS, 1920.

Boys' Brigade. *The Boys' Brigade in the United States of America.* San Francisco: Brigade Council, 1891.

Brent, Charles H. *Adventure for God.* New York: Longmans, Green & Co., 1905.

———. *The Splendor of the Human Body.* New York: Longmans, Green, 1908.

Bridgman, Howard. *Real Religion: Friendly Talks to the Average Man on Clean and Useful Living.* Boston: Pilgrim Press, 1910.

Brown, Arthur J. *The Why and How of Foreign Missions.* New York: Domestic and Foreign Missionary Society of the Protestant Episcopal Church, 1911.

Brown, Charles R. *Faith and Health.* New York: T. Y. Crowell & Co., 1910.

———. *The Making of a Minister.* New York: The Century Co., 1927.

Brown, E[mma] E., ed. *True Manliness: From the Writings of Thomas Hughes.* Boston: D. Lothrop & Co., 1880.

Brown, William A. *General War-Time Commission of the Churches: Its Organization and Its Purpose.* New York: The Commission, 1917.

Burr, H[anford] M. *The Calling of Boyman.* New York: Association Press, 1916.

——. *Studies in Adolescent Boyhood.* Springfield, Mass.: Seminar Publishing Co., 1910.

Burrell, David J. *For Christ's Crown and Other Sermons.* New York: W. B. Ketcham, 1896.

Bushnell, Horace. *Christian Nurture.* New York: C. Scribner, 1861.

Butler, Samuel. *The Way of All Flesh.* London: Grant, Richards, 1903.

Calkins, Earnest E. *Business the Civilizer.* Boston: Little, Brown & Co., 1928.

Camp Fire Girls. *The Book of the Camp Fire Girls.* New York: National Headquarters, 1915.

Case, Carl D. *The Efficient Young People's Society.* Philadelphia: American Baptist Publication Society and Northern Baptist Commission on Young People's Work, 1915.

——. *The Masculine in Religion.* Philadelphia: American Baptist Publication Society, 1906.

——. *Men and the Church.* Philadelphia: American Baptist Publication Society, 1914.

Chapel of the Comforter [New York City]. War Committee. *The Causes of the War.* War Paper no. 3. Brooklyn: The Committee, 1918.

Chesley, Albert. *Social Activities for Men and Boys.* New York: Association Press, 1910.

Choate, Anne, and Helen Ferris, eds. *Juliette Low and the Girl Scouts: The Story of an American Woman, 1860–1927.* New York: Doubleday, Doran & Co., 1928.

Clark, Francis E. *Christian Endeavor in All Lands.* [Philadelphia: United Society for Christian Endeavor], 1906.

——. *The Gospel Out of Doors.* New York: Association Press, 1920.

——. *The Great Secret: Health, Beauty, Happiness, Friendmaking, Commonsense, Success.* Boston: United Society for Christian Endeavor, 1897.

——. *Some Christian Endeavor Saints.* Boston: Congregational Sunday-School and Publication Society, 1892.

——. *World Wide Endeavor: The Story of the Young People's Society of Christian Endeavor.* Philadelphia: Gillespie & Metzger, 1895.

——. *The Young People's Society of Christian Endeavor: Where It Began, How It Began, What It Is, How It Works.* Boston: United Society of Christian Endeavor, 1895.

Committee on the War and the Religious Outlook. *The Missionary Outlook in the Light of the War.* New York: Association Press, 1920.

——. *Religion among American Men.* New York: Association Press, 1920.

Conant, Robert. *The Virility of Christ.* Chicago: The Author, 1915.

Congregational Church. Executive Council. *Brotherhood of Andrew and Philip?* [Boston, 1901.]

Coubertin, Pierre de. *L'Education en Angleterre*. Paris: Hachette et Cie, 1888.

Cressey, Frank G. *The Church and Young Men*. Chicago: Fleming H. Revell Co., 1903.

Curtis, Henry S. *The Play Movement and Its Significance*. New York: Macmillan Co., 1917.

Cuyler, Theodore L. *Sermons on Christian Recreation and UnChristian Amusement*. New York: E. D. Barker, 1858.

———. *Well-Built: Plain Talks to Young People*. Boston: United Society of Christian Endeavor, 1899.

Davidson, Henry. *The American Red Cross in the Great War*. New York: Macmillan, 1919.

Davis, Ozora. *The Gospel in the Light of the Great War*. Chicago: University of Chicago Press, 1919.

Dennen, Ernest J. *Knights of King Arthur, Department of the Order of Sir Galahad: A Club for Boys and Young Men, Especially Those of the Episcopal Church*. New York: Church Literature Press, 1915.

Doggett, Laurence L. *History of the Young Men's Christian Association*. New York: Association Press, 1922.

———. *Life of Robert A. McBurney*. Cleveland, Ohio: F. M. Barton, 1902.

Dole, Charles F. *The Religion of a Gentleman*. New York: T. Y. Crowell & Co., 1900.

Donald, E. Winchester, et al. *Ministers' Meeting of Protest against the Atrocities in the Philippines*. Boston, 1902.

Dresser, Horatio. *A History of the New Thought Movement*. New York: T. Y. Crowell Co., 1919.

Drury, Samuel S. *Backbone, the Development of Character*. New York: Macmillan Co., 1923.

Eddy, Mary Baker. *Science and Health with Key to the Scriptures*. Boston: Christian Science Publishing Co., 1918.

Eddy, Sherwood. *The Right to Fight: The Moral Grounds of War*. New York: Association Press, 1918.

Eddy, Sherwood, and Kirby Page. *The Abolition of War*. New York: George H. Doran Co., 1924.

Emerson, Ralph W. *English Traits*. Boston: Phillips, Sampson & Co., 1857.

Evans, Daniel. *Some Religious Problems Created by the War*. Boston: n.p., 1917.

Faunce, William H. P. *Religion and War*. New York: Abingdon Press, 1918.

Federal Council of Churches. Commission on International Justice and Good-Will. *The Church and a Warless World*. New York: The Commission, 1921.

Ferris, Helen. *Girls' Clubs, Their Organization and Management*. New York: E. P. Dutton & Co., 1918.

Fisher, George J., and Martin I. Foss, eds. *Physical Work: Management and Methods*. New York: Association Press, 1913.

Fiske, George. *Finding the Comrade God: The Essentials of a Soldierly Faith*. New York: Association Press, 1918.

Forbush, William B. *The Boy Problem: A Study in Social Pedagogy.* Boston: Pilgrim Press, 1907.
———. *The Boy's Life of Christ.* New York: Funk & Wagnalls Co., 1908.
———. *Church Work with Boys.* Boston: Pilgrim Press, 1910.
———. *The New Round Table: The Order of the Knights of King Arthur.* Taunton, Mass.: Charles W. Davol, 1925.
Fosdick, Harry E. *The Challenge of the Present Crisis.* New York: Association Press, 1917.
———. *The Manhood of the Master.* New York: Association Press, 1913.
———. *Shall We End War?* New York: Clearing House for the Limitation of Armament, 1921.
Foster, Eugene C. *The Boy and the Church.* Philadelphia: Sunday School Times Co., 1909.
Foster, William T., ed. *The Social Emergency: Studies in Sex Hygiene and Morals.* Boston: Houghton Mifflin Co., 1914.
Fulton, Robert, and Thomas Trueblood, eds. *Patriotic Eloquence Relating to the Spanish-American War and Its Issues.* New York: Scribner, 1900.
Gage, Albert H. *Evangelism of Youth.* Philadelphia: Judson Press, 1922.
Gates, Herbert. *Recreation and the Church.* Chicago: University of Chicago Press, 1917.
Gibson, Henry W. *Boyology; or Boy Analysis.* New York: Association Press, 1916.
———. *Camping for Boys.* New York: Association Press, 1911.
———. *Services of Worship for Boys.* New York: Association Press, 1914.
———. *Twenty-five Years of Organized Boys' Work in Massachusetts and Rhode Island, 1891–1915.* Boston: State Executive Committees of the Massachusetts and Rhode Island YMCAs, 1915.
Gilman, Charlotte P. *The Man-Made World.* New York: Charlton Co., 1911.
———. *The Yellow Wall Paper.* Boston: Small, Maynard & Co., 1899.
Gladden, Washington. *Amusements: Their Uses and Abuses.* North Adams, Mass.: James T. Robinson & Co., 1866.
———. *Straight Shots at Young Men.* New York: T. Y. Crowell & Co., 1900.
———. *The Young Men and the Churches: Why Some of Them Are Outside and Why They Ought to Come In.* Boston: Congregational Sunday-School and Publication Society, 1885.
Goodwin, Daniel. *Thomas Hughes of England and His Visits to Chicago in 1870 and 1880.* Chicago: Chicago Literary Club, 1896.
Gordon, George A. *The Claims of the Ministry on Strong Men.* Claims and Opportunities of the Christian Ministry [Series], ed. John R. Mott. New York: Student Dept. of the YMCA, 1909.
Gulick, Luther H. *The Dynamic of Manhood.* New York: Association Press, 1918.
———. *The Efficient Life.* New York: Doubleday, Page & Co., 1907.
———. *Morals and Morale.* New York: Association Press, 1919.

———. *Popular Recreation and Public Morality*. New York: Playground Association of America, 1909.

Gulick, Sidney. *The Fight for Peace: An Aggressive Campaign for the American Churches*. New York: F. H. Revell, 1915.

Guy, Cuthbert. *Scouting and Religion*. New York: Macmillan Co., 1924.

Hale, Edward E. *If Jesus Came to Boston*. Boston: Lawson & Wolffe, 1895.

———. *A New England Boyhood*. New York: Cassell, 1893.

———. *Public Amusement for Poor and Rich*. Boston: Phillips, Sampson & Co., 1857.

Hall, G[ranville] Stanley. *Jesus, the Christ, in the Light of Psychology*. Garden City, N.Y.: Doubleday, Page, 1917.

———. *Morale: The Supreme Standard of Life and Conduct*. New York: D. Appleton, 1920.

———. *Youth: Its Education, Regimen, and Hygiene*. New York: D. Appleton & Co., 1906.

Harper, W. A. *The Making of Men*. Dayton, Ohio: Christian Pubblishing Association, 1915.

Harrison, Frederick. *Studies in Early Victorian Literature*. London: E. Arnold, 1895.

Hobart, Alvah S. *Religion for Men*. New York: Association Press, 1912.

Hoben, Allan. *Why Boys and Girls Go Wrong*. Philadelphia: American Baptist Publication Society, 1912.

Holmes, John H. *New Wars for Old*. New York: Dodd, Mead, 1916.

Home Missions Council. *New Americans for a New America*. New York, n.p., 1913.

Hughes, Edwin H. *A Boy's Religion*. New York: The Methodist Book Concern, 1915.

Hughes, Thomas. *The Manliness of Christ*. Boston: Houghton, Osgood, 1880.

———. *Tom Brown at Oxford*. Philadelphia: Henry T. Coates & Co., [1861].

———. *Tom Brown's School Days*. Boston: Ticknor & Fields, 1868.

Iglehart, Ferdinand C. *Theodore Roosevelt: The Man as I Knew Him*. New York: Christian Herald, 1919.

James, Henry. *The Bostonians*. New York: Dial Press, 1945.

James, William. *On Vital Reserves*. New York: Henry Holt, 1911.

Jefferson, Charles E. *The Character of Jesus*. New York: T. Y. Crowell & Co., 1908.

———. *What the War Has Taught Us*. New York: Fleming H. Revell, 1919.

Johnson, Owen. *Stover at Yale*. New York: F. A. Stokes, 1912.

Johnston, Mercer Green. *Patriotism and Radicalism*. Boston: Sherman, French & Co., 1917.

Kellogg, Walter. *The Conscientious Objector*. New York: Boni & Liveright, 1919.

Kelman, John. *The War and Preaching*. New Haven: Yale University Press, 1919.

King, Henry C. *How to Make a Rational Fight for Character*. New York: International Committee of the YMCAs, 1902.

——. *The Moral and Religious Challenge of Our Times*. New York: Macmillan Co., 1911.

——. *The Seeming Unreality of the Spiritual Life*. New York: Macmillan, 1908.

Kingsley, Charles. *Hereward the Wake*. London: Macmillan and Co., 1866.

——. *Hypatia*. London: J. W. Parker and Son, 1853.

——. *The Roman and the Teuton: A Series of Lectures Delivered Before the University of Cambridge*. London: Macmillan & Co., 1875.

——. *Sanitary and Social Lectures and Essays*. London: Macmillan, 1880.

——. *True Words for Brave Men*. New York: Thomas Whittaker, 1886.

——. *Two Years Ago*. Cambridge: Macmillan and Co., 1857.

——. *Westward Ho!* Cambridge: Macmillan, 1855.

——. *Yeast*. London: John W. Parker, 1851.

Kingsley, F. E., ed. *Charles Kingsley: His Letters and Memories of His Life*. 2 vols. London: H. S. King & Co., 1877.

Lansing, Isaac. *Why Christianity Did Not Prevent the War*. New York: George H. Doran Co., 1918.

Lawrence, George A. *Guy Livingstone*. New York: Harper and Brothers, 1857.

——. *Sword and Gown*. Boston: Ticknor and Fields, 1859.

Lee, Joseph. *Play in Education*. New York: Macmillan, 1915.

Leete, Frederick D. *Christian Brotherhoods*. New York: Eaton & Mains, 1912.

Lewis, Sinclair. *Elmer Gantry*. New York: Harcourt, Brace, 1927.

Lindsey, Ben, and Harvey O'Higgins. *The Doughboy's Religion and Other Aspects of Our Day*. New York: Harper and Brothers, [1920].

Lunn, Arnold. *The Harrovians*. London: Methuen & Co., 1913.

Lynch, Frederick. *The Peace Problem*. New York: Fleming H. Revell, 1911.

——, ed. *President Wilson and the Moral Aims of the War*. New York: Fleming H. Revell, 1918.

Lynch, Frederick, et al. *The Christian in War Time*. New York: Fleming H. Revell Co., 1917.

Lytton, Edward George Bulwer-. *Kenelm Chillingly*. Edinburgh: William Blackwood and Sons, 1873.

Macfadden, Bernarr. *The Virile Powers of Superb Manhood*. New York: Physical Culture Publishing Co., 1900.

Macfarland, Charles S. *The Churches of Christ in America and International Peace*. New York: Church Peace Union, 1914.

——. *Spiritual Culture and Social Service*. New York, etc.: Fleming H. Revell Co., 1912.

——, ed. *The Christian Ministry and the Social Order*. New Haven: Yale University Press, 1909.

——, ed. *The Churches of Christ in Time of War*. New York: Federal Council of Churches of Christ in America, 1917.

Mahan, Alfred T. *The Harvest Within: Thoughts on the Life of the Christian*. Boston: Little, Brown, 1909.

——. *The Interest of America in Sea Power*. Boston: Little, Brown, 1897.

Massee, Jasper C. *Men and the Kingdom.* New York: Fleming H. Revell, 1912.

Mathews, Shailer. *Patriotism and Religion.* New York: Macmillan Co., 1918.

McCauley, William. *Why: Reasons for the Christian Endeavor Movement.* Cincinnati, Ohio: Standard Publishing Co., 1894.

McCormick, William. *Fishers of Boys.* New York: Hodder & Stoughton and George H. Doran Co., 1915.

McDowell, William F. *A Man's Religion: Letters to Men.* New York: Eaton & Mains, 1913.

———. *The Right Sort of Men for the Ministry.* Ed. John R. Mott. The Claims and Opportunities of the Christian Ministry [Series]. New York: Student Dept. of the YMCA, 1909.

McKeever, W. A. *Training the Boy.* New York: Macmillan Co., 1913.

———. *Training the Girl.* New York: Macmillan Co., 1914.

Men and Religion Forward Movement. *Men and Religion Songs.* New York: Association Press, 1912.

———. *The Message and Program of the Men and Religion Forward Movement.* New York: Association Press, 1911.

———. *Messages of the Men and Religion Forward Movement.* 7 vols. New York: Association Press, 1912.

Mencken, H[enry] L. *The Vintage Mencken.* Ed. Alistair Cooke. New York: Vintage Books, 1990.

Meredith, Isaac H., ed. *The Boys' Hymnal.* New York: Tullar-Meredith Co., 1913.

Meredith, Isaac H., and Grant C. Tullar, eds. *Manly Songs for Christian Men: A Collection of Sacred Songs Adapted to the Needs of Male Singers.* New York: Tullar-Meredith Co., 1910.

Merrill, Lilburn. *Winning the Boy.* New York: F. H. Revell, 1908.

Michael, Charles D., ed. *Missionary Heroes: Stories of Heroism on the Mission Field.* Kilmarnock, Scotland: John Ritchie, 1905.

Morse, Richard C. *My Life with Young Men: Fifty Years in the YMCA.* New York: Association Press, 1918.

Mott, John R. *Addresses and Papers.* 6 vols. New York: Association Press, 1946–1947.

———. *The Evangelization of the World in This Generation.* New York: Student Volunteer Movement, 1900.

———. *The Future Leadership of the Church.* New York: Student Dept. of the YMCA, 1908.

———. *The World's Student Christian Federation.* [London]: WSCF, 1920.

Myers, Courtland. *Why Men Do Not Go to Church.* New York: Funk & Wagnalls, 1899.

Newman, John H. *Apologia Pro Vita Sua: Being a History of His Religious Opinions.* Ed. Martin J. Svaglio. Oxford: Clarendon Press, 1967.

———. *Callista: A Sketch of the Third Century.* London: Burns and Lambert, 1856.

Niebuhr, Reinhold. *Leaves from the Notebook of a Tamed Cynic.* San Francisco: Harper and Row, 1980.

Ober, Charles. *Adventures in Faith.* New York: Association Press, 1915.

———. *Luther Wishard, Projector of World Movements.* New York: Association Press, 1927.

Page, Kirby. *War: Its Causes, Consequences and Cure.* New York: George H. Doran Co., 1923.

———, ed. *Recent Gains in American Civilization.* New York: Harcourt, Brace & Co., 1928.

Patten, Gilbert. *Frank Merriwell's Faith.* Philadelphia: D. McKay, 1900.

Peabody, Francis G. *Jesus Christ and the Christian Character.* New York: Macmillan, 1905.

———. *Mornings in the College Chapel.* Boston: Houghton, Mifflin, 1907.

———. *The Religious Education of an American Citizen.* New York: Macmillan Co., 1917.

Pell, E. L. *What Did Jesus Really Teach About War?* New York: Fleming H. Revell Co., 1917.

Pentecost, George. *The Coming Age of America: A Retrospect and a Forecast.* New York, n.p., 1898.

Pierce, Jason W. *The Masculine Power of Christ.* Boston: Pilgrim Press, 1912.

Poling, Daniel. *Huts in Hell.* Boston: Christian Endeavor World, 1918.

Powell, Lyman. *The Emmanuel Movement in a New England Town.* New York: G. P. Putnam, 1909.

Puffer, J. Adams. *The Boy and His Gang.* Boston: Houghton Mifflin Co., 1912.

Rainwater, Clarence E. *The Play Movement in the United States: A Study of Community Recreation.* Chicago: University of Chicago Press, 1922.

Rauschenbusch, Walter. *Christianity and the Social Crisis.* New York: Macmillan Co., 1913.

———. *Christianizing the Social Order.* New York: Macmillan Co., 1912.

Reisner, Christian F. *Roosevelt's Religion.* New York: Abingdon Press, 1922.

Reynolds, James B., et al., eds. *Two Centuries of Christian Activity at Yale.* New York: G. P. Putnam's Sons, 1901.

Rice, Emmett. *A Brief History of Physical Education.* New York: A. S. Barnes & Co., 1929.

Richardson, Norman. *The Religion of Modern Manhood; or, Masculine Topics for Men's Bible Classes.* New York: Eaton and Mains, 1911.

Richardson, Norman, and Ormond Loomis. *The Boy Scout Movement Applied by the Church.* New York: C. Scribner's Sons, 1915.

Rihbany, Abraham. *Militant America and Jesus Christ.* Boston and New York: Houghton Mifflin Co., 1917.

Roosevelt, Theodore. *Fear God and Take Your Own Part.* New York: George H. Doran Co., 1916.

———. *The Great Adventure: Present-Day Studies in American Nationalism.* New York: C. Scribner's, 1918.

———. *The Strenuous Life: Essays and Addresses*. New York: Century Co., 1901.

———. *Theodore Roosevelt: An Autobiography*. New York: Charles Scribner's Sons, 1920.

Sallmon, William H., ed. *The Culture of Christian Manhood*. New York: Fleming H. Revell, 1897.

Saunders, J. R. *Men and Methods that Win in the Foreign Fields*. New York: Fleming H. Revell, 1921.

Scott, William H. *Men in the Church: An Address Delivered before the [Presbyterian] Synod of Pennsylvania*. Philadelphia: Allen, Lane & Scott, 1909.

Sheldon, Charles. *In His Steps: "What Would Jesus Do?"* Chicago: Advance Publishing Co., 1897.

Shelton, Don O. *Men and the Christian Conquest of America*. New York: Congregational Missionary Society, 1906.

Smith, Fred B. *A Man's Religion*. New York: Association Press, 1913.

Sneath, E. Hershey, ed. *Religion and the War*. New Haven: Yale University Press, 1918.

Speer, Robert E. *The Christian Man, the Church, and the War*. New York: Macmillan, 1918.

———. *The New Opportunity of the Church*. New York: Macmillan Co., 1919.

———. *Paul, the All-Round Man*. New York: Fleming H. Revell, 1909.

———. *The Stuff of Manhood: Some Needed Notes in American Character*. New York: Fleming H. Revell, 1917.

———. *Young Men Who Overcame*. New York: Fleming H. Revell, 1905.

Stagg, Amos A. *Touchdown!* New York: Longmans, Green & Co, 1927.

Stelzle, Charles. *Boys of the Street: How to Win Them*. New York: F. H. Revell Co., 1904.

Sterling, John. *A Correspondence between John Sterling and Ralph Waldo Emerson*. Ed. E. W. Emerson. Boston: Houghton Mifflin, 1897.

Stewart, George, and Henry B. Wright. *The Practice of Friendship: Studies in Personal Evangelism with Men of the United States Army and Navy in American Training Camps*. New York: Association Press, 1918.

Stone, John T. *Recruiting for Christ: Hand to Hand Methods with Men*. New York: Fleming H. Revell, 1910.

Storrs, Richard S. *Manliness in the Scholar*. New York: A. D. F. Randolph, 1883.

Strachey, Lytton. *Eminent Victorians*. New York: G. P. Putnam's Sons, 1918.

Strong, Josiah. *The Challenge of the City*. New York: Young People's Missionary Movement, 1907.

———. *The New Era; or, The Coming Kingdom*. New York: Baker & Taylor, 1893.

———. *Religious Movements for Social Betterment*. New York: Baker & Taylor, 1900.

———. *The Times and Young Men*. New York: Baker & Taylor, 1901.

Sunday, William [Billy]. *The Moral Leper.* Ft. Wayne, Ind.: E. A. K. Hackett, 1908.

Super, Paul. *Formative Ideas in the YMCA.* New York: Association Press, 1929.

Taft, William H. *Political Issues and Outlooks.* New York: Doubleday, Page & Co., 1909.

Taft, William H., et al., eds. *Service with Fighting Men: An Account of the American Young Men's Christian Associations in the World War.* 2 vols. New York: Association Press, 1922.

Talbot, Eugene S. *Degeneracy: Its Causes, Signs, and Results.* New York: C. Scribner's Sons, 1898.

Taylor, Charles K. *Character Development.* Philadelphia: John C. Winston Co., 1913.

Thompson, Fayette L., et al. *Men and Religion.* New York: Association Press, 1911.

Tippy, Worth. *The Church and the Great War.* New York: Fleming H. Revell Co., 1918.

Twain, Mark. *Christian Science.* Buffalo, N.Y.: Prometheus Books, 1986.

Tyler, Moses C. *The Brawnville Papers.* Boston: Fields, Osgood, 1869.

Vance, James I. *Royal Manhood.* New York: Fleming H. Revell, 1899.

Veach, Robert W. *The Meaning of the War for Religious Education.* New York: Fleming H. Revell, 1920.

Veblen, Thorstein. *The Theory of the Leisure Class.* New York: New American Library, 1953.

War Addresses from Catholic Pulpit and Platform. New York: Joseph F. Wagner, [n.d.].

Waugh, Alec. *The Loom of Youth.* London: G. Richards, 1921.

Wayne, Kenneth. *Building the Young Man.* Chicago: A. C. McClurg, 1912.

Wells, Amos R. *Citizens in Training: A Manual of Christian Citizenship.* Boston: United Society of Christian Endeavor, 1898.

White, Bouck. *The Call of the Carpenter.* New York: Doubleday, Page & Co., 1912.

Wilson, Elizabeth. *Fifty Years of Association Work among Young Women, 1866–1916.* New York: National Board of YWCAs of the USA, 1916.

Wilson, Frank E. *Contrasts in the Character of Christ.* New York: F. H. Revell, 1916.

Winsor, Wiley, ed. *The Leaders' Handbook for the Young Men's Christian Associations of North America.* New York: Association Press, 1922.

Worcester, Elwood, et al. *Religion and Medicine: The Moral Control of Nervous Disorders.* New York: Moffat, Yard, 1908.

YMCA International Committee. *American Standard Program for Boys.* New York: Association Press, 1918.

———. *Association Hymn Book.* New York: Association Press, 1907.

———. *Handbook for Comrades: A Program for Christian Citizenship Training for Boys 15–17 Years of Age.* New York: Association Press, 1920.

————. *The Jubilee of Work for Young Men in North America*. New York: International Committee, 1901.

————. *Physical Education in the YMCAs of North America*. New York: Association Press, 1914.

YMCA Philadelphia Association. *War and Peace: A Quaker City Narrative*. Philadelphia: Edgell Co., 1899.

Index